D1608028

ADVANCES in
SCHOOL PSYCHOLOGY
Volume I

ADVANCES in SCHOOL PSYCHOLOGY
Volume I

edited by
THOMAS R. KRATOCHWILL
University of Arizona

LEA LAWRENCE ERLBAUM ASSOCIATES, PUBLISHERS
1981   Hillsdale, New Jersey

Lawrence Erlbaum Associates, Inc., Publishers
365 Broadway
Hillsdale, New Jersey 07642

Advances in School Psychology
ISSN 0270-3920

Printed in the United States of America

This series is dedicated to improved services to children and to schools, and especially to Tyler Thomas.

List of Contributors

Numbers in parentheses indicate the pages on which the authors' contributions begin.

Howard B. Ashby (307)
Division of Child Psychiatry
University of Iowa College of Medicine
Iowa City, Iowa 52242

John R. Bergan (255)
Department of Educational Psychology
University of Arizona
Tucson, Arizona 85721

Anthony A. Cancelli (217)
Department of Educational Psychology
University of Arizona
Tucson, Arizona 85721

Thomas R. Kratochwill (1,217)
Department of Educational Psychology
University of Arizona
Tucson, Arizona 85721

Sharon Landesman-Dwyer (281)
Child Development and Mental Retardation Center,
   and Regional Primate Research Center
University of Washington
Seattle, Washington 98196

Charles A. Maher (169)
Graduate School of Applied and Professional Psychology
Rutgers University—Busch Campus
P.O. Box 819
Piscataway, New Jersey 08854

Joel Meyers (133)
Department of School Psychology
Ritter Hall Annex
Temple University
Philadelphia, Pennsylvania 19122

Victor N. Morin (281)
Child Development and Mental Retardation Center,
    and Regional Primate Research Center
University of Washington
Seattle, Washington 98196

Beeman N. Phillips (19)
Department of Educational Psychology
University of Texas
Austin, Texas 78712

Gene P. Sackett (281)
Child Development and Mental Retardation Center,
    and Regional Primate Research Center
University of Washington
Seattle, Washington 98196

Gerald N. Senf (83)
Journal of Learning Disabilities
1331 Thunderhead Drive
Tucson, Arizona 85718

Mark A. Stewart (307)
Division of Child Psychiatry
University of Iowa College of Medicine
Iowa City, Iowa 52242

Advisory Board

Contents

Preface

Schools continue to play a major role in the educational and social development of children and youths. Recognizing that these influences have profound and lasting effects on our young, psychologists, educators, and other professionals have increasingly spent time analyzing these settings and the individuals that function within them. In recent years, more diverse groups of professionals have been interested in schools and their effects on students. Psychologists practicing in schools or providing services to schools continue to face an increasing amount of theoretical, practical, and research literature relevant to this practice. An ever increasing proliferation of research and writing on professional, legislative, and ethical issues has also occurred within the field of school psychology. This increased attention to issues relevant to school psychology has resulted in a rather large body of literature, making it difficult for professionals working within the field to keep abreast of all the new developments. Psychologists practicing within the field as well as those involved in training school psychologists have a number of journals, monographs, and books that greatly assist in integrating research and theory in practice, but there is a marked need for a volume in school psychology that will publish original volumes on an *annual* basis.

Advances in School Psychology is a serial publication designed to integrate original review of important developments each year relevant to the field of school psychology. Many and diverse topics are pertinent to the practice of psychology in the schools. Indeed, school psychology cuts across and impinges upon other important psychological fields including clinical, counseling, developmental, learning, and educational psychology. Thus, a periodic examination of significant developments, procedures, and issues in a more detailed fashion than is possible in journals and many textbooks seems imperative. Certain topics pertaining to school psychology also reach beyond the common domain of psychology and education, as usually conceived. An attempt will be made to sample widely from diverse areas of relevance to school psychology. I plan, on occasion, to solicit discussion from theoreticians, researchers, and practitioners not directly associated with school psychology. The series will encompass the contributions of psychology, psychiatry, social work, education, rehabilitation, law, and medicine. This cross-fertilization of ideas from diverse fields can lead to better theory, research, and practice in school psychology, especially when an empirical basis has been established for the issues advanced.

To provide this evaluation and review of topics and issues relevant to the field of school psychology is the primary function of the *Advances in School Psychology* series. Each chapter is written by individual(s) who have expertise in a topic of relevance and importance to the field. Contributing authors are encouraged to develop specific topics in greater detail than is commonly allowed in journal publications. It is expected that statements made and conclusions reached will guide future research, practice, and/or training in school psychology.

The birth of this series was possible through the efforts of a number of individuals. My sincere appreciation is extended to the members of the advisory board for their suggestions on authors and topics for the series. I am also indebted to my colleagues, John R. Bergan, Anthony A. Cancelli, and David C. Berliner for their thoughtful comments during the formative stages of this series. Appreciation is also given to Russell A. Barkley, John R. Bergan, Richard J. Morris, and Rosemary Rosser for their review efforts. My students also deserve a special note of appreciation for offering their perspectives on the field of school psychology.

My own work with the first volume was supported by several individuals to whom I owe a debt of gratitude. My wife, Carol Ann, supported my work throughout the volume. Special appreciation goes to Naomi Van Gilder and Judy Landrum for their editorial assistance on the volume. Larry Erlbaum and the staff at Lawrence Erlbaum Associates were very helpful and supportive in my work. Finally, I thank the authors of Volume 1 for your contributions, which will advance our knowledge of school psychology.

Thomas R. Kratochwill

December, 1980

Tucson, Arizona

ADVANCES in SCHOOL PSYCHOLOGY
Volume I

1

Advances in School Psychology: A Preview of the Contents and an Overview of the Chapters

Thomas R. Kratochwill
University of Arizona

INTRODUCTION

The field of school psychology is one of the most important and active areas in contemporary psychology. Yet, school psychology is undergoing a critical period in its development. It has been and continues to be extraordinarily diverse in its training programs, theoretical approaches as represented in practice, and service-delivery systems. Information relevant to theory, research, and practice in school psychology also cuts across many different professional fields. Such diversity may be a strength because the field must take into account the wide range of problems existing in applied educational settings. However, meeting the diverse needs existent in applied settings has been and will be a practical issue with respect to the survival and growth of the field.

School psychology has shown sensitivity to survival issues that are emerging in psychology and education. In 1954 the American Psychological Association (APA) held a conference at The Hotel Thayer, in West Point, New York. The published report of this conference, *School Psychologists at Mid-Century* (Cutts, 1955) provided an important document discussing roles, ethics, practice, research, and interprofessional relationships of school psychologists. In 1973, the APA, with support of the National Institute of Mental Health, held a conference in Vail, Colorado which had important implications for professional training in school psychology. Among the many professional issues discussed at Vail, an endorsement of the professional training model (i.e., Psy.D. degree) emerged as an alternative to the traditional Ph.D. degree.

A most recent demonstration that school psychology continues to critically examine itself and factors related to its development was the *Spring Hill Sym-*

1

posium on the Future of Psychology in the Schools held at Wayzota, Minnesota in June, 1980. This symposium was sponsored by the National School Psychology In-Service Training Network, the Bureau of Education for the Handicapped, the National Association of School Psychologists, and Division 16 of APA. The focus of the symposium was designed to develop a blueprint for the future of psychology in the schools. Stimulus papers were presented by Gil Trachtman, Jeff Grimes, and Don Baer. Reaction papers were also presented and roundtable and group discussions were used to evaluate various perspectives and issues in the field. Proceedings of the symposium will be disseminated through the *School Psychology Review*. The conference was attended by approximately 75 individuals representing various areas of school psychology. A follow-up conference incorporating a larger representation of the field is planned for late 1981.

PERSPECTIVES ON SCHOOL PSYCHOLOGY

The diversity apparent in school psychology has raised problems in generating a uniform definition that adequately reflects the multifaceted nature of the field and at the same time accurately portrays the many different conceptions. Over the history of school psychology, many and varied definitions have been offered of what school psychologists are and what they should do (e.g., Bardon & Bennett, 1974; P. Eiserer, 1972; Monroe, 1979; Taylor, 1977; Tindall, 1979; Wallace & Ferguson, 1967). If one examines the various works specifically focused on school psychology or the provision of psychological services in schools, this diversity over definition, scope, and purpose clearly emerges. Table 1.1 shows some major works in the field of school psychology in which the authors and/or contributors have taken somewhat different perspectives on the field over its relatively short period of development.[1] Various issues and perspectives concerning definition, role, and function have also appeared in professional journals that publish articles directly relevant to the school psychologist (see Table 1.2). Each journal has taken a similar perspective on publishing work of relevance to the field of school psychology (see Appendix A later in this chapter).

Definitions of school psychology are also known to be influenced by professional organizations, local, state, and federal boards of education and special education, as well as by university training programs. Moreover, such factors as the origins of the field, roles, and factors influencing roles have their unique contributions. School psychology has its origins in historical psychology and philosophy, the testing movement, special education, the mental health movement, and early learning theory (Tindall, 1979; Wallace & Ferguson, 1967).

---

[1]This is not to imply that school psychology is a new field. Indeed, school psychology is nearly as old as psychology in the United States, having its roots in those early psychologists concerned with the academic learning and adjustment of school-age individuals (cf. Tindall, 1979).

TABLE 1.1
Major Works in School Psychology

Author(s)	Title	Date
Cutts	School Psychologists at Mid-Century	1955
Mullen	The psychologist on the school staff: Report of the committee on reconsideration of the functions of the school psychologist	1958
White & Harris	The school psychologist	1961
Eiserer	The school psychologist	1963
Gottsegen & Gottsegen	Professional and school psychology	1963
Gray	The psychologist in the schools	1963
Hirst	Know your school psychologist	1963
Valett	The practice of school psychology: Professional problems	1963
Reger	School psychology	1965
Phillips	Perspectives on school psychology	1966
Magary	School psychological services in theory and practice, a handbook	1967[a]
Herron, Green, Guild, Smith, & Kantor	Contemporary school psychology	1970
Holt & Kicklighter	Psychological services in the schools: Readings in preparation, organization and practice	1971
Attwell	The school psychologist's handbook	1972
Bardon & Bennett	School psychology	1974
Fein	The changing school scene: Challenge to psychology	1974
Carroll	Contemporary school psychology: Selected readings from psychology in the schools	1978
Meyers, Parsons, & Martin	Mental health consultation in the schools	1979
Phye & Reschly	School psychology: Perspectives and issues	1979
Conoley	Consultation in schools: Theory, research, technology	1980
Kratochwill	Advances in school psychology (Volume 1)	1981
Reynolds & Gutkin	Handbook of school psychology	1981
Bergan	School psychology in contemporary society	1981

[a]Published again in 1972.

Some of the ambiguity about the domain of school psychology can also be inferred from the many different types of practice that exist. Roles have been and continue to be diverse, including, but not limited to, counseling/therapy, psychoeducational assessment, consultative child study, inservice traning, and research (Monroe, 1979). Moreover, community needs, and issues within the profession, and professional perspectives (P. Eiserer, 1972) have influenced the roles as determined by individuals within the field. The enactment of Public Law

TABLE 1.2
Major Journals in School Psychology

Journal	Dates
Journal of School Psychology	1963–present
Professional Psychology	1969–present
Psychology in the Schools	1964–present
School Psychology Digest (Review)[a]	1972–present
School Psychology International	1980–present
School Psychology Monograph[b]	1973–present

[a] Format change in 1979.
[b] Publication has been periodic rather than yearly.

(PL) 94–142 has had a major impact on school psychological practice in some areas of the field and represents one "external" influence that will have far-reaching consequences for the future. Many of these factors and variations will continue to exist and, consequently, the proper domain of school psychology continues to be a source of some debate.

Current perspectives on the future of school psychology parallel the diversity of the past and present. The identification of school psychology with professional psychology (e.g., as represented in the American Psychological Association) is perceived as critical to some (e.g., Bardon, 1979; Tindall, 1979), but this also remains debatable (cf. Brown, 1979). A major source of controversy in this area has been whether and how school psychology in the future will resolve the somewhat opposing positions enunciated by the American Psychological Association (APA) and the National Association of School Psychologists (NASP). Whether or not school psychology will be a subdiscipline of generic psychology or will become an independent profession remains a point of sometimes heated controversy. Even if these issues are resolved, there is the question of whether a new model of professional psychology will evolve that will replace current subdisciplines or distinct specialities (Bardon, 1976).

Continuing collaboration between NASP and APA will likely lead to the resolution of many important differences between the two organizations. In addition to the cooperative efforts in the development of the Spring Hill Symposium, the formation of the NASP/APA Task Force on Accreditation and Credentialing shows promise of continued cooperation in development of the field. For example, both NASP and APA may formalize joint structures for the accreditation of school psychology training programs at the doctoral and non-doctoral levels.

Whatever school psychology is, some authors have noted that a common feature of the field is training in psychology and professional employment in the schools (Tindall, 1979). Training programs in school psychology have been surveyed for the past 14 years (e.g., Bardon, Costanza, & Walker, 1971; Bardon & Wenger, 1974; Brown & Lindstrom, 1977; French, Smith, & Cardon, 1968;

Smith, 1964; White, 1963–1964). Bardon and Wenger (1974) noted that at least 618 faculty were involved either full time or with major graduate commitment to the speciality. Brown and Lindstrom (1977) identified 203 school psychology programs. Yet, it must be recognized that however one defines the field, variations in training across speciality areas (e.g., school, clinical, counseling, special education, and related areas) contribute to diversity with their entry into school psychology practice. It is well known and documented that individuals enter the practice of school psychology from many and different areas of training. It was estimated that the number of practicing school psychologists in the United States and Canada is approximately 12,000 (Ysseldyke, 1978). Professional certification provides some unification, but even here there is much variation. Even within the speciality of school psychology, considerable diversity exists across and within "designated" school psychology training programs.[2]

Recently, the status of school psychology as a professional specialty has been formalized. In January of 1980 the Council of Representatives of the APA adopted the Guidelines for Delivery by Providers of School Psychological Services. Similar guidelines were developed for practice in clinical, counseling, and organization/industrial psychology. Within APA, school psychology now represents, along with the other three areas, a distinct and defined specialty for the practice of psychology. Following the Specialty Guidelines, school psychological services refer to a number of services offered to individuals involved in educational settings from pre-school through higher education for the protection and promotion of mental health and learning.

Nevertheless, the conception of training in psychology and employment in educational settings as a major characteristic of the field could be compatible with a perspective that the future will see a new model of professional psychology involving broad-based training that permits psychologists to adapt to many different settings. In this regard, training may involve (Bardon, 1976) "understanding the importance of knowing a lot about *where* one works as well as *what* one does [p. 790]." If this more general trend occurs, it will likely open up the possibilities for broader theoretical and conceptual bases for practice. Such a trend will probably also be controversial.

PERSPECTIVES ON THE FUTURE

The purpose of noting the forementioned areas of ambiguity within the field of school psychology is not to exhaust divergent positions, views, and controversies. However, this brief glimpse of the issues represented conveys something of

---

[2]Designation as a "school psychology training program" comes from the American Psychological Association and the National Association of School Psychologists through accrediation efforts. Some programs are "self-designated" school psychology training programs in that they offer training leading to certification as a school psychologist in a particular state, but do not have formal endorsements of the two major organizations.

the nature of the issues remaining in the field and what they will be in the future. Presentation of controversial issues need not detract from conveying the larger picture of what school psychology is and what contribution it can make in theory, research, and practice. Indeed, what was said only a few years ago still has much merit (Bardon, 1976):

> The years ahead are full of promise for improved service to children and to schools. It is believed that there is much to be gained by continuing analysis of the speciality of school psychology, which, perhaps, more than any other speciality in psychology mirrors the times and serves as an indicator of what may be ahead for all of professional psychology [p. 790].

One perspective that may provide some consistency within the field of school psychology pertains to an empirical basis for effective techniques implemented in providing services to children and schools. Such a perspective should transcend some of the noted areas of controversy within the field. Although there will continue to be debates about the effectiveness of various models of treatment, service-delivery systems, and focus of intervention efforts, the continued critical analysis of these and other emerging issues in the field will remain one of its strongest features. It is in this tradition that the *Advances in School Psychology* series is designed to function. More specifically, the series is intended to present several different types of information. Chapters will be included that evaluate existing literatures on important topics relevant to diagnosis, assessment, and treatment, as well as innovative directions within these areas. Chapters will be included that review the literature and update our knowledge of related disciplines that may have contributions to theory, research, and practice in school psychology. Chapters of a more diverse nature that provide a substantive background to school psychologists for practice will also be included. Such contributions will cover theoretical, conceptual, methodological, as well as legal, ethical, and philosophical contributions to school psychology. Although a trend may appear to emerge within a particular volume or from one volume to the next, it should be noted that this is probably reflective of timely topics in the field, availability of authors to address a particular topic, as well as material being given coverage in other areas of the professional literature. The series should be perceived as an ongoing analysis of the field of school psychology and its dynamic character.

AN OVERVIEW OF THE CHAPTERS

The present volume covers a number of diverse topics of relevance to the field of school psychology. The nine chapters each deal with a different topic, and each can be read as a timely and up-to-date contribution in the area on which it focuses. The chapters have been ordered in a sequence that seemed to make salient their meaningfulness. Some conceptually similar topics (e.g., assessment) have been grouped together, but the book could be read in any sequence depending on the particular interests of the reader.

The growth of school psychology has brought with it a set of problems that will need our most careful attention as the profession moves through the 1980's. In Chapter 2, "School Psychology in the 1980's: Some Critical Issues Related to Practice," Beeman N. Phillips raises 10 issues that will undoubtedly have a profound impact on the future of school psychology. These include professionalization, licensing, mental-health services in the schools, psychoeducational rehabilitation, ethical practice, coping with professional stress, control and regulation in school psychology, professional associations and political activism as the means to career and status support, the role of school psychologists in legal advocacy, and job and career dissatisfaction among school psychologists. These issues relate specifically to the growth of school psychologists as individuals, and collectively to school psychology as a profession. Phillips has specified the conditions under which the issues should be examined, and what directions might be taken to resolve the problems. A major statement made is that the burden of problem solving lies with school psychologists, rather than with outside factors. A major problem faced by the profession is to develop concepts and services that are responsive to the needs of society and the schools, as well as the special interests of the diverse constituency. Phillips concludes that resolution will be speeded if struggles for power and control are avoided and efforts are focused on institutional reforms that lead to improvement in practice, education and training, and the profession as a whole. This chapter deserves careful reading by all those concerned with the future of school psychology.

School psychology has always had a close affiliation with special education and the provision of special-education services. This affiliation has not always been a stable and pleasant relationship. Frequently, the relationship has been characterized by professional role problems and controversy over function in the provision of services. In Chapter 3, "School Psychology: An Instrumental Service for the Handicapped," David A. Sabatino reviews the history of services to the handicapped and presents an overview of school psychology. He takes the position that school psychology, in its inception and continued development, is inseparable from the public-school delivery of services to the handicapped. Within the context of modern school psychology's search for professional identity, three major topics are discussed: the professional preparation of school psychologists in special education; communication between special education and school psychology, and the involvement of school psychologists in PL 94-142.

Professional activities of school psychologists have been greatly influenced by PL 94-142. Sabatino suggests that PL 94-142 typically forces special educators to accept data from school psychologists as part of a team involved in implementing the individualized education program plan. This entry of school psychology into educational service delivery provides the opportunity to promote instructional and management objectives. Sabatino takes the position that a consultation role can provide the model for delivery of services when three areas are incorporated—namely, an increased role with preschool and secondary-aged handicapped children, the development of monitoring systems (accountability), and systematic identification processes for unserved and underserved handicapped children. A team relationship with special educators is lauded as an effective and efficient means for implementation of this approach to special services.

One area in the field of special education that has been characterized by considerable debate and controversy over diagnosis and assessment is the area of learning disabilities. School psychologists have had a central role in the diagnosis and assessment of this special-education category of handicapped children. In Chapter 4, "Issues Surrounding the Diagnosis of Learning Disabilities: Child Handicap versus Failure of the Child–School Interaction," Gerald M. Senf reviews the major issues surrounding the diagnosis of learning disabilities and the role of the school psychologist in this activity. Problems in diagnosis, assessment, and service are related to the underlying assumptions of the term "disabled learner" and the assumptions concerning education in the United States.

The complex field of learning disabilities is traced along the dimensions of the function and ramifications of definition, historical perspectives, and problems with definitions. Thereafter, the *dilemma* for education with learning disabilities is discussed within the context of regular and special education. Senf takes the position that an educational handicap must be demonstrated to be a characteristic that inhibits the realization of a child's potential within the goals of the educational system. This, of course, presents major challenges in the use of traditional categories of handicap. Challenges occur on three dimensions—namely, that the learning problem lies in the learner, that there exists a group of children who possess a similar disability that makes them qualitatively different from normal, and that there exists a group of normal children lacking handicaps.

An alternative conception based on the "Child–School Interaction Model" is proposed. This conception differs from traditional approaches and is focused on the specific adjustment tasks for all children in educational systems. This approach differs from traditional conceptions in that the problem is defined in terms of relative school adjustment and not only the child's characteristics; the false dichotomy between "normals" and "handicapped" is not forced, and does not allow professionals to brand anyone as handicapped, viewing instead the problems as adjustments between child and school. A detailed presentation of the components of the child–school interaction model is the focus of the remainder of the chapter.

Consultation remains a primary mode of psychological service delivery in school psychology. Several different models (approaches) to consultation have been presented, including mental health, organizational, and behavioral. In

Chapter 5, "Mental-Health Consultation," Joel Meyers provides a comprehensive overview of the writing and research in the mental-health consultation field. Many school psychologists were introduced to this area of consultation by Meyers and his associates in the recent book entitled *Mental Health Consultation in the Schools* (Meyers, Parsons, & Martin, 1979). In his chapter, Meyers updates work in the mental-health consultation area by reviewing the most current theory and research with an emphasis on practice in the schools. The chapter focuses on three major topics—namely, an overview of mental-health consultation, a model for mental-health consultation in the schools, and direct service to teachers.

Mental-health consultation is defined as a "problem-solving process that occurs between two professionals where one (the consultant) tries to help the other (the consultee) maximize the social–emotional development of the clients (e.g., students) under the consultee's care." The consultee may be a teacher, administrator, or other school personnel. Mental-health consultation is perceived as a voluntary relationship in which the consultee learns to handle current and future problems in a more skillful and sensitive manner. Based on a modification of Caplan's (1963, 1970) mental-health consultation, four categories of consultation are provided, including direct service to the child, indirect service to the child, direct service to the teacher, and service to the organization. Finally, direct service to the teacher is used to illustrate mental-health consultation.

Program-evaluation services are increasingly playing an important role in the school psychologist's professional activities. One reason for this interest in program evaluation is the developing emphasis on accountability in the provision of psychological and special services. In Chapter 6, "Program Evaluation and School Psychology: Perspectives, Principles, Procedures," Charles A. Maher provides an overview of program evaluation. Program evaluation is examined in relation to school psychology, from historical, conceptual, and practical perspectives, with respect to evaluation principles and procedures. Maher provides a broad view of program evaluation, which has great relevance to practitioners interested in many and diverse applications of program evaluation in applied settings.

Recent advances in program-evaluation thinking and technology are reviewed, the relevance of these developments for school psychologists are discussed, a problem-solving approach to school program evaluation delineated, issues in the training of school psychologists in program evaluation explicated, and future directions for program evaluation and school psychology noted. The information provided in the chapter serves heuristic and practical purposes for school psychology trainers, who are interested in incorporating program evaluation into their training programs, and for school psychology practitioners, who are interested in learning about, or who are responsible for, program evaluation.

As school psychology moves through the 1980's, we will see an increased emphasis on accountability in psychological services in schools. School psychologists appear to be in an excellent position to design programs and evaluate them on a number of dimensions. Maher has provided a framework for knowledge and skills in this area. Practicing psychologists and training programs must now incorporate program evaluation into their work in the field of school psychology.

Criterion-referenced assessment continues to be an area of interest for school psychologists. In Chapter 7, "Advances in Criterion-Referenced Assessment," Anthony A. Cancelli and I review several of the advances made in criterion-referenced assessment that are useful for the practice of school psychology. Three areas are identified and reviewed because of their unique contributions to the development of criterion-referenced assessment: instructional psychology, psychometric theory, and behavior therapy. In the area of instructional psychology, the contributions of intellectual skills and learning hierarchies, in the tradition of Gagné, to the conceptualization of criterion-referenced tests are reviewed. Although work in this area has had only indirect impact on the design of criterion-referenced tests, informal procedures governed by the concepts of intellectual skills and learning hierarchies appear to be influencing the assessment activities of school psychologists. The use of task-analysis procedures presents one example of this wherein school psychologists can incorporate such assessment information into the design of individual education programs.

In the area of psychometric theory, those developments pertinent to the design of criterion-referenced tests are reviewed. Moreover, the advances in the explanation of content and item domain through the use of domain statements are presented. Finally, the issues surrounding the selection of items, reliability, validity, and selection of performance standards is also examined. Significant advances have been made in our understanding of the underlying assumptions governing the construction of criterion-referenced tests. An area identified for future development relates to a technology for the adequate design and interpretation of criterion-referenced tests that can be easily implemented.

An often-overlooked area of psychology in which significant advances in the development and use of criterion-referenced assessment has occurred is in behavior therapy. In this section of the chapter, we examine how assessment is conceptualized within the behavioral approach and how individual assessment services can be delivered. An important theme of this section is that various setting factors and situation-specific influences must be considered in the use of criterion-referenced tests in assessment and program monitoring. It is noted that continued exploration of the congruence between criterion-referenced measurement and the methods of behavioral assessment will further advance our understanding of the utility of criterion-referenced assessment in school psychology.

Major concerns have been raised over the assessment procedures used in educational settings. At the forefront of controversy has been the issue of whether norm-referenced or criterion-referenced tests should be used to identify learner needs. Yet, this may be the wrong question given certain priorities in schools and the different kinds of data generated by these two testing procedures.

In recent years, new mathematical techniques have been developed that help psychologists represent behavioral structures involved in learning and behavior. These have provided a basis for development of new kinds of assessment procedures called path-referenced assessment. In Chapter 8, "Path-Referenced Assessment in School Psychology," John R. Bergan reviews the new developments in the area of path-referenced assessment. This type of assessment refers to the strategy of describing test performance by indicating the client's position in a structural model specifying relations among classes of behavior. For example, on a learning task consisting of three specific subtasks, one could describe how learning task A affected performance on task B, and how task B influenced performance on task C.

In this chapter, Bergan reviews the foundations for a technology of path-referenced assessment within the context of a structural analysis of behavior. In addition, path-referenced psychometrics are presented. Like other assessment procedures, the properties of these procedures must be established within the context of reliability and validity. The psychometric properties of these assessment procedures differ, however, from techniques employed in other areas of assessment. The chapter further describes the implications of adopting a path-referenced approach to assessment for test bias. Specific uses of path-referenced assessment in school psychology practice, including screening, placement, diagnostic testing, and program evaluation, are presented. Finally, the implications of adopting a path-referenced approach in school psychology practice are discussed.

Many of the developments in path-referenced assessment are exciting and have important implications for school-psychology practice. The reader will also learn that much remains to be accomplished in this area if these developments are to be translated into practical assessment procedures. Hopefully, Bergan's suggestions will prompt the further development of a technology and the kind of research that further attests to the efficacy of path-referenced assessment.

Naturalistic observation of academic and social behavior is increasingly recognized as an important assessment skill for the practicing school psychologist. A growing literature has expanded the methodological and conceptual issues in behavioral assessment generally (e.g., Haynes, 1978; Haynes & Wilson, 1979; Johnson & Bolstad, 1973; Jones, Reid, & Patterson, 1975; Kent & Foster, 1977; Wildman & Erickson, 1977), and school psychology specifically (e.g., Alessi, 1980; Hunter, 1977; Keller, 1980b; Kratochwill, 1981; Lynch, 1977). Development of a technology in observational assessment is timely because school psychologists must attend to the evaluation of special-education programs. In Chapter 9, "Naturalistic Observation in Design and Evaluation of Special Education Programs," Gene P. Sackett, Sharon Landesman-Dwyer, and Victor N. Morin advance reasons why it is necessary to measure the impact of educational programs on the everyday lives of retarded individuals. Specifically, the chapter reviews problems concerning maintenance and generalization of training programs, provides an overview of the importance of observational assessment in this area, and presents an applied example of the use of observational assessment of retarded individuals in training and generalization settings.

In the section on transfer and maintenance of learning of retarded people, Sackett and his associates review some of the major issues involved in educational programming for retarded individuals. A prominent theme developed in this section is that school psychologists cannot assume that special programs established in school settings will ensure that skills acquired will generalize to settings in the natural environment. Given that a primary objective of special education of the retarded is to increase the person's "quality of life and independence of action and choice," school psychologists and other professionals must document that these goals are being met.

One assessment technology that can provide the kinds of data necessary to evaluate special-education programs on the generalization dimension is quantitative observational methods. In the next section of the chapter, the authors provide an overview of the contributions naturalistic observation assessment can make to evaluation of mental retardation programs. The authors advance several dimensions of quantitative observational methods that have been useful in work with the mentally retarded. Specifically, they discuss what to observe, sampling strategies, reliability, statistical analysis of data, and applications of observation in educating retarded people. This section builds upon the rather extensive work done in the area of applications of observational methods in the mental-retardation field (see Sackett's 1978a and 1978b work in this area).

To demonstrate the importance of naturalistic observational assessment in work in the mental-retardation area, an applied program-evaluation project is presented. The data reported are part of a study measuring the effects of residence changes on the behavior of 165 severely and profoundly retarded adults in an institutional setting. Results of the evaluation indicated that the training program was not effective; repeated monitoring showed that the people's performance deteriorated as training progressed. Especially important, the data suggested that even for those individuals for whom the program was effective, transfer of skills to another setting did not occur.

The chapter concludes with a discussion of the importance of observational assessment in applied treatment-oriented settings. More importantly, the authors demonstrate that quantitative observational assessment can be used to evaluate programs and generate hypotheses for future programming. The authors have presented major challenges for school psychologists and other professionals responsible for the design and implementation of special programs.

In Chapter 10, "Treatment of Hyperactive, Aggressive, and Antisocial Children," Mark A. Stewart and Howard B. Ashby take the position that although our understanding and treatment of children's behavior disorders has progressed, these advances have not always *secured* regions of new knowledge. With this conservative stance, the authors present an overview of the definitions of children commonly labeled ''hyperactive,'' ''aggressive,'' and ''antisocial.'' A major issue presented in the chapter is that there have been problems in defining these behavior patterns. The chapter focuses primarily on ''behavior problem'' or chronically disruptive children.

The authors first provide a general overview of the nature of these problems. They take the perspective that these childhood problems are multifaced and related to psychological, environmental, and biological factors. Given the current state of knowledge in this area, the authors recommend that we be skeptical about all treatments. Especially important in treatment is the recognition that there are biologic limits to the changes that can be made in a child's behavior. With this perspective, the authors review the limits to behavior therapy. Behavior therapy is the more generic terminology and does not refer to only those procedures commonly affiliated with behavior modification procedures (Kazdin, 1978).

Recognizing these possible biological limitations, the authors review types of treatment for children who have aggressive conduct disorders. These treatments include training in self-awareness and in monitoring one's own behavior, coaching in specific social skills, training in normal assertiveness, training in impulse control and problem solving, and wilderness survival training. Next, the authors review treatment with stimulant drugs, emphasizing some of the issues that have still to be resolved in this area. The chapter concludes with a presentation of treatments involving members of the child's family and teachers. Stewart and Ashby have presented many issues that are disquieting to practicing school psychologists. Much remains to be done in the treatment of behavior-problem children, and this chapter is a refreshing and candid statement of the empirical work in this area.

APPENDIX A

The *Journal of School Psychology* publishes articles on research, opinions, and practice in school psychology, with the aim of fostering its continued development as a scientific and profesisonal speciality. It was the first journal specifically devoted to the speciality of school psychology. Similarly, *Psychology in the Schools* is devoted to research, opinion, and practice, and includes manuscripts from those ''that range in appeal from those that deal with theoretical and other problems of the school psychologist to those directed to the teacher, the counselor, administrator and other personnel workers in schools and colleges, public and private organizations.'' Manuscripts that clearly describe implications for the practitioner in the schools are given preference.

From 1972 through 1978, the *School Psychology Digest* published original articles through arrangement with the Editor. Relevant articles recommended by the publication Editorial Board were condensed or abstracted by the authors or the editorial staff. In 1979, the *Digest* involved a format change as a result of opinions expressed in a NASP survey. The *Digest* (now called the *School Psychology Review*) "publishes original research, reviews of theoretical and applied topics, and descriptions of intervention techniques of interest to school psychologists." The *Review* is the official journal of the National Association of School Psychologists.

The Division of School Psychology (16) of the American Psychological Association has also sponsored a publication called the *School Psychology Monograph*. The objectives of the Monograph series were and continue to be:

1. To present current broad issues in school psychology in depth.
2. To serve as an essential current reference work for practitioners.
3. To offer critical evaluation of topical areas, with both integration and synthesis included.
4. To be application oriented, offering a data base for decision making; when expert opinion is presented, differential evaluation will be made.
5. To present material with wide appeal to school psychologists, school teachers, special educators, administrators, and students. The evidence is expected to be made up of psychologists concerned with education and educators concerned with psychology.
6. To present material not readily available in other publications (Bardon, 1973, preface).

Professional Psychology, an APA-sponsored publication outlet, has published articles primarily on the application of psychology, and particularly on techniques and practices used in the application of psychology. The journal publishes articles of interest to all professional psychologists, and not just school psychologists. Specifically, the journal publishes articles on:

1. Standards of professional practices and delivery of services, and especially empirical research on such standards and services.
2. Applications of psychology in a variety of contexts: industries, institutions, and other organizations.
3. Education and training of professional psychologists at the graduate level and in continuing education (1979, editorial policy).

A newcomer to the publications devoted specifically to school psychology is the *School Psychology International.* As the title implies, the journal (magazine) has an international editorial board and publishes articles dedicated to a worldwide readership. The specific aims of the journal are to:

1. Provide a channel of communication, especially of practical procedures and ideas, for psychologists working in schools and for teachers.

2. Stimulate the use of new techniques that are not universally known, and apply them to problems commonly faced by psychologists and teachers.

3. Develop a rallying point through which psychologists and educators from around the world can identify with the growing international movement in their profession.

4. Provide a medium for encouraging improved educational/psychological approaches by parents and to help children in every nation.

REFERENCES

Alessi, G. J. Behavioral observation for the school psychologist: Responsive-discrepancy model. *School Psychology Review,* 1980, *9,* 31–45.

Attwell, A. A. *The school psychologist's handbook.* Los Angeles: Western Psychology Services, 1972.

Bardon, J. I. Preface. *School Psychology Monogrpah,* 1973, *1*(1), iv.

Bardon, J. I. The state of the art (and science) of school psychology. *American Psychologist,* 1976, *31,* 785–791.

Bardon, J. I. Debate: Will the real school psychologist please stand up? Part 1: How best to establish the identity of professional school psychology. *School Psychology Digest,* 1979, *8,* 162–167.

Bardon, J. I., & Bennett, V. C. *School psychology.* Englewood Cliffs, N.J.: Prentice-Hall, 1974.

Bardon, J. I., Costanza, L. J., & Walker, N. W. Institutions offering graduate training in school psychology, 1970–71. *Journal of School Psychology,* 1971, *9,* 252–260.

Bardon, J. I., & Wenger, R. D. Institutions offering graduate training in school psychology, 1973–74. *Journal of School Psychology,* 1974, *12,* 70–83.

Bergan, J. R. (Ed.). *School psychology in contemporary society.* Columbus, Ohio: Charles E. Merrill, in press.

Brown, D. T. Debate: Will the real school psychologist please stand up! Part 2: The drive for independence. *School Psychology Digest,* 1979, *8,* 168–173.

Brown, D. T., & Lindstrom, J. P. *Directory of school psychology training programs in the United States and Canada.* Stratford, Conn.: National Association of School Psychologists, 1977.

Caplan, G. Types of mental health consultation. *American Journal of Orthopsychiatry,* 1963, *3,* 470–481.

Caplan, G. *The theory and practice of mental health consultation.* New York: Basic Books, 1970.

Carroll, J. L. (Ed.). *Contemporary school psychology: Selected readings from psychology in the schools.* Brandon, Vt.: Clinical Psychology Publishing, 1978.

Conoley, J. C. (Ed.). *Consultation in schools: Theory, research, technology.* New York: Academic Press, 1980.

Cutts, N. (Ed.). *School psychologists at mid-century.* Washington, D.C.: American Psychological Association, 1955.

Eiserer, E. *The School psychologist.* New York: Center for Applied Research in Education, 1963.

Eiserer, P. The school psychologist. In B. B. Wolman (Ed.), *Manual of child psychopathology.* New York: McGraw-Hill, 1972.

Fein, L. G. *The changing school scene: Challenge to psychology.* New York: Wiley, 1974.

French, J. L., Smith, D. C., & Cardon, B. W. Institutions offering graduate training and financial assistance in school psychology. *Journal of School Psychology,* 1968, *6,* 261–267.

Gottsegen, M. G., & Gottsegen, G. B. (Eds.). *Professional and school psychology.* New York: Grune & Stratton, 1963.

Gray, S. W. *The psychologist in the schools.* New York: Holt, Rinehart, & Winston, 1963.

Haynes, S. N. *Principles of behavioral assessment.* New York: Gardner, 1978.

Haynes, S. N., & Wilson, C. C. *Behavioral assessment*. San Francisco: Jossey-Bass, 1979.

Herron, W., Green, M., Guild, M., Smith, A., & Kantor, R. *Contemporary school psychology*. Scranton, Pa.: International Textbook, 1970.

Hirst, W. E. *Know your school psychologist*. New York: Grune & Stratton, 1963.

Holt, F. D., & Kicklighter, R. H. (Eds.). *Psychological services in the schools: Readings in preparation, organization, and practice*. Dubuque, Iowa: William C. Brown, 1971.

Hunter, C. P. Classroom observation instruments and teacher inservice training by school psychologists. *School Psychology Monograph*, 1977, *3*, 45-88.

Johnson, S. M., & Bolstad, O. D. Methodological issues in naturalistic observation: Some problems and solutions for field research. In L. A. Hammerlynck, L. C. Handy, & E. H. Mash (Eds.), *Behavior change: Methodology, concepts and practice*. Champaign, Ill.: Research Press, 1973.

Jones, R. R., Reid, J. B., & Patterson, G. R. Naturalistic observation in clinical assessment. In P. McReynolds (Ed.), *Advances in psychological assessment* (Vol. 3). San Francisco: Jossey-Bass, 1975.

Kazdin, A. E. *History of behavior modification: Experimental foundations of contemporary research*. Baltimore: University Park Press, 1978.

Keller, H. R. Behavioral consultation. In J. C. Conoley (Ed.), *Consultation in schools: Theory, research, technology*. New York: Academic Press, 1980. (a)

Keller, H. R. Issues in the use of observational assessment. *School Psychology Review*, 1980, *9*, 21-30. (b)

Kent, R. N., & Foster, S. L. Direct observational procedures: Methodological issues in naturalistic settings. In A. R. Ciminero, K. S. Calhoun, & H. E. Adams (Eds.), *Handbook of behavioral assessment*. New York: Wiley, 1977.

Kratochwill, T. R. Advances in behavioral assessment. In C. R. Reynolds & T. B. Gutkin (Eds.), *Handbook of school psychology*. New York: Wiley, 1981.

Lynch, W. W. Guidelines to the use of classroom observation instruments by school psychologists. *School Psychology Monograph*, 1977, *3*, 1-22.

Magary, J. F. (Ed.). *School psychological services in theory and practice, a handbook*. Englewood Cliffs, N.J.: Prentice-Hall, 1967.

Meyers, J., Parsons, R. D., & Martin, R. *Mental health consultation in the schools*. San Francisco: Jossey-Bass, 1979.

Monroe, V. Roles and status of school psychology. In G. D. Phye & D. J. Reschly (Eds.), *School psychology: Perspectives and issues*. New York: Academic Press, 1979.

Mullen, F. (Ed.). *The psychologist on the school staff: Report of the Committee on reconsideration of the functions of the school psychologist*. American Psychological Association, 1958.

Phillips, B. N. (Ed.). *Perspectives on school psychology*. Austin: University of Texas Press, 1966.

Phye, G. D. School psychologists as consultants in the evaluation of learning and intervention outcomes. In G. D. Phye & D. F. Reschly (Eds.), *School psychology: Perspectives and issues*. New York: Academic Press, 1979.

Phye, G. D., & Reschly, D. J. (Eds.). *School psychology: Perspectives and issues*. New York: Academic Press, 1979.

Reger, R. *School psychology*. Springfield, R.I.: Charles C. Thomas, 1965.

Reynolds, C., & Gutkin, T. (Eds.). *Handbook of school psychology*. New York: Wiley, 1981.

Sackett, G. P. (Ed.). *Observing behavior: Data collection and analysis methods* (Vol. 2). Baltimore: University Park Press, 1978. (a)

Sackett, G. P. (Ed.). *Observing behavior: Theory and applications in mental retardation* (Vol. 1). Baltimore: University Park Press, 1978. (b)

Smith, D. C. Institutions offering graduate training in school psychology. *Journal of School Psychology*, 1964, *3*, 58-66.

Taylor, D. F. (Ed.). Explorations in role and function of the school psychologist. *Viewpoints: Bulletin of the School of Education, Indiana University*, 1977, *93*, V-69.

Tindall, R. H. School psychology: The development of a profession. In G. D. Phye & D. J. Reschly (Eds.). *School psychology: Perspectives and issues*. New York: Academic Press, 1979.

Valett, R. E. *The practice of school psychology: Professional problems*. New York: Wiley, 1963.

Wallace, J. E. W., & Ferguson, D. G. The development of school psychological services. In J. F. Magary (Ed.), *School psychological services in theory and practice, a handbook*. Taipei, Taiwan: Meiya Publications, 1967.

White, M. A. Graduate training in school psychology. *Journal of School Psychology*, 1963–1964, *2*, 34–42.

White, M., & Harris, M. *The school psychologist*. New York: Harper & Row, 1961.

Wildman, B. G., & Erickson, M. T. Methodological problems in behavioral observation. In J. D. Cone & R. P. Hawkins (Eds.). *Behavioral assessment: New directions in clinical psychology*. New York: Brunner/Mazel, 1977.

Ysseldyke, J. E. Who's calling the plays in school psychology? *Psychology in the Schools*, 1978, *15*, 373–378.

2 School Psychology in the 1980's: Some Critical Issues Related to Practice

Beeman N. Phillips
University of Texas at Austin

INTRODUCTION

School psychology has had phenomenal growth in the last two decades, especially in the last 10 years. But, continued growth and expansion in the next 10 years is problematic, partly due to the downward trend in school enrollments, conflicted relations with psychology and education, and internal divisions. Even in this context, however, it is worthwhile to look at the future, particularly with the view of identifying the most central issues or problems that need to be resolved, and what solutions to them are most likely to benefit school psychology, and hopefully are most likely to occur in the next decade.

Any predictions about school psychology involve some assumptions about the schools and their changes. There has been much discussion about the coming shortage of jobs for school psychologists; those making such predictions usually base them on the decreasing birth rate and subsequent school enrollment decreases. Whether this relation holds, however, depends on other factors. For example, if the American Psychological Association guidelines for psychological service units are adopted, requiring at least one "qualified" psychologist in each psychological services unit, up to a total of 10,000 positions for doctorally trained, or otherwise qualified, school psychologists would be available, assuming that at least one-fourth of the present school districts that provide psychological services do not have a qualified psychologist on the staff. This compares with an estimated 16,000 presently employed in schools, using Kicklighter's (1976) and Meacham and Peckham's (1978) figures, which are based on state education department reports that in some states grossly underestimate the actual numbers. In view of this, and the acceleration of employment during this period, the preceding estimate is an extrapolation. Furthermore, the number of students in training at the present time is estimated to be 5,000, using French and McCloskey's (1979) figures for 1978, which includes part-time students, and the number of graduates each year is estimated to be about 2,500, with 10% receiving doctorates.

The commitment of American society to education also enters into such extrapolations. If quality education continues to be valued, we can assume further upgrading of schooling and greater efforts to meet the educational needs of all children. This, of course, would enhance future prospects for psychologists in the schools. The nature of schooling is also likely to change, including further integration of the schools and social services, which will increase the need for school psychologists to fulfill a broader role, or, conversely, to be trained in one of several subspecializations within school psychology, in order to maximize the chances of taking full advantage of the employment opportunities that become available. To some extent, these possibilities are already evident in the role/functions assigned to school psychologists in the literature (Hunter & Lambert, 1974) and in the emphases of training programs (Goh, 1977).

Overall, there are grounds for being enthusiastic and optimistic about future prospects for school psychology. We, as academic and professional psychologists, will affect our own future, because it not only depends on factors outside of school psychology. How we deal with issues *inside* of school psychology, as well as our relations with professional psychology, and our interface with education, will have an important impact.

PROFESSIONALIZATION OF SCHOOL PSYCHOLOGY

Assumptions about the identity of school psychology as a profession are fundamental to many issues that will concern school psychologists in the 1980's. In the process of defining itself as a profession, school psychology has to first resolve whether it seeks identity as part of the psychology profession, or as an independent profession. If one begins with a prior question—that is, "What is the nature of a profession?"—then the resolution of this identity issue can be made in terms intrinsic to professionalization itself, assuming that there is consensus that school psychologists want greater professionalization.

Many writers have described the characteristics of a profession, one of the earliest being Flexner (1915), who is best remembered for his work in developing guidelines for the professionalization of medicine. More recently, Hickson and Thomas (1969) have examined a number of different definitions of a profession and have abstracted a set of criteria that specify their common characteristics. Utilizing similar criteria, Howsam, Corrigan, Denemark, and Nash (1976) have taken up the issue of whether teaching qualifies as a profession. Still more recently, Morell and Flaherty (1978) applied the criteria to the development of evaluation as a profession.

These conventions about the nature of professions represent sociological criteria in large measure, and in this sociological approach, there is the implicit

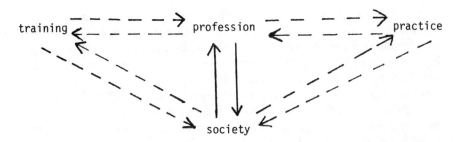

FIG. 2.1.   Schematic representation of interacting factors in a profession.

and sometimes explicit recognition that a profession develops out of a complex of relationships between society, training, and practice. This interactive and evolutionary process is schematically represented in Fig. 2.1. For example, a profession is an occupationally related social institution with a high level of public trust that provides essential services to society. Furthermore, it is based on undergirding disciplines from which basic insights are drawn and applied knowledge and skill are obtained. There is also a body of knowledge and skills *specific to the profession,* and not available to laypersons, that is acquired through protracted training and is accompanied by a strong service commitment and a lifetime commitment to competence. The profession is organized into professional associations that, although socially accountable, function to control standards for admission to, and work and continuance in, the profession. This is accompanied by accountability to the profession rather than to the public, and relative freedom from *direct* on-the-job supervision.

Examining school psychology with respect to these criteria, it can be argued that school psychology will continue to professionalize in the next decade. But in the process, some of the issues that must be faced and resolved include:

1. What particular set of essential services will school psychology lay claim to? How will territoriality issues be dealt with?

2. Will justification of the scientist–practitioner model of training be maintained? How will psychology and/or education as the knowledge and skills base of school psychology be dealt with? Can school psychologists identify a body of knowledge and skills *specific* to school psychology, and to school psychology as a professional psychology specialty?

3. How will school psychology resolve the master's versus doctorate entry-level issue? The state education department versus state psychology board role in certification and licensing? The American Psychological Association versus the National Council for Accreditation in Teacher Education role in accreditation of programs?

4. How will school psychology deal with consumerism? Legal factors in providing school psychological services? Role of professional associations in school psychology? Support of scholarly activities?

Although no strong claim can be made for the professional status of school psychology at this time, there are encouraging signs. A claim for such professional legitimacy can be made, for example, on the basis that there is an emerging body of special knowledge in school psychology—that is, knowledge that is specific to the psychological aspects of schooling. In addition, there has been a rapid development of training programs (French & McCloskey, 1979), and there is a growing specification of who is competent to perform what school-psychological services. Further, those who have looked at psychology recently (e.g., Peterson, 1976) tend to conclude that it is well on its way to becoming a profession. School psychology, as a professional psychology specialty, would appear, therefore, to be on the same road. At least, one might argue that psychology, and thus school psychology, will qualify as a profession during the 1980's.

LICENSING FOR SCHOOL PSYCHOLOGISTS?

One important aspect of the present education and credentialing scene is professional licensing. It is a potent issue in psychology (Gross, 1978; Matarazzo, 1977) and in other helping professions, such as among social workers (Hardcastle, 1977) and counselors (Forster, 1977). In view of the conflicts surrounding licensure, one might assume that there is great controversy over the value of professional licensing. But, this does not seem to be the case, because the belief that licensing is a way to protect the public against incompetent professionals appears to be widely shared among professionals and the public at large. Although this appears to be the case in most of the 50 states, some professionals who have carefully reviewed the literature on licensing strongly disagree with this almost universal assumption. Gross (1978), for example, is very critical of professional licensing. Using research and scholarly opinion primarily on the medical profession, because that is what most of the literature has focused on, and because it is the model being followed by other helping professions, Gross argues that there is a specious relation between licensing and professional competence. He further argues that the myth of the presumed value to the public of professional licensing is maintained by collusion between the states and the professions. His discussion, however, is restricted to the legislative aspect of licensing, including certification and other forms of legal restraints on entry into and practice in a profession. He further excludes occupations where autonomy is restricted by legislative mandate, as in the case of master's level psychologists (in most states), dental hygienists, nurses, and so on, and where the institution maintains control over the service setting, as in the teaching profession. In effect, Gross focuses on independent practice.

Because the practice of school psychology is mostly in an institution that maintains control over the service setting, and few school psychologists are in independent practice, one might conclude that licensing would *not* be a "hot" issue among school psychologists. However, this is not the case at the present time, so that many school psychologists must see licensing as central to professional interests.

The explanation for this interest may lie in the role of licensing in the development of professions. For example, Gerstle and Jacobs (1976) draw an analogy between professions and guilds, pointing out that guilds restricted competition, set prices, defined the qualities of craftsmanship, and controlled entrance and training. Although guilds and professions differ in essential ways, they see similarities that are important in understanding the centrality of licensing to professional practice. As Gross (1978) points out, licensing is a charter of autonomy that is based on public acceptance of professional expertise and altruism. With it, the power of the professional is legitimized, and the profession gains a monopoly over practice. It is not surprising, therefore, that such power is widely sought, that many occupations want to become professions, or that school psychologists are interested in licensing.

Although the evidence does not indicate that licensing is effective in preventing incompetent practice (Gross, 1978), there is a relation between licensing and training that may appeal to school psychologists supporting licensing efforts. As Spector and Frederick (1952) note, licensing leads to the raising and tightening of standards, including the lengthening of the period of training, and the adding of extended internship experience. This, and the presumed link between training, professional competence, and quality of service, may be the basis for school psychologists' support of licensing arrangements for the profession.

Ultimately, the issue for school psychologists may be political in nature. It is not so much that they want to be licensed, because licensing does not appear to be a necessity for the profession. What is at issue is our identity as a profession, either as a part of professional psychology or as an independent profession allied to both the psychology and teaching professions. There is a fear of *exclusion* from licensing rather than a strong urge to be licensed. In a fundamental sense, the pressure for licensing of school psychologists is reactive—to avoid prohibitions on practice and dependence on others, and to restrict the rights of other professionals to define the boundaries of school-psychology practice. Because licensing is so potentially powerful and serves so many professional and self-interest purposes, this concern is very real, and necessary.

To synthesize many of the issues and problems in licensing, one can focus on the one overriding question, which is: What do we do about the master's level psychologist? Without reexamining this issue in all its ramifications, because this has been done many times over a number of years, it instead would be helpful to state how this challenge should be met. That is, if current developments in this fundamental area are indicative of an emerging resolution, it appears to be this:

First, career tracks should be implemented for those with less than a doctoral degree who wish to work and progress upward in status and responsibility in school psychology. This will require increased accessibility to doctoral training, more emphasis on continuing education, and the establishment and implementation of national standards for school psychology, while preserving doctoral-level training as the ultimate goal.

Second, in recognition that there are and will continue to be a need for different levels and patterns of training, as well as practice, in school psychology, training and practice should emphasize specialization, with practice limited by training emphases and competencies. As reinforcement of such differentiated training and practice, state education departments, national psychological examining boards, and professional accrediting bodies should limit credentialing and program evaluation to such subspecialty training and practice, leaving generic licensing to state psychology boards.

Third, school psychologists should work for the reform of licensing laws, while not, however, working for deprofessionalization. More reliance should be placed on accreditation of training programs and credentialing of individuals through professional groups rather than licensing statutes.

Fourth, school psychologists should become a major force in promoting cohesiveness among professional psychologists, as opposed to fractionation and insularity, even though recognizing substantive specialization and differentiation by levels of training and role functions. They also should take a politically and professionally active role in promoting psychology in the schools, and school psychology within psychology.

MENTAL-HEALTH SERVICES IN THE SCHOOLS, AND SCHOOL PSYCHOLOGISTS AS HEALTH-SERVICE PROVIDERS

One of the hottest legislative topics confronting psychology is national health insurance. It affects all psychologists in one way or another, and many professional psychologists directly, including some school psychologists. Psychologists have quite different views of the issue, however, and there are probably wide variations in school psychologists' views of it, including variations in how *other* psychologists view our role as health-service providers.

In a recent study, Gottfredson and Dyer (1978) present a basic description of health-service providers who are members of APA, utilizing a stratified random sample of 10,002 APA members, with a 74% return. Of interest was the finding that school psychologists were the third most common specialty of psychologists, behind clinical and counseling psychologists. School psychology was the specialty of 24% of the master's-level and 5% of the doctoral-level service providers, in addition to representing 36% of the "other postbaccalaureate" degree psychologists, this latter group including MD, JD, and presumably EdSp degree holders.

Using their analysis of the primary settings in which psychologists provide health services, 28% of master's-level psychologists, 6% of doctoral-level, and

41% of "other postbaccalaureate" degree psychologists reported that they provide health services primarily in schools. Presumably, these are mostly school psychologists, which reinforces the idea that school psychologists are substantially involved in providing mental-health services. As to licensure/certification status, 56% of those identifying school systems as their primary service setting (for providing mental-health services) stated that they were licensed and/or certified.

Whether school psychologists have a future role in national health insurance, and the nature of that role, will depend to some extent on the role of the schools in the delivery of mental-health related services to children. If a comprehensive delivery system develops as Ramey (1974) advocates, its main function will be to monitor the mental and physical health of all children, and provide the needed preventive and remedial services. In Ramey's proposed model, local schools would be used as the front-line screening, assessment, and treatment center, being staffed with a team of professionals including school nurses, school counselors, psychological examiners, and other staff. Problems that require more sophisticated diagnosis and treatment, or that for other reasons prove to be intractable to local efforts, would be referred to the second level of services, this group consisting of psychologists (including school psychologists), doctors, dentists, and so on. The advantages of using schools is that they provide the easiest accessibility to children and families, schools usually serve contiguous neighborhood areas, and the facilities already present can serve such functions with minimal modification or improvement.

Such a comprehensive delivery system, which utilizes local schools, would, of course, have a preventive orientation. But this raises the question of what detrimental behaviors are to be prevented, and whether there are effective means to achieve such prevention, once the mental and emotional problems that are to be given priority are identified. A corollary to this proposal, which rests upon the same general logic, is that preschool programs should be universally available. For reasons of comprehensiveness and overall effectiveness, preschool programs would be included in the general model, providing the same screening, assesssment, and treatment services from a very early age onward. In Ramey's (1974) view, the child would be enrolled in the system during the mother's pregnancy and would remain in it until adulthood. However, the likelihood of such a comprehensive health-services system being incorporated into a national health-insurance program appears to be slight. At least, the chances appear bleaker now than they may have appeared in the early 1970's when the Joint Commission on Mental Health of Children report (1970) that was the stimulus for Ramey's article was published.

A related development is the concept of developmental review of all children that has as its impetus the Early and Periodic Screening, Diagnosis, and Treatment Program (EPSDT), which became a mandated service under the Medicaid program through an amendment of Title XIX of the Social Security Act. It became effective in July, 1969, and required early screening and diagnosis of individuals eligible for Medicaid or under the age of 21, to ascertain physical and mental defects and to provide such health care, treatment, and other measures as needed to correct or ameliorate the defects and chronic conditions discovered. More recently, there has been a major proposed shift in this program's emphasis to one that develops a system of health care that treats the person rather than the dysfunction or disease. An example of this orientation, with its obvious implications for schools, is the report of the February, 1977, Conference on Developmental Screening and Assessment assembled by the American Association for Psychiatric Services to Children (Huntington, 1977).

To a considerable degree, the potential role of school psychologists in national health insurance depends on the definition of mental-health services, and the nature of the health-services delivery model that is ultimately developed. If mental-health services are primarily defined in terms of psychotherapy, then the participation of school psychologists is necessarily limited. This is the position espoused in the special issue of the *American Psychologist* on national health insurance (Cummings, 1977). Throughout this special issue, the term mental-health services is rarely used, whereas psychotherapy appears over and over in the articles presented, and the point at issue is never explicitly raised. As to the model that is to be followed in national health insurance, a distinction can be made between a health model as opposed to a medical model, although the medical model is also used in a metaphorical sense, as when it refers to underlying pathology. In a medical approach, emotional problems that have a basis in organic brain disease, or that are classifiable as psychosis, would be included in the plan. This is essentially a psychiatrically oriented view of mental illness. In contrast, the community mental-health center concept fits well into the health model, as does the idea that psychological problems are closely interrelated with physical problems, and that mental-health interventions can effectively treat emotional aspects of physical illness.

More recently, a special issue of *Professional Psychology* (Budman & Wertlieb, 1979) was devoted to psychologists in health-care settings. The orientation of this issue is broad and diverse, with considerable coverage of children in health-care settings. There is also greater attention to a wider variety of interventions, and more emphasis on the training needed by psychologists who work in such settings. Overall, this special issue implicitly presents a more promising view of the potential for involvement of school psychologists in health-care settings.

A practical question looming ever larger in deliberations on national health insurance, and which will be of central importance in policy decisions, is the cost effectiveness of mental-health services. At this time, provision of such services is increasingly becoming an economic as well as a political issue. The argument generally made by psychologists is that the inclusion of mental-health services will enable the entire health-care system to operate on a more cost-effective basis because of the presumed benefits of mental-health intervention in reducing physical health costs. The special issue of the *American Psychologist* previously referred to strives to provide detailed documentation of such benefits, with some success. Throughout these discussions, however, there is the recognition that mental-health services would need to be greatly curtailed—e.g., brief psychotherapy rather than extended psychotherapy—as well as other limits put on the utilization of such services. In essence, the developments occurring imply that only severe emotional illness and emotional aspects of physical illness will ultimately be "insurable" in a national health plan.

These developments taken together would seem to minimize the role of the schools in health care, and reduce the potential role of school psychologists in a comprehensive health-care system, because such a system will not be nearly as comprehensive as initial discussions and planning envisioned. Nevertheless, some school psychologists will want to prepare themselves to participate in the system, and in some schools, comprehensive health services will become a viable aspect of the educational enterprise, utilizing school psychologists as well as other health-care personnel.

PSYCHOEDUCATIONAL REHABILITATION: KEY TO THE RELEVANCE OF SCHOOL PSYCHOLOGY TO THE NEW EDUCATIONAL PRIORITIES?

The research indicates that schools are not doing an adequate job of rehabilitating students with severe handicaps (Dunn, 1968; Reynolds, 1978). The goal of psychoeducational rehabilitation should be to provide these children with the intellectual, emotional, and physical skills needed to function in the school, family, and community with the least amount of support from the family, the community, and support services personnel. In other words, it is the development of skills, not just environmental manipulations and adjustments, that is the determining factor in a *rehabilitation* outcome. There are a myriad of skilled behaviors that such children must perform if they are to function effectively in the school, family, and community. The quality and complexity of these skills vary with respect to the particular environment in which the child is functioning. In such a skills-training approach, the rehabilitation diagnosis attempts to identify those specific skills deficits that are preventing these children from functioning more effectively and at a level commensurate with their potential. A requirement of the skills-training model is the *systematic use* of existing rehabilitation environmental support settings. These rehabilitation settings provide the means by which teachers, school psychologists, collaborating parents, and others involved in the rehabilitation process can gradually increase the environmental demands placed upon the handicapped child as the child develops increasingly higher levels of skilled performance. In this way, the child has the opportunity to practice his/her developing skill in an environmental setting that is suitable to the child's present skill level.

Table 2.1 provides an outline of the psychoeducational–environmental support settings available to such children. They are sequenced in terms of the child's dependency, which is defined in terms of his/her need for special settings and professional school-related manpower. Even though Public Law 94–142 and other statutory and court mandates have given widespread support to the development and growth of these settings, the failure to develop specifically *rehabilitative* programs for these psychoeducational support settings has been conspicuous. The psychoeducational programs provided are those typically provided in any remedial situation. For the most part, teachers, school psychologists, and other professional support personnel have continued to rely too much on a psychodynamic–personalistic approach to intervention. There is a failure, in part, to recognize that placing the handicapped child in alternative psychoeducational settings is not rehabilitative *in itself*. Placing a child in a rehabilitative setting is only the initial step, and if the child has not been taught to be more capable *in such settings*, once the support system is withdrawn, the child will be no better off. The psychoeducational setting is more than just a place to put the handicapped child. The important factor is whether the child is rehabilitated in the sense of increased capability to adapt in *that* setting, and has acquired the *potential* for adapting in a higher order setting.

It must be noted, therefore, that if school psychologists are to be relevant to the educational priorities of the 1980's, they must have the skills required by a psychoeducational–rehabilitation approach. Essentially, these are skills to diag-

TABLE 2.1
Psychoeducational Rehabilitation Environments Ordered in Terms
of the Handicapped Child's Dependency[a]

Level of Independence[b]	Psychoeducational–Environmental Support Settings	
	Living	Schooling
Total Independence	1. Home, with parents	1. Regular school and classroom
	2. Home, with parents + Preschool center	2. Regular school and classroom, with special tutoring, etc.
	3. Residential day center, with nights, and weekends at home	3. Regular school, with special class
	4. Residential institution	4. Special day school
Total Dependence		5. Residential school

[a] After Anthony, 1977.
[b] Level of independence refers to need for special settings and professional assistance and support.

nose exactly what skills the handicapped child has, what skills are needed in *each* psychoeducational support environment, and what is needed to intervene and develop and implement programs leading handicapped children to acquire these necessary skills.

A combination of behavior-therapy approaches (Marholin, 1978), and Bloom's (1976) philosophy and theory of school learning can provide the underpinning for such a psychoeducational–rehabilitation model. In this version of mastery learning, cognitive entry behaviors, affective entry characteristics, and the quality of instruction are important variables. However, quality of instruction is the particular aspect of Bloom's theory that has the most potential impact, and by serving in a behavioral consultative role (Bergan, 1977) to teachers, and so on, the school psychologist has the opportunity to make a real difference in the skills learning of handicapped students. In addition to contributing to the choice of environmental setting goals, which need analysis in terms of specific elements and their interrelationships, diagnostic and assessment tools need to be developed.

Psychoeducational rehabilitation also requires interprofessional collaboration, and in this connection much has been made of PL 94–142's injunctions concerning evaluation by a "multidisciplinary team or group of persons" and placement decisions "by a group of persons, including persons knowledgeable about the child, the meaning of the evaluation data, and the placement options (Section 121a)." In addition to such legal mandates, there are a variety of other bases for interprofessional collaboration. For example, Smith (1973) writes to this point and argues that psychologists need to work routinely with other professionals. Within school psychology, Thomas (1972), Smith and DiBacco (1974), and others have put forward the idea that joint responsibility for evaluation and intervention decisions and activities is a desirable and necessary goal. The learning-disabilities movement has also provided strong advocacy for a "team" approach (Wallace, 1976).

What is at issue here, however, are two different matters. One concerns the decision-making model, which involves the need to collaborate and to function *as a team,* and the other concerns the professions, and indirectly the disciplines, involved in such collaboration. A "discipline" is a field of study, a branch of knowledge, or a systematized body of knowledge; presumably, different disciplines are important to the diagnostic–intervention process. In contrast, a profession, even though it draws from one or more disciplines, includes much more, such as role definitions, legislative sanctions, and a number of other characteristics. Strictly speaking, therefore, "disciplines" do not collaborate, but professionals do.

The decision-making model itself also raises some problems because it is variously construed in the school-psychology literature. Although the PL 94–142 mandate is only for collaboration, many writers discuss it as if team or group decisions are mandated. Patton (1976), for example, found that individuals making such decisions could, or did, not function as a team, and construes this as an unsatisfactory situation. Others have examined child-study teams in greater detail, as in the case of Hyman and his colleagues (Hyman, Carral, Duffey, Manni, & Winikur, 1973), who examined conflict resolution, whereas Yoshida, Fenton, Maxwell, and Kaufman (1978) looked at the kind of participation and satisfaction of team members. From these and similar studies, one gets the impression that the adequacy of team functioning is the criterion against which success is to be judged, which leads to the further impression that it is presumed, by these writers, that collaboration *requires* a team approach and group-derived decisions.

In summary, although psychoeducational rehabilitation requires a multidisciplinary base, and considerable interprofessional collaboration, the decision-making model that is becoming widespread in school psychological practice should be viewed with grave reservations, not only in terms of its impact on psychoeducational rehabilitation specifically, but school psychology generally. For example, the consultation model of providing services is compatible with interprofessional collaboration (Meyers, Parsons, & Martin, 1979), and it is a necessary aspect of psychoeducational rehabilitation, while at the same time being inherently inhospitable to group decision-making paradigms and team functioning.

ETHICAL PRACTICE IN SCHOOL PSYCHOLOGY

Most school psychologists try to uphold the ethical principles of their profession. These principles entail a commitment to promote the welfare of clients, as defined in the ethical standards of the APA (1977). However, the recent emphasis on the rights of consumers, and the increasing involvement of legislative and court mandates in education (Bersoff, 1975), make it important that school psychologists in the 1980's extend their thinking about ethical standards and practice.

Dealing with the rights of clients, of course, presupposes that who is the "client" is always obvious. This is not the case, although the argument might be made that ultimately the child is the client. In some cases, the child is the client directly, but in many cases, the client is a parent, teacher, or other school person. One might even consider that the school system is the school psychologist's "client" in some cases. In a functional sense, and in terms of actual services being provided, the "client" may be any one of the forementioned. Most often, however, it is the child, teacher, or parent, or another specific *individual* to whom service is provided. In addition, in regard to most services to children, the parents or legal guardian must be considered at least coequally as the client, and as the legal "surrogate client." This complicates the task of the school psychologist who attempts to integrate ethical rights and responsibilities with school-psychological services.

Ethical principles require that clients be provided with sufficient information to make informed decisions about the services that might be provided. For example, if a school psychologist is proposing a particular intervention in a school, the principal needs knowledge of the procedures involved, the probable benefits and possible side effects of the proposed intervention, and information on alternatives that might be used instead. When the client is the child and parent, information about the qualifications of the school psychologist to carry out a proposed intervention may be important to an informed decision. Information about the goals of the intervention, length or duration, and the limits on confidentiality also need to be considered.

Whereas the focus just discussed is on the school psychologist's goals, procedures, and so on, the client may have goals incompatible with the school psychologist's. When this is the case, the school psychologist and client need to examine together the likely consequences of pursuing the school psychologist's and the client's goals. If an agreement cannot be reached, then the school psychologist cannot work with the client, and will seek alternative arrangements. An example would be if the school psychologist finds it hard to support the parents' goals for the child, or if parents seek to waive rights of children that cannot be waived by parents.

An issue that sometimes comes up involves challenges to the school psychologist's competence by parents, the child, or other clients. Although direct challenges to one's competence are highly threatening, and it is easy to dismiss such criticism, the school psychologist who is concerned with ethical practice must consider the validity of such criticisms, and respond appropriately. In some instances, the school psychologist receives complaints from clients about other school psychologists. In such cases, ethical practice requires that the school psychologist attempt to rectify the situation, keeping in mind the corollary responsibility of protecting the reputation of professional colleagues.

In the future, more discussion of the specific ways in which ethical principles should be put into practice will be necessary. If ethical codes represent principles that guide practice, more will need to be done in training as well as in continuing professional development. For example, it is unethical for school psychologists to practice beyond the limits of their competence, but more needs to be done in the future to teach school psychologists to recognize when they have reached those limits. In addition, training and continuing-education activities need to provide the knowledge sufficient to practice competently. In effect, we must rethink and retool our training, continuing-education, and professional-development activities in the 1980's if the practice of school psychology is to be consistent with ethical principles.

COPING WITH PROFESSIONAL STRESS:
THE "HIDDEN" CHALLENGE OF THE 1980's?

The thrust toward recognizing stress and taking collective professional responsibility for coping with it may be one of the revolutionary changes in school psychology in the 1980's. This effort would seek to prevent needless distress and professional dysfunction and to build the strengths and increase the competence and coping skills of school psychologists.

Although an understanding of etiology is necessary in order to develop adequate strategies of intervention, the literature on stress of school psychologists is almost nonexistent, so that we presently know little about the sources, incidence, and effects of stress among school psychologists. In contrast, there has been extensive research on the stress of children in school (e.g., Phillips, 1978), and the stress of teachers has been under increased investigation (Keavney & Sinclair, 1978; Phillips & Lee, 1980). In the best of circumstances, however, the search for the causes of stress would be a difficult challenge, because stress is usually the outcome of multiple interrelating personal and situational factors, including professional factors that are recognized as important contributors to the incidence of stress among professionals.

To some extent, our profession will be crisis oriented in the 1980's, and a number of developments that are anticipated in this decade may contribute to school psychologists' distress. New roles are emerging for school psychologists (Hunter & Lambert, 1974), along with considerable divergence as to priorities among these roles (Kaplan, Clancy, & Chrin, 1977; Meacham & Peckham, 1978). This ambiguity and the demands for adapting to such changing roles represent important stressors. Moreover, as courts and legislative bodies take an increasingly active interest in psychological and educational practices, further legal impingements on the work of the school psychologist will occur; such intrusions have considerable potential for increasing the ambiguity of the school psychologist's role (Cardon, Kuriloff, & Phillips, 1975). With the expected decline in school enrollments, increased job insecurity is likely as a result of pressures to reduce the size of support-services staffs. In addition, the concept of accountability will continue to have increased application to education, and applying the concept to school psychologists will raise issues of special concern. Finally, school psychologists, as increased professionalization occurs, will increasingly seek autonomy, quality services, and other professional goals that will clash with the bureaucratic requirements of school systems.

The pattern, therefore, is one of increasing uncertainty and difficulties for school psychologists, so that making help available to those trying to cope with distress needs to become a responsibility of the profession. In particular, strategies should be encouraged for the prevention of distress, and such efforts should have a high priority, for such activities are justified both by their efficacy and by the personal, professional, and economic costs of relying only on remedial and corrective programs.

CONTROL AND REGULATION IN SCHOOL PSYCHOLOGY: TOWARD A NATIONAL STANDARD OF TRAINING AND PRACTICE?

At this point in time, a description of the school-psychology enterprise is exceedingly complex because it is rife with Byzantine organization, governance, and decision-making structures. A case in point is that controls and regulations in school psychology are ubiquitous, which is not surprising, emerging as they do from this labyrinthine structure of forces. The ultimate justification of such control and regulation, however, is seemingly self evident: to promote the public welfare by protecting the schools, children, and parents from gross incompetents; by improving the quality of training and practice, and by maximizing cost–benefit service delivery outcomes.

In examining and dealing with the issues and problems of regulation and control, it is important to have a conceptual as well as a practical understanding of the factors involved. If we do not know and understand what these factors are and how they work, both overtly or explicitly and covertly or implicitly, then we may not realize just how we are controlled and regulated in school psychology. The factors that are involved are varied and a number of them are depicted in Fig. 2.2. For example, control and regulation originates at the local, state, or federal *level;* there are legal (statute, administrative regulations, or court rulings), institutional (training and services-delivery settings), professional, and nonprofessional *sources* of control; and regulatory *mechanisms* such as accreditation, codes of ethics, and licensing. In addition, the point at which control and regulation are exercised is perhaps most critical because exercising control at the level of training, through entry into the profession, or at the level of practice may influence school psychology in profoundly different ways.

To see the nature of control and regulation most clearly, we need to raise the two basic questions about regulation and control, and then apply them to subdoctoral psychology, an issue that has had great prominence in psychology. The basic questions are: Regulation and control toward what ends? And, regulation and control through what means? To cull out and underline the thesis of much of the past discussion on this controversial topic, which in reality centers around these two basic questions, it would appear that, in retrospect, the fight and the struggle concerning master's-level psychologists has been fought on narrow grounds. The battleground has been private practice, and whether psychologists with master's degrees can practice independently. Even more narrowly conceived, the battleground has been psychotherapy. The issue has been framed in

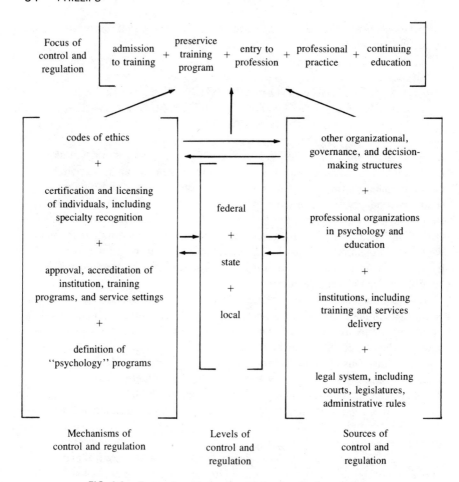

FIG. 2.2.   Factors in control and regulation in school psychology.

state statutes, however, in terms of supervision, rather than practice, and by restricting the use of the title "psychologist." As a matter of fact, there are no restrictions on the practice of master's-level psychologists that do not apply equally to the doctoral-level psychologist, *except* that such practice must be done under supervision, making the supervisory mechanism, therefore, the primary means of regulating and controlling practice.

As to the future of control and regulation in school psychology, two concurrent models of change seem to be supported. One is that control and regulation will become increasingly nationalized under pressures from developments in education and psychology. Within education, one can include effects of the body of federal statutes, regulations, and court rulings that have limited both state and local policy options; collective bargaining and the political influence of organized teachers (e.g., NEA); and the federal role in categorical and targeted funding and other financial support of education, and in coordination activities, through the new Department of Education. In psychology, a number of developments are occurring that reinforce this nationalization theme. The APA Council of Representatives adopted generic guidelines for providers of psychological services in January, 1977, and this committee is now drafting guidelines for specialties in psychology. Similarly, the APA Committee on State Legislation is working on a national model for state legislation regulating the practice of psychology. The proposed National Commission on Education and Credentialing in Psychology is another milestone in this effort to unify the education and credentialing system in psychology, as is the Council for the National Register of Health Service Providers in Psychology. The "Criteria for Accreditation of Doctoral Training Programs and Internships in Professional Psychology," approved by the APA Council of Representatives in January, 1979, and the National Association of School Psychologists (NASP) Standards for Training Programs in School Psychology, approved in February, 1978, represent a similar development specifically in the area of training standards.

But, there is evidence of other important changes in regulatory and control processes in psychology, and this model of change is represented by those who are proposing deprofessionalizing the professions. Advocates of this radical approach oppose, for example, licensure generally, believing that anyone who wants to practice psychology, law, medicine, or other professions should be permitted to. The proposition behind this position is that licensing is not done to protect the public, but to control entry into the profession, thus creating a monopoly. The Department of Justice and the Federal Trade Commission are in some ways allied with this position, and may aggressively enter this arena on the basis of antitrust considerations and federal statutes. A related threat to licensure is posed by the Equal Employment Opportunity Commission (EEOC), which may seek to bring the licensed professions under the terms of civil-rights legislation. However, the emergence of this kind of influence on the professions is likely to only *redirect* the trend toward nationalization of training and practice standards, because the federal government will be the primary force behind such efforts.

Thus, in summary, these two sets of events, forces, and developments, even though they appear to have oppositional characteristics, may over time coalesce around a national perspective on training and practice. Although the direction, but not the substantive character, of these changes can be predicted, it can be more safely concluded that the debate will be sharp, the conflict overt, and the changes evolutionary.

PROFESSIONAL ASSOCIATIONS AND POLITICAL ACTIVISM AS THE MEANS TO CAREER AND STATUS SUPPORT IN SCHOOL PSYCHOLOGY

School psychologists are identified with both psychology and education. They serve children as only one among several professional groups that work in supportive services roles in the schools. Among the others are the school counselors, the school social workers, and speech, school nurse, and other specialists. In the 1980's, if funds for education become scarcer and demands for accountability increase, the employment and role/functions of school psychologists may be increasingly influenced by political rather than professional factors.

The relation between school psychology and psychology represents a similar situation. School psychology as a specialty competes with other professional psychology specialties, especially clinical psychology, the dominant group in professional psychology. There is, in this relationship, as in those involving other school professionals, a question of a "territorial imperative" mentality involving jurisdictional disputes and issues of competence for particular role/functions. Typically, the issues ultimately involve funding, training standards, qualifications for providing psychological services, and certification criteria.

Division 16 of the APA and the NASP have for years been heavily involved in efforts to confirm the competence, status, and professional autonomy of school psychologists. Concern with legislation, negotiations with school systems and government agencies, and workshops and other forms of continuing education reflect these efforts. School psychologists in academic settings, however, have, to some extent, been privileged in not having to deal with these issues to the extent that practicing school psychologists have had to. In contrast, school psychologists in nonacademic settings have lacked the forms of protection and mutual support found in academia. They have, therefore, increasingly turned to professional associations to represent them in conflicts with other segments of psychology, other professions, and educational institutions.

To a greater degree than in academia, the context in which school psychologists function in schools is also not of their own making, so practitioners have had to further their careers by opposing and trying to change conditions in schools that are the products of tradition and practices influenced by a diversity of groups. For the practitioner's status to change, therefore, a number of current practices, beliefs, and traditions about the schools require change. The same might also be said about some of the conditions of professional psychology. Implicit in such change is the recognition of school psychology as a professional psychology specialty by both psychology and education. If such changes can be brought about, practicing school psychologists, no longer beleaguered, could relinquish the role of activist. It is likely, with their professional status confirmed, they could devote more effort toward their school endeavors, with the freedom to apply their unique professional knowledge and skills more effectively to school learning and behavior problems. At least, such an achievement would lead to a displacement of special professional interest by a more general concern with the interests of psychology as a science and profession, as well as the educational and general public interest.

Ultimately, however, these matters will be resolved in the professional and political arena, and professional organizations and politics become the means through which school psychologists will achieve career and status support. The APA, particularly the Division of School Psychology, and such affiliated groups as the Council of Directors of School Psychology Programs, and the various state psychological associations, and such other groups as the NASP, The American Personnel and Guidance Association, the various special-education groups, and such education groups as the American Association of School Administrators and the National Educational Association will mold and shape the future of school psychology. The vulnerability of school psychology is that it has allegiances to both psychology and education, and must therefore actively work with both education and psychology organizations. To achieve its legitimate goals, it must collaborate and work through such groups, while at the same time dealing with the rivalries and conflict of interests that exist, and achieving cooperation and mutual objectives whenever possible. Unfortunately, the amount of work that must be done increases geometrically with the number of groups involved, the difficulty of the issues and problems to be resolved, and the degree to which legislative and other political realities enter into the outcomes that are sought.

THE ROLE OF SCHOOL PSYCHOLOGISTS IN ADVOCACY

In the 1980's, school psychologists will find many reasons to affirm their concern for children through meaningful advocacy actions and programs. The scope of these actions will reflect the diversity of the groups, professions, and disciplines through which children's psychological and educational interests are represented. Because much of the advocacy for psychological and educational reforms will be controversial, a child-advocacy system needs to be created. Specifically, arrangements need to be made at the local, state, and national level to ensure a collective and cohesive response to the needs of children.

In the process of developing a child-advocacy system, it is important that long-range planning, policy making, and programming be given high priority. Special emphasis also needs to be given to the interrelationships of professional groups, agencies, and other entities serving children and their families, and to their working together, rather than competing or overlapping, in such advocacy efforts. The consumers of school psychological services also must be heard,

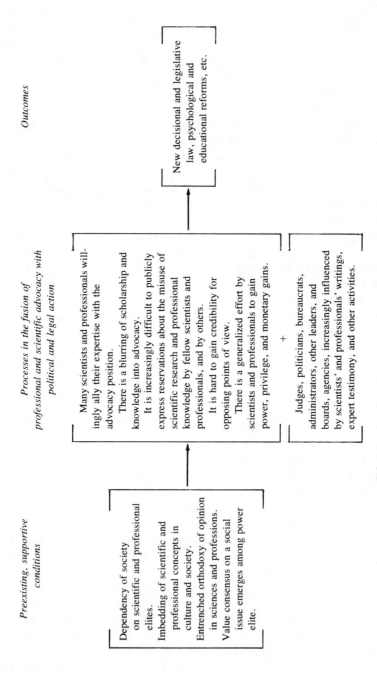

Preexisting, supportive conditions

Processes in the fusion of professional and scientific advocacy with political and legal action

Outcomes

Dependency of society on scientific and professional elites.
Imbedding of scientific and professional concepts in culture and society.
Entrenched orthodoxy of opinion in sciences and professions.
Value consensus on a social issue emerges among power elite.

Many scientists and professionals willingly ally their expertise with the advocacy position.
There is a blurring of scholarship and knowledge into advocacy.
It is increasingly difficult to publicly express reservations about the misuse of scientific research and professional knowledge by fellow scientists and professionals, and by others.
It is hard to gain credibility for opposing points of view.
There is a generalized effort by scientists and professionals to gain power, privilege, and monetary gains.

+

Judges, politicians, bureaucrats, administrators, other leaders, and boards, agencies, increasingly influenced by scientists' and professionals' writings, expert testimony, and other activities.

New decisional and legislative law, psychological and educational reforms, etc.

FIG. 2.3.   Paradigm of advocacy by scientists and professionals.

especially the parents of children, because children are unable to speak effectively for themselves.

Those who have addressed themselves to the problems and promise of advocacy have considered the factors that militate for and against successful sociopolitical and legal advocacy. In addition to looking at the significance of particular factors in specific advocacy situations, they have examined the fundamental dimensions, general conditions, and general processes that are involved. Some of these insights are represented in the paradigm shown in Fig. 2.3, which in turn is derived from the writings of Young and Bress (1975), Coleman (1975), Bazelon (1973), Bersoff (1975), Krass (1976), Kamin (1975), Rist and Anson (1977), and Bersoff and Prasse (1978).

What has been said by these writers, and hopefully what is reflected in the paradigm, is that advocacy by scientists and professionals can have considerable impact on basic sociopolitical decisions. In the final analysis, therefore, scientists and professionals who have been involved in, and who have examined, advocacy confirm what common sense tells us: Advocacy has a legitimate, and an increasingly important, place in the future of school psychology.

The emphasis on legal advocacy, however, raises many corollary issues. For example, what are the implications of legal advocacy when viewed in terms of particular applications? This is clearly a question that relates to, among other matters, the implications of school psychologists' "testifying," with equal conviction, to opposing conclusions about the same situation. It also relates to whether there are some areas in which school psychologists should not be involved in legal advocacy, and whether legal advocacy is an appropriate process for dealing with some issues and problems. In essence, legal advocacy places a heavy burden on school psychologists, and there is the real danger that it will be misused. Given the realities projected for the 1980's, however, such burdens and potential dangers need to be accepted, for the risks are outweighed by the gains that can be achieved.

JOB AND CAREER DISSATISFACTION AMONG SCHOOL PSYCHOLOGISTS: A RESPONSIBILITY OF THE PROFESSION?

There is a great deal of documentation of dissatisfaction and alienation among blue-collar workers, and even white-collar workers in business and industry (Dunnette, 1976). But, there is almost nothing on the satisfactions and dissatisfactions of people in the major professions—i.e., law, medicine, psychology, and so on. In a recent book, however, Sarason (1977) found virtually no difference between professionals and other occupational groups in level of job satisfaction. In effect, the belief that professionals would find their work more satisfying than blue-collar workers seems to be a myth. Although the author

knows of no research specifically on school psychologists, except the study
recently reported by Berman, Gottlieb, and Hornick (1979), which surveyed
master's-degree graduates of one program in New York City, there is no reason
to believe that their occupational situation is any different than that of other
professionals. Instead, one might think that dissatisfaction is more widespread
and intense than it is in the more prestigious, societally recognized and rewarded
professions such as medicine and law.

The problem is exacerbated in the professions by the "one life–one career
imperative," which in a sense traps professionals in a career in which they no
longer find identity, satisfaction, and fulfillment. The problem is further com-
pounded because professionals are more likely than other workers to say that they
want self development, enjoyment, and meaning in their work. Added to this is
the large increase in numbers of professionals relative to pre-World War II
numbers, and to the population as a whole, which enlarges the size of the
problem, at least in quantitative terms.

What is needed is not only an increased awareness of the problem among
school psychologists, but further, that it be recognized and accepted as a problem
that should be addressed by school psychology *as a profession*. With this will
come research on the scope and dimensions of the problem, and understanding of
how dissatisfaction and alienation is handled by school psychologists. In relation
to this latter point, Sarason provides impressionistic data that indicate denial
and withdrawal are the major strategies used by professionals to manage their
career-related despair. We also need answers in regard to how this state of affairs
has come about. Here again, Sarason makes a telling observation, pointing out
that the changing role and status of the professional, especially in the human-
services or helping professions, has been a major contributing factor in the
development of occupational malaise. Other factors related to the psychology of
work and social changes are also implicated by Sarason, and those knowledgeable about the practice of school psychology can relate to these, as well as
identify others. In fact, other sections of this chapter provide such information,
and some answers to this question.

With such a context for viewing job and career dissatisfactions among school
psychologists, there can be a better articulation of the linkages and the cause-
and-effect relationships involved. And, with such facts in hand, the profession
can then thoughtfully consider solutions that involve immediate, crisis-oriented,
as well as long-range recommendations, plans, and programs.

SUMMARY

In summary, this chapter has singled out a number of professional issues that
seem critical to school psychology's future. In doing so, it is acknowledged that
other issues might have been included. In a fundamental sense, all the issues

selected relate to the pursuit of professional growth—as individuals, and collectively as a profession. With each issue that was raised, an attempt was made to clearly specify the conditions under which the issue should be examined, and what directions resolution might take. Furthermore, in every case, responsibility was ultimately placed on school psychologists themselves, although there was recognition of the impact of outside factors, and the dynamic tension that exists between school psychology, psychology, and education.

The major problem we face as school psychologists is to develop concepts and related mechanisms that are responsive to the needs of society and its schools, and the special interests of our diverse constituency. The essence of such actions is the avoidance of needless struggles for power and control, while working to encourage institutional reforms that lead to improvements in school-psychological practice, education and training, and the profession as a whole. Fortunately, the opportunities for school psychology to create its own future are excellent. Unfortunately, some school psychologists may not use them unless our leaders speak and act wisely.

REFERENCES

American Psychological Association. *Ethical Standards of Psychologists* (rev. ed.). Washington, D.C.: American Psychological Association, 1977.

Anthony, W. A. Psychological rehabilitation: A concept in need of a method. *American Psychologist,* 1977, *32,* 658–662.

Bazelon, D. L. Psychologists in corrections—Are they doing good for the offender or well for themselves? In S. Brodsky, *Psychologists in the criminal justice system.* University of Illinois Press, 1973.

Bergan, J. *Behavioral consultation.* Columbus, Ohio: Charles E. Merrill, 1977.

Berman, H., Gottlieb, S., & Hornick, K. M. A 15-year follow-up study of graduates of a master's degree program in school psychology. *Professional Psychology,* 1979, *10,* 347–356.

Bersoff, D. N. Professional ethics and legal responsibilities: On the horns of a dilemma. *Journal of School Psychology,* 1975, *13,* 359–376.

Bersoff, D. N., & Prasse, D. Applied psychology and judicial decision making: Corporal punishment as a case in point. *Professional Psychology,* 1978, *9,* 400–411.

Bloom, B. S. *Human characteristics and school learning.* New York: McGraw-Hill, 1976.

Budman, S. H., & Wertlieb, D. (Eds.). Special issue on "Psychologists in health care settings." *Professional Psychology,* 1979, *10,* 397–644.

Cardon, B. W., Kuriloff, D. J., & Phillips, B. N. (Eds.). Special issue on "Law and the school psychologist: Challenge and opportunity." *Journal of School Psychology,* 1975, *13,* 281–392.

Coleman, J. Social research and advocacy: A response to Young and Bress. *Phi Delta Kappan,* 1975, *57,* 166–169.

Cummings, N. (Guest Ed.). Special issue on "National health insurance." *American Psychologist,* September, 1977.

Dunn, L. M. Special education for mildly retarded—is much of it justified? *Exceptional Children,* 1968, *35,* 5–22.

Dunnette, M. D. (Ed.). *Handbook of industrial and organizational psychology.* Chicago: Rand McNally, 1976.

Flexner, A. Is social work a profession? In *Proceedings of the National Conference of Charities and Corrections*. Baltimore, Md.: Social Work, 1915.

Forster, J. R. What shall we do about credentialing? *Personnel and Guidance Journal*, 1977, *55*, 573-576.

French, J. L., & McCloskey, G. Characteristics of school psychology program directors and program production. *American Psychologist*, 1979, *34*, 710-714.

Gerstle, J., & Jacobs, G. *Professions for the people*. Cambridge, Mass.: Schenkman, 1976.

Goh, D. S. Graduate training in school psychology. *Journal of School Psychology*, 1977, *15*, 207-218.

Gottfredson, G. D., & Dyer, S. E. Health service providers in psychology. *American Psychologist*, 1978, *33*, 314-338.

Gross, S. J. The myth of professional licensing. *American Psychologist*, 1978, *33*, 1009-1016.

Hardcastle, D. A. Public regulation of social work. *Social Work*, 1977, *22*, 14-19.

Hickson, D. J., & Thomas, M. W. Professionalization in Britain: A preliminary measurement. *Sociology*, 1969, *3*, 37-53.

Howsam, R. B., Corrigan, D. C., Denemark, G. W., & Nash, R. J. *Educating a profession*. Washington, D.C.: American Association of Colleges of Teacher Education, 1976.

Hunter, C. P., & Lambert, N. M. Needs assessment activities in school psychology program development. *Journal of School Psychology*, 1974, *12*, 130-137.

Huntington, D. *Developmental review in the early and periodic screening, diagnosis, and treatment program* (Report to Conference of American Association for Psychiatric Service to Children, No. 77-24537). HEW Medicaid Bureau (HCFA), 1977.

Hyman, I., Carral, R., Duffey, J., Manni, J., & Winikur, D. Patterns of interprofessional conflict resolution on child study teams. *Journal of School Psychology*, 1973, *11*, 187-195.

Joint Commission on Mental Health of Children. *Crisis in child mental health: Challenge for the 1970's*. New York: Harpers, 1970.

Kamin, L. Social and legal consequences of I.Q. tests as classification instruments: Some warnings from our past. *Journal of School Psychology*, 1975, *13*, 317-323.

Kaplan, M. S., Clancy, B., & Chrin, M. Priority roles for school psychologists as seen by superintendents. *Journal of School Psychology*, 1977, *15*, 75-80.

Keavney, G., & Sinclair, K. E. Teacher concerns and teacher anxiety: A neglected aspect of classroom research. *Review of Educational Research*, 1978, *48*, 273-290.

Kicklighter, R. H. School psychology in the U.S.: A quantitative survey. *Journal of School Psychology*, 1976, *14*, 151-156.

Krass, M. S. The right to public education for handicapped children: A primer for the new advocate. *University of Illinois Law Forum*, 1976, 1016-1079.

Marholin, D., II (Ed.). *Child behavior therapy*. New York: Gardner Press, 1978.

Matarazzo, J. D. Higher education, professional accreditation, and licensure. *American Psychologist*, 1977, *32*, 856-859.

Meacham, M. L., & Peckham, P. D. School psychologists at three-quarters century: Congruence between training, practice, preferred role and competence. *Journal of School Psychology*, 1978, *16*, 195-206.

Meyers, J., Parsons, R. D., & Martin, R. *Mental Health Consultation in the Schools*. San Francisco: Jossey-Bass, 1979.

Morell, J. A., & Flaherty, E. W. The development of evaluation as a profession: Current status and some predictions. *Evaluation and Program Planning*, 1978, *1*, 11-17.

Patton, C. V. Selecting special students: Who decides? *Teachers College Record*, 1976, *78*, 101-124.

Peterson, D. R. Is psychology a profession? *American Psychologist*, 1976, *31*, 572-581.

Phillips, B. N. *School stress and anxiety: Theory, research and intervention*. New York: Human Sciences Press, 1978.

Phillips, B. N., & Lee, M. The changing role of the American teacher: Current and future sources of stress. In C. L. Cooper & J. Marshall (Eds.), *White collar and professional stress*. London: Wiley, 1980, 93–111.

Ramey, C. T. Children and public policy: A role for psychologists. *American Psychologist*, 1974, *29*, 14–18.

Reynolds, M. R. (Ed.). *Futures of education for exceptional children: Emerging structures*. Reston, Va.: Council for Exceptional Children, 1978.

Rist, R. C., & Anson, R. J. Social science and the judicial process in education cases: An introduction. *Journal of Law and Education*, 1977, *6*, 1–2.

Sarason, S. B. *Work, aging and social change: Professionals and the one life–one career imperative*. New York: Free Press, 1977.

Smith, B. Is psychology relevant to new priorities? *American Psychologist*, 1973, *28*, 463–471.

Smith, K. E., & DiBacco, J. The multidisciplinary training team: Issues and problems. *Journal of School Psychology*, 1974, *12*, 158–167.

Spector, S., & Frederick, W. *A study of state legislation licensing the practice of professionals and other occupations*. Chicago: Council of State Governments, 1952.

Thomas, B. K. Collaboration of pupil services and instructional personnel. *Journal of School Psychology*, 1972, *10*, 83–87.

Wallace, G. Interdisciplinary efforts in learning disabilities: Issues and recommendations. *Journal of Learning Disabilities*, 1976, *9*, 59–65.

Yoshida, R. K., Fenton, K. S., Maxwell, J. P., & Kaufman, M. J. Group decision making in the planning team process: Myth or reality? *Journal of School Psychology*, 1978, *16*, 237–244.

Young, B. W., & Bress, G. B. Coleman's retreat and the politics of good intentions. *Phi Delta Kappan*, 1975, *57*, 159–165.

3

School Psychology: An Instrumental Service For The Handicapped

David A. Sabatino
Southern Illinois University

INTRODUCTION

It is difficult to distinguish the growth and development of school psychology from the delivery of programs and services to handicapped children and youth (Bennett, 1970). School psychology's very existence has been and continues to be closely associated with the identification of handicapped children and youth for placement into special-education service delivery modes (Catterall, 1972; Lambert, 1974; Sabatino, 1972). Indeed, the funds provided by most state legislatures for school psychological services are channeled through the State Educational Agency and, in the majority of states, the Department of Special Education. In spite of this procedure, school psychologists, in the view of many special educators (Alevy, 1964; Lesiak, 1973), have great difficulty accepting an identity with special education.

One of the reasons for rejecting a closer identity with special education appears to be an adherence to the traditional psychometric role. Newland (1970) described ''psychometric robotism'' as the inability of school psychologists to function apart from the time-honored role of testing and placing handicapped children into special education. The gatekeeping role of regulating the flow of children from regular education into special education requires the establishment of a legal definition for children earmarked to receive special-education services, and a school official to apply the definition. Historically, a categorical label for each handicapping condition was mandated by most states, and the school official entrusted with applying the appropriate label was the school psychologist. It was not the fault of the school psychologist that: (1) only a two-box (regular and special-education) model existed for years (Reynolds, 1962), limiting educational placement options for handicapped students; (2) growing resentment resulted from disenchantment with placing many handicapped children into special-education classes (Dunn, 1968); or (3) labeling of handicapped children was challenged as a nonproductive educational practice (Foster, Schmidt, & Sabatino, 1976).

As Kirp and Kirp (1976) have indicated, it is difficult to recognize that the client's best interests are being served when children are placed into special education because they do not speak the same language as the examiner (Diana vs. State Board of Education), or when partial tests are administered (Kirp, Buss, & Kuriloff, 1974), or when the placement is to accommodate the school and not the child (PARC vs. Commonwealth of Pennsylvania). Then, too, there are problems associated with the testing role, the use of an IQ test as a criterion for placement decisions (Larry P. vs. Riles), and seeing to it that confidential data are carefully placed into school records (Lister, Baker, & Milhouse, 1975).

It is not surprising that school psychology has developed intense feelings of being "unloved and unlovely" (Kirp & Kirp, 1976). Whether the criticisms were valid or not, practices of labeling and placing children into restricted environments, as well as an overemphasis on testing has resulted in an awkward relationship between school psychologists and special educators. The oldest hack in education must be that "all school psychologists do is test." The corollary, to every school psychologist's displeasure, is that every test necessitates a psychological report.

School psychology has always been in an awkward position within the school environment. A psychologist working in the school is, at best, poorly understood, especially when educational administrators are reluctant to accept professionals often perceived as noneducators working in an educational setting (Manley & Manley, 1978). Similarly, the profession of psychology may also have provided a junior-partner status to the discipline of school psychology. Most states do not equate the teaching licensure or certification of the school psychologist with that of the licensed clinical psychologist. Therefore, unless a school psychologist also has a psychology license, he or she is prohibited from private practice. Thus, school psychologists are placed into a "no-win" situation, simply because they serve two masters (Musto, 1975): the profession of psychology and the public-school bureaucracy.

It is not difficult to understand the discomfort school psychologists associate with their traditional service roles to the handicapped. The question that drives this chapter concerns an examination of the historic influences as well as the current practices in the field of school psychology and special education, and the role of school psychologists in the delivery of services to handicapped children and youth in vocational, special, and regular education. Traditionally, school psychologists have not viewed themselves as members of the special-education service delivery system, at least not by choice. The change in the school psychologist's role relationship with special educators resulting from PL 94–142 legislation suggests that the school psychologist may no longer function as the sole decision maker in placement decisions involving handicapped students. Instead, the psychologist must become a team member with the capability of contributing psychological data to a team-derived diagnostic–management statement. From this point in time on, diagnosis requires that placement become a committee decision with one vote for each member. As a result, school psychologists are and shall be required to change their role relationships with special educators.

In the next section, the importance of interindividual comparisons are reviewed as an outgrowth of service to the handicapped. The following section reviews the role alternatives, training, and communication of school psychologists with special educators in particular, and educators in general. The final section examines the current status of school psychology in response to PL 94–142, with observations regarding its future in a multidisciplinary team relationship with special education.

A HISTORY OF SERVICE TO THE HANDICAPPED

Recorded history places the beginning of sustained efforts for the handicapped in the early 16th century (Hewett & Forness, 1977). Louis XIV of France established a vocational training center for the blind in the early 1500's. That center also served his Majesty's less altruistic purposes by providing blind musicians for the royal orchestra. During that same time period, a Spanish nobleman taught his hearing-impaired son a manual communication system, and in Germany, an educator of deaf individuals developed an oral rehabilitation approach to communication with the hearing impaired. By 1876, the British government passed the first compulsory-education act. The passage of that act brought, for the first time in recorded history, a sharp focus on children who failed to learn. The British noted that many children did not learn well in school, but were not of the idiotic or imbecilic (feeble-minded) classification requiring institutionalization. That finding prompted a two-year study by the Ministry of British Education. The results revealed that 10% of the school-age population functioned between the imbecilic classification and those of dull normal intelligence.

This led to the formation of special classes for a new classification of children, known as mentally defective. These students were identified by a general inability to profit from an ordinary school program (Tredgold & Soddy, 1956). By 1913, the Royal British Commissioner of Education relabeled the mentally deficient group of children as feeble minded, or persons having the most mild degree of mental retardation.

Meanwhile, in Germany, special-education classes for the feeble minded began in Hallen-der-Saale in 1859. By 1905, Saxony alone had some 500 special-education classes, educating nearly 10,000 handicapped children with teaching methods similar to the perceptual–motor curricula found in today's kindergartens.

Following the wake left by the French Revolution, which raised questions regarding the previously undisputed genetic nature of humankind and led to a new emphasis on education, Phillipe Pinel differentiated between the criminal and the insane, leading to the opening of the doors of the prisons for the insane. It is probably safe to presume that Pinel's book on psychiatric diagnosis had a powerful influence on at least one of his students, Jean-Mark Gaspard Itard. Lane (1976) notes that the 26-year-old Itard, having just completed his medical studies, began work with a preadolescent boy who roamed the forests around Aveyron in southern France. The "wild boy," as he was known, had sought human interaction, and finally accepted residence with a local farm family.

Itard soon undertook the boy's training in the National Institute for Deaf–Mutes. The importance of the environment (nurture) became apparent as the boy's behavior changed, contradicting the unanimous medical opinion that the case was hopeless. This furthered Itard's stand against those who contended that the boy was left in the wild because he was an idiot, not that he was an idiot because he was left in the wild. It was these methods of teaching that Itard's student, Edward Sequin, would later use at the Hospital for Incurables to prove that even the most desperate cases can be changed by education. Simultaneously, Esquirol, a leading psychiatrist in that same period, removed for the first time idiocy and imbecility from a list of known chronic diseases, attributing their causes to poorly or underdeveloped "intellectual faculties" (Esquirol, 1838). The change in such predominant views was supported by a French neurologist, Charcot, who developed sophisticated examination techniques and a systematic classification of central nervous system pathologies as they relate to handicapping conditions.

The combined work of these French pioneers resulted in the necessity for diagnostic procedures, classification systems, and treatment methods based largely on sensory (physiological) stimulation in order to "cure" the mentally retarded. Special education had received its beginning, for it was in the Hospital for Incurables that George Sumner and Maria Montessori witnessed Itard's techniques for judging the degree of educability in a population of low-functioning children and youth. The need for ascertaining the "type" and "amount" of "special education" had been born.

While the 1860's and 1870's marked the initial transition in this country from custody in institutions to training, a new site of treatment of the mildly handicapped was evolving. By 1875, public-school classes for the "backward" (mildly mentally retarded) were begun in Cleveland; and by 1905, Chicago, New York, Providence, Springfield (Massachusetts), Philadelphia, and Boston had such classes as well. In the rapid expansion of special classes in the public schools, Wallin (1949) identified two parallel forces: (1) the work in psychology that attempted to determine traits and classify people according to their ability to function (one person in comparison to another); and (2) remedial approaches to the education of handicapped students, employing physiological stimulation, controlled socialization experiences, and educational approaches that tried to develop functional skills emphasizing preparation for life. Thus, even from the beginning of public special-education programs, the measurement of human performance had a profound impact.

At the turn of the 20th century, the French Minister of Public Instruction was still wrestling with an age-old problem: how to consistently identify the mentally handicapped. Having agreed upon the terminology to be used (idiot, the lowest level; imbecile, the intermediate level; and moron, or mildly mentally retarded), a psychologist, Alfred Binet, and physician, Theatré Simon, were commissioned to develop a consistent means of classifying children. Binet and Simon (1905, 1908) produced, through a standardized procedure of observation, a psychological classification of quantifiable differences in children's intellectual characteristics (traits).

No individual was more aware of these trends than Henry Goddard, Director of Research at the Vineland Training School. Goddard uncovered the Binet tests in 1908 and subsequently published the 1905 scales in the hope that they would assist American educators and psychologists in the most important objectives of measurement (Goddard, 1919): "to obtain a general knowledge of the capacities of man by sinking shafts, as it were, at a few critical points [p. 37]." Binet, the creator of a global measure of intelligence, was really a faculty psychologist and the man who should be credited with the tradition of evaluating or defining processes through psychometric measurement. Goddard also translated and developed an American standardization for the 1908 scales, and, using this standardization (completed in 1910), he prepared a classification of feeblemindedness for the American Association of Mental Deficiency.

The continued development of the Binet test resided in the hands of Louis Terman. Not content with previous advances, Terman released a new version of the original scales based upon his definition of intelligence, which, for the concise Terman, was simply the ability to "think abstractly." The scale, known as the Stanford–Binet (Doll, 1917), was revised into separate forms (L and M) (Terman & Merrill, 1937) and subsequently was recombined into a single form in 1960 (Terman, 1960). Almost immediately, Terman's version of the Stanford–Binet showed the ability to produce a high positive relationship with reading comprehension, other academic achievement measures, and general school success. To say that the Stanford–Binet tests were widely accepted and highly regarded would be an understatement of considerable degree. In fact, early special-class placements for exceptional children, particularly the mentally retarded, were so dependent on the single Binet criteria that they were called "Binet classes." The impact was so great that by 1927, 11 years following the introduction of Terman's new Stanford–Binet instrument, 15 states had developed special-education laws for the mentally retarded. Soon, even more precise measurements were necessary and the Stanford–Binet was rapidly augmented by other measurement devices. The precise assessment of characteristics of handicapped learners had begun in earnest.

The early enthusiasm for the Stanford–Binet and similar tests was in no small way related to a professional enthusiasm for diagnostic categories. Paralleling the scientific method, it was sometimes vehemently held that diagnosis led to classification that formed the basis for developing (and implementing) habilitative procedures. But, by the mid-20th century, direct linkage had not been found between diagnosis and educational interventions, an event that brought diagnostics into a state of low credibility. Part of the problem lay in a confusion of purpose. Engelmann (1967) states that: ". . . Diagnosis has become synonymous with testing, and this is part of many contemporary shifts away from substance to technology, in this shift the 'how' defines the 'what' and task defines the questions to be asked of nature, as though the technology of science has pre-existed to science itself and is not really born of it [p. 199]." Engelmann's statement reflects precisely the fact that diagnosis is often synonymous with testing, a confusion of purpose and technology. This event has resulted in the development of psychoeducational diagnostic tests that are studied for their own sake, wherein the tests themselves often determine what is being sought. In short, the irrational purpose of much diagnostic effort was to permit diagnosticians to build a better diagnostic methodology, with or without purpose.

Identifying characteristics that inhibit the learning or adjustment process has become secondary in importance to determining how well (reliable or valid) these characteristics are measured or observed. One point is, however, quite clear: The early special-education classes for the mildly retarded were, in fact, "Binet classes," as the Binet instrument was the device used to identify children. School psychology, its early role relationship to handicapped children and special education, was established. If special education was a warehouse for the handicapped schoolage child, school psychologists were indeed the gatekeepers.

As Sarason (1976) points out, school psychology was "born in the prison of a test [p. 584]," and despite attempts at remodeling, it is still a prison. Binet, who was a developmental psychologist, not merely a tester with a penchant for report writing, saw testing as a means to educating individual potentials, not as an end in itself. The current frustration of many school psychologists centers around the failure of the discipline to make sufficient progress since the time of Binet toward bridging the gap between the instructional passive-testing role and an active participation in education and behavioral management. Only through a broadening of scope can the role of the school psychologist become effective in educational planning, policy, and practice (Sarason, 1976).

AN OVERVIEW OF SCHOOL PSYCHOLOGY

As early as 1732, Christian Wolfe defined imagination, memory, the power of sensory discrimination, and the traits of intelligence in *Psychologic Empirica* (Mann, 1974). Other faculty psychologists were interested in the *power* and *faculty* of the mind; Reid (1710–1792) wrote (quoted in Mann, 1974):

> the words power and faculty, which are often used in speaking of the mind, need little explication. Every (mental) operation supposes a power in the being that operates; for to suppose anything is operate, which has no power to operate, is manifestly absurd [p. 89].

Franz Joseph Gall (1758–1828) was the modern father of phrenology, a doctrine that advanced a belief that different psychological faculties are located in specific parts of the brain and that their strength and weaknesses can be judged by the size and location of protrusions on the skull. Boring (1950), in an evolutionary statement of the importance of phrenology, noted "... it is almost accurate to say that scientific psychology was born of phrenology, out of wedlock with science [p. 473]." It may also be correct to assume that Gall is the early progenitor of modern learning disabilities (Mann, 1974), as well as the founder of modern brain localization theory.

It is believed, by those who carried the torch of phrenology, that faults in pupil learning were simply due to undeveloped faculties that were diagnosed by skull depression. Famous early educators such as Barnard, Many, and Howe continued to guide the practice of special education in this country by a doctrine and educational practice of assessing abilities and disabilities through study of the proportions of the skull, and remediating it accordingly. In addition, Vives, Pestolozzi, Froebel, Rosseau, Itard, Sequin, and Montessori adapted to some degree the practices of faculty psychology (Mann, 1974).

By the early 1800's, faculty psychology had received serious challenges from the most prominent psychologists of the times. Herbart (1776–1841), followed by James (1912), Thorndike (1913), and Woodworth (1939) advanced the belief that independent faculties were nonexistent in isolation. Mann, in reviewing these early philosophers–psychologists noted that the position advanced assumed cognitive acts, without differentiating specific cognitive powers or abilities. By Galton's time, a stable approach had emerged that capitalized on early faculty psychology by a ceaseless search for those traits, aptitudes, or abilities that underlie learning. This emphasis was soon complemented by attempts in English psychology to establish reliable measures of individual differences. Galton's work in England exemplified the development of rigorous, standardized procedures in measuring individual differences, a point that has led some authors (White & Harris, 1961) to conclude that his efforts represent the prototype activities of the school psychologist. At any rate, Galton's brilliance was manifested in part, during the next dozen years (circa 1884–1896), by continual insights into the refinement of measurement practices.

As services began to appear toward the end of this period, psychologist practitioners recognized the potential uses of measurement. In this country, the first laboratory–clinic was established at the University of Pennsylvania by Lightner Witmer. Although Witmer's clinic was devoted to child "guidance," the individuals operating the clinic maintained close ties with public education. Therefore, Witmer's efforts are cited as a first example of psychology being applied to educational problems within the public school.

Soon after these events, "school psychologists" began to appear, the first recorded use of the term being the title given to Arnold Gesell in 1915. Holt and Kicklighter (1971) have indicated that the State of Connecticut Board of Education granted the title to Gesell to: "travel throughout rural Connecticut and examine children who were performing poorly in school. He consulted with school personnel, with parents and with child care agencies [p. 1]." With the introduction of Gesell's work, school psychology arrived on the American educational scene.

Bardon and Bennett (1974) have discussed the movements within the field of school psychology, emphasizing the sporadic nature of professional development across the country. School psychologists were responsive to local needs, which in turn were quite different from one geographic region to another in various parts of the country. Although "roles" varied considerably, school psychologists generally progressed from "testers" in the first quarter of the 20th century to more clinically oriented professionals concerned with mental-health issues in the second quarter. Roles changed dramatically again in the 1960's. School psychologists began to recombine the testing and clinical–mental-health activities to meet the new pressures of the period. Role characteristics between this camp and that camp of school psychologists became less absolute when a greater saturation of diverse activities similar to all camps (e.g., consultation in behavioral techniques) began to appear.

To summarize some of those changes, in less than half a century, school psychologists have expanded on their primary role in individual assessment (Bernauer & Jackson, 1974) to a systems orientation, in which they functioned as consultants (Lambert, 1974), behavioral interveners (Kratochwill & Bergan, 1978a), and in curriculum development (Winett, Battersby, & Edwards, 1975). More recently, according to Maher (1973), school psychologists have become specialists in program evaluation (e.g., Granger & Campbell, 1977).

In the following sections, I examine the relation between school psychology and the handicapped, discussing the current search for viable role options in service to the handicapped. Finally, I reexamine those alternative role options against PL 94–142 compliance assurances. A theme not developed, but alluded to, is that not every school psychologist should work with the handicapped. But, those who decide to do so need additional training and clearer missions, clarifying their roles as behavioral scientists with specialized populations. The future looks to be exceedingly bright if some school psychologists are willing to assume new and expanded roles in service-delivery systems to the handicapped and become conversant with special, vocational, and regular-education curricula. The techniques for adapting and adopting behavioral and instructional management for the handicapped must be developed and validated, expanding the scientific role of the school psychologists. The daily work will be on joint multidisciplinary teams working to assist the handicapped, especially at the pre- and postschool-age levels.

MODERN SCHOOL PSYCHOLOGY:
SEARCH FOR PROFESSIONAL IDENTITY

Probably the most persistent concern of school psychologists has been that of their role and function. The balance sought has been to retain their identity as psychologists while serving in a public educational setting.

This delicate balance has become more tenuous in recent years, as the American Psychological Association has adopted the official policy in Standards for Providers of Psychological Services that the doctoral degree is the minimal or entry degree for the use of the term "psychologist" (Bardon, 1976). Many school psychologists holding state department certification who have only 2 years of training or its equivalent must consider the impact of this policy on their professional identity. To add to this "identity crisis," many state departments of education view school psychology not as "psychology" but as simply a convenient label to describe pupil personnel service functions and skills (Bardon, 1976) taking place within the schools. Caught in the middle of changing times and standards and faced with increasing demands for a broader interpretation of their role in the school setting, school psychologists have had to reexamine and redefine their professional identity.

Evidence of the search for professional identity is clearly reflected in no less than three national conferences: the 1954 Thayer Conference (Cutts, 1955), the Boulder Conference (Raimy, 1950), and the Vail Conference (Korman, 1974). What resulted from these conferences was a listing of activities that school psychologists perform. There is little question from even a cursory review of that list that activities providing services to the handicapped represent, or at least incorporate, a majority of those professional endeavors performed by school psychologists.

In part, one aspect of the issue is that the school psychologist, an employee of the public school system, is expected to meet the job expectancies of the employer as either previously established or agreed. There can be little doubt that one of the major expectancies from the federal, state, and local educational agencies is the continued identification (child find) of handicapped children. Therefore, the inordinate amount of rhetoric on the role and function of the school psychologist has been for all practical purposes considered futile by many in the field (e.g., Pielstick, 1970).

Pielstick's (1970) point is that the variance in the role of the school psychologist may be greater between buildings in the same district than among school districts in a given state. The tack suggested by Pielstick is that the tasks themselves should be the prime concern and not the search for an optimum role. He perceived the responsibility for a specific task residing within the person on the school staff with the greatest competencies, interests, and available time to do the job. That position would, of course, resolve some of the territoriality questions that are boiling out of the interdisciplinary relationship between specialists serving the handicapped in the schools. Such questions include: Who assesses language—the school psychologist or the learning-disabilities resource teacher?

Gilmore (1974) concluded that the field of school psychology has been far more capable of defining what it is not than what it is, and likened the field's anxiety over defining its role to the adolescent who is uncomfortable in answering questions of who and what he or she is. Further, the author stressed the need for role models that reflect the combination of settings and situations within which they are to function. Gilmore agrees with Pielstick (1970), and cautions that a single model is inappropriate and suggests that major models could be categorized under the two headings of operations and sources. The operations or "practices" refers to two dimensions: (1) the directness or indirectness of services provided; and (2) the degree to which a model is more service or science oriented. The second heading, sources, refers to the basis of the model according to each of three dimensions: (1) education or psychology as the parent discipline; (2) adopted or developed, which refers to the acceptance of information; and (3) the relative emphasis on the theoretical as opposed to the applied practices inherent in the model. The combined use of these five dimensions provides a sophisticated scale by which models can be compared.

Using the just described framework, Gilmore (1974) analyzed the following five historically significant models: (1) Bardon's (1965) application in the school setting model, which attempts to serve individual children through techniques developed in clinical psychology; (2) Vallett's (1963) diagnostic–prescriptive model, which also attempts to serve children through an individual approach that emphasizes academic remediation; (3) Reger's (1965) educational programmer model in which the school psychologist's primary focus is on academic learning and the child's response to the curricula; (4) Gray's (1963) systems-level problem solver, which views problems and their solutions beyond the individual child in the context of the entire system; and (5) the preventative mental-health model of Bower (1965), which stresses activities of school psychologists being oriented to prevention rather than primary remediation.

Trachtman (1971) proposes a combination of roles by drawing heavily upon

systems interventions (e.g., Gray, 1963) and individual inter
don, 1965; Vallett, 1963). Bennett (1976) emphasized the sc
role in research, which in many respects may be seen as com
(1974) program-consultant and Granger and Campbell's
evaluator role.

Tracy and Sturgeon (1977) recognize the need for the school psychologist to
assess and understand the educational service-delivery system. Hyman and
Schreiber (1975) and Mearig (1974) describe a role that emphasizes the benefits
to youth of relieving selective pressures through child advocacy. Abidin (1972)
stresses consultation within the school to change the general contingency system
that teachers employ daily whereas McDaniel and Ahr (1965) emphasize staff
development through inservice. More futuristic articles emphasize an increase in
school-psychology activities in community liaison and interagency planning
(Brantley, Reilly, Beach, Cody, Fields, & Lee, 1974; Steinberg & Chandler,
1976).

Although the time-honored search for professional identity has been productive from time to time, it also has imposed realistic limits. Is it possible that the
time is past for academic rhetoric concerned with the role of the school psychologist? Or, has there been a gradual shift in role relationships as the various
specialists examine task and population in light of Pielstick's search for the "best
professional for the job" response? If school psychologists do what their competencies dictate, then they are dependent on their training to establish those
competencies.

The question to be asked is whether most school psychologists understand the
primary dimensions that compare the three major curricular divisions in the
schools: (1) regular education; (2) vocational education; and (3) special education. Furthermore, are they prepared to recommend adoption or adaptation of
curricula (alteration necessary to adjust one or all of these three curricula) for the
handicapped person, their family, or teacher? The point is that the school psychologists' function is dictated by a traditional approach that they are trained to
provide. The average school psychologist develops high-level report-writing
skills that promote communication of their findings, but fail to relate those
findings to the major curricula dimensions and a service delivery system within
the schools. A case in point is Maher's (1973) position paper on a role for school
psychologists as evaluators of special-education programs. Maher quotes Bardon
and Bennett (1974), noting that a school psychologist should develop skills as an
education evaluator to provide the information on the success of special-
education programmic efforts. As yet, there is no literature in response to an
evaluation format for IEP's mandated by PL 94–142. Would not the school
psychologist be a likely person to develop accountability processes for instructional objectives and enabling steps prepared (supposedly) from learner characteristic data?

Candidly, it would appear that, traditionally, school psychologists have been prepared as clinicians, and not as educators. That fact may be problematic, because it would appear that school psychologists are being prepared in an archive of outmoded activities for today's schools.

The time for "role" rhetoric has passed. Those concerned with the professional preparation of school psychologists must deal with the practical concerns of the school psychologist attempting to move beyond the "prison of the test" (Sarason, 1976), into the wider realm of effective interaction and communication with teachers and other school personnel (Kratochwill & Bergan, 1978b). Unfortunately, at present, there are an excess of groups representing the training of school psychologist's. Hyman (1979) charges that no consensus on necessary degree requirements will be achieved unless these groups unite in a common voice that can be heard and responded to by existing training institutions.

Hayes and Clair (1978) advance the argument that the education and training of school psychologists by universities must deemphasize the psychology-clinical model and prepare psychologists to focus on "the educational process as it involves learning, instruction, and children's specialization and individual sensitivity [p. 519]." Attention should be given those aspects of PL 94-142 regarding equal access to educational opportunities and parent's and children's rights via due process. The school psychologists must expand their knowledge for the expanded age range including the preschool child and young handicapped adult (Kabler, 1977). Specified by law, the role has evolved to include a complex array of legal issues and responsibilities, all with the potential of threatening active litigation (Kaplan, Chrin, & Chancy, 1977; Kirp & Kirp, 1976).

During the course of this section, I have reviewed, in a cursory fashion, a few of the more popular interpretations of the role and functions of the school psychologist in relationship to the handicapped. However, the reader should be aware that the position of the writer is that school psychologists have confused function with service-delivery mode. The confusion results from the training that compartmentalizes skill development in didactic courses with poorly integrated and supervised clinical activities, especially with the handicapped.

Specific training activities are addressed on several occasions in the following section of this paper. It is simply a topic that cannot be sidestepped. This is especially true when one examines the limited course content and even more limited practicum involvement of school psychology students with the handicapped.

The Professional Preparation of School Psychologists in Special Education

Propaedeutic to this discussion is the issue of professional preparation. Could it be that the arcane professional preparation of school psychologists plants the problem squarely in the universities' backyard?

Keogh, Kukic, Becker, McLoughlin, and Kukic (1975) interviewed 85 school psychologists in 10 districts examining four major areas: background and training; professional duties; techniques with children, and options and recommendations concerning school psychological services.

Only a few school psychologists surveyed reported extensive training in educational intervention, remedial curriculum planning, special education, or the study of exceptional children. In addition, school psychologists' lack of affiliation with national professional organizations focused on psychology or on exceptional children was striking. This raises serious questions as to the sources of updating of information for practicing school psychologists.

Other findings reported by Keogh et al. (1975) indicated that although recent role development has emphasized the educational consultant and remedial program planner models, time and effort studies continue to delineate the primary function of the school psychologist as psychometrics and test-related activities. Other program aspects (i.e., research, inservice training, evaluation, and curriculum development) remain minimal at best.

School psychologists surveyed also expressed concerns for the adequacy of their own training, especially in educational areas. A number of the school psychologists recommended inservice or preservice training focused on educational techniques for exceptional children, related to curricular matters, as well as school psychologists' more traditional techniques.

The significance of the Keogh et al. (1975) study is simply that the school psychologists surveyed revealed that they were functioning from a traditional if not archaic platform. Once again, the question arises: Does the professional training available adequately prepare the school psychologist to work with the handicapped?

The literature over the past 15 years examining school psychology training is rather substantial. There is data to indicate that the number of programs has increased to the point that 40 states are now training school psychologists in 70 master's programs, 151 sixth-year programs, and 66 doctoral programs (Brown & Lindstrom, 1978). Brown, Sewell, and Lindstrom, (1977) reported that master's programs generally require 44 or less hours of courses, with six-year programs ranging from 45 to 72 hours beyond the master's degree.

All the states, except one, certify a school psychometrist, educational examiner, or school psychologist (Brown et al., 1977). Nine (9) reported a master's degree, 28 states require a sixth-year program, and eight states require a form of field experience, whether it be practicum, internship, or externship.

Twenty-seven states require a supervised internship beyond the work of the university. Other coursework varies from state to state, although a general pattern recommended by the American Psychological Association is followed. Brown, Sewell, and Lindstrom (1977) categorize the course patterns into groups of: (1) consultation and intervention; (2) educational foundations; (3) psychological foundations; (4) special education; (5) tests and measurements; and (6) miscellaneous. Of these categories, courses in special education are required. The most frequent one is the survey course (introductory course), which reviews the various categories of exceptional children in a highly cursory fashion. Special educators will follow this type of course with others that emphasize characteristics, diagnosis, and management of one or more of the specialized handicapped groups. School psychologists rarely take a second course in either the characteristics or management of a specialized population, but rather opt for a course concerned with the diagnostic use of specialized tests. To the best of this writer's capability to isolate course patterns in special education beyond the survey course, it would appear that only seven states require a characteristics, method, or assessment in learning disabilities as a second course, four states require a curricular or diagnostic course in mental retardation, and four specify a course in special-education program development or supervision. Three additional states require three courses in special education, but do not specify them. Only one state specified four courses in special education.

It is apparent that school psychologists are not generally trained to recognize the behaviors associated with specific handicaps, nor are they trained in specialized assessment procedures needed to describe the difficulty in assessing handicapping conditions. More importantly, their knowledge of intervention, including applied behavioral analysis, if learned, frequently results from on-the-job training (OJT). In fact, OJT may be a major source of preparation assisting school psychologists with either the sensory, motor, or multiply handicapped students. The reason for that belief is that none of the states require a student in school psychology to enroll in a special-education practicum experience of any kind. How can either communication or remedial skills be well developed? As a result, few school psychologists have the highly developed skills necessary to work with specific populations of handicapped children.

In one comprehensive study, W. Levine (1974) completed a review of the psychological performance of psychologists with deaf children. Her brilliant and much-needed piece of work on psychological practices with the deaf should be replicated with other groups of handicapped students. Levine (1974) surveyed 151 educational facilities and 11 agencies serving the deaf. The highest percentage of returns came from schools exclusively for the deaf—of the 135 listed in the 1971 American Annals Directory, 102 responded. Of the 102 who responded, 28 reported having no psychologist in their school at the time of the survey.

Of the 153 psychologists who responded, only 28% reported psychological testing experience prior to testing the deaf. Sixty-five percent reported no experience with deafness prior to their work. Although 65% of the institutions surveyed were using language of signs in combinations with words, only 50% of the psychologists could use (or read back) sign language. The inference is that about 90% of the respondent group are unable to communicate effectively, if at all, in sign language with a manually oriented clientele.

Eighty-three percent of respondents reported on-the-job learning as their only preparation for psychological work with the deaf. Ancillary help was obtained from readings, observations of teaching and testing the deaf, courses and discussions with experienced workers.

The "preparation" reported by the remaining 17% was quite varied and included: multidisciplinary training programs for workers with the deaf; inservice training; supervised practicum; workshops on the deaf including a 6-hour workshop on counseling and testing; clinical internships; the opportunity to work as assistant to highly experienced psychologists for the deaf; "instruction from predecessor," and deaf family background. The training data supports the concern that school psychologists are not generally prepared at the preservice level to employ special-education instructional or behavioral management principles with many types of exceptional children.

An additional problem is that few school psychologists are trained initially in multidisciplinary settings, therefore having little opportunity to learn skills to facilitate communication with the other disciplines required to arrive at a management plan for handicapped children.

S. M. Levine (1977) states that school psychologists have found themselves in disequilibrium with the passing of "The Education for all Handicapped Children Act" (PL 94–142), because they are required to perform tasks they are not trained to do. School psychologists feel this most keenly in attempts to assess and prepare management plans for preschool, adolescent, and the severely handicapped (PL 94–142).

Kratochwill and Bergan (1978b) point out that the practice of defining the role of the psychologist primarily by setting must be restructured to emphasize the psychologist's impact on the setting and ultimately on clients and society. Trainers of psychologists must respond to this demand by reconceptualizing curricula, internships, and competency levels of the school psychologist in the school environment.

There is no reason to berate the training issue, but in the absence (if not deterioration) of an attempt to develop and improve communication between special education and school psychology, professional preparation becomes a major issue. In the next section, an aspect of the relation between special education and school psychology is discussed in detail.

Communication between Special Educators and School Psychologists

School psychology's relationship with special education has been tenous at best. Gallagher (1969) writes: "... (these disciplines) have always had a symbiotic relationship because the psychologist was, and is, a necessary first step in any special program [pp. 219–220]."

Other authors have discussed the school psychology–special education relationship at length: Lambert (1974) concluded that the traditional sources of school psychologists' influence lay in special-education related activities whereas Sabatino (1972), though critical of psychologists for the manner in which the work relationship with special education had developed, called upon the profession to acknowledge a genuine professional relationship. Catterall (1972) indicated the economic ties of the professions by suggesting that over half of the finances for school psychology are accrued through its relationship with special education. Quite recently, Ysseldyke (1978) cited eight potentially influential sources of change that may require dramatic alterations in the practice of school psychology during the next decade. All eight points could be seen as partially reflective of change occurring in special education, five points seem to *stem directly from within special education.*

These points include: (1) the disillusionment of teachers with the kinds and quality of services provided by school psychologists; (2) increased emphasis on the rights of children; (3) the mandate via PL 94–142 of nondiscriminatory assessment of all handicapped children; (4) mainstreaming activity; (5) more individualized instruction for increasing numbers of children; (6) due process procedures; (7) new constituencies of previously unserved populations; and (8) increased use of medication.

In short, the profession of school psychology has demonstrated a long-term commitment to working with special children and, by extrapolation, with special educators.

Because the public schools' commitment to handicapped children has now been mandated by legislation, it is reasonable to expect that school psychologists will figure prominently in these newly affirmed responsibilities.

Unfortunately, Baker (1965), writes that data he obtained indicates that the "largest single weakness of psychological services in the public schools was poor communication between the classroom teacher and the school psychologists [p. 10]." His data indicated that the "willingness" of a teacher to activate a psychologist's recommendations was directly related to the "quality" of the face-to-face interaction that took place between them. He surmises that the breakdown in communication is due in great part to the fact that the behaviors the psychologist sees in a one-to-one individual assessment situation are entirely different than those behaviors displayed by the same child in the classroom. The psychologist is generally too busy to make direct observations in the classroom and the teacher sees that as a dissonance-producing mechanism. The dissonance often results from the response to the teacher request, "Please see what it is like in my environment" with the implied response, "I am too busy to visit in your classroom."

Teachers' responses to collaborative consultation were studied by Wenger (1979). School psychologists rate consultation with the teacher as the most valuable model of program delivery (Bardon & Bennett, 1974; Footman, 1973; Roberts, 1970; Tan, 1969). The reason for its importance is that it provides the opportunity for a close relationship between teacher and psychologist (McClung & Studen, 1970). It would appear that there are at least two styles of consultation: (1) collaborative; and (2) expert. The essential difference is the communication process, as collaborative consultation requires a basic dialogue between parties, whereas expert consultation is a fairly directive monologue. Wenger hypothesized that teachers would favor the expert style of consultant attitudinally, but would apply more active follow-through on the recommendations that grow from collaborative relationships. The results were not as expected. Teachers did not favor the expert consultation model, but instead preferred the collaborative role. However, there was no difference in the amount of follow-up between the two styles of consultation. The implication is clear: Special educators want a relationship, not a set of cold, hard recommendations. Furthermore, it also seems likely that in order to be carried out, recommendations must be custom tailored for the classroom environment, and the teacher's style, or they have no meaning.

It is also true that special educators feel that the realism with which the psychologist understands the problem referred is reflected in the specificity, and therefore usability, of the recommendation. As early as 1945, Cason observed that the major complaint of special educators was the generality, and therefore lack of applicability, of the recommendation being reported. Rucker (1967) also noted that the quality of recommendations was the most important factor in how both special and regular educators judged the usefulness of the report. Mussman (1964) found the recommendation portion of the psychological report to be one of primary interest to regular educators.

Similarly, Lucas and Jones (1970) studied the attitudes of special educators toward psychological reports and services. A questionnaire was administered, first in pilot form to 50 special-education teachers, and then in finalized form to special educators and 37 school psychologists. The data reflected contrasting rankings given various aspects of the school psychologist's role as viewed by the two groups, and the likes and differences on attitude and information based on given demographic characteristics (e.g., educational background). The psychologists and special educators differed greatly on most of the variables surveyed, in terms of the degree of helpfulness. The most outstanding finding was that as the contacts between the two increased, the teachers reported an increase in the amount of helpfulness.

In a similar study, Gilmore and Chandy (1973b) classified teachers according to (1) their years of teaching experience; and (2) frequency of professional contacts with school psychologists. The results revealed that school psychologists were viewed primarily as specialists who work with students with emotional problems. Both groups of teachers viewed the school psychologist as having little time or tolerance with either academic problems or the skills to assist them in classroom management. Regardless of the amount of teaching experience, the amount of direct contact with the school psychologist did improve the teachers' perceptions and also their need for such service. In a second study, reported in the same year (1973a), Gilmore and Chandy again investigated the perception of the role of the school psychologist as viewed by teachers, principals, and school psychologists. The data suggest: (1) experienced teachers expected less consulting and more testing from the school psychologist than did newer teachers; (2) teachers with a high frequency of contact with the school psychologist viewed the psychologist in a less restrictive role than did teachers with prior contact; (3) school size did not affect perceptions of the school psychologist; (4) socioeconomic status of the school did affect perceptions; specifically, personnel from lower-income schools attributed fewer and more restricted skills to the school psychologist than did personnel from upper-income schools.

Kahl and Fine (1978) expanded the number of items in the Gilmore and Chandy (1973b) work. They attempted to study: (1) how teachers viewed the role of the school psychologist, and their helpfulness; and (2) what effect socioeconomic status of the school had on teachers' perception of the roles of school psychologists. Teachers were grouped consecutively on two dimensions: (1) number of years of teaching experience (three groups); and (2) number of contacts (low, moderate, and high) with school psychologists. Schools were grouped according to socioeconomic status. Although the sample size was small ($N = 54$), several interesting results were observed.

The socioeconomic status of the school and the frequency of teachers' contact with the school psychologist were related. Lower-income schools report more professional contact with school psychologists than high socioeconomic schools.

A second observation was that as teaching experience increased, so did the teachers' view of the psychologist in a consulting role. That difference contrasts sharply with previous studies (Gilmore & Chandy, 1973a, 1973b), which report that more recently employed teachers saw consulting as part of the school psychologist's role. That difference in findings may in fact reflect the increase in consultation in a 4-year (1973–1977) period.

Whereas a previous study (Gilmore & Chandy, 1973a) found that teachers reporting high contact with the psychologist tended to view him/her as a consultant rather than merely a tester (this was termed a "broader" view of the psychologist), the present investigation found no differences here according to degree of contact. However, the present findings did suggest that as the amount of contact increased, so did the teachers' view of the school psychologist as being more helpful to the following children: (1) underachievers; (2) learning disabled; (3) emotionally maladjusted; and (4) those presenting problems at home.

The significant two-way interaction (Degree of Contact × Socioeconomic Status) on the dependent variable helpfulness suggested the following: Teachers from upper-income schools reporting high contact with the school psychologist viewed the psychologist as the most helpful to the greatest number of children. At the same time, however, it was found that teachers from these same upper-income schools who reported only moderate contact were among two of the groups who viewed the psychologist as the least helpful.

The other group who viewed the psychologist as less helpful were teachers from lower-income schools who reported low contact. It could be suggested that because of the low amount of contact, these teachers were not aware of many of the functions of the psychologist; therefore, they had difficulty picturing the school psychologist as helpful in many instances. However, the low-contact teachers from the upper-income schools did not share this view of school psychologists; instead, they saw him/her as relatively helpful (Kahl & Fine, 1978).

Lucas and Jones (1970) summarize:

> ... lack of contact with the psychologist appears to be the major source of dissatisfaction with psychological services. Special educators who had little personal contact with the psychologist saw psychological services as much less helpful than did those who felt the psychologist was available on request... If psychologists wish to change this image, and the literature indicates that many do, new means of increasing contact with teachers must be developed. Special education teachers and school administrators need additional clarity on the service (other than testing) which the psychologist can render. Teachers themselves have indicated they feel testing is insufficient and that consultation is often an unmet need. The consultation function of the psychologist needs to be given more consideration both at university training levels and in professional practice [p. 130].

The vagueness with which the role of the school psychologist is viewed may be related to the wide range of tasks that psychologists in the school typically perform. Medway (1977) analyzed the amount of time 15 school psychologists spent on seven specific roles and functions during a 6-week period. The seven activities included:

1. Administration and scoring of formal and informal psychological tests.
2. Writing psychological reports.
3. Interviewing principals, counselors, or teachers.
4. Observing in the classroom.
5. Consulting with a principal or counselor about ways in which to remediate a problem of psychological nature.
6. Consulting with a teacher about ways to remediate a problem of psychological nature.
7. Counseling students either individually or in groups.

In one day, a school psychologist may function as a psychometrician, a program evaluator, a counselor, a public-relations specialist, or in several other very particular specialties. (See Bersoff [1975] and Gray [1963] for particularly lucid descriptions of the daily demands on school psychologists.) Special educators invariably view school psychologists as they have *seen* them function, in providing services to handicapped children, not, perhaps, as they *can or should* function in different capacities.

In most instances, the dominant activity (time-wise) has the greatest probability of influencing the role ascribed to the psychologist. Yet, when special educators observe other activities performed by the school psychologist over time, the mystery surrounding the role of the school psychologist becomes more perplexing. Much of the ambiguity could be alleviated by recognizing that school psychology is not a unilateral role composed of a few activities, but instead denotes a range of possible activities depending on circumstances and needs. By analogy, special educators have tended to describe themselves more fully in terms of the population that they work with or the setting/arrangement within which they work, such as "resource teacher for the learning disabled," or the broad function they perform, such as "special education administrator." School psychologists generally have not categorized themselves in the same manner. Perhaps special educators now find themselves too well defined on restrictive criteria, as one may witness in the move toward noncategorical teacher preparation, whereas school psychologists may tend to be misunderstood because of the very vagueness of the title under which they operate.

The data suggest that teachers' perceptions of psychological services do not agree with the opinions maintained by the psychologists themselves (Gilmore & Chandy, 1973a; Roberts, 1970). Teachers' attitudes appear to be based on little direct information and do not appear to be strongly held, suggesting that school psychologists desiring to change their professional roles may do so without undue teacher resistance.

It may be relatively safe to conclude that a teacher's direct experience with a given school psychologist is the most important single ingredient in determining the attitude and judgment that the one professional has for the other. Times have changed; the placement role of testing and placing the handicapped has given way to consultation with teachers on a wide array of behavioral and learning problems in the classroom. In becoming a team member, the school psychologist may be viewed by teachers as less of an expert. This perceived change in status should not be seen in a negative sense, but rather as a means of footing improved communication among professionals in order to facilitate appropriate educational services to handicapped students.

What, then, of the role perceptions of those who employ the school psychologist—the superintendents? Manley and Manley (1978) surveyed the personal value structure and operative goals of 96 school psychologists and 75 superintendents. To conduct this research, an instrument was developed containing 56 value concepts classified by England (1967) into: ideas associated with people, personal goals of individuals, and groups of people. In addition, 21 goals directly related to school psychology were included. The resulting instrument reflected five classes of goals. They were: community-oriented goals, internal goals, consultation goals, functional goals, and professional-development goals. One of the primary areas of interest was to determine the degree to which the organization succeeds in achieving its goals (Price, 1968) as a measure of organizational effectiveness.

The two purposes of the research were to determine the agreement between school psychologists and school superintendents and to determine how school psychologists and school superintendents differ in their rankings of the goals of school psychology.

The rankings of the value concepts and goals between psychologists and superintendents were found to be highly correlated. Two goals were ranked higher by school superintendents than by psychologists. They were:

1. Referral and follow-up on cases handled by child guidance clinics, community classes, and other community agencies.
2. The identification of factors that influence learning efficiency and classroom behavior—i.e., pupil–teacher interaction.

The four goals ranked higher by school psychologists than by superintendents were:

1. To conduct parent counseling involving communication of psychological findings, behavior management, and implementation of recommendations.
2. To conduct parent interviewing and counseling and education.
3. To attend university seminars and workshops for school psychologists.
4. To activate assessment and placement teams that make decisions on the placement of exceptional children.

Noticeable differences were found to exist in the respective rankings for only a few value concepts of: concern; empathy; flexibility; rationality; and autonomy (ranked higher by school psychologists than superintendents). Superintendents, on the other hand, gave higher rankings to: faculty, ambitions, loyalty, principals, administrative staff, and school boards than did psychologists.

An extensive survey of school superintendents was undertaken by Kaplan, Chrin, and Chancy (1977) to evaluate school administrations' priorities for school psychologists. A 21-item questionnaire was sent to all members ($N = 1100$) of the Buckeye Association of School Administrators (Ohio). Four-hundred-eighteen of the responses were returned. The results indicated that superintendents rated the activities of diagnosis and child study the highest and they rated research and evaluation of curricula the lowest. These results are consistent with the Keogh (1977) study of school psychologists' self evaluations and the results of a previous study of administrators (Senft & Clair, 1972). However, it does not appear to be consistent with the Manley and Manley (1978) study, which found little support for school psychologists in a child appraiser role.

Communication, in its broadest aspects, was reviewed in this section. It would appear that the variance in roles and tasks have confused teachers on the exact role of the school psychologists. Teacher familiarity and the direct value of the recommendations' section of the psychological reports contribute to the communication process when it is an open, nonmandated structure. The discussion in the next section examines in particular three aspects of the school psychologist's role post-PL 94–142.

The School Psychologist and PL 94–142

What is Public Law 94–142? A quote directly from the law may clarify its purpose (from the Federal Register, August 23, 1977):

> It is the purpose of the Act to assure that all handicapped children have available to them a free and appropriate public education which emphasizes special education and related services designed to meet their unique needs, to assure that the rights of handicapped children and their parents or guardians are protected, to assist States and localities to provide for the education of all handicapped children, and to assess and assure the effectiveness of efforts to educate handicapped children.

The major elements of PL 94–142 are:

1. Individualized education program.
2. Parental participation.
3. Due process.
4. Access to student records.
5. Education of handicapped with nonhandicapped to maximum extent appropriate.
6. Child find.
7. Inservice training.
8. Nondiscriminatory testing.
9. Barrier-free schools.
10. Inclusion of handicapped in physical education programs.
11. Financial support to schools.

Abeson and Zettel (1977) described PL 94–142, or the Education of All Children Act, as the turning of a significant corner in the delivery of special-education services. The law probably has had more impact on school psychology as a discipline than any other single endeavor since the profession's inception in the early 1900's. Early reports on PL 94–142 in school psychology literature, such as Kabler's (1977) response, focused primarily on nondiscriminatory evaluation procedures, parental access to research, parental rights to challenge placement, and the other highly structured legal safeguards described implicitly in the law. In short, the legal safeguards simply require the school psychologist to perform in a professional manner that involves keeping the channels of communication open between the school and the parent, protecting records from general review by nonauthorized persons, assuring that parents are well informed, and by inviting parental decision on placement prior to placing the child in an educational environment.

Special education, on the other hand, has existed in an atmosphere in which program accountability, or compliance in meeting mandatory special-education legislation, has been slow to occur. Recent articles (Saretsky, 1973; Sugarman, 1974) have emphasized accountability—or lack of it—in the school and the alternative, accountability through the courts. The press for accountability is justified and may provide the opportunity for all areas of education to meet the challenges that have been emphasized for decades. This fact is especially true for school psychologists, for in many school systems, there is no other professional so well equipped to measure the sine qua non of school accountability—behavioral change. It is important to note, however, that behavioral change can be measured in multiple ways and that the target of measurement should be comprehensive. Traditional procedures and traditional targets may need to be augmented by alternative measurement requirements and practices.

In this section, I examine three aspects of PL 94–142 and expanded role developments that could be trend setters in protecting the future of school psychology and the handicapped. The three areas of focus are: the consultant role and the Individualized Educational Plan (IEP) process, IEP monitoring, and an exploration of a few of the major-systems contributions school psychologists can make to old problems by evolving a management/systems approach to problem solving.

The Consultant Role and IEP Process.   PL 94–142 has placed important new role demands on the school psychologist, requiring the school psychologists to vary their traditional skills. An example is the deemphasis on formal assessment, removing the "do not disturb" signs hung on the door to private rooms. The school psychologist is now part of the assessment team and, as such, must answer questions leading to the preparation of the Individualized Educational Plan (IEP). The IEP requires information about "what has been taught" and how it was taught as data entry when the student is recommended for placement. Thus, the short- and long-term instructional, behavioral, management statements must be in place before the student can be reassigned a placement/change in program.

The traditional emphasis of psychoeducational testing and clinical intervention have been discussed in recent years; some (e.g., Bersoff, 1971) have likened many past practices to "institutional psychiatry," whereas others (Hayes & Clair, 1978) suggest that to continue in the process of the past could lead to the death of the profession. A review of school psychologists' perceptions of their role demonstrates either difficulty with time constraints or a genuine reluctance to work within the ecological setting of the school, e.g., in consultation with parents and others in the community. The history of special education reminds us that parent and community support have been essential for the growth and development of programs and, in many cases, the success of programs for exceptional children and youth. Therefore, school psychologists must begin to emphasize work within the ecology beyond the school.

Yet, most special educators feel school psychologists have much more to offer than test scores. The direction school psychology has taken in its development of the consultative role can be a very good one in special-education service delivery. However, the manner in which the literature describes the consultation model is just not very exciting. Once again, it appears to be another all-or-nothing role model, not an alternative applicable to particular settings or referral problems. The principle that drives consultation cannot simply be a deemphasis on testing, but must include an increase in classroom observation and collaboration with other school and community agencies and staff. The model is certainly not new, and, in fact, is an outgrowth of the "mental-health movement in the schools," which dates back to the 1950's. It is predicated on the fact that test scores do not communicate instructional and behavioral management plans. Unfortunately, the primary criticism of school psychologists—their poor level and pattern of communication with both special and regular teachers—has not mitigated the problem.

Consultation may include two additional principles when handicapped children are involved. Consultation concerning exceptional students, particularly preschool and secondary school-age youth, must include agencies external to the school.

The relationship between school and other agency personnel is a sensitive issue at best. What agencies and who in those agencies should be involved, the communication safeguards between agencies on matters of release of confidential information, and who chairs the committee on the handicapped meeting must be considered. These are critical issues that cast long shadows on any role relationships school psychologists may wish to play with handicapped students in the future.

Lovan (1978), in writing on alternative approaches to family/school liaison notes, "frequently, the child identified is viewed as the sole 'owner' of a problem [p. 585]." Handicapping conditions are simply not the child's fault, or his or her problem; they are also not the fault of the family, or their problem. Handicapping conditions are a community-wide responsibility, and must be managed as such. The consultant role must be broadened to include the preparation of the community, attitudinally and informationally, for its role in the life of a handicapped person.

Lovan describes four steps in the consultative process. The first three are: (1) information gatherer–imparter; (2) facilitator, primarily of communication among the family and other agencies; and (3) consultant, which itself has two operational steps: (1) a problem-solving focus on the consultee's management plan; and (2) a consultation educator, or the communication link between family members, other agencies, and the school. The fourth step is one of primary importance with the handicapped, and one that should be increased significantly at this time. It is: (4) counselor–educator, which is described (Lovan, 1978) as parent–educator charged "... to teach parents a specific approach to parent/child conflict resolution, specific techniques for parents to use in modifying problematic child behavior or a specific interaction style [p. 557]."

Handicapping conditions place families into crisis and require that parents receive long-term and crisis-intervention services. The handicapped child presents management needs that exceed what the family normally can provide. Serious problems begin when parents deny the handicap, repressing the very existance of the child into a nondescript personalogical being without family characteristics or individual identity. Guilt can accompany the denial, resulting in severe self blame or the search for someone or some person to blame. Work with parents requires specific skills learned by studying the process and applying the process in supervised settings.

The second relatively unexplored area important to the management of the handicapped through consultation is that of career education. Career planning begins early and should have a set of stated objectives just as one would develop for academic planning and social–personal development. The point is to create a continuum of programs and service that permits alternatives to placement in regular education on the far right, and special-education classes in the middle, and residential programs on the extreme left. What is needed are age-specific goals leading to life goals, beginning in early childhood and following throughout the life of the child.

One of the objectives would be that of career education. What is career education? Hoyt (1977) has formulated one definition that appears to be receiving considerable attention:

> Career education represents the total effort of public education and the community to help all individuals become familiar with the values of a work oriented society, to integrate those values into their personal value structure, and to implement those values in their lives in ways that make work possible, meaningful, and satisfying to each individual [p. 3].

There seems to be so little known in the area of career education that it is as if once a handicapped youth reaches a certain age, s/he is no longer of any significant concern to special education. About all that has been available are collections of job descriptions based on personal experiences of writers in the field (Kokaska, 1964; Kolstoe & Frey, 1965; Younie & Clark, 1969).

However, career education has been in effect a number of years for handicapped students through the secondary-level work–study program. A basic criticism of these secondary-level programs in special education has been the continuance and promulgation of "watered down" curricula focusing on academic content rather than the relevant skill areas necessary for handicapped people to function vocationally and socially in their respective communities. Our educational system is just beginning to view employment as an important subgoal (Martin, 1972).

The impetus to develop new, innovative delivery systems designed to service handicapped students in regular and vocational programs of which school psychology is a team member needs further exploration. If the consultation role is applied to vocational education, Hohenshil (1975) notes that the school psychologist can greatly aid in the process:

> The psychologist, with extensive knowledge of human development, the learning processes, personality development, and experience with atypical students, could be an invaluable consultant to vocational educators in the development of appropriate instructional programs for disadvantaged and handicapped students. He could provide in-service training to acquaint these vocational teachers with the types of behavior and learning rates to expect from students with various types of handicapping conditions; he could also suggest effective behavior management techniques. The importance of this type of consultation cannot be overestimated, for the most frequent cause of a vocational instructor's failure is not his lack of skill in the trade areas but rather his failure to take into consideration the learning and/or behavioral characteristic of the handicapped or disadvantaged students [p. 61].

However, Hohenshil points out that specialized knowledge and training are necessary for the school psychologist to function in special education programs. The school psychologist should have a working knowledge of the variety of vocational offerings and the types of aptitudes required for each.

In short, the consultation role, if used in the delivery of services to the handicapped, requires fair familiarity with preschool regular and special-education curricula, and vocational program components, methods, and techniques. It would appear that the times are right, the need is clearly evident, and there is a desire on the part of the profession to address these concerns. What, then, is missing? Is it the attitude that school psychologists are psychologists and not educators, or simply that school psychologists do not currently possess the skill and time to assume new "role" responsibilities? Is it that a redefined role is absent from formalized job descriptions or, could it be that school psychologists can go, if they want to, but are caught in the "why change trap?"

The School Psychologist and IEP Monitoring.   The school psychologist is now expected to contribute information to a team of regular and special-education (and sometimes vocational) educators, administrators, parent and community agency personnel, and then monitor (account for) the results of those activities. Decisions on the education of the handicapped are now outgrowths of data derived from all those support persons who can contribute to that data. The school psychologist must link information (Miller, 1978), facilitating team function, because their training cuts across the widest array of disciplines.

White (1968–1969) in a position paper entitled *Will School Psychology Exist?* made clear that the schools have changed dramatically over the past few years, but school psychology has not. She projects, and quite accurately, that the school psychologists *must* enter a role of research and development.

Kratochwill and Bergan (1978b) see this role best fulfilled through a focus on evaluation research and suggest the need for school psychologists to receive specific training in this area. Glaser and Backer (1972) describe three district classes of evaluators: (1) self-evaluation staff team (i.e., an evaluation conducted by program workers themselves); (2) inside evaluation team (evaluators who are employed by the institution of which the program is a part, but are not themselves part of a particular program); (3) an outside evaluation team (a consultant or team of consultants brought in from some other organization to perform the assessment). Kratochwill and Bergan (1978a) suggest that the school psychologist can provide the technical expertise to function as a system-change agent within a behavioral consultation model that corresponds to Glaser and Bacher's type-2 classification.

The school psychologist can provide monitoring processes on the growth of handicapped children and youth, and function as an advisor to educators in a team relationship, as well as construct custom-tailored school programming around available service-delivery capabilities. White's projection of the future made some 19 years ago is still a topical concern in the current PL 94–142 environment.

School psychologists now have the opportunity to break from traditional roles and engineer processes that can identify children as handicapped, constructing a system process, for finding children, that is sensitive to compliance with the law while remaining cost efficient. That effort should develop into a research/ evaluation to capability serving to provide IEP monitoring structures that enable the psychologist to work in a data-based scientific role of feeding back information useful to the teacher. In short, the school psychologist can become the applied scientist, interested in advancing the art of teaching the handicapped.

The School Psychologist as a Systems Engineer.   School psychologists are unique by the very fact that although prepared professionally as psychologists, they work in the public-school setting with a professional peer group predominated by educators. In this setting, school psychologists can contribute a thorough knowledge of human growth, development, and aberrations that impact children. PL 94–142 is explicit in its requirement that all handicapped children are to receive at least as much service as any "normal" child in a school district. It is quite clear that a 5½-hour school day is mandated for all handicapped children, and children is defined as ages 3 to 21. Stipulated by the law, services are to extend to those handicapped children who are unserved or underserved, including the seriously handicapped who were (and are) institutionalized.

One of the systems school psychologists can build are child-find procedures to identify the unserved and underserved. Historically, school psychologists have been involved in child-find procedures since Binet's time. The psychological referral procedure is one type of child-find process. The difference is that the referral procedure places the school psychologist as a primary decision maker in the flow of referral process. The problem is that the communication flow from teacher to psychologist is frequently subjective. The first-order opinion is that of the teacher—should the child be referred. The classic study on teacher recognition of emotional problems (Wickman, 1928) suggests that teachers are not foolproof. In fact, they are only as good as the quality of inservice they are receiving (Boeck, Allione, Mochnaley, Toomey, & Kaplan, 1973).

The initial endeavor in a screening system is to develop who is to do what, establishing the criteria at which point a child is in or out of the screening flow. A task flow of the referral process is therefore necessary. The initial role of the school psychologist is to provide inservice to persons who will contribute data to that process. An example of a screening system for learning-disabled children is shown in Fig. 3.1. The importance of the inservice is to inform people of their responsibility and establish the criteria for selection. The use of a screening system places the psychologist into a new role with two primary dimensions.

First, because the school psychologist is the expert on the school staff in measurement, child growth, and development, it is not unlikely that the psychologist will engineer the system, at least in great part. Secondly, the initial function of the school psychologist in the system is to assist other staff to develop competencies in observing, measuring, and recording data in keeping with the emphasis of their training and discipline. A systems approach advances the capability of all who use it when well engineered, augmenting efficiency. For example, should psychologists administer academic achievement tests? Could not the formal and informal academic-achievement assessment procedures be administered by the regular and special educators who need those results more urgently? If other disciplines were involved in the screening and diagnostic systems, it could reduce the amount of time school psychologists spend on that task, and increase the number of children they can serve.

More importantly, the communication between psychologists and educators should increase significantly as a result of a shared responsibility in the screening procedure. Child-find systems should be designed to increase communication from the point of initial teacher referral to the most exacting diagnostic detail concerning learner characteristics. Traditionally, the referral device has been anything but exact.

Communication among disciplines, and observational skills on target behaviors can be increased when a structured referral form initiates the process. When teachers pinpoint the grade or age equivalent for a specific learner charac-

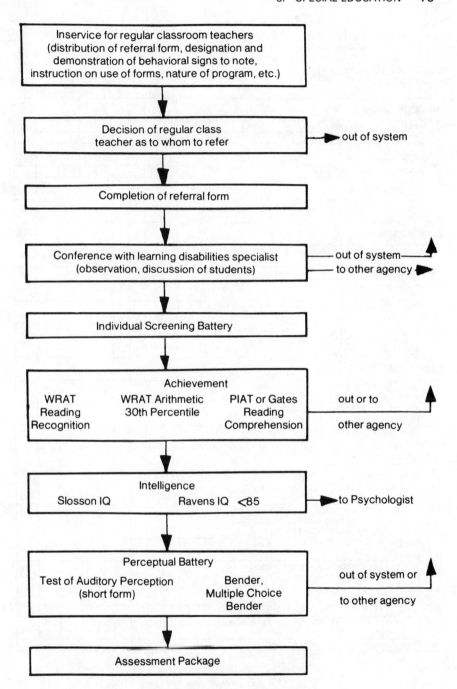

FIG. 3.1.   Example of a screening system.

TEACHER INDEX

Please indicate the age level at which you feel this child is functioning. Keep in mind his (her) age and the level of his (her) fellow students. Place an X in the appropriate box.

AGE LEVELS

	4-5	5-6	6-7	7-8	8-9	9-10	10-11	11-12	12
A. ACADEMIC SUBJECTS									
1. Arithmetic reasoning									
2. Arithmetic computation									
3. Word recognition									
4. Word meaning									
5. Reading comprehension									
6. Spelling									
7. Handwriting									
8. Written expression of thought									
9. Oral expression of thought									
B. SPEECH AND LANGUAGE									
10. Comprehension of verbal directions or explanations									
11. Speech intelligibility (articulation)									
C. AUDITORY PERCEPTION									
12. Ability to discriminate between similar sounding letters and words									
13. Ability to remember verbal directions									
14. Ability to associate meaning with auditory stimulus									
D. VISUAL PERCEPTION									
15. Ability to discriminate between similar visual stimuli									
16. Retention of visual images (letters and words)									
17. Ability to associate meaning with visual stimuli									
E. SOCIAL - EMOTIONAL									
18. Agressiveness - tendency toward hitting, spitting, pushing, teasing, and/or hostility									
19. Withdrawing behavior - incidence of staring, awareness of surroundings, attention to directions									
20. Mood - unpredictability of mood changes									
21. Depressive behavior - happiness, activity level, tension, anxiety, morbidity of thoughts or themes, reality of fears									
22. Hypoactivity - tiredness, energy level									
23. Hyperactivity - tendency to be always on the go									
24. Relationships with other people									

FIG. 3.2. Teacher Index.

teristic, they are forced to observe that skill, trait, or aptitude carefully. Fig. 3.2 provides a display of a specific referral form. The reasons for its use are:

1. Gibberish used by most examiners can be eliminated.
2. Inservice training can be developed to promote consistent communication between examiner and teachers using learning characteristics descriptors.
3. Consistent use of terminology should enhance the explicit use of instructional and behavioral management.
4. The time and dollar effectiveness of using a behavioral descriptive profile system can be a very important consideration.
5. Important, too, however, are the implications for assisting the teachers to tie into the formal assessment process by having them provide observational and informal assessment data as a diagnostic team member.

Similarly, reporting the results of the screening process in profiles of learning characteristics greatly aids communication over the current narrative reports.

Fig. 3.3 shows a profile for reporting the results of a systematic assessment procedure as an alternative to a written report. In fact, why not impose a 1-year moratorium on all written psychological reports, and upgrade the level of communication (and therefore cooperation) between special educator and school psychologists by using a profile as the reporting mechanism?

PL 94–142 requires school psychologists to abandon their traditional ring seat on the edge of the special educator arena and enter as partners into the various service-delivery systems for handicapped children in school and community. Some parts of the law are very restrictive, requiring reevaluation every 3 years for all handicapped children in specialized placement. However, the law provides psychologists the opportunity to develop the consultant model into a set of activities that can serve the handicapped. By letter and intent of the law, the school psychologist can become an important team member, mapping custom-tailored programs for handicapped children and youth (to age 21) through a broad base of community school services. This section has drawn on the child-find process as one example.

SUMMARY

The message herein is simple. School psychology, its inception, and continued development is inseparable from the public-school delivery of services to the handicapped. PL 94–142 forces special educators to accept the data from school psychologists as part of a team-driven Individualized Educational Plan (IEP). School psychology can now use that entry into educational service delivery to offer a custom-tailored set of instructional and management objectives. The

MODEL LEARNING DISABILITY SYSTEMS
INDIVIDUAL PROFILE RECORD

PUPIL NAME _____

I.D. NUMBER _____SEX_____BIRTHDATE _____

I. SCREENING PROFILE: DATE _____

ACADEMIC ACHIEVEMENT

K 1.0 1.5 2.0 2.5 3.0 3.5 4.0 4.5 5.0 5.5 6.0

Spelling
Arithmetic
Word Recognition
Reading Comprehension

LANGUAGE

Verbal Conceptualization
Non-Verbal Conceptualization

VISUAL PERCEPTION

Discrimination
Retention
Sequencing

AUDITORY PERCEPTION

Discrimination
Retention
Sequencing

II. HANDICAPPING CONDITIONS:

A. Physical —Upper Involvement: _____
            —Lower Involvement: _____
B. Vision —Corrected: _____
            —Uncorrected: _____
C. Hearing —Corrected: _____
            —Uncorrected: _____

III. SCHOOL AND HOME INFORMATION:

A._____ Present Grade
B._____ Classroom Teacher
C._____ If child has ever been retained, list grades.
D._____ What special services is the child presently
                 receiving?
E._____ Parent Name and Address

_____

_____

F._____ Home Telephone Number

IV. ADDITIONAL INFORMATION

_____
_____
_____
_____
_____

V. ASSIGNMENT:

	Date Enrolled	Date Withdrawn
A. Assessment Class	_____	_____
B. Resource Room	_____	_____
C. Strategist	_____	_____
D. Other	_____	_____

VI. PROGRAM OBJECTIVES:

Objective 1: _____
_____

Objective 2: _____
_____

Objective 3: _____
_____

Objective 4: _____
_____

Objective 5: _____
_____

Objective 6: _____
_____

Objective 7: _____
_____

Objective 7: _____
_____

Objective 8: _____
_____

Objective 9: _____
_____

Objective 9: _____
_____

Objective 10: _____
_____

FIG. 3.3. Model Learning Disability Systems Individual Profile Record.

objectives can be augmented through the consultation model by: (1) including an increased role with preschool and secondary-aged handicapped children; (2) developing monitoring (accountability) systems; and (3) systematic structures to augment effective and efficient identification (child-find) processes for unserved and underserved handicapped children. There must exist a realization on the part of school psychologists that they can greatly improve the quality of comprehensive special-education services through a team relationship with special educators.

REFERENCES

Abeson, A., & Zettel, J. The end of the quiet revolution: The education for all handicapped children act of 1975. *Exceptional Children*, 1977, *44*(2), 114–130.

Abidin, R. R. A psychosocial look at consultation and behavior modification. *Psychology in the Schools*, 1972, *9*, 358–363.

Alevy, D. A psychologist in the schools. *Psychology in the Schools*, 1964, *1*, 412–414.

Baker, H. L. Psychological services: From the school staff's point of view. *Journal of School Psychology*, 1965, *3*, 36–42.

Bardon, J. E., & Bennett, V. C. *School psychology*. Englewood Cliffs, N.J.: Prentice-Hall, 1974.

Bardon, J. I. Problems and issues in school psychology. *Journal of School Psychology*, 1965, *9*, 252–260.

Bardon, J. I. The state of the art (and science) of school psychology. *American Psychologist*, 1976, *31*, 785–791.

Bennett, V. C. Who is a school psychologist and what does he do? *Journal of School Psychology*, 1970, *8*, 166–171.

Bennett, V. C. Applied research can be useful: An example. *Journal of School Psychology*, 1976, *14*, 67–73.

Bernauer, M., & Jackson, J. H. Review of school psychology for 1973. *Professional Psychology*, 1974, *5*, 155–165.

Bersoff, D. N. School psychology as "institutional psychiatry." *Professional Psychology*, 1971, *2*, 266–270.

Bersoff, D. N. Professional ethics and legal responsibilities: On the horns of a dilemma. *Journal of School Psychology*, 1975, *13*, 359–376.

Binet, A., & Simon, T. Methodes nowvelles pour le diagnostic elu niveau intellectual des anormaux. L'Annee Psychologique, 1905, 11, 93, 191–244.

Binet, A., & Simon, T. Le développement de l'intelligence chez les enfants. *L'Annee Psychologique*, 1908, *14*, 1–94.

Boeck, D., Allione, J., Mochnaley, S., Toomey, R., & Kaplan, J. Instructional objectives and prescriptive materials. In D. A. Sabatino (Ed.), *A systems approach to provide educational services to children with learning disabilities*. University Park, Pa.: Model Learning Disabilities Systems of Pennsylvania, 1973.

Boring, E. W. *A history of experimental psychology*. New York: Appleton-Century-Crofts, 1950.

Bower, E. M. *The significance of the public school in shaping the life of the child*. Address on Mental Health, Wheeling, West Virginia, November 1965.

Brantley, J. G., Reilly, D. H., Beach, N. L., Cody, W., Fields, R., & Lee, H. School psychology: The intersection of community, training institution and the school system. *Psychology in the Schools*, 1974, *11*, 28–31.

Brown, D. T., & Lindstrom, J. P. Training of school psychologists. *Psychology in the Schools,* January, 1978, *15*(1), 37–45.

Brown, D. T., Sewell, T. J., & Lindstrom, J. P. *The handbook of certification licensure requirements for school psychologists.* National Association of School Psychologists, January 1977.

Catterall, C. D. Special education in transition—implications for school psychology. *Journal of School Psychology,* 1972, *10,* 91–98.

Cutts, N. E. (Ed.). *School psychologists at mid-century.* Washington, D.C.: American Psychological Association, 1955.

Doll, E. A. A brief Binet–Simon scale. *Psychological Clinic,* 1917, *11,* 197–211; 254–261.

Dunn, L. Special education for the mildly retarded: Is much of it justifiable? *Exceptional Children,* 1968, *35,* 5–22.

Education for All Handicapped Children Act of 1975, Public Law 94–142, 89 STAT. 773, November 28, 1975, Federal Register, 1975.

Engelmann, S. Teaching reading to children with low mental ages. *Education and Training of the Mentally Retarded,* 1967, *2,* 193–201.

England, G. W. Personal value systems of American managers. *Academy of Management Journal,* 1967, *10,* 53–68.

Esquirol, J. E. *Des mentales consideries les rapports medical hygienique et medico–legal.* Paris: Bailliere, 1838.

Footman, G. E. An analysis of the tastes and roles of the school psychologist in the state of California (doctoral dissertation, University of Southern California, 1972). *Dissertation Abstracts International,* 1973, *33,* 3379A. (University Microfilms No. 73–736).

Foster, G. G., Schmidt, C. R., & Sabatino, D. A. Teacher expectancies and label, "Learning Disabilities." *Journal of Learning Disabilities,* February 1976, *9*(2), 111–114.

Gallagher, J. J. Psychology and special education—the future: Where the action is. *Psychology in the Schools,* 1969, *6,* 219–226.

Gilmore, G. E. School psychologist–parent contact. *Psychology in the Schools,* 1974, *11,* 170–174.

Gilmore, G. E., & Chandy, J. Educators describe the school psychologist. *Psychology in the Schools,* 1973, *10,* 397–403. (a)

Gilmore, G. E., & Chandy, J. Teachers' perceptions for school psychological services. *Journal of School Psychology,* 1973, *11,* 139–147. (b)

Glaser, E. M., & Backer, T. E. Outline of questions for program evaluations utilizing the clinical approach. *Evaluation,* Fall 1972, *1*(1), 58–60.

Goddard, Henry Herbert. *Psychology of the normal and subnormal.* New York: Dodd, Mead, 1919.

Granger, R., & Campbell, P. The school psychologist as program evaluator. *Journal of School Psychology,* 1977, *15,* 174–179.

Gray, S. W. *The psychologist in the schools.* New York: Holt, 1963.

Hayes, M. E., & Clair, T. N. School psychology—why is the profession dying? *Psychology in the Schools,* 1978, *15,* 518–521.

Hewett, F., & Forness, S. R. *Education of exceptional learners* (2nd ed.). Boston: Allyn and Bacon, 1977.

Hohenshil, T. H. Call for redirection: A vocational educator views school psychological services. *Journal of School Psychology,* 1975, *13*(1), 58–62.

Holt, F. D., & Kicklighter, R. H. (Eds.). *Psychological services in the schools Readings in preparation, organization and practice.* Dubuque, Iowa: William C. Brown, 1971.

Hoyt, K. B. *A primer for a career education,* Washington, D.C.: U.S. Government Printing Office, 1977.

Hyman, I. A. Debate: Will the real school psychologist please stand up? Part 3: A struggle of jurisdictional impenalism. *School Psychology Digest,* 1979, *8*(2), 174–180.

Hyman, I. A., & Schreiber, K. The school psychologist as a child advocate. *Psychology in the Schools,* 1975, *12,* 50–57.

James, W. *Essays in radical empiricism*. New York: Longmans, Green, 1912.

Kabler, M. L. Public Law 94-142 and school psychology: Challenges and opportunities. *School Psychology Digest*, 1977, *7*, 19-30.

Kahl, L. J., & Fine, M. J. Teachers' perceptions of the school psychologist as a function of teaching experience, amount of contact, and socioeconomic status of the school. *Psychology in the Schools*, 1978, *15*(4), 577-582.

Kaplan, M. S., Chrin, M., & Clancy, B. School psychological services. *Journal of School Psychology*, 1977, *15*(1), 15-80.

Keogh, B. K. Working together: A call for greater and more creative teamwork between researchers and clinicians. *Journal of Learning Disabilities*, 1977, *10*(8), 478.

Keogh, B. K., Kukic, S. J., Becker, L. D., McLoughlin, R. J., & Kukic, M. B. School psychologist's services in special education programs. *Journal of School Psychology*, 1975, *13*(2), 146-147.

Kirp, D., Buss, W., & Kuriloff, P. Legal reform of special education empirical studies and procedural proposals. *California Law Review*, 1974, *62*, 40-155.

Kirp, P. L., & Kirp, L. M. The legalization of the school psychologist's world. *Journal of School Psychology*, 1976, *14*, 83-89.

Kokaska, C. A tool for community adjustment. *Mental Retardation*, 1964, *2*, 365-368.

Kolstoe, O. P., & Frey, R. M. *A high school work study program for mentally subnormal students*. Carbondale, Ill.: Southern Illinois University Press, 1965.

Korman, M. National conference on levels and patterns of professionals training in psychology. *American Psychologist*, 1974, *29*, 441-449.

Kratochwill, T. R., & Bergan, J. R. Evaluating programs in applied settings through behavioral consultation. *Journal of School Psychology*, 1978, *16*(4), 375-386. (a)

Kratochwill, T. R., & Bergan, J. R. Training school psychologists: Some perspectives on a competency-based behavioral consultation model. *Professional Psychology*, February 1978, *73*, 71-82. (b)

Lambert, N. M. A school based consultation model. *Professional Psychology*, 1974, *5*, 267-276.

Lane, A: *The wild boy of Aveyron*. Cambridge: Harvard University Press, 1976.

Lesiak, W. The Michigan school psychologist, 1960-1970. *Michigan Association of School Psychologists*, 1973, *2*,4.

Levine, S. M. Disequilibrium and growth. In American Psychological Association. *School Psychology Newsletter*, 1977, *31*(4), 2-3.

Levine, W. Psychological tests and practices with the deaf. A survey of the state of the art. *The Volta Review*, 1974, *76*, 298-314.

Lewis, C. R. The school psychologist as program consultant. *Psychology in the Schools*, 1974, *11*, 294-295.

Lister, M., Baker, A., & Milhouse, R. L. Record keeping, access and confidentiality. In N. Hobbs (Ed.), *Issues in the classification of the children*. San Francisco: Jossey-Bass, 1975.

Lovan, D. M. Four alternative approaches to the family. School liaison role. *Psychology in the Schools*, October 1978, *15* (4), 553-559.

Lucas, M. S., & Jones, R. L. Attitudes of teachers of mentally handicapped children toward psychological reports and services. *Journal of School Psychology*, 1970, *8*, 122-130.

Maher, C. A. A synaptic framework for school program evaluation. *Journal of School Psychology*, 1973, *16*, 322-333.

Manley, T. R., & Manley, E. T. A comparison of the personal values and operative goals of school psychologists and school superintendents. *Journal of School Psychology*, 1978, *16*(2), 99-109.

Mann, L. *Cognitive training: A look at the past and some concerns about the present*. State of the Art Review, Reston, Virginia, 1974. Paper presented at National Regional Resource Convention, Reston, Virginia, September 1974.

Martin, E. Individualism and behaviorism as future trends in educating handicapped children. *Exceptional Children*, 1972, *38*, 517-525.

McClung, F. B., & Studen, A. A. *Mental health consultation to programs for children: A review of data collected from selected U.S. sites.* USPHA Publication No. 2066, 1970.

McDaniel, L. J., & Ahr, E. The psychologist as a resource person conducting inservice teacher education. *Psychology in the Schools,* 1965, *2,* 220–224.

Mearig, J. S. On becoming a child advocate in school psychology. *Journal of School Psychology,* 1974, *12,* 121–129.

Medway, F. J. Teacher's knowledge of school psychologists' responsibilities. *Journal of School Psychology,* 1977, *15*(4), 301–307.

Miller, W. E. A new role for the school psychologists—who needs it? *Psychology in the Schools,* October 1978, *15*(4), 514–517.

Mussman, M. C. Teachers' evaluations of psychological reports. *Journal of School Psychology,* 1964, *3,* 35–37.

Musto, D. F. Whatever happened to "Community Mental Health"? *Public Interest,* 1975, *39,* 53–79.

Newland, T. E. The search for the new: Frenzied, faddish, or fundamental. *Journal of School Psychology,* 1970, *8,* 242–244.

Pielstick, N. L. The appropriate domain of the school psychologist. *Journal of School Psychology,* 1970, *8*(4), 317–319.

Price, J. L. *Organizational effectiveness: An inventory of propositions.* Homewood, Ill.: Irvin, 1968.

Raimy, V. C. (Ed.). *Training in clinical psychology.* Englewood Cliffs, N.J.: Prentice-Hall, 1950.

Reger, R. *School psychology.* Springfield, Ill.: Charles C. Thomas, 1975.

Reynolds, M. C. A framework for considering some issues in special education. *Exceptional Children,* 1962, *28,* 369–370.

Roberts, R. D. Perceptions of actual and desired role functions of school psychologists by psychologists and teachers. *Psychology in the Schools,* 1970, *7,* 175–178.

Rucker, C. W. Report writing in school psychology: A critical investigation. *Journal of School Psychology,* 1967, *5,* 101–108.

Sabatino, D. A. School psychology—special education: To acknowledge a relationship. *Journal of School Psychology,* 1972, *10,* 99–105.

Sarason, S. The unfortunate fate of Alfred Binet and school psychology. *Teachers College Record,* 1976, *77,* 579–592.

Saretsky, G. The strangely significant case of Peter Doe. *Phi Delta Kappan,* 1973, *54,* 589–592.

Senft, L., & Clair, T. N. Iowa survey reveals principals' perceptions of school psychologists. *School Psychologist Newsletter* (American Psychological Association), 1972, *27,* 34–35.

Steinberg, M., & Chandler, G. Coordinating services between a mental health center and public schools. *Journal of School Psychology,* 1976, *14,* 355–362.

Sugarman, S. Accountability through the courts. *School Review,* 1974, *82,* 233–259.

Tan, J. S. B. Role of the school psychologist as perceived by the Illinois school psychologists and directors of special education (doctoral dissertation, Illinois State University, 1968). *Dissertation Abstracts,* 1969, *29,* 3010–3011A. (University Microfilms No. 72-11, 721)

Terman, L. M. *The measurement of intelligence.* Boston: Houghton Mifflin, 1960.

Terman, L. M., & Merrill, M. A. *Measuring intelligence.* Boston, N.Y.: Houghton Mifflin, 1937.

Thorndike, E. L. *Educational psychology.* New York: Teachers College, Columbia University, 1913.

Trachtman, G. Do your thing in school psychology. *Professional Psychology,* 1971, *2,* 377–381.

Tracy, M., & Sturgeon, S. The school psychologist as program evaluator: A comprehensive note in the 1980's. *Viewpoints,* 1977, *53,* 49–69.

Tredgold, R. F., & Soddy, K. *A text-book of mental deficiency.* London: Bailliere, Lindall, and Cox, 1956.

Vallett, R. E. *The practice of school psychology: Professional problems.* New York: Wiley, 1963.

Wallin, J. E. *Wallace children with mental and physical handicaps.* Englewood Cliffs, N.J.: Prentice-Hall, 1949.

Wenger, R. D. Teacher response to collaborative consultation. *Psychology in the Schools,* January, 1979, *16*(1), 127–131.

White, M. A. Will school psychology exist? *Journal of School Psychology,* 1968–1969, *7*(2), 53–57.

White, M. A., & Harris, M. *The school psychologist.* New York: Harper, 1961.

Wickman, E. K. *Childrens' behaviors and teachers' attitudes.* New York: Commonwealth Fund, 1928.

Winett, R. A., Battersby, C., & Edwards, S. M. The effects of architectural change, individualized instruction and group contingencies on the behavior and academic production of sixth graders. *Journal of School Psychology,* 1975, *13*, 23–40.

Woodworth, R. S. *Psychological issues: Selective papers of Robert S. Woodworth,* New York: Columbia University Press, 1939.

Younie, W. J., & Clark, G. M. Personnel training needs for cooperative secondary school programs for mentally retarded youth. *Education and Training of the Mentally Retarded,* 1969, *4*, 184–196.

Ysseldyke, J. E. Who's calling the plays in school psychology? *Psychology in the Schools,* 1978, *15*, 373–378.

4

Issues Surrounding the Diagnosis of Learning Disabilities: Child Handicap versus Failure of the Child–School Interaction

Gerald M. Senf
Journal of Learning Disabilities

INTRODUCTION

The past decade—the 1970's—has seen the fledgling concept of learning disabilities, born the previous decade, become a statutory term with legal imperatives attached equal to those of the concepts of blindness, deafness, mental retardation, emotional disturbance, crippled and other health impaired, and associated disorders. Although diagnosis of physically based handicaps affords more definitive standards for identification, perhaps owing to their long standing and their clearer biological basis, learning disabilities remain ambiguous.

School psychologists and others in education agree that psychoeducational diagnosis is a primary—if not the central—occupational responsibility. In fact, some school psychologists have told me—as have some others working in educational settings—that there is too much psychometry (and report writing) and too little psychology in the school psychologists' role.

Inasmuch as the school psychologist, as diagnostician, typically serves a labeling function closely tied to administrative/fiscal concerns, the occupational affiliation is typically located at some level "above" the local education agency (LEA). Simple accuracy of diagnosis—though accuracy is no simple matter with learning disabilities (Bryant, 1972)—becomes complicated by limited funds, program availability, area priorities, local politics and personalities, and a host of other and derivative considerations.

Even more problematic, perhaps, is the ever-increasing insistence by educators that diagnoses have a strongly prescriptive focus. Administration may need categories for funding, but teachers need direction for instruction. These two diagnostic goals are not necessarily incompatible—but the administrative demand to accomplish many diagnoses takes precedence over time-consuming prescriptiveness. After all, the school psychologist is typically hired by a supra-LEA administrator; repeated child and teacher contacts are necessary for con-

83

structive, ongoing prescriptive diagnosis; and, even were the time available, few school psychologists know the classroom or the child in the classroom context sufficiently to be of substantial service. In effect, job demands of labeling keep most school psychologists from learning how to apply their psychological knowledge or adapt their skills for direct service to the child and his/her teacher. Even parent contact is typically limited to the now ubiquitous IEP meeting. The loss of a direct-service function is extremely costly in my opinion, restricting service and promoting job dissatisfaction and "burn out" among the psychometrically oriented school psychologist.

I return to these concerns at the end of this chapter. It need only be noted here that the school psychologist's role is determined heavily by the school's organizational structure and, specifically, by the bureaucratic needs of that organization. This fact, if my analysis is correct, provides some hope for increasing the vitality and depth of contribution of the school psychologist.

A concern preliminary to the school psychologist's specific role involves the definition of learning disabilities: Who should and who should not be so called? This chapter deals primarily with this issue from a perspective not presently represented in the literature, but many of the ideas and the conditions discussed are not entirely new. In examining the frustrations involved in diagnosing a child as learning disabled (LD), I have come to question the efficacy of the LD diagnosis apart from the educational failure it is supposed to cause. As Lieberman (1980) points out regarding funding for the handicapped: "When this mandate was given, a handicapped child was not handicapped because he was failing at school. he was failing in school because he was handicapped [p. 66]." Consequently, we need to examine in a broader context whether learning disabilities, historically and sociologically, are true handicaps or are simply indicative of unexpected failure in school. I dwell less on the future technical potential in diagnosing the "true" learning disability than on the sociological implications that the term presents for all of us concerned with the education of our children.

The Context

The paradox of learning disabilities is that as a professional discipline it is so small, yet as a focal point for educational reform it holds great potential. Learning disabilities is the link between regular and special education, the gray area between the child whom we see as functioning normally and the child who needs special assistance in order to realize his or her educational potential. Learning disabilities, by virtue of the way we think about them, are handicapping conditions. We think something must be done about children having such conditions in order that the child's handicap will not prevent him or her from realizing his or her potential. But, unlike other handicapping conditions such as deafness, blindness, cerebral palsy, and severe mental retardation, the signs by which we recognize the child's handicap are not at all so clear to us.

The learning-disabled child presents all of us concerned with the education of children with a monumental dilemma: How can we provide all of our children an equal educational opportunity? The plight of the learning-disabled child is, I believe, symptomatic of some of the most central problems that presently plague our educational system. Dissatisfaction with our schools is widespread. Children are said not to be learning the basic skills of reading, writing, and arithmetic. Seemingly more and more children are said to create discipline problems. According to some experts, as many as 15 to 30% are said to be learning disabled. So-called cultural disadvantagement creates enormous problems for educators and, in turn, for the poverty and minority groups whose disadvantagement creates problems for themselves and for the schools. Never have the schools been so attacked through the courts. Suits alleging improper administration of funds, utilization of special class placement as a tool of racial segregation, failure to provide handicapped children with services necessary for their education, and inability to educate normal pupils in the basic skills are not uncommon. Teachers are equally dissatisfied, and strike for better working conditions and higher pay. Parents are also demanding to be heard and frequently find themselves at loggerheads with the school administration. While trying to keep the lid on, and also to hold the line on the quality of instructional programs for the children, administrators seek extra funds to meet teacher demands. Legislatures are reluctant to appropriate more money because they do not obtain mandates from the people to provide the (failing?) schools with more funds. Half of the school bond issues are now being defeated.

The picture I am painting is bleak indeed, but I am not so much concerned here about arguing the severity of the present problems as much as recognizing that the problems appear to permeate the system rather than being something that will either pass in time or be solved by a council of experts.

The concept of learning disabilities plays a key role in many of the issues concerning diagnosis and placement. For example, all of the core problems previously mentioned can be phrased to include the term learning disability. Are not those children failing to learn the basic skills of reading, writing, and arithmetic learning disabled? Are not those children who demonstrate acting-out behavior reacting to an underlying learning disability? Does not the labeling of so many minorities and poverty children as mentally retarded reflect a cultural bias, and are not many of these children simply learning disabled?

The answers to these and other perplexing questions about the problems schools face and the problems of the disabled learner can only be discussed within a context of certain basic assumptions about education that utilize a set of words whose meanings likely vary from one reader to the next In order to solve problems, we must recognize their true scope. We must recognize the number of persons whose interests should be served by the "solution" to the problems we face. Defining terms is only an initial step in solving problems, as it only provides a means of discussing them.

Some words are very easy to define so that their meaning is clear, direct, and widely shared. Other terms are not so readily defined, and "learning disabilities" is one of them. Our present inability to agree on a definition of this term derives in part from its relative newness, but more so from the complexity of its referent, and the variety of conceptual frameworks from which various professionals and parents view the term. Neither the complexity of the conditions to which the term learning disabilities might be applied nor the differences in the conceptual frameworks within which different individuals come to understand learning disabilities can be clarified simply by proposing an arbitrary definition of terms. No matter how carefully the definition is phrased, agreement cannot be obtained, because the term, in fact, means different things to different people. To assert the correctness of a given definition can only hamper our understanding by limiting perhaps both the domain of concern and the various ways different people come to understand that domain.

How, then, can we clarify our understanding of learning disabilities and allow for communication between people concerned with them so that solutions to the problems that the term now designates can be found? Parents, teachers, psychologists, allied professionals, administrators, legislators, and most of all children, have an immense stake in our shared understanding of learning disabilities. Each has different interests and concerns. In addition, every one of us also has unique interests and concerns that may not be specifically related to our role as psychologist, educator, parent, child, or legislator.

I cannot possibly represent all the views of so wide a range of persons, nor do I set for myself that task. Although I can listen to the diverse viewpoints, I can only hear them within the context of my own experience and values. I can, therefore, speak only from that same position and feel only justified to describe as accurately as I can what that position is. I would like to see every child happy with himself/herself and with his/her relationship to others and to society. My talents, professional training, and the realities of the social institutions within which I work have caused me to approach this goal by attempting to understand children's development and the organizations we use (primarily schools) to foster their development. I could describe to you my specific affiliations and past occupational roles, the labels we use to communicate and infer experience, interest, and competence among adults. However, from the point of view from which this chapter is written, these would be unimportant and likely misleading. The affiliation that organizes this chapter for me is with children.

PROBLEMS OF THE SCHOOL PSYCHOLOGIST IN DEALING WITH THE LEARNING DISABLED

The problems of educating the learning disabled child are inextricably intertwined with the problems of regular education. The learning disabled, by whatever definition, place added demands on an educational institution already in desperate trouble. The solution to these children's problems and to those of their peers must take place in that problem-riddled context. The societal focus on the learning disabled, reflected in the rapid growth of the Association for Children with Learning Disabilities, the passage of the Learning Disability Act of 1969, and the incorporation of LD into the Education for All Handicapped Children Act (PL 94–142), represents the broader educational concerns of responsible adults. Learning disabled youngsters are symptomatic of more basic educational problems; the solution to the learning-disabled child's plight cannot be achieved through a patchwork of special services, for, at the optimistic extreme, one can only hope to subject the child once again to the same regular-education program to which the child was previously unable to adjust.

Learning disabilities could be defined very narrowly, this restricting our domain of concern. For example, we could define learning disabilities so as to require "proof" of neurological involvement. The alleged benefits of such a tack might be reduced special-education costs resulting from the restrictive definition, relative ease of program administration, greater homogeneity in remedial programs and needed materials, conceptually simpler professional training programs, and so forth. I believe restrictive definitions of learning disabilities or any other educational disability only multiply our problems. The problems of those persons disenfranchised by the restrictive definition do not go away—nor do they themselves. We must ask ourselves how large special education must become, how many handicaps we will need to identify and program for, until we recognize the unending nature of this endeavor.

Nevertheless, by statute, learning disabilities are thought to encompass a wide range of school problems characterized by failure or underachievement. Many of you will disagree emphatically with such a conceptualization, much as Lieberman (in press) does, but I ask you to suspend your definition of LD in order to understand the implication of alternatives. I have selected the broadest possible definition not because I think it is right, but because it serves best to illustrate how the very concept of handicap itself has created more problems than it has solved.

Though you may define learning disabilities quite restrictively, you will still most likely agree that many of the core educational problems in the following lists are epitomized or at least represented by the learning disabled:

1. How can education help each child realize his/her potential? The LD concept reflects failure in this regard.

2. How can education assure that each child capable of acquiring the basic skills does so? LD children typify the school's difficulty in achieving this goal.

3. How can schools deal with pupil negativism and "acting out"? LD children frequently present these problems.

4. How can schools minimize the stigma and emotional damage that stem from children's failure? LD children face both the emotional repercussions of their failures and the stigma of inadequacy.

5. How can schools utilize individual differences productively as opposed to "homogenizing" children of different talents, interests, and backgrounds? LD children are sufficiently atypical that the school must deal with their individuality.

6. Can diagnosis come to serve children rather than the administration of school systems? Will certification for extra assistance continue to be the focus of diagnosis as opposed to the foundation for intervention planning? The roles and skills of school psychologists and other educational diagnosticians are of questionable efficacy in this regard, especially when dealing with the learning disabled.

7. How can schools become more responsive to parents' wishes concerning their child's education? Programs for the LD child include an unprecedented degree of parent involvement. The central issue here is whether today's huge educational institution is capable of carrying out the educational goals of the tax-paying parent rather than becoming involuted and self serving.

8. Can we learn how to organize and administer educational programs so that they truly serve children and do not become inextricably bound up in "red tape"? The complexity of special-education funding at federal, state, and local levels seriously challenges our present administrative systems.

9. Can teachers who have lost their enthusiasm for education regain the depth of purpose and rewards of accomplishment? Can all persons involved in education feel proud of their efforts? Can the isolation and alienation that both teachers and administrators report ever be purged in the often demeaning and sometimes tyrannical bureaucracies in which they must work? The LD child and other problem children more than test educators. As individuals, these children seem to create more than their share of despair and less than their share of rewards for educators.

10. If it is correct that the problems of LD children are inextricably bound up with those of other educational systems, how can we reconceptualize learning disabilities in order not to perpetuate these problems? We must analyze in some detail the problems that we encounter in defining learning disabilities so that we will recognize the difficulties a new conceptualization must avoid.

ANALYSIS OF PROBLEMS

Underlying Assumptions

Definitions typically rest on underlying assumptions. Together with the conceptual framework within which the definition is cast, these assumptions structure and direct our thinking. Just as the 17th-century Puritan belief that deviant individuals were witches was based on underlying assumptions drawn from a demonological interpretation of the Bible, viewing some learners as disabled stems from basic underlying assumptions. The issue is less whether the assumptions are right or wrong than it is that they implicitly organize our thinking.

What are the underlying assumptions when we chose the term "disabled learner"? The specific assumptions are as follows:

1. The problem lies in the learner, specifically with the abilities of the learner's brain.

2. There exists a group of youngsters, each of whom possesses a (conceptually) similar disability that makes the group members more similar to each other than to normals—i.e., a qualitative difference exists.

3. Additionally, there exists a group of children called "normals" who neither possess learning disabilities nor any other handicaps.

4. Because he/she allegedly has normal ability potential, the disabled learner should aspire to overcome his or her disability or at least not let it deter his or her acquisition of the basic school skills; i.e., the child should aspire to the education goals society poses for normals.

5. The adults, parents and educators alike, should likewise maintain normal educational goals for the learning disabled.

6. Being disabled is a condition requiring remediation; both adults and the disabled pupil should work to attain normal functioning. To do less represents failure, either the child's or the school's, but in either case it represents a loss to society.

In addition to these specific assumptions, other general assumptions concerning education in America also apply:

1. Educational potential is more or less normally distributed, most of the children being average, with the rest falling in graded degrees above and below the mean.

2. Educational potential is relatively well estimated by the IQ (This legacy given us by Binet was fortunately showing signs of old age, but was revived by PL 94–142 regulations concerning LD.)[1]

---

[1]This revival of the IQ may prove to be short lived (*APA Monitor*, 1979):

In a case that goes back to 1972, a federal district court (in California) has finally ruled invalid California's use of standardized IQ testing for assigning black children to remedial programs for the educable mentally retarded.

In a massive 130-page opinion in Larry P. v. Riles filed October 16, district court judge Robert Peckham ruled that the disproportionate number of blacks pressed into EMR programs, widely labeled "dead end" tracks, was discriminatory and illegal.

Should the case go to the Supreme Court, as some speculate, a similar ban on IQ testing could be spread nationwide [p. 8].

3. Achievement in basic skills and later in content subjects correlates positively with potential so that it is only reasonable to expect that those pupils with high potential will achieve higher absolute levels of achievement.

4. Absolute achievement is valued to the degree that we give A's (or some equivalent) to the "best" students, C's to the average students, and failing grades to the "worst" students. A student with average potential can seldom meet the absolute standard set by the superior students and, hence, seldom receives commendation (an A).

5. The concept of IQ is respected to the extent that a child achieving more poorly than his or her IQ would have predicted is termed an "underachiever," whereas the counterpart who outperforms the prediction is called an "overachiever." This manner of thinking places more confidence in the predictor (IQ) than in the criterion (school achievement)—i.e., the prediction is assumed to be perfect; the child's performance is seen as awry. This fallacy is the essence of the federal and many state definitions of learning disability—i.e., the capacity-performance discrepancy.

6. A regular-education curriculum, costing the same for all children (within an educational unit—usually a district), is provided to all normal children. Methods of tracking are used to provide instruction to the brighter, average, and duller students though the goals for all remain basically the same, as does the instructional mode of a teacher, a curriculum, and the class of pupils.

7. Some children, by virtue of a handicapping condition, cannot be viewed in the context of the normal curve of ability. Special education for which eligibility must be certified is required for those handicapped.

I repeat that the importance of these assumptions lies not in whether they are correct, but in their influence on our conceptualization of problems. The notion of disabled learners requires the assumptions pertaining to academic standards. Without standards, there is no failure. How few children, for example, have to languish past kindergarten as "singing disabled," though a significant number certainly persist in being nearly tone deaf. Because it does not place a high value on musical attainment for all its members, our society does not categorize children or try to remediate them either on the basis of absolute singing ability or on the relative difference between their IQ and singing competence.

One obvious implication of this line of argument would be to eliminate academic standards and thereby eliminate learning disabilities. Such would only be a semantic solution, of course, because the valuation of academic achievement is inextricably woven into society's fabric. However, the problems that the concept of learning disabilities produces give me every reason to question the paramount importance placed on so-called academic success. Some other conceptualization may satisfy our desire to see our children achieve that will be more congenial with some of our other concerns for them.

LEARNING DISABILITIES TODAY

The defining of an entity has widespread ramifications. When that entity is a complex of little-understood "disorders," the ramifications are especially widespread and significant.

The Function of Definition

It is important for the present discussion to understand the function that definition serves and the ramifications of the definitional process. The formulation of a definition formalizes awareness. Although there have undoubtedly been learning-disabled children by whosever definition in schools for decades some types for as long as schools are old . . . it was the defining of these children as constituting a class of individuals that allowed for organized action on their behalf. The surrounding terminology that grows up around definitions serves further as a communication vehicle both to extend awareness of the condition to others and to communicate more clearly.

When a definition gains statutory status, its significance is greatly enhanced. By law, those who come under the definition become entitled to special services that will likely have a profound impact on their lives. In addition, the statutory status of a definition requires the organization of mechanisms to carry out the statutes and for the development of attendant administrative procedures. Our awareness of the LD group and statutes mandating service for them require complex adjustments within the total educational system. The implications of the existence of a learning-disability statute for education at all levels of administration cannot be minimized. It can be summarized by the perplexing questions, "Who are these children, how many of them are there, what kind of services do they need, how can we deliver the services, and how can we learn more about their school problems?"

The Ramifications of Definition

As though the perplexing quesitons surrounding delivering services to learning-disabled youngsters were not complex enough, the ramifications of a statutory definition are truly mind-boggling in scope. Consider, for example, the creation of institutions that derive from the formalization of the learning-disability definition: the Association for Children with Learning Disabilities, presumed to have over 30,000 members; learning-disability programs sponsored at the federal, state, and local levels; learning-disability divisions within special education departments at universities throughout the country; the formation of a learning-disability division within the Council for Exceptional Children; the creation of the *Journal of Learning Disabilities*. In addition, sociological institutions pertaining to professional standards and practices are created by virtue of the defining statutes.

There are other sociological implications of definitions. As we are all aware, learning disabilities do not exist, nor were they created, within a vacuum. These children must compete for resources with others who are needy, thereby acquiring detractors as well as supporters. By defining the field of learning disabilities narrowly, its leadership can more readily acquire alliances that will help stabilize and support the concept. Further, an excessively broad definition will increase the probability of internal factions that might negatively effect the concept's longevity. These and a host of surrounding issues point to the realization that learning disabilities are not simply a disorder that afflicts children, but have themselves become a social institution related to government, public instruction, and professional endeavor. Many people have a very large stake in the definition of learning disabilities, for it influences not simply the well being of children, but the professional aspirations, interests, and, in fact, the very livelihood of thousands of professionals.

Viewed in this context, it is little wonder that agreement cannot be obtained on what the definition of learning disabilities should be. And, it is for these very same reasons that it is fruitless to try to assert the correctness of one semantic definition over another. To repeat the theme mentioned earlier, there are too many persons extremely interested in learning disabilities to think that at this stage of development we can solve any of the problems we face by rewording the definition.

There is one further implication of definition that is critical to the ensuing discussion. There is a tendency for our language system to reify the constructs to which it refers. For example, it used to be thought that there existed witches who were agents of the devil. In God's name, these witches were captured and brought to trial. We now recognize that many of these so-called witches were simply socially deviant individuals, in many cases those we now call "mentally ill." Those who burned witches at the stake were, nevertheless, quite convinced of the correctness of their conceptualization. The point here is not that the Puritans were incorrect, but that the concept became reality and was acted upon. It is equally arguable, as in fact it has been argued in psychiatry and clinical psychology in recent years, that the "mental-illness" conceptualization is itself inappropriate (Szasz, 1961). The point, then, is that we must be very careful not to let our thinking become slavish to our own concepts, but instead consider alternative ways of conceptualizing the problems that confront us.

Present Status of the Definition of Learning Disabilities

There was a marked decline during the past decade in the number of papers devoted to discussions of the definition of learning disabilities. Yet, my experience dealing with persons in all stations within the educational community indicates that concerns about definition are still very much alive. In fact, educational administrators at all levels of government express apprehension that the most serious problems still lie ahead. I believe the realization has come that the problems of learning disabilities will not be solved by convening another council of experts. The experts had their days in the mid- to late 1960's. Task forces, advanced-study institutes, conferences, and independent writers worked and reworked definitions of learning disabilities. With the passage of the federal Learning Disability Act of 1969, state legislation mandating special services for the learning disabled, and the incorporation of LD into PL 94–142, certain definitions became statutes. The conceptual issues were put to rest, and the task of delivering services was begun.

Though few states adopted outright the definition of the National Advisory Committee on Handicapped Children (1968), the influence of the federal definition on the field has been significant. Largely because special-education services are organized at the state level, federal input to states is facilitated through its funding to state offices of education. Though federal funding for learning disabilities has been meager, almost every education department and those of the Bureau of Indian Affairs and Puerto Rico have received funding since 1971. However, by 1982, the federal government plans to increase its fiscal role from approximately 5% to 40% of monies spent on special education.

Historical Perspective

The current status of definition can best be understood through the historical background of the field of learning disabilities. (The reader interested in a lengthier treatment of the field's history is referred to a review by Wiederholt [1974].) I have previously summarized the recent history and quote that treatment here (Senf, 1973):

> The milestones which define the field of learning disabilities as it is constituted today began in 1963. Then a steering committee sponsored by the National Society of Crippled Children and Adults, Inc., in cooperation with the Neurological and Sensory Disease Control Program of the Division of Chronic Diseases, United States Public Health Service, met to plan a symposium on the "Child with Minimal Brain Dysfunction." The committee recommended small groups (task forces) to study each of three aspects of the problem: (1) terminology and identification, (2) services, and (3) research. The agencies eventually responsible for supporting the task forces and their reports included (1) National Institute of Neurological Diseases and Stroke, National Institutes of Health, (2) Easter Seal Research Foundation, National Society of Crippled Children and Adults, (3) Bureau of Education for the Handicapped, United States Office of Education, Department of Health, Education and Welfare, and (4) Neurological and Sensory Disease Control Program, Health Services and Mental Health Administration, Department of Health, Education and Welfare.

Though mobilization of interest in the learning disabled child most certainly is reflected in these early collaborative efforts, the medical orientation of the first report on terminology and identification appears to have limited its impact on the developing field of learning disabilities.

In the same year, 1963, Congress passed Public Law 88-164 providing funds for training and research in special education. Though no funds were specifically earmarked for the learning disabled, programs were initiated under the rubric "crippled, or other health impaired, who by reason thereof require special education and related services."

At about the same time, in 1964, a national parent group, The Association for Children with Learning Disabilities (ACLD), was formed for the purpose of "advancing the education and general well-being of children with adequate intelligence who have learning disabilities arising from perceptual, conceptual or subtle coordinative problems sometimes accompanied by behavior difficulties." This parent group now records a membership of over 20,000 parents and professionals. Through a network of local and state associations, ACLD has had a broad impact on legislative and funding decisions and has also provided an interdisciplinary forum for exchanging professional thinking in the area of developmental disabilities. The choice of the term "learning disabilities" to name the association rather than "minimal brain dysfunction" or some other medical-organic term has been influential in drawing the Association closer to the field of special education than to medicine and in promoting the growth of the field of learning disabilities within education. The choice of the term reportedly derived from its focus on "education and training rather than on etiology."

In 1966 a unit on Learning Disorders and Interrelated Areas was added to the Division of Training Programs, Bureau of Education for the Handicapped, United States Office of Education. Funding for children with learning disabilities was, therefore, for the first time distinguished from "crippled and other health impaired." Federal funding of training programs within 11 universities immediately followed, as did a federally supported conference of these programs' administrators to exchange information.

A milestone in defining learning disabilities within an educational perspective was reached through an Advanced Study Institute held at Northwestern University in 1967. This institute, attended by 15 special educators, forged an educational definition to supersede the existing multidisciplinary definitions. The resulting definition and discussion are reported in Kass and Myklebust's paper (1969), published in the *Journal of Learning Disabilities,* which itself had been instituted only the previous year.

> Learning disability refers to one or more significant deficits in essential learning processes requiring special education techniques for remediation.
>
> Children with learning disability generally demonstrate a discrepancy between expected and actual achievement in one or more areas, such as spoken, read, or written language, mathematics, and spatial orientation.
>
> The learning disability referred to is not primarily the result of sensory, motor, intellectual, or emotional handicap, or lack of opportunity to learn.
>
> *Significant deficits* are defined in terms of accepted diagnostic procedures in education and psychology.

Essential learning processes are those currently referred to in behavioral science as involving perception, integration, and expression, either verbal or nonverbal.

Special education techniques for remediation refers to educational planning based on diagnostic procedures and results [p. 39].

The preoccupation with definition continued in the face of pending legislative decisions. Later the same year, the National Advisory Committee to the Bureau of Education for the Handicapped, chaired by Samuel A. Kirk who had previously suggested the name Learning Disabilities to the parent group, ACLD, prepared the following definition which has become a guideline for both federal and State legislation.

Children with special learning disabilities exhibit a disorder in one or more of the basic psychological processes involved in understanding or in using spoken or written language. These may be manifested in disorders of listening, thinking, reading, writing, spelling, or arithmetic. They include conditions which have been referred to as perceptual handicaps, brain injury, minimal brain dysfunction, dyslexia, developmental aphasia, etc. They do not include learning problems which are due primarily to visual, hearing, or motor handicaps, to mental retardation, emotional disturbance, or to environmental disadvantage (National Advisory Committee on the Handicapped, 1968) [pp. 609-611].[2]

According to Bryant and Kass (1972): "In 21 studies of incidence of learning disabilities using various groups and criteria, the values range from 3 percent to 28 percent, half being above 13 percent [p. 31]." These early 1970's attitudes prompted Congress to place a "cap" of 2% average daily attendance (ADA) on the number of children designated LD prior to the incorporation of learning disabilities into PL 94-142. With the publication of regulations in December, 1977 (*Federal Register,* December 29, 1977), the 2% cap was removed, but it was made clear that federal monies would extend only to 12% of ADA for all handicapping conditions combined.

Some Problems with Learning-Disability Definitions

An optimistic viewpoint would note that in the relatively short span of a decade, the 1960's, services have been mandated, organized, and delivered to many school children under the rubric learning disabled. The 1% service figure now

---

[2]The PL 94-142 definition is essentially the same with minor textual editing—except for the expansion of "environmental disadvantage" as an exclusion criterion to read "environmental, cultural, or economic disadvantage." In any case, the reader must distinguish the *definition* as a statutory description with the *regulations* that describe the methods of child identification. The regulations (*Federal Register,* December 29, 1977) emphasize underachievement, though the statistical formula defining the severe discrepancy level between IQ and achievement was dropped from the initial regulations (*Federal Register,* November 26, 1976)—c.f. Danielson and Bauer (1978) for a discussion of the regulations. The final regulations state (*Federal Register,* December 29, 1977): "A team may determine that a child has a specific learning disability if: (1) The child does not achieve [in any of seven skill areas] commensurate with his or her age and ability levels [p. 65,083]."

estimated is unquestionably high, and it is also debatable how extensive the service has been for many of the children. Nevertheless, it is undeniable that some very profound changes have resulted in local schools as a result of the learning-disability movement.

This optimistic viewpoint would continue with a belief that, in time, some of the present problems that I describe will disappear. If my thesis is correct that the problems evidenced by the learning disabled are symptomatic of more basic problems facing the schools, no amount of streamlining of administration or even serving all 2% of the ''hard-core'' learning-disabled children will make the problems we face go away. Any such success must recognize the bittersweet quality of having labeled 1.5 million children as handicapped.

Communication

One of the premier reasons for utilizing a formal category system is that it fosters communication. Although a term certainly will not tell us everything we want to know about a given condition, it should, at the very least, give other persons knowledgeable about the condition an opportunity to communicate more efficiently and with a greater clarity. As such, category names can serve as a communication shorthand. The concept of learning disabilities has surely failed miserably in this regard. Simply reviewing the variations in incidence figures offered both by research studies and the experts tells us that there must exist different underlying conceptions—i.e., different meanings ascribed to the term by different individuals.

The problem is not so simple as the possibility that different persons might be using different semantic definitions of the term. Bryant (1972) cites a study of incidence estimates of 100 leaders in the field of learning disabilities, 39 of whom responded: "Half of the respondents estimated between 2 to 5 percent while almost a third estimated 15 percent or higher [p. 53]." Given that the essence of the statutory definition has not changed since then, we can only suspect that there still exist large discrepancies in the incidence estimates. Though allied with the field and cognizant of its organizing definitions, the experts disagree as to prevalence by literally millions of children.

It is important to remember that we are not dealing here with a semantic game. A child may or may not be assisted by virtue of the way the diagnostician chooses to interpret the meaning of such terms. The highly variant incidence rates reflect the grossest form of diagnostic unreliability. Without imputing to any practitioner ill-motive, the possibility is likely that a child will be served not by virtue of whether he or she meets or does not meet the definition, but by whether he or she happens to be so certified by the school district. Even though we maintain the concept of the disabled learner as one whose own internal disabilities inhibit school achievement, admission to service depends as much on the interpretation of the definition, the availability of services, and all too often on the attitudes and social competence of the parents or the teacher or psychologist who intervene on the child's behalf.

Operational Definitions

A lack of reliability in applying the learning-disability label simply means that a child thought to be learning disabled by one professional might not be thought to be learning disabled by another. The child should or should not meet the criteria. Obtaining consistency from one professional to the next is important for a variety of reasons. In addition to promoting better communication concerning the entity being labeled, reliability at least makes it technically possible to distribute services in a fair and unbiased manner. Diagnostic reliability also allows for the orderly accumulation of knowledge through programmatic research.

When unreliability of classification exists (as I assume it does due to the variable incidence figures, though I was unable to find any reliability studies in a thorough manual and computer search of over 200 journals), the appropriate solution is to define more carefully in observable terms the conditions under which utilization of the category is appropriate. Specifically, with respect to learning disabilities, an operational definition would spell out exactly what conditions a child would need to meet—i.e., what behaviors a child would need to exhibit—in order to be so classified. In this fashion, the reliability of assignment to the class learning disabled would be greatly increased.

Not the Solution.   I do not think that constructing one or more operational definitions would go very far in solving the problems that the learning-disability concept raises.[4] There is a desire among educational planners and administrators at the federal and state levels to limit the learning disability incidence figure to approximately 2%. The population that would thereby be called learning disabled would represent the "hard core," those with the most severe disabilities. It is unquestionably possible to define learning disabilities operationally to produce whatever incidence figure one wishes (McLeod, 1979) and to limit services by virtue of that definition.

The concerns associated with the desire to limit the use of the term learning disabled to this "hard-core" group involve primarily fiscal and administrative realities. The states are simply faced with the untenable position of labeling large portions—e.g., 15% or more—of the student population as handicapped. Were they to do so, many states would be under their own statutory mandates to provide special-education services to these children. Estimates of the cost of special education for children with "special learning disorders" exceed twice the cost of educating a "normal" youngster (Frohreich, 1973). Without a restrictive enough definition, the double costs of learning-disability education could result in the tail (special education) wagging the dog, to use one state's special-education director's metaphor.

An operational definition restricting the population of learning-disabled youngsters to 1 to 3% of the student enrollment still represents a tremendously

---

[4]Portions of this section, somewhat edited here, including the Fig., first appeared in Senf and Sushinsky, 1975. Used with permission.

difficult administrative task for state government. At the same time, the parents of a less-severely handicapped child, who nevertheless know that their child could benefit from more intensive instruction, will be disenfranchised by restrictive operational definitions. By establishing operational definitions upon which service decisions would be made, parents who have worked hard to obtain such services run the risk that their child will not qualify under the stringent regulations. As an aside, it must be recognized that services to the learning disabled are in their infancy and, as a consequence, services paradoxically are now more easily obtained for the mild-to-moderate disabled learner than they will be in the future. Because of the shortage of trained personnel, many districts have no programs at all for the learning disabled, allowing other, more experienced (and typically richer) districts to provide services to more children without exceeding the state "quotas." In time, states will have to deal with the problems more *affluent* districts will present them.

I doubt, also, that operational definitions would be particularly welcome by local school administrators. Although a firm operational definition would provide a principal an objective basis for denying extra services when none are available, s/he would at the same time lose many degrees of freedom in making decisions about the distribution of education resources under his/her charge. Because services for learning-disabled children typically are not reimbursed at a 100% rate, local districts incur extra costs whenever a learning-disability case is identified. The looseness of the present definition has the questionable virtue of allowing administrators to maintain control over their expenditures and keep peace in their school boards through failure to notice learning-disability cases (Luick & Senf, 1979). It must be recognized that the misuse of such discretionary power can be detrimental to many children in need of service.

Technical Problems.   There are technical problems involved in defining who should or should not be called a learning-disabled child that should be noted though not discussed in any detail in the present context. One approach to operationalizing learning disabilities involves calculating the discrepancy between a child's estimated achievement potential (measured by an IQ test) and his/her achievement in the basic school subjects. Such procedures, with many variations, are frequently utilized in the research literature (e.g., Myklebust, 1968; Vande Voort, Senf, & Benton, 1972). Although acceptable for research purposes where decisions concerning individual children are not being made and where testing error tends to average out over sampling groups, the measurement of differences between IQ and achievement is not as reliable as we would like it to be in order to make judgments about individual children. An article by Salvia and Clark (1973) demonstrates that despite the fact that intelligence and achievement tests are our most sophisticated and stable psychometric instruments, the error that results from the process of subtracting two test scores is considerable. According to their calculations, 1.9% of the children would show an achievement "deficit" of 1 year simply by chance alone. McLeod (1979) discusses other such realities concerning psychometric definitions.

The problem here may be more than psychometric. We noted earlier that one of the underlying assumptions of education in this country was that IQ was an appropriate and generally accurate predictor of achievement to the extent that we label those who fail to live up to their intelligence prediction "underachievers" and those who further excel as "overachievers." Looked at in a more neutral light, because the correlation between intelligence and achievement is not a perfect one, there must exist children whose IQ rankings are relatively higher than their achievement rankings, and vice versa. The degree of difference may simply reflect the lack of correspondence between the global skills assessed by the intelligence instrument and the more specific ones assessed by the achievement instrument. No necessary correlation must exist. To assert that the lack of correspondence between the two measures represents a pathological condition is, in the very least, an assumption. The uncertainty of this assumption coupled with the psychometric problem that almost 2% of the children, ironically the suggested maximum, will have a 1-year discrepancy in the two measures simply by chance makes basing our definition of handicap on such a procedure ethically questionable.

Of course, other definitions of learning disabilities do not hinge on the discrepancy notion. Such is particularly the case when preschool or kindergarten learning disabilities are considered and no achievement data exist against which to determine whether the child is meeting his or her potential. In such cases, it is more typical to conceptualize the learning disability in terms of a deficit in one of the underlying psychological processes.

Psychometric problems exist here as well. Our understanding of basic psychological processes is not so sophisticated that we presently have unitary measures of those processes necessary for skills as complex as reading, writing, mathematical computing, reasoning, thinking, and so forth. Modern psychology certainly has many theories with supportive research (cf. Lindsay & Norman, 1972; Neisser, 1967; Torgesen, 1975, 1979), but there is by no means consensus concerning the description or measurement of the basic underlying psychological processes. One can certainly take the position that we must do the best job we can with the instruments we have now and, in fact, we are doing just that. At the same time, it is important to recognize that the instruments we use are of questionable validity in making predictions about underlying abilities. A much safer tactic, I believe, if we are to continue singling out children for special services, would be to utilize academic and adjustment criteria that we can agree upon and develop predictive instruments that will signal later failure in these skill and adjustment areas rather than to assert the existence of some underlying disorder as a statutory endeavor.

Arbitrariness.   A more basic argument against instituting operational definitions of learning disabilities is that they are typically, by their very nature, arbitrary and capricious. To concoct a formula that will yield a 2% incidence figure statewide is both intellectually dishonest and ethically questionable. Used correctly, an operational definition specifies the presence or absence of a condition that has conceptual integrity. If there exists a group of disorders of the underlying psychological processes involved in the basic school skills, we should go about instrumenting an operational definition to measure this construct in a valid manner and then determine empirically what percentage of our children possess these conditions. The operational definition must derive from the concept and the incidence figure result from its application, and not vice versa.

Overriding Considerations. The problem with the term learning disability derives not from the lack of clarity of the words used in the various definitions so much as what those words mean to people and what people would wish their educational system to do for their children. When I see learning-disabilities incidence estimates as high as 30%, I think that people are saying that there are many children whose needs are not being met by our schools and to whom they would be willing to ascribe a handicap label in order to see something done about the situation. Neither the states nor the local districts nor parents and teachers disgruntled with the educational system will find any solution in a mechanism that limits learning disabilities arbitrarily to a 2% figure.

Differential Diagnosis

The task of operationalizing a definition of learning disabilities is truly formidable. I have already noted the problems of measurement surrounding an IQ-achievement difference definition and the problems that derive from our lack of knowledge concerning the basic underlying processes necessary for success in the school-related skills of reading, writing, arithmetic, and so on. By looking at the list of alternative diagnoses from which a diagnosis of learning disability must be distinguished, it is no wonder that this task is extremely difficult and leads to vastly different incidence estimates. The learning-disabled child must be distinguished from the educable mentally retarded child, the emotionally disturbed child, the culturally disadvantaged child, the child who has had inadequate instruction, the child who is simply a slow learner, *and* from children who are so-called "normal." Such a task presents the diagnostician, be she/he a learning-disability specialist or a school psychologist, with an extremely complex problem for which we lack the necessary instruments and, as previously noted, sufficient criteria for making these differential judgments.

LD versus EMR

Distinguishing learning disabilities from the educable mentally retarded is less difficult with the older child in whom an achievement–IQ discrepancy can be assessed. If this discrepancy is sufficiently large—e.g., 2 plus years for the fourth grader—one could discount the mentally retarded diagnosis with reasonable confidence. However, remember that most of the state definitions and the federal regulations speak of the differences between actual and realized potential, but this concept is inapplicable to younger children who have not yet had the opportunity to fail. Making the differential diagnosis between learning disabilities and the educable mentally retarded on the basis of whether there exists ''a disorder in one or more of the basic psychological processes . . .'' necessary for the acquisition of school skills becomes terribly judgmental. In fact, we have found in Illinois (Senf & Grossman, 1975) that some localities have an extremely high relative proportion of mentally retarded students, whereas an adjacent geographic area has a much higher proportion of learning disabled. Do these truly reflect differences in the children, or bias in the diagnostic process? It is my understanding that many of the parents involved in the Association for Children with Learning Disabilities have children previously diagnosed as mentally retarded. In this context, a learning-disability label, though also designating a handicap, represents a more acceptable label than that of retardation, which is generally considered more stigmatic. Neff (1973) reports the case of his son who had been diagnosed mentally retarded. When the child was diagnosed instead as learning disabled, the expectations were apparently markedly changed; according to Neff, the learning-disability diagnosis was important in altering the child's educational milieu, program, and expectations. Some years ago, I learned that the son was in graduate school. Certainly, if the difference in outcome between the learning-disabled and educable mentally retarded definition can make such a difference, we had best be sure we can apply these diagnoses reliably and validly.

It is my understanding from talking with learning-disability specialists and psychologists that this distinction is in practice often extremely hard to make, resulting in the classification chosen being contingent upon the nature of the services available. If there is no learning-disability program available, but there is a program for the mentally retarded, the child will typically find his or her way into the retardation group. One must recognize that this diagnostic distinction is complicated by the fact that the same problems that inhibit the child's achievement scores may also play upon the IQ score as well (Bryant, 1974), implying that the IQ may be an instable index of the child's potential.

From the foregoing discussion, I would contend that there is a more basic issue illustrated by the case of Dr. Neff's son: If it took a correct diagnosis of learning disabilities to save his son from the tragedy of unrealized potential, it implies that the way we think about a child—specifically, the label we employ and the resulting treatment of the child—is what determines the child's educational future and not his or her characteristics per se. One wonders how many allegedly mentally retarded children there are who are not realizing their potential because of the minimal expectations of the adult community. The Neff case appears to be a very clear-cut instance of labels intervening between the adult and the child to produce mutual expectations that limit the realization of the child's potential. It is ironic, indeed, that another handicapping label, that of learning disabilities, was required in order to save the boy from the results of the previously rendered and apparently more detrimental label, mental retardation.

LD versus ED

The differential diagnosis between learning disabilities and emotional disturbance is no more clear. It is a rarity indeed for the learning-disabled child not to have emotional concomitants to his or her problems. Discerning whether the emotionality derives from the learning problem or vice versa is the crux of this differential diagnosis. The diagnostician is called upon to unravel the chicken-and-egg problem, typically without the necessary information such as knowledge of the family situation, the child's peer relationships, and so forth (if, in fact, this information would provide a basis for a reliable distinction). It is in difficult diagnostic cases such as this that we frequently hear the recommendation that multidisciplinary teams be employed to understand accurately the child's problem and confer upon the child the proper diagnosis. I shudder to think of the costs involved in such multidisciplinary teams, not simply due to the number of hours the personnel must work on the case, but also the hours required in conferring with one another to determine the correct labeling of each child's disability. Those that have had experiences working on multidisciplinary teams know that it is seldom that communication across professions is very facile. Even for well-functioning teams, diagnosis is, as it is presently conceived, of questionable utility in planning the child's remedial program. Although interesting cases have been discussed over the years by such teams and distinctions drawn that illustrate the different conceptual backgrounds engendered by various professions (Meehl, 1973), I wonder how cost effective such teams are in providing services to children.

The fact is that most of these multidisciplinary teams are diagnostic in nature. A multidisciplinary treatment team, were it to provide a coordinated intervention service, would be at least more justifiable, although no less expensive. It is paradoxical that one of the chief concerns of learning disabilities' prime advocate (Samuel A. Kirk) was to avoid the time and money wasted in the diagnostic process. Instead, the diagnostic–prescriptive approach was stressed and the Illinois Test of Psycholinguistic Abilities (ITPA) was developed with therapeutically relevant information (at least from the viewpoint of Osgood's now-outdated psycholinguistic model, which underlies the ITPA). It is impossible to know how frequently, but it appears that quite often, the ITPA is now incorporated in the diagnostic assessment battery much as the Wechsler Intelligence Scale. Scores generated are listed in the child's school record and a lengthy diagnostic report, which has little relevance or input to the remedial effort, is prepared. In most cases, local reimbursement depends on certification of a handicapping condition as specified by state statute. Consequently, a full diagnostic work-up, whether useful for the child's remediation or not, is necessary. It is less a question of whether the differential diagnosis between learning disabilities and emotional disturbance must be made. I believe this to be an extremely wasteful and demeaning process to subject children to and derives from our conceptualization of the differences we perceive as "handicaps" rather than recognition of them as part of the range of individual differences that children exhibit. I expand on this point later.

LD versus Environmental Disadvantagement

The distinction between the learning disabled and the environmentally disadvantaged are no more easily made and are complicated by the social issues surrounding such an endeavor. The crux of the cultural–economic disadvantagement diagnosis is similar to that of emotional disturbance in that the diagnostician must determine for each individual case the *cause* of the disorder. It is problematic enough to arrive at a descriptive statement and determine whether one's descriptive statement is sufficiently close to that of the class principles characteristic of a diagnostic category (cf. Zigler & Phillips, 1961, for terminology and related discussion). To have the additional problem of determining whether one's description of the child's functioning then derives from a certain historical cause is almost impossible to do in a reliable and consequently valid fashion. Herrick (1973) raises the question of whether valid differences exist between the learning-disabled and disadvantaged population. Herrick (1973) asks rhetorically:

> If extensive research and documentation can demonstrate that culturally deprived children behave educationally, emotionally and socially in the school similarly to the learning-disabled child, that culturally deprived children are linguistically impaired in the eyes of the school, that cultural deprivation causes degrees of mental dysfunction, and that search for etiology can be dismissed, why is the culturally disadvantaged student excluded from consideration by the field of special education [p. 385]?

Fantini (1972) has taken no less assertive a stance. He notes that the minorities have been the first to point out that the problems they face may lie as much with the educational institution as with the learner. In calling for reform, several different steps have been taken. One is desegregation, which Fantini (1972) describes as allowing the "minorities to 'cash-in' on the benefits presently available in the middle-class white schools [p. 93]." Decentralization in community schools providing the minorities the right to increase their voice in school affairs has been another reform. Alternative schools, developing new patterns of education, have been yet another reform.

The problem facing the diagnostician in the form of a racial minority child from a poor background is that s/he must determine whether state funding will be extended to this child under the rubric of learning disabled, whether s/he will have the child served under the rubric of mental retardation, or whether s/he will assume that the child's background has caused the educational problems, and, hence (unless Title I funds are available), return the child to his/her classroom and to obscurity.

As I see the problem, the issue is not so much whether a diagnostician can reliably distinguish between the learning disability of the advantaged child and that of the culturally disadvantaged child, but whether s/he should attempt such a differential diagnosis. There may have been a time in this country's social history not too long ago when it was sound operating procedure for the white middle-class community to seek services from their schools without complicating their petitions with the needs of minority pupils. It is a wish and a dream to think that a coherent definition of learning disabilities can be evolved that will serve the white middle-class community and exclude the racial minorities and the poor. The social reality is that redress through the courts is being used more and more frequently as a means of requiring the educational system to treat all children equally and fairly. It is no secret, though the embarrassment causes us not to speak too much of these issues, that a disproportionate number of children in our special-education classes for the mentally retarded are minority children[3] (Dunn, 1971). If the differential diagnosis between mental retardation and learning disabilities is as critical to the child's self concept and eventual performance as Neff (1973) believes, what a great disservice we are doing in attempting to maintain a distinction that is most likely culturally discriminatory, intellectually dishonest, and morally indefensible. Obviously, we must all care for the needs of our children and vie for the benefits of the limited resources. These efforts must still respect the United States Constitution, however, or we will have won a very small battle and lost the war.

An excellent though now somewhat dated article by Ross, DeYoung, and Cohen (1971) provides a summary of the confrontation between special-education placement and the law. They cite Judge Wright's remarks in ruling on the cultural bias of tests (Hobson v. Hansen, 1967), which are frequently used to demonstrate a low intellectual potential on the part of racial minorities and hence relegate them to classes for the mentally retarded. Judge Wright states (Hobson v. Hansen, 1979):

It is regretable, of course, that in deciding this case the court must act in an area so alien to its expertise. It would be better indeed for these great social and political problems to be resolved in the political arena by other branches of government. But these are social and political problems which seem at times to defy such resolution. In such situations, under our system, the judiciary must bear a hand and accept its responsibility to assist in the solution where constitutional rights hang in the balance [page 517].

---

[3]See Footnote 1.

I do not believe that learning disabilities can long disassociate itself from the parallel demands of the so-called disadvantaged. It is ironic that the racial minorities are resisting the helping hand of special education, for to them it means the unjust application of a stigma branded upon their children by the white community, whereas the white middle-class parents actively seek special services for their children. To them, apparently, a handicap label is acceptable if it is the avenue for assistance.

An understanding of these two different attitudes is facilitated by the recognition that, for the minority, the school run by the racial majority is viewed as an institution unheeding of the real cultural differences that exist. It is demeaning and unjust within that frame of reference to be called handicapped, for it is to brand one's cultural heritage as inferior. The white middle-class parents have less redress, for they cannot see the school as an agent of another culture. They must accept the handicap label as their ticket for special services. How bitter a pill to swallow it is for both white and minority parents in order to obtain an adequate education for their children.

LD versus "Normals"

The differential diagnosis between the learning-disabled child, the child whose failure is due to the accumulation of poor or missing instruction, the slow-learning child who is nevertheless allegedly "normal," and other normal children brings us to the crux of the diagnostic issue. If it takes an intensive psychoeducational diagnosis to determine whether a child is failing because he or she has some subtle deficit versus whether a child is failing simply because he or she is "slow" or has had inadequate instruction, I believe we must honestly ask the question as to what difference the answer to the question makes. Regrettably, the difference the anser to the question makes, of course, involves extra service versus regular placement. Somehow, we are able to justify to ourselves as a society that, if the child has had 4 or 5 years of inadequate instruction that account for the failure, the child is most likely *not* handicapped and as a consequence need *not* be given service despite the fact that the prognosis is probably as poor as that of any child labeled learning disabled. Similarly, the slow learner is not to receive the help he or she might need to realize his or her less lofty potential because we have decided that the child has no specific handicap: S/He is "normal." These distinctions are not only conceptually distasteful, but cannot be made with any degree of certainty.

The concept of normalcy confines our thinking no less than does that of handicap. The existence of a concept ascribable to nearly 90% of our nation's children is staggering to the imagination. We have difficulty enough conceptualizing the similarities between a small group of children such as the mentally retarded—who allegedly have some characteristic in common—let alone conceptualizing the similarities inherent in the remaining 90%.

Normalcy, in perspective, is not a state of being, nor is it a characteristic of a person. It is, rather, a statement about the character of the interaction between the individual and some other person or institution. To say that a child is normal in school is to say that he or she can adapt to the conditions therein. One can be nonnormal by demonstrating inability or unwillingness to adapt to the institutional demands. Consequently, the same child can be normal in one context and not in another, as for example the child who is a hellion at school, but angelic at home, or vice versa. Rather than crediting our children for their willingness to subvert their own interests to those of the school, we label them as normal, just as we label as handicapped those who cannot or will not make the adaptation. What allows us to call these children normal is that they share the common feature of their adaptation to the educational process and context and/or the ability of the educational system to adapt to them. We brand as handicapped—with good intent—those children who do not adapt.

It is unfortunate that money is linked to the decision as to whether a person is handicapped or normal, for were there no money linked to that decision, I do not believe it would be being made. I am asserting essentially that, no matter how physically based or how unique a child's characteristic is, it is not the difference per se that prompts us to call the child handicapped, but it is the effect that the difference has on the child's ability to adapt to the school curriculum that causes us to use the label.

Let me relate a true story that illustrates this point. A friend described to me in a bemused way an auditory screening program in which her child had participated. An alarmed school audiologist reported back to her by anxious phone call that her child was totally deaf in the one ear. Though the child was in the third or fourth grade at the time, this "disability" had not previously been noticed by the school. The parent's bemusement derived from the fact that the child from birth had had only one ear; the child's long hair had obscured her "idiosyncrasy."

There was no reason for alarm; there was no disability; the child was doing quite well in school. Both parents were professionals in the health sciences and had deemed the child's "difference" unimportant to her school attainment, as, in fact, it was proving to be.

A similar example may clarify the point even further. Blindness is not an all-or-none state. There are degrees of blindness, just as there are "degrees" of height and weight. Legal blindness constitutes an arbitrary categorization so as to distinguish for Internal Revenue Service purposes those who are and those who are not eligible for an extra deduction. The utilization of these same definitions in the educational arena proved unworkable, because the difference between one child who was marginally blind but not legally so and the pupil who fell just within the cut-off did not have differential educational prognoses. The partial blindness constitutes only one variable contributing to the child's educational success. An intellectually capable child possessing a strong interest in learning may not find blindness certified by the Internal Revenue Service a serious educational impediment, whereas a child no more severely blind but lacking the same talents or desire for knowledge may find the blindness more of a "handicap."

When we assert that a child is learning disabled and hence handicapped, we fall victim to our own ways of thinking about problems. The difficulty faced by the diagnostician when s/he must decide between the diagnosis of learning disabilities versus the diagnosis of normalcy is that the difference may be only a hair's breadth wide. In fact, the judgment that is being made is not whether the child has a disability, but whether the individual differences the child possesses make him or her more or less incapable of adjusting to the educational environment. The child who is extremely active, the child who has trouble attending in the classroom situation, the child who is partially sighted, the child who reacts with anger and defiance to authority, the child who is motorically expressive and acts in a boisterous manner, the child whose values run counter to those of the school, the child who has cerebral palsy and hence cannot adapt to the physical demands of the school, the child whose visual system has great difficulty discriminating between graphic symbols and hence is frustrated and stressed by the demands of the reading program—these are all examples of children with individual differences that complicate their adjustment to regular education as it is now constituted. If a child's adjustment is extremely impaired, to the extent that the parent or the school becomes alarmed, or to the extent that the child begins to show distress in a rebellious or destructive way, his or her chances of being called handicapped are increased. To the extent that the child is willing and capable of subverting his or her individual needs and interests to the school program, or is able to survive within the educational system, or to the extent that the school program can be adapted to his or her individual characteristics, needs, and interests, the child will be called normal.

This assertion is not to deny that some children are blind, that some children are hard of hearing, that some children do contract diseases, that some children act deviantly with respect to the behavior of their peers, that some children are less capable than their peers at auditory and visual information processing, or any of the other differences that we find are signals for what we now call handicaps. These differences are not denied; instead, they can be seen as part of a broad set of individual differences that characterize all children.

Children differ in a lot of ways, some of which have prompted us to view children as handicapped because the problems were so obviously a characteristic of the person, such as blindness, and an impediment to life's pleasures. However, we did not recognize that the relevance of the blindness to the educational institution was the impact it had on the child's ability to adapt to the regular curriculum. It is in this sense that the child is handicapped. In this same sense, many children whom we are not now calling normal are sacrificing to some degree the realization of their potential to adapt to school curricula. The difference between the so-called handicapped children and normal children is consequently one of degree, not kind; it is the degree to which children are able to adjust to school without causing obvious trouble to themselves, their parents, or the school. It is no wonder that diagnosis, based as it is on the assumption of qualitatively different conditions, presents so many perplexing problems. The alternative conception of a child's school problem as an interaction between the child's characteristics and those of the school system rather than as solely a characteristic of the child obviously has widespread implications.

Labeling

Why do we feel required to label our children prior to adjusting the school program to fit their needs? The answer to this question is extremely complex, because it involves the whole administrative structure of special education at the federal, state, and local levels. Although some states have designed their reimbursement procedures to localities so that specific children do not have to receive diagnostic labels in order to qualify *programs* for reimbursement, many states do require certification according to state guidelines that the child is handicapped in order for the local district to receive reimbursement for the extra cost of adjusting curricula to meet a child's needs. The ramifications of such funding patterns are enormous. The most basic one is the institutionalized assertion that there exists two classes of children, those who are handicapped and hence eligible for special education and those who are normal and who consequently are expected to learn adequately within the regular-education program. Such an assumption is fantastically optimistic and simplistic.

In historical perspective, the present existence of regular education supplemented by special education is perfectly understandable. It was logical enough to recognize early on the severe disjunctions between certain children's abilities and those required for adequate adaptation for the regular-education program. Such children as the profoundly retarded, the deaf, the blind, and those with cerebral palsy obviously needed curriculum modifications. Given the obvious nature of their differences, the assertion that they were not normal and the assertion that they needed extra assistance were both reasonable and appropriate. As more and more problems arose in dealing with pupils in the regular classroom, exacerbated by the increase in class size, the aging of our schools and facilities, the increase in our population and the attendant demand for more teachers, and the subsequent necessity for larger and more complex administrative structures to manage the growing public-education institution, greater pressures were placed on the regular classroom teacher. More and more students were unable to adapt successfully to the curriculum plan of the class. With as few as two or three nonadjusting children in a class of 30 or more, only the most capable of teachers can effectively maintain an educationally conducive atmosphere. Mainstreaming—now termed ''downstreaming'' by cynics (or realists?)—represents an ironic semantic denial of the original problems.

I believe the problems reached their peak with the learning disabled. Though the words used in the federal and state definitions convey restrictive meaning to some professionals, those very same words are being construed by others as including a whole host of children who create problems for the classroom teacher. It is no wonder that to seek relief from the increasingly unrewarding task placed upon them, teachers looked to special education. Learning disabilities represented an avenue for such relief. And, it is not so much that teachers were shirking a responsibility by attempting to obtain a handicap label for a child and, hence, rid themselves of the responsibility for the child's education. It was reasonable to see that many children, perhaps as high as 30 to 40%, could be construed as having problems in the basic psychological characteristics required for adequate school performance. After all, who knows what these skills are and how to assess them while standing in front of a class of 30 children?

If you can see yourself as a parent of a disgruntled child who is failing at school and whose problems are spilling over into the home and disrupting its harmony, if you can see yourself in the role of a teacher whose occupational rewards are being thwarted by children who appear incapable of dealing with the structures required by a curriculum administered in a setting of 30 other children, you can see how learning disabilities could represent a sign of hope for the daily problems parents and teachers confront. It is for this reason that I have argued that the problems surrounding the definition of learning disabilities will not be solved by an arbitrary redefinition that operationally excludes service to most of the children for whom the parents and teachers are seeking assistance.

LEARNING DISABILITIES: A DILEMMA FOR EDUCATION

My overriding concern is the question, "What clarification of the definition of learning disabilities will be of assistance to children?" I have great respect for the stability of social institutions and, therefore, shudder to think that the problems, of which the learning-disability child is symptomatic, reflect the institutionalization of the "handicap model" and the resulting dichotomy of regular and special education. But, I do believe such is the case.

Regular Education/Special Education

As represented in the American public-school system, regular and special education have distinct functions. Whereas regular education is expected to bear the responsibility for the normal child's education, special education is intended to deal with the idiosyncrasies of the handicapped that prevent them from benefiting from the regular school program. Such a dichotomy rests on the assumption that there exists a group of children who are normal and groups of children who are handicapped. Such an assumption is untenable. It is certainly the case that there are many children who are not benefiting optimally from the regular education program, some of whom benefit so minimally and/or become so disruptive that alternative placement appears mandatory both for the child's sake and for that of the peers and teacher. Whether such children reasonably can or should be viewed as handicapped is another issue.

An excellent study by Rubin and Balow (1971) adequately documents the fallacy of this dichotomy. This longitudinal study included the offspring of mothers who had received prenatal care and delivered their offspring at the University of Minnesota Hospitals in the Collaborative Parinatal Research Project. The authors present data to indicate that this population of 967 subjects was essentially normal on socioeconomic, medical, intellectual, and school-readiness characteristics. During the spring of the 1969 school year, 178 of the subjects were completing third grade, 252 were completing second grade, 294 were completing first grade, and 243 were about to conclude kindergarten.

Were one to rely on generally accepted prevalence estimates of special-education populations (Mackie, 1969), one would conclude that the figure runs approximately 12% for all areas of exceptionality. However, this longitudinal study, ranging over 8 years, shows a very different picture. Of the 967 children, 2.5% were receiving special class placement during the 1968–1969 school year. Another 84 children, or 11.6%, of the 726 study subjects who had completed 1 or more years of school had repeated at least one grade. (The authors present data to indicate that this percentage is not out of line with those of other studies.) Also, teachers were asked to report whether or not a child showed problems of attitude and/or behavior at school. Teachers identified 28% of the study subjects as manifesting such problems. According to the study by Rubin and Balow (1971):

> Action involving retention, special class placement, or referral for special services had been taken for 102 children (39 percent) who were identified as behavior problems in the present survey. As the children progress out of the primary grades, there is every likelihood that additional members of the group will be identified as problem children.
>
> Eighteen percent of the total group of regular class children had been recipients of one or more special services, with boys outnumbering girls approximately two to one.
>
> *A total of 397 different subjects (41.1 percent of the study population) were identified in one or more of the problem areas under investigation* . . . [pp. 297–298, italics added].

I doubt that these figures are surprising to school psychologists or teachers working at the local level. It is simply the fact that *many* children are sufficiently unique that at some point in their educational careers they are unable to adapt themselves to the demands of the school curriculum. Special education, in fact, does not deal with isolated, distinct categories of handicapped children. Though some of its services are of this kind, such as the special schools for the deaf and blind, they are the exception rather than the rule. Rather, special education is more and more taking on the role of a general problem solver for regular education. By virtue of its supposed greater knowledge of individual differences and the benefits of more favorable teacher–pupil ratios and special equipment, special education increasingly finds itself in the role of "trouble-shooter" for regular education. Sometimes, this role involves counseling regular educators, but all too often, the role requires the special educator to "take the problems off the hands" of the classroom teacher.

Locus of the Problem

There is another basic assumption, which is equally untenable, that has been referred to earlier. This is the assumption that the problems encountered in school by child and school alike reside in the child rather than in the relationship between the child and the school. School handicaps and medical handicaps are of a different order: A medical handicap is defined in terms of an individual organism's physical intactness relative to norms, whereas an educational handicap must be shown to be a characteristic that inhibits the realization of the individual's potential within the goals of the educational system. *An educational handicap is based not in the factual existence of a deficit (or difference), but in the degree to which the deficit (or difference) will create problems for the child's attainment of his or her educational potential.*

For example, although partial blindness is certainly a biological disability, the degree of blindness may make it less of an educational handicap than one might think. Paradoxically, the inability to sit still, listen to directions, and follow the dictates of the curricula may represent more serious educational handicaps than partial blindness and partial deafness. My point is not so much to argue which individual differences are more or less educationally detrimental, but to point out that our notions of who needs help should be defined in terms of the difficulty the child encounters in successfully realizing his or her potential in the educational system to which s/he is exposed and not on the degree of biological difference.

Such a reorientation of assumptions has a number of implications critical to our programming for children who are having difficulty with the education process. An organizing implication is that the differences between so-called handicaps are more of degree than of kind. Though partial sightedness is certainly different than hyperactivity, the relevant issue is the degree to which this deviance hinders the child's realization of his or her educational potential. As Rubin and Balow (1971) point out, whether the teacher's belief that there is a problem is correct or not, the child has a problem—namely, that the teacher believes the child has a problem. The problem need not lie in the child, nor need it conceptually be viewed as so. If the educational system is attempting to educate children and we find that many children are not becoming educated, it is a generous assumption to suggest that the failure lies in the interaction between child and school and is not a failure of the school—let alone a failure solely of the child.

The Problem of Categories

New conceptualizations of problems can cause problems. One can run off a series of staggering questions posed by a "child-school interaction model" of education failure that pose no problem to the "handicap model." For example, what shall be the role of psychologists in the schools, and what implication will this role have for university training programs and the need for inservice training? Would the legal statutes, both federal and state, need revision? How would others' roles be affected? Would the psychologist take on responsibilities more immediately relevant to educating children? What would be the response of groups organized around specific handicapping conditions? Would they form broader alliances to achieve greater benefits for all children or would they accept continued stigmatization of the handicap labels as an acceptable price for a greater share of the education resources?

The biggest question of all might be, "What would regular education do were the American people to come to believe that it is the right of their children to be unique and the duty of the school to educate them in a manner so that each realizes his or her potential?" I raise these questions so as not to appear obtuse to the implications of my own argument.

I have argued in other papers (Senf, 1972, 1973, 1974a, 1974b, 1976) that categories are an inevitable and necessary component of our research and service endeavor in learning disabilities. The contradiction with the present stance is only apparent. In order to facilitate a child's learning, an educator must understand the developmental tasks the child faces so that s/he can organize the learning of social and academic skills without dampening the child's natural desire to know and to achieve. In order to be truly facilitating rather than directive and restrictive, an educator must develop a better understanding of the basic processes underlying the acquisition of these new behaviors. Such an understanding, I have argued, must come through the study of many children who share common characteristics, and who, in a sense, constitute a "category" or "type" of child. Without disputing the child's individuality, I believe that there exist similar children for whom similar educational experiences will be most conducive to their cognitive and social development.

The analogy to medicine is apparent: Through the careful study of repeated cases of similar symptom characteristics, physicians have been able to determine the remedies that will work best. Rather than making the assumption that all humans are unique, a philosophical assumption that makes for a good bedside manner but not the accumulation of knowledge about remedies, physicians have been able to learn enough about certain diseases that what were once serious health problems are now routinely cured. I have argued that individuality is a two-edged sword; though one wishes to be treated by one's physician as a unique human being, one much prefers one's disease to be routine in the doctor's experience and the treatment already prepackaged. For education, we look for categories that we have termed disabilities or handicaps that children possess, and study those handicaps in order to bring to bear derived knowledge on new cases. Such an effort is, I believe, structurally correct, and should be maintained. However, I do not believe that learning disabilities represents an appropriate category for such research, nor by extension is it appropriate for conceptualizing the problems that have become subsumed under that label.

All learning disabilities are, of course, not alike. Nor, for that matter, are all cases of partial deafness alike, nor are all cases of partial blindness alike. It falls to researchers in these areas to determine the types of problems that these children are encountering in becoming educated. We need a flexible typology that will have as correlates educational recommendations that are valid (cf. Senf, 1976). Just as the master teacher recognizes similarities between a child having problems at school and another child s/he instructed perhaps years ago and utilizes this experience to maximize the child's educational potential, so the researcher must seek categories of individual differences that have reality for the educational enterprise. The categories or types need not be seen as handicaps; they are patterns of individual differences that make it more or less easy for the child to learn in certain kinds of educational environments. We need to match these child types with the optimum instruction system (recognizing the limiting factors of our present knowledge and fiscal resources).

The handicapping conditions presently utilized for funding purposes do not serve either research or educational practice well. They may be quite adequate as administrative mechanisms, but they fail miserably as conceptual devices for organizing our thinking or our delivery of services to children. Because the assumption is that these conditions reside in the children and a diagnostic evaluation is necessary to certify that the child does, in fact, possess the problem, stigmatization and associated loss of self esteem often exacerbate the child's already tenuous adjustment.

The Response of Special Education

Special education need not be upset by this alternative conceptualization, though, if my arguments are correct, the face of special education will change in time. Special education could withdraw to a position where those it serves are willing to accept the stigma of handicap in order to receive their educational rights. However, I believe that educators at the grass-root level are more interested in educating children than in maintaining a traditional orientation to education.

The allegedly handicapped individual and his or her spokespeople also may see virtue in destigmatizing individual differences. The area of the physically handicapped is a case in point. Though the physically handicapped have had a long time to adapt to the idea that the locus of their problems is internal, they now mount ever more effective campaigns against those who would construct physical barriers that limit their potential. The very existence of such a stance reflects the understanding that the alleged handicap lies not simply within the individual, but represents a problem (mostly shouldered by them) that is created when they interact with other institutions. Public institutions, often by state statute, have responded by building ramps, lowering telephones and drinking fountains, altering bathrooms, and so on, which allow the physically disabled greater access to society's resources. Whether those with other so-called handicapping conditions will continue to accept the stigma of handicap in exchange for services is indeterminate. Specifically, will the learning-disabled child bear the stigma of handicap in order to realize his or her educational potential? It is interesting to consider what can happen to our conceptualization of a problem when just a few organizing assumptions are changed. I would like to formalize an alternative conceptualization that has been emerging from this critique of the present status of learning-disability definitions.

THE CHILD–SCHOOL INTERACTION MODEL: AN ALTERNATIVE CONCEPTION

The assumption that the problem lies in the learner, the assumption that there exists a group of youngsters each of whom possesses a similar disability that makes him or her qualitatively different from normal, and the assumption that there exists a group of normal youngsters lacking handicaps can be replaced by a single alternative assumption.

Assumption

Each child possesses certain capabilities, characteristics, and interests that make his or her adjustment to public education more or less successful. The lack of certain abilities, the exhibition of certain behavioral characteristics, such as an extreme activity level, the possession of interests or values at variance with the school curriculum, or a combination of these factors, even though none is particularly exceptional in and of itself, create an adjustment task for all children.

This organizing assumption has a number of implications that differ significantly from current assumptions. First, it defines the problem relative to school adjustment and not solely in terms of the child's characteristics. In so doing, it acknowledges that schools make demands on children, so that responsibility for any failure that results in this relationship between child and school must be shared by both parties.

The assumption does not force a false dichotomy between so-called normals and so-called handicapped youngsters. It instead acknowledges problems as they are; to be called normal and thereby be ignored, simply because a diagnostician was unable to discern some physical or functionally based disorder residing in the child, is logically avoided.

Third, the assumption does not allow us to brand *anyone* as "handicapped," but instead views all problems as the natural adjustment between child and school. In "dehandicapping" children, the assumption recognizes the existence of individual differences not as deficits, but as legitimate features of children.

The three additional assumptions previously asserted as applying to learning-disabled children were: (1) that the disabled learner should aspire to overcome his or her disability or at least not let it deter acquisition of the basic school skills; (2) that parents and educators alike should maintain the educational goals appropriate for normals; and (3) that the disability requires remediation in order the educational goals appropriate for normals to be achieved. These assumptions all hinge on an acceptance of the "handicap model" and make sense only within that framework. Though a category of handicap, learning disabilities are thought not to necessitate an alteration in the basic educational goals. The assumptions furthermore assert that the child, school, and parents should engage in a remedial effort to achieve "normal functioning" in the child.

No parallel set of assumptions would exist in the child–school interaction model because it does not assert the existence of qualitatively different children—i.e., the normal and the handicapped. Instead, the issue of educational goals for the handicapped and the need for "remediation" (education) would not be distinguished from these same issues as applied to all children. An alternative assumption concerning educational goals should be derived from a consideration of the general assumptions that pertain to all children in our educational system.

In relating the general assumptions concerning education in America today, I noted the reliance on the concept of the normal curve as a representation of the population's educational potential. I saw this underlying assumption about the normal distribution of talent to be basic to our competitive orientation to education as well as to most all endeavors. The attendant assumptions to this organizing concept of a normal distribution of talent were that the IQ could be used to measure this distribution of talent, that we could expect achievement in basic skills to correlate positively with this achievement index, that absolute achievement was valued, thereby accounting for our interest in norm-referenced tests that indicate a child's relative standing, and that the IQ was so accepted that it has been afforded more validity than it is capable of demonstrating.

Somewhat paradoxically, given the belief in this distribution of talent, we have nevertheless maintained the belief that because children are all "normal," they should be given a "regular" education costing about the same per pupil. (In practice, of course, we have looked for ways of regrouping students based on the notion of differential talent. We have, in fact, viewed our IQ tests with such respect that they have been used in total disregard for the individual differences presented by children, particularly those from minority groups, resulting in tracking systems based on IQ scores being declared unconstitutional by virtue of their violating the right to an equal educational opportunity.) (See Hobson v. Hansen, 1967; cf. also Larry P. v. Riles, 1979.)

The organizing assumption of the normal distribution of talent clearly falters when confronted with handicaps. The blind, deaf, and so on, could not reasonably be scaled on this normal curve. Obviously requiring a "special" instructional program, the physically disabled were seen as conceptually different. It fell, then, to special education to determine the educational goals and procedures for these children.

Child–School Interaction Model

An alternative conceptualization requires a replacement of this absolute achievement orientation and our reliance on normative thinking as the underpinnings of our educational goals. A viable alternative would be as follows: The goal of the interaction between the child and the school would be to maximize each child's educational and personal potential.

The difference between this goal and the assumptions they replace is graphically illustrated in the following figures. Fig. 4.1 represents our present conceptualization. Regular education and special education are separate. Regular education bases its thinking on normative capabilities utilizing academic ability as its unifying concept. All children are assumed to be essentially normal although varying in innate or acquired ability. Most children are "average," others are "brighter," others "duller." This dimension is correlated with academic achievement, which seems to legitimize the initial conceptualization. (Parenthetically, it should be noted that the correlation between ability and achievement is artifactual. We *construct* our achievement measures so that the resulting distribution of scores will be normal, thereby reinforcing our belief in the normal distribution of talent dogma. More seriously, our curricula are structured to attain

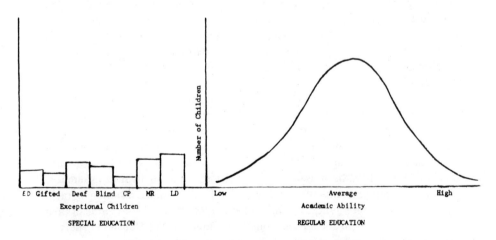

FIG. 4.1.   Illustration of the present model of education.

a normal distribution of achievement by requiring all children to work on the same time schedule. By allowing the so-called duller pupils more time, their achievement comes to resemble more closely that of the brighter children—and the empirical correlation between IQ and achievement is dramatically reduced, though that between achievement and study time equally dramatically increases [cf. Klaus, 1969, p. 95].)

Special education is separate from regular education primarily because the so-called handicap makes the child unable to compete in the regular-education program. It is organized into handicap categories primarily because of gross physical and/or mental similarities and because alternative services are theoretically linked to these handicap categories. In fact, a much more thorough analysis of individual differences is actually required in order to prescribe appropriate alternative education methods.

The separation shown graphically in Fig. 4.1 is real, not metaphorical. To get from the regular-education group and normalcy to the special-education category, a costly certification process must ensue and the price of admitting the inferiority of handicap must be paid prior to obtaining "remedial assistance." Crossing the gulf is long, arduous, and costly. To return is equally painful and not very likely. Though the separation graphically portrayed in Fig. 4.1 is real, not metaphorical, the reality derives from our conceptualization of individual differences and not from their inherent characteristics.

The Child–School Interaction Model illustrated in Fig. 4.2 looks essentially like the regular-education portion of Fig. 4.1, but on closer inspection, one finds a number of important differences. Note that the dimensions along which children are distributed in the Child–School Interaction Model is the "degree of potential realized" rather than the absolute academic potential of the children. Because I am somewhat pessimistic about the present state of public education, I have drawn the curve with a positive skew to illustrate that a greater proportion of the children now fall below a hypothetical neutral point—i.e., they are finding school detrimental to the realization of their potential. However, there *are* some children to the right side of the curve who are finding their school program highly congenial to their talents, characteristics, and interests. Those who do fall to the right of neutral are, of course, not necessarily those who are on the right of average in the distribution of academic potential shown in Fig. 4.1. In fact, careful examination of the special-education portion of Fig. 4.1 will show that many of the most extreme scores on the academic potential dimension are being served by special education as "gifted," an acknowledgment that the regular-education program is unable to meet the unique characteristics not only of the disabled children but also of other "exceptional" children. My guess would be that many of those who are on the right side of the Child–School Interaction Model distribution, indicating the maximization of potential, are those with average intellect coupled with an ability to work under highly structured conditions—but the conceptualization does not rest on such conjecture.

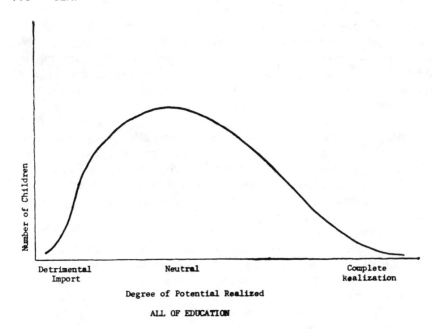

FIG. 4.2.   Illustration of the Child–School Interaction Model. A theoretical curve representing the average impact of all education programs.

Another aspect by which Fig. 4.2 and Fig. 4.1 differ is the greater breadth of distribution of potential (Fig. 4.2) than that of academic potential (Fig. 4.1). Because the units of these two distributions are different, it is not technically accurate to describe one distribution as having a wider range than the other. However, what I am suggesting in this graphic illustration is that the range of academic potential illustrated in Fig. 4.1 is smaller by virtue of its being only one of the characteristics that relate to a child's realization of potential. Consequently, the range of realization of potential is conceptually broader than that of the single dimension of academic potential. In more concrete terms, there are some children for whom school is doing more to actualize their potential than may be manifested by a high IQ score, whereas there are many children for whom school is an unmitigated disaster.

Because of our present provision for special-education services to some of our children, it is likely that some of those children who would have fallen far to the left of neutral, had they been provided with a standard instructional program, would be found to the right of neutral on the Child–School Interaction Model of Fig. 4.2. In essence, the individualized instruction provided some of our (exceptional) children is able to create a higher degree of potential realized than that realized by (allegedly) more able "normal" pupils.

There is nothing surprising in this observation: Special educators have long expressed the belief that many of their methods and, in particular, their focus on the individual characteristics of each child (unfortunately termed "strengths" and "weaknesses") provide the child with a greater opportunity for realizing his or her educational potential. In fact, this recognition finds its way into special-education statutes. For example, Chapter 89 of the Laws of the State of Wisconsin state: "It is the policy of this state to provide as an integral part of free public education, special education to *meet the needs and maximize the capabilities of all children with exceptional educational needs* (italics added)." The notion that education should be provided to maximize the capabilities of children by meeting their needs is certainly not revolutionary. It is simply tragic that this conceptualization is limited only to children who have to undergo the stigma of being handicapped in order to receive such humane understanding. The Child–School Interaction Model implies that the state has no less responsibility to meet the needs and maximize capabilities of *all* children, with or without exceptional needs.

As already implied, the function shown in Fig. 4.2 represents only one of a set of curves. It is the theoretical function of the mean degree of potential realized by children in all regular-education programs in the United States. As such, there are two major classes or variables that together interact to determine the function presented: those contributed by the child and those contributed by the school.

Fig. 4.3 shows the theoretical distributions representing the average impact of three different educational systems and three randomly assigned groups of children. By arbitrarily holding the student variables constant, the conclusions to be drawn from Fig. 4.3 would be that System 1 is on the average quite detrimental to

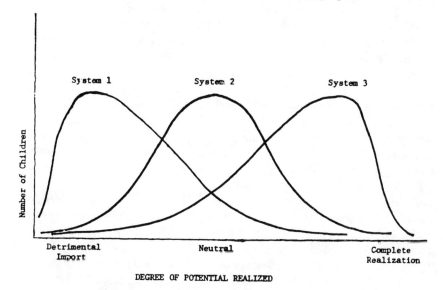

FIG. 4.3.   Theoretical curves representing the average impact of three different educational programs on three randomly assigned groups of children.

most pupils, whereas System 2 is neither generally facilitating nor generally detrimental to most of the students, and System 3 is superior to the other two.

The constitution of the educational systems is no less complex than that of the children. Educational systems have different organizational characteristics, different teachers, different curricula and materials, different classroom organization, and different classroom composition in terms of the backgrounds, talents, interests, and values of the pupils. Each classroom, primarily by virtue of the teacher's values and/or those of the school's administration, has specific rules of operation that specify appropriate behavior for pupils. Each of these characteristics, in turn, represents a cluster of variables that interact among themselves, interact with other system characteristics, and with the pupils' characteristics to determine the degree to which each pupil maximizes his or her potential. Consequently, there does not exist *a* correct educational system. Rather, certain system characteristics will be more or less fruitful for some students. The three curves presented in Fig. 4.3 illustrate that different kinds of systems may, on the average, be more or less fruitful, but, still, no one system is optimal for all children.

The reality of cost factors and our lack of knowledge about the role of individual differences in the learning process prohibit us from matching a specific instructional system to each child. However, the Model requires that we attempt such maximization whenever possible rather than search for a new system appropriate for all. A specific example illustrates this point: The wave of "open-space" educational structures, characterized by team teaching as many as 100 pupils in the same physical space, represents an attempt to find a new instructional structure (a major educational system variable) better suited to all children. Even though open space may (or may not) be a better procedure on the average, it commits the same error as the "traditional" structure of the unit classroom it replaces by implicitly assuming that some new structure will be at least somewhat better for all pupils. Evidence (Reiss, 1974) indicates that this assumption is false: For many children, the "open-space" educational structure is significantly more detrimental to their learning basic academic skills and to their personal adjustment. It is not surprising to find such a result; what is surprising is that the educational planners persist in their search for a new structure without considering the individual differences presented by the pupils who the new structure is allegedly to serve.

Figure 4.4 represents a theoretical curve illustrating the effect of selecting educational systems to maximize the needs of all students. Almost all of the pupils receive a greater than neutral impact. Most of the pupils are receiving definitely positive effects. Those for whom school is still not assisting in realizing their potential should represent our locus of concern. Is some modification in the instructional system possible that will improve the situation? For example, would the child profit more from a teacher with other personal characteristics? Would s/he profit more from a more- (or a less-) structured curriculum? Would

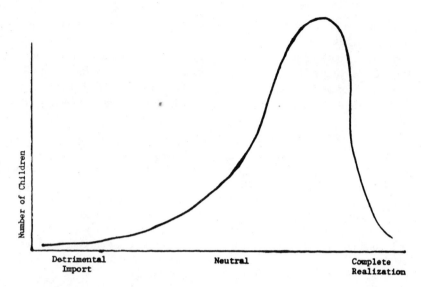

FIG. 4.4. Theoretical curve resulting from selecting instructional programs to meet the needs of all students.

s/he profit more from a modification of the instructional goals that would allow his/her interests more expression? Perhaps no modification that the school could accomplish with all our knowledge and even unlimited resources might make a difference. Perhaps the major portion of the variance in his/her inability to realize his/her potential in school resides in aspects of personality, in problems in the home situation, or in general with variables more associated with the pupil than with the school system. But even in these cases, there probably exist ways in which the school could modify its approach. *The critical issue is not the labeling of some disorder, but the localization of the problem(s) through an analysis of the child–school interaction so that a more optimizing interaction cannot be found.* Although realistic limits on the degree to which the school can modify its approach must exist, the responsibility must lie with the adults representing society to maximize each child's potential. Locating the educational failure in the child represents an abdication of this responsibility.

Goals of Education

The notion of meeting children's needs and maximizing their potential can be embraced without actually acting to improve the child's situation; obviously, more than the semantics must be changed. We must reexamine what it means to "educate" a child and, in this context, what it means to assist each child in realizing his or her potential. The broader issue boils down not simply to individualized instruction, although such would be an important ingredient in instrumenting the Child–School Interaction Model, but to an individualization of educational goals.

Take the case of the learning-disabled child in seventh grade with second- or third-grade reading skills. The child understandably hates reading, feels like a failure, has poor peer relationships because of continued failures at school, acts antisocially, and so forth. Gever (1970) describes the affects of failure well:

> School failure experiences often result in extreme feelings of discomfort, tension, and anxiety. In some children, the negative affect is clearly observable in their nervous, restless activity. In other children, the underlying discomfort is not nearly so apparent. However, hazing and dazing affects of anxiety quietly cloud the intellect. Often a penetrating self-consciousness floods the child so that he becomes too aware of the mechanics of his performance or the reactions of others. Illustrative of this experience is the child who carefully decodes each word with perfection in his oral reading yet has no recognition of the thoughts that were communicated by the words. Perhaps the voice within him blares, "You're making a fool of yourself," hopelessly distracting him from the task at hand [p. 315].

Gever goes on to present an interesting discussion of the role of failure in learning disabilities.

I have asked many professionals whether they think the goals of the learning-disabled child's education should be any different than those for the normal child. There is frequently quite a long latency of response. The usual response is that there is not a change of goals until the child reaches secondary school. Then, parent and school alike begin to consider the realistic options available—more academic training or vocational training. It is tragic that goal alternatives are thought of only at the time when the child is no longer a child and is about to exercise his or her own choice, that of "dropping out." We are all too willing to give a child the "right to read," but are we willing to give the child the right *not* to read? Locked into an ethic that makes academic achievement the presumed road to wealth and social acceptance, we are unwilling to accept the diversity that exists within our own people. We want children to read, to arithmetically calculate, and to spell correctly to the extent that we are willing to take an otherwise happy, loquacious child and steal from him or her the happiness of childhood in order that s/he might become proficient at skills valued by the adult community. How much grief, stress, and anger does a child need to exhibit before we change our goals for him/her? How many of us as parents or professionals are actually looking at the child's discomfort in terms of a cry for help, asking us not to make him or her have to do it any longer?

The acceptance of individual differences is more than just a slogan. It is a genuine ability to allow others to exercise choices that run counter to one's own value system. Children have few rights and, hence, few choices. It is my belief that, unwittingly, education has acted in the disinterest of many children by adopting a common set of standards against which all children are measured, perhaps because the history of education in this country is one of increasing bureaucratization as the only method of dealing with the magnitude and complexities of the public educational system. With the increasing size and resulting anonymity of our public-school institutions, schools have had to adopt curricula acceptable to an increasingly wide range of parental values. Rather than having the wide range represented in the schools, the administrative expedient for having common curricula has resulted in our accepting the lowest common denominator, specifically the teaching of the basic skills of reading, writing, arithmetic, and so on. The pressures placed upon schools resulting in this delimitation of educational goals is epitomized by the rulings barring prayer in the schools and local restrictions against sex education. One simply cannot please all the people all the time and so schools, rather reasonably, have retreated to a position of providing the basics (without apparently considering whether this stance represents an implicit violation of the children's rights. Ironically, schools have failed in this self-restrictive approach—would there be a ''back-to-basics'' movement today had the schools succeeded in this effort?).

A Critical Role for the Parents

I firmly believe that the goals of education should be determined by parents. They are the ones who predominantly pay for the service, the service is rendered to their children, and it is supposed to be *a service* to them. (Despite the fact that education attendance is mandatory, the process is construed as a priviledge rather than a requirement of citizenship.) Teachers and school administrators are hired by and are responsible to the people. It is an important component not only of the Child–School Interaction Model, but of sensible educational policy to have parents involved in the educational choices made for their children. In fact, litigation charging that failure to involve parents when educational decisions affect their child represents violations of due process (Arreola v. Board of Education, 1968; The Education for All Handicapped Children Act, 1975).

Though there are many reasons why it would be difficult to involve parents in choosing the educational goals for their child, I believe it is nevertheless mandatory that such be done. It is more important, in my view, to have the school, parents, and child committed to the educational objectives, even if time were to be taken from the instructional day to accomplish this task, than to maintain the distance that now exists between schools and their constituency.

I recognize that these attitudes will not be congenial with many teachers, with many school administrators, nor with school psychologists. However, I believe that in the long run, favorable relationships with parents will result in a much more positive atmosphere beneficial to all. It is troublesome to consider the possibility of allowing a potentially disruptive parent into one's school, but, ultimately, a truce might return to the children, to the teachers, and to those who operate the educational systems a sense of meaningful accomplishment and comraderie.

Some Real Problems

Lest I appear a Pollyanna, I acknowledge that the Child–School Interaction Model would represent a different way of thinking and, therefore, a source of problems to institutions based on present conceptualizations. At the same time, I contest blanket statements of pessimism about such a conceptualization, for I know that schools exist in which not only "handicapped" children are treated like individuals, but so are all children. These schools have fine relationships between their teachers, administrators, and parents. In one specific case, in deciding the question of whether a child could miss a week of school in order to travel with his parents through the Southwest, the mother and teacher together agreed that the educational opportunities available on the trip outweighed those available in the school, particularly because the child had attained a level of mastery of his subjects acceptable to the parents and himself and, in fact, was showing signs of boredom late in the school semester.

Special-Education Funding

One of the state learning-disability consultants mentioned to me in our interviews that surely I understood that were I to go to a legislature seeking funds for a program that would adjust school characteristics to the needs of children and were he to go to that same legislature seeking money for *handicapped* children, he would receive funding whereas I would not. I suppose this is true, but I also believe it to be true only because it represents our present conceptualization. We used to treat those having medical handicaps with social ridicule and exclusion from our system of education; now, we serve them under the condition that they admit to their handicap and "wear it" in return for service. The difference between these two conceptualizations of the problem is like night and dawn. It represents a significant advance in our acceptance of others' differences. Can we not let the clock advance further into daylight and recognize that the differences that we now call handicaps simply represent the most extreme physical conditions that characterize all children, differences that make them more or less capable of interacting successfully with the public school? I cannot believe that the limits of our humanity have been reached in our obvious stigmatization of physically and emotionally disabled children. I believe that reform of public education has a much better chance than reform of some of the other institutions that have become equally bureaucratized and involuted (see Blatt, Ozolins, & McNally, 1979).

This belief stems from the fact that parents remain concerned about their children and more and more of the so-called radicals of the mid- to late 1960's now have or are soon to have school-aged children. Together, parents create a pressure group more powerful than those concerned about any of the other social institutions of our society in need of overhaul—e.g., the welfare system, public transit, social security, and so forth.

But, the problem remains as to how special educators and those parents who have been concerned and involved for years obtaining funds for handicapped children would react to the idea of expanding their efforts to attack the more basic problem—whether our educational system truly provides an opportunity for all our children to realize their potentials. Because the field of learning disabilities as construed by the laity represents a much broader pool of potential child failure and parental discontent than the 2% expected by federal regulations, I believe that many parents will be looking for other avenues to make schools more responsive to their children's needs. I think that parents of allegedly handicapped children would do just as well were they to remove the stigma from their children and allow the public institution that was unable to accommodate their needs to share the burden of the problem. In fighting for funding for the handicapped, there are few true allies, though many sympathetic listeners. My prediction may be wrong and for a while yet special interest groups representing children with biological handicaps and resulting educational problems may band together in the fear that the expansion of the concept of individuality to all children will diminish the resources available for the more severe problems their children face. In time, however, I believe the new technological advances that make possible the individualization of instruction will create an atmosphere that allows teachers to be more open with parents and accepting of the individual differences that children possess. The potential rewards for teachers in being able once again to teach children rather than curricula will more than make up for the trials of dealing with (little) people.

Our administrative machinery for special education need not be replaced; biological disabilities will not disappear, so there will remain an increasingly important role for what we now know as special education to refine and expand the techniques of individualized instruction and parent involvement and to share these advances with regular education. All that the Child–School Interaction Model requires is that the middle ground between special and regular education be recognized and the false dichotomy that now exists be bridged. The individualization of instructional goals and instructional methods that have been pioneered by special educators and others interested in the educational needs of the individual child can be used to create new areas of study: development of creativity; utilization of child-based interests in facilitating educational development; the sharing and development of cultural heritages rather than their subjugation; the impact of different cognitive styles; adapting media methods to the individual learning styles of children; developing teacher sensitivity to the role emotions play in the learning process so that they can be fostered and used productively rather than be seen as a destructive influence. There is so much teachers, school psychologists, and other auxiliary school personnel could do and want to do. I have met few teachers who really want to be *regular* teachers and no school psychologists who want only to test and write reports, but the impact of required curricula and administrivia stifles them. Teachers uniformly apologize for their roles as "just regular teachers" when I meet them on site visits, when, in fact, I have much more respect for them than I do for their so-called leaders. To borrow Dylan's verse, school psychologists too often appear "burned out from exhaustion, burried in the hail, poisoned in the bushes, blown out on the trail."

Special education may choose for its role concentration on what are now recognized as medical handicaps. As one director of special education stated, he would prefer to recommend to the legislature that learning disability money be turned over to regular education and "let them clean their own house" than to continue the process of taking on more and more of the problems fostered by an educational establishment insensitive to the individual differences among children. Such a stance of more restrictively defining the domain of special education abdicates responsibility. Others might take the reverse tactic and expand by consciously including the study of individual differences. Such a special-education department would not be organized around biological disorders, though course offerings specific to these pupils' individual differences would remain as important as ever. Instead, the focus would be on the broader dimensions of individuality and methods of channeling and fostering them in the interests of the child and society. (Cf. Reynolds & Balow, 1972, whose excellent article I was advised of by a state LD consultant after preparing the initial draft of this chapter. Many of the ideas expressed here are inherent in their position.)

A department having such an orientation would represent an applied psychology of education unit whose purpose would be to study and teach how to utilize individual characteristics of children and how to organize education flexibly enough so that workable means of bringing the most efficacious educational programming to each individual child can be determined and taught. As such, the role of such a special-educational psychology department would be to study not only the learner–system interactions, but also to consider the organizational problems, as well as train teachers and administrators to carry out the recommendations derived from their continued study.

For the sake of the biologically disabled, I would certainly prefer to see the study of individual differences carried on within such a department, so that individualized programming for children in schools would help destigmatize those with such disabilities. Were special education to restrict its domain to biological handicaps and maintain its funding base through certification of handicap, I fear we would continue to stigmatize those whose physical disabilities have already created for them more than their share of misery.   .

The Cost

I suppose it is inevitably the case that something that sounds better must cost more. New ideas do cost more, simply because changes would be required and changing anything costs money. At the same time, in my visits with regular-education teachers who have interaction with the learning-disability programs to which I consulted, I was impressed by the ingenuity they show in restructuring their own internal resources to provide more and more children with the benefits they saw accruing to children in the learning-disability program. How nice, for example, it would be to have "normal" children be able to utilize the special machinery and media available in the resource room! But, certainly such is impossible if the Frohreich (1973) data are correct—that special education costs for disabled learners run more than twice those of "normals." Or, is this in fact true? Cost studies can only examine what is, not what might be. I would bet that a huge portion of the extra cost derives from *administering* special education and in certifying eligibility. A careful study of possible means of reorganizing resources should be undertaken so that more children can benefit from our "special-education" resources.

For example, if resource rooms would be useful for all children, providing them with extra materials and greater teacher attention and encouragement to pursue their interests, could this not be accomplished by a reorganization within a school? Would not teachers be willing to take on five extra students were this to leave one out of every four rooms capable of having a 1-to-10 teacher–pupil ratio and a resource room atmosphere and materials (assuming that all four teachers have the opportunity to teach in that classroom for one-quarter of the time)? How well it would break up their routine, provide a much better opportunity to get to know more pupils, and to see them in an environment where strict discipline and control were not so necessary to the maintenance of an educationally viable environment. In such an atmosphere, the school psychologist could become integrated into the educational effort, and come to know the students beyond the bounds of test scores and assist the students using their psychological expertise. In fact, so-called "regrouping" programs are now in operation whereby two teachers take on portions of a third teacher's class, thereby providing the third teacher with greater ability to deal with some of the learning problems (uncertifiable handicaps) that some of the pupils are facing. There is no extra cost to such reorganization, only ingenuity.

A thorough study of such organizational modifications should be undertaken. Organizational changes have an additional benefit besides their cost: They tend to be more lasting because the new structure helps maintain change, whereas change directed toward individuals' personal characteristics tends to wane over time. I am not saying that there would not be added costs, but only that we need not think of every change as adding to the costs that we have. If the intellectual ingestibles that comprise the educational diet are so lousy now, should we complain about them being served in small portions? We do not have to add to what we are doing; we have to change it. With a growing technology making us ever more capable of individualized instruction (cf. Klaus, 1969), we should be able to relate to children as though they were individual people without having it cost us an arm and a leg. Indeed, if we do not relate to children as if they were individual people, it will certainly cost us much more in the long run.

Although there must surely be problems for our present educational policies resulting from (1) a full recognition of the individual talents, behavioral characteristics, and interests of children; and (2) an acknowledgment that it is the school's responsibility to help each realize his or her potential, the positive values for children, for those educating them, and for their parents would be immense. Though individual differences that are restricting (presently called handicaps) obviously would still exist, they would not need to be seen as shameful. (If individualization were for everyone, no one would be stigmatized.) These children would certainly place the greatest demand on the educational system to modify itself, as they do now, if they were going to be able to realize their potential; certainly, the public must provide extra funds for such conditions. However, those who are not biologically disabled but nevertheless need a modification of their instructional program in order to realize their potential, which probably involves all children to some degree, no less deserve some personalization of their education. A sliding scale of services from individualization in the classroom to extra resource-room activities covering a wide variety of skills and interest areas could be provided for many more children than is presently the case.

The Reward

The legitimatization of individual differences coupled with the individualization of learning goals would be able to encompass the diversity represented in cultural groups, cognitive styles, unique talents, behavioral variation, and special interests. Here, the door to an exciting, vital job for psychologists would open. Children would learn to value uniqueness and the "handicapped" child would learn to focus on talents rather than becoming obsessed with deficits. By the example set by adults, the child would see uniqueness respected. The desire for the invisibility of normalcy would eventually give way to the realization that even biologically disabled people have individuality that extends beyond their physical or mental atypicality. They would see other children being treated as individuals and provided an education suited to their needs. The unfortunate disassociation of psychology from pedagogy has proven too costly *not* to repair.

The interests of children as well as their differential talents require notice. The present reduced ability of our schools to allow children to follow their interests and retain their true involvement with learning is one of the greatest wasted resources in this country. By allowing differential interests to be valued within the school setting, children could learn to take pride in their individuality. An added derivative benefit is that the acknowledgment of differences as acceptable and valuable undercuts the need for children to compete with one another. By removing a single standard against which all children are measured, we allow them to take interest in the activities of others and learn from the differences they see in others, rather than to model adults' tendency to cultivate an atmosphere where differences are subject to ridicule.

Most critically, though, the recognition of responsibility on the part of the school to accept differences in children and to see it as the school's goal to foster the individual potential of each child allows the child to maintain an innate drive to know and to achieve.

The preciousness of the inquiring child seems so quickly lost in our huge impersonal educational system that sets its standards and, in its effort to discipline, tries to homogenize children and scale them along a single standard. By maintaining their inquisitiveness, the children will retain responsibility for learning. Though they may all come out looking different and though some of them may not be the kind of children you or I might choose to have as our own, they will all be much happier. And in time, they will have fewer concerns about sending their own children to the public schools.

REFERENCES

APA Monitor, 1979, *10*(11), 8.

Arreola v. Board of Education, 160 577 (1968).

Blatt, B., Ozolins, A., & McNally, J. *The family papers: A return to purgatory.* New York: Longman, 1979.

Bryant, N. D. Learning disabilities. *Instructor,* 1972, *81,* 49–56.

Bryant, N. D. Learning disabilities: A report on the state of the art. *Teachers College Record,* 1974, *75,* 395–404.

Bryant, N. D., & Kass, C. E. *Leadership training institute in learning disabilities* (Vols. 1 and 2). Tucson Department of Special Education, University of Arizona, and Program Development Branch, Division of Educational Services, Bureau of Education for the Handicapped, United States Department of Health, Education, and Welfare, 1972.

Danielson, L. C., & Bauer, J. N. A formula-based classification of learning disabled children: An examination of the issues. *Journal of Learning Disabilities,* 1978, *11,* 163–176.

Dunn, L. M. Special education for the mildly retarded—is much of it justifiable? *Exceptional Children,* 1971, *37,* 537–538.

Education for All Handicapped Children Act, 1975, PL 94–142.

Fantini, M. D. Education of the economically disadvantaged. *National Elementary Principal,* 1972, *51,* 93–94.

Federal Register. November 26, 1976.

Federal Register. December 29, 1977.

Frohreich, L. E. Costing programs for exceptional children: Dimensions and indices. *Exceptional Children,* 1973, *39,* 517–524.

Gever, B. E. Failure and learning disability. *Reading Teacher,* 1970, *23,* 311–317.

Herrick, M. J. Disabled or disadvantaged: What's the difference? *Journal of Special Education,* 1973, *7,* 381–386.

Hobson v. Hansen, 269 F. Supp. 401 (1967).

Kass, C. E., & Myklebust, H. R. Learning disability: An educational definition. *Journal of Learning Disabilities,* 1969, *2,* 37–43.

Klaus, D. J. *Instructional innovation and individualization.* Pittsburgh: American Institutes for Research, 1969.

Larry P. v. Riles. *APA Monitor,* 1979, *10*(11), 8.

Lieberman, L. M. The implications of non-categorical special education. *Journal of Learning Disabilities,* 1980, *13,* 65–68.

Lindsay, P. H., & Norman, D. A. *Human information processing: An introduction to psychology.* New York: Academic Press, 1972.

Luick, A. H., & Senf, G. M. Where have all the children gone? *Journal of Learning Disabilities,* 1979, *12,* 285–287.

Mackie, R. P. *Special education in the United States: Statistics 1948–1966.* New York: Teachers College Press, 1969.

McLeod, J. Educational underachievement: Toward a defensible psychometric definition. *Journal of Learning Disabilities,* 1979, *12,* 322–330.

Meehl, P. E. Why I do not attend case conferences. In P. E. Meehl, *Psychodiagnosis: Selected papers.* Minneapolis: University of Minnesota Press, 1973.

Myklebust, H. R. Learning disabilities: Definition and overview. In H. Myklebust (Ed). *Progress in learning disabilities. I.* New York: Grune & Stratton, 1968.

Neff, H. The child who wasn't retarded. *PTA Magazine,* 1973, *67,* 20–23.

Neisser, U. *Cognitive psychology.* New York: Appleton-Century-Crofts, 1967.

Reiss, S. *Educational and psychological effects of open space education in Oak Park, Illinois.* Unpublished paper submitted to the Board of Education, District 97, Oak Park, Illinois, 1974.

Reynolds, M. C., & Balow, B. Categories and variables in special education. *Exceptional Children,* 1972, *38,* 357–366.

Ross, S. L., Jr., DeYoung, H. G., & Cohen, J. S. Confrontation: Special education placement and the law. *Exceptional Children,* 1971, *38,* 5–12.

Rubin, R., & Balow, B. Learning and behavior disorders: A longitudinal study. *Exceptional Children,* 1971, *38,* 29–29.

Salvia, J., & Clark, J. Use of deficits to identify the learning disabled. *Exceptional Children,* 1973, *39,* 305–308.

Senf, G. M. An information integration theory and its application to normal reading acquisition and reading disability. In N. D. Bryant & C. E. Kass (Eds.), *Leadership training institute in learning disabilities* (Vol. 2). Department of Special Education, University of Arizona, Tucson, and Program Development Branch, Division of Educational Services, Bureau of Education for the Handicapped, United States Department of Health, Education, and Welfare, 1972.

Senf, G. M. Learning disabilities. In H. J. Grossman (Ed.), *Learning disorders. Pediatric clinics of North America,* 1973, *20,* 607–640.

Senf, G. M. Future research needs in learning disabilities. In R. Anderson (Ed.), *Texas Tech Invitational Conference on Learning Disabilities/Minimal Brain Dysfunction.* Springfield: Thomas, 1974. (a)

Senf, G. M. *Issues surrounding classification in learning disabilities.* Association for Children with Learning Disabilities National Convention, Houston, March 1974. (b)

Senf, G. M. Some methodological considerations in the study of abnormal conditions. In R. Walsh & W. T. Greenough (Eds.), *Environment as therapy for brain dysfunction.* New York: Plenum, 1976.

Senf, G. M., & Grossman, R. P. State initiative in learning disabilities: Illinois' project SCREEN. Report 3. Local and state opinion regarding the concept of learning disabilities. *Journal of Learning Disabilities,* 1975, *8,* 587–596.

Senf, G. M., & Sushinsky, L. W. State initiative in learning disabilities: Illinois' Project SCREEN. Report 2. Definition and Illinois practice. *Journal of Learning Disabilities,* 1975, *8,* 524–533.

Szasz, T. S. *The myth of mental illness: Foundations of a theory of personal conduct.* New York: Hoeber-Harper, 1961.

Torgesen, J. K. Problems and prospects in the study of learning disabilities. In E. M. Hetheringtron (Ed.), *Review of child development research.* Chicago: University of Chicago Press, 1975.

Torgesen, J. K. What shall we do with psychological processes? *Journal of Learning Disabilities,* 1979, *12,* 514–521.

Vande Voort, L., Senf, G. M., & Benton, A. L. Development of audiovisual integration in normal and retarded readers. *Child Development,* 1972, *43,* 1260–1272.

Wiederholt, J. L. Historical perspectives on the education of the learning disabled. In L. Mann & D. Sabatino (Eds.), *The second review of special education.* Philadelphia: JSE Press, 1974.

Zigler, E., & Phillips, L. Psychiatric diagnosis, a critique. *Journal of Abnormal and Social Psychology,* 1961, *63,* 607–617.

5 Mental-Health Consultation

Joel Meyers
University of Minnesota[1]

INTRODUCTION

This is an exciting time to be a school psychologist. The profession has evolved into a unique discipline of applied psychology. There has been a geometric increase in the number of school-psychology training programs since the Thayer Conference was held in 1954 (Cutts, 1955), and this has resulted in a large number of practicing school psychologists who have received training in this specific field. With this increase in professionals trained as school psychologists, there is no longer a need for schools to rely on clinical psychologists for the bulk of school psychological services. As a result, it is no longer a major goal to define the role and function of school psychologists. Although there will always be different emphases as well as continued modifications in the school psychologist's role, most school psychologists now have a well-developed conception of the possibilities and limitations of the role based on their training.

There is reason to be optimistic now, as school psychologists attempt to move beyond general role descriptions to the specification of techniques based on current developments in applied psychology and in psycho–educational research (e.g., the recently developed applied behavior analysis technology). In addition to these scientific and applied advances, recent legislation is having a tremendous impact on the field and on education in general. Just one recent example is PL 94–142, which has mandated education in the least restrictive environment for all children regardless of their handicaps. By mandating a team concept for evaluation, the use of nondiscriminatory assessment devices, and active parental in-

---

[1]On study leave from the Department of School Psychology, Temple University.

133

volvement, this legislation has many specific implications for the work of school psychologists. In this climate of scientific advances in psychology coupled with increased legislative influence and community involvement, effective research is essential. Strong data are needed to demonstrate effectiveness of specific techniques so that professionals will be in a position to influence their roles in a positive manner. Not only is this a period that has witnessed *Advances in School Psychology,* but the next decade demands much more of the same.

It is in this context that the present chapter seeks to consider mental-health consultation. The goal of this chapter is to consider the ways in which mental-health consultation has produced *and* holds promise for advances in school psychology. This is accomplished by reviewing the most current theory and research with an emphasis on the practice of mental-health consultation in the schools. The chapter reviews the three following topics: (1) introduction to mental-health consultation; (2) a model for mental-health consultation in schools; and (3) direct service to the teacher.

Although the aim is to provide a comprehensive overview of the writing and research in this field, this is done from the author's frame of reference. This viewpoint reflects the author's experience as a practitioner, a researcher, and a trainer, and it borrows extensively from ideas that were developed in a recent book entitled *Mental Health Consultation in the Schools* (Meyers, Parsons, & Martin, 1979).

INTRODUCTION TO MENTAL-HEALTH CONSULTATION

Although mental-health consultation has been defined in many diverse ways, for the purposes of this chapter, it is defined as follows: Mental-health consultation is a problem-solving process that occurs between two professionals when one (the consultant) tries to help the other (the consultee) maximize the social–emotional development of the clients (i.e., students) under the consultee's care. In school consultation, the consultee might be a teacher, administrator, or other school personnel. For the purposes of this chapter, mental-health consultation is defined as a voluntary relationship in which a current work problem of the consultee is considered. When this relationship is effective, the consultee (e.g., teacher) handles both current and future problems in a more skillful and sensitive manner.

Brief Historical Perspective

Mental-health consultation has received attention in recent years as an alternative system for the delivery of psychological services in schools, and it has been very much a part of the debates about the role of the school psychologist. Those favoring the mental-health consultation role have cited numerous reasons: (1) the medical model that conceptualizes psychological problems as an internal disease process has received much recent criticism and alternatives are needed that emphasize the impact of the environment; (2) professionals are not convinced about the effectiveness of traditional therapeutic techniques and alternative approaches to intervention are needed; (3) there has been recent emphasis on indirect rather than direct-service models, and mental-health consultation is one approach to indirect service; (4) there is an inadequate number of professionals available to provide psychological services, and therefore more efficient approaches are needed.

The basic problem is that many educators feel that they do not receive meaningful help from psychologists. This feeling is so widespread that it is expressed by a range of people including teachers, administrators, and funding agencies. Frequently, informal discussions reveal that educators have never even met the school psychologist; in urban school systems, this problem has been particularly acute. When teachers have had contact with psychologists, criticisms often note that too much time is spent in diagnosis and report writing, whereas little time, if any, is spent trying to provide meaningful help in the classroom.

A basic premise of traditional psychological service models is that both diagnosis (e.g., psycho–educational diagnosis) and treatment (e.g., psychotherapy) are provided directly by the psychologist. The problems associated with such direct-service models have been experienced by anyone who has worked in the schools. This system is often so inefficient that some children wait as long as 1 year for a psychological evaluation; in addition, diagnostic work can be so time consuming that little time or energy is left for effective communication with children, parents, teachers, and others. Moreover, after an evaluation, the child is often referred to a special-education class, a school counselor, or a psychotherapist outside of the school. Yet, there are not enough special class placements, counselors, or psychotherapists available within or outside of the school system to provide the help to all children who need it.

This criticism does not apply to all school systems. There are many that have provided efficient and valued service for years. Nevertheless, these systems are in the minority. The effectiveness of mental-health consultation as a model for the delivery of services needs to be examined empirically in the future. Currently, there are not sufficient data to present this as a definitive answer to the problems that have just been elaborated. However, it does provide an alternative approach that at least holds the promise of reaching more children indirectly by influencing teachers and schools. It is a technique designed to prevent future problems and is, therefore, not limited to the remediation of current problems.

By providing service indirectly, mental-health consultation offers the opportunity of reaching more children and effecting a reduction in long waiting lists for evaluations. Yet, frequently when consultation is discussed as an alternative system for the delivery of service, psychologists and administrators respond that although it sounds nice in theory, they do not have time to implement it due to large backlogs of referrals. As an example, a large urban school system reported a backlog of 16,000 evaluations during 1979 (Ysseldyke, 1979). Because of the current system, these psychologists have been too busy testing to offer alternative services. However, there may be something to be learned from historical experience. Gerald Caplan first initiated mental-health consultation in an attempt to cope with inordinately long waiting lists. In 1948, he was responsible for the mental health of 16,000 new immigrant children in Israel with a small staff of psychologists and social workers. Traditional direct-service approaches were inadequate to cope with the more than 1000 referrals received during the first year. By chance, the staff noticed patterns in the referrals coming from specific institutions. Certain institutions reported difficulties with specific types of children—for example, acting out, bed wetting, or learning problems.

Caplan used these observations as a basis for experimenting with indirect approaches to the delivery of service. The reasoning was simple: School A referred aggressive children; if that school could learn to cope more effectively with aggressive children, the referral list might be reduced significantly. Far from considering mental-health consultation a luxury, he used it as a pragmatic technique to deal with the large numbers of referrals that otherwise would have remained unanswered.

After returning to the United States in 1952, Caplan continued his work on mental-health consultation at Harvard University and his book, *The Theory and Practice of Mental Health Consultation* (Caplan, 1970), has had a major impact. He has made three primary contributions. First, he describes mental-health consultation as a nonhierarchical, *coordinate relationship* between two professionals. The consultant has expertise about mental health and the consultee has expertise in his or her field. The teacher, for example, should be perceived by the consultant as an expert in the classroom. Second, Caplan considers it counterproductive for the consultant to confront the consultee directly, because he supposes that confrontation will destroy the consultee's defenses. Caplan feels that the consultation relationship, unlike psychotherapy, does not provide the time to rebuild defenses. Instead, he discusses *indirect techniques* such as theme-interference reduction. Third, Caplan's *four-part categorization* of consultation approaches provides the foundation for much of the work that has been done in mental-health consultation. These four categories of consultation are client-centered case consultation, program-centered administrative consultation, consultee-centered case consultation, and consultee-centered administrative consultation. Each of these contributions is elaborated on later in this chapter.

Both Kurt Lewin and Seymour Sarason have also had an impact on the development of mental-health consultation. Lewin has had two important effects. One derived from the National Training Laboratories T-group (training group) movement. In 1946, Lewin and his staff at the Massachusetts Institute of Technology developed a T-group approach in which trainees were placed in small groups and given personal feedback about their behavior in groups. The premise underlying this approach was that if people were brought together from different levels of the organization and were given feedback, then communication on the job could be improved. His second major influence was the application of attitude-survey research and data feedback to organizational problems. Typically, attitude-survey data were gathered from members of the organization. These data would then be discussed with these members in an effort to determine the key organizational difficulties and determine possible action plans. Lewin's work places clear emphasis on the environment of the organization as well as on the importance of indirect service. His ideas have had most influence on the approach to consultation labeled Service to the Organization, which is discussed later in this chapter.

Sarason's work at Yale's Psychoeducational Clinic has also had an impact. This clinic was concerned with preventive mental health in the school and community, and instead of having clients coming to the clinic, the goal was to provide help in the community and the school. By stressing the importance of providing service in the client's environment rather than at the clinic, Sarason's work has suggested the importance of environmental factors in mental-health consultation.

A Brief Overview of Research

Although consultation has been considered formally as a professional technique since about 1950, research in this area has been a recent development. The reader interested in more detailed considerations of this research literature is referred to several recent reviews (Mannino & Shore, 1975; Medway, 1979; Meyers et al., 1979; Meyers, Pitt, Gaughan, & Freidman, 1978).

One frequent topic of research has been to determine how various professional groups, such as administrators, school psychologists, and teachers, view the consultation role. Although there is still occasional debate about whether school psychologists should use a consultation role, the results of this survey research have been consistently positive. Both teachers and psychologists view this role favorably (e.g., Cook & Patterson, 1977; Fairchild, 1976; Gilmore & Chandy, 1973; Gutkin, 1980; Lambert, Sandoval, & Corder, 1975; Manley & Manley, 1978; Martin, Duffey & Fischman, 1973; Szmuk, Docherty & Ringness, 1979; and Waters, 1973). In fact, when consultation approaches are compared to traditional referral modes, both teachers and psychologists report a preference for consultative services (e.g., Gutkin, Singer, & Brown, 1980).

There are some data indicating the extent to which school psychologists use consultation techniques. In one report, Farling and Hoedt (1971) indicated that the professional activity of most school psychologists was essentially oriented toward direct-service techniques, and that nondoctoral school psychologists provide essentially psycho-diagnostic service. Similarly, Cook and Patterson (1977) found that although school psychologists viewed consultation as their most important function, most of their time was devoted to individual assessment. Martin et al. (1973) did a time line analysis of the time spent in consultation activities by school psychology interns in an internship emphasizing consultation. They found that only 28.3% of the interns' time was spent doing consultation. A more recent survey suggests similar results for school psychologists (Martin & Meyers, 1978). Thirty-three percent of those responding indicated that they spend 31% or more of their time consulting. However, 44% spend between 11 and 30% of their time consulting, and 23% of those responding indicated that they spend less than 10% of their time consulting. Although more data are needed, it can be concluded tentatively that despite the favorable view of consultation, many school psychologists do not implement this model sufficiently in practice.

One factor that may influence the implementation of consultation is the extent to which it is thought of as an effective technique. Although there is a clear need for more research on this question, there have been several relevant studies to date; many of these indicate that consultation can have a positive impact (Gutkin et al., 1980; Hops, 1971; Meyers, 1975; Meyers, Freidman, & Gaughan, 1975; Ritter, 1978; and Ruckhaber, 1975). Two different reviews have concluded from published research that consultation has a success rate of about 69% (Mannino & Shore, 1975; Medway, 1979). Much of this research can be criticized for its consideration of global outcomes of consultation and the frequent failure to use behavioral measures of effectiveness. Nevertheless, taken as a whole, it is reasonable to conclude that consultation can be an effective technique. Future investigations must try to determine the precise conditions necessary for consultation to be effective. This can be done by assessing more specific consultation techniques as well as by trying to answer more specific questions that have a practical value for the practice of consultation. Some investigations that have at least attempted this goal are considered in later sections of this chapter.

A MODEL FOR MENTAL-HEALTH CONSULTATION IN SCHOOLS

Caplan's (1963, 1970) four-part categorization of mental-health consultation has been the most influential framework in this field throughout the past 15 years. The terminology that he developed for this framework is used frequently in the professional literature on mental-health consultation. Because this work forms at least a partial basis for most discussions of the consultation process, his four categories are defined briefly here.

Client-centered case consultation is Caplan's first category, and it occurs when the focus is on the consultee's difficulty with a professional case. The primary goal is to help the consultee (e.g., teacher) find the most effective treatment for the client (e.g., student). A secondary goal is to help the consultee become better prepared for similar clients in the future. Because attention is focused on the client, the consultant would often use a variety of psycho–educational diagnostic techniques and develop specific remedial plans.

The second category of consultation described by Caplan is *program-centered administrative consultation*. This occurs when the consultant is requested to help solve current problems in the administration of a program (for our purposes, these would be educational programs even though Caplan considers a variety of other programs that relate to mental health). In this approach, the consultant assesses the current program and recommends a plan to resolve the problem. As with the first category, a secondary goal is to educate the consultees so that they will be able to deal with similar problems in the future without consultation.

Consultee-centered case consultation is the third type discussed by Caplan. This approach focuses on the consultee (e.g., teacher) rather than the client (e.g., student). The primary goal is to improve the consultee's (e.g., teacher's) functioning rather than the specific client (e.g., student). The consultant may help to improve the skill, knowledge, objectivity, or self confidence of the consultee by discussing the consultee's role in the problem. This particular approach provides the cornerstone for much of the discussion in the section *Direct Service to the Teacher* later in this chapter.

The last type of consultation discussed by Caplan is *consultee-centered administrative consultation*. The primary goal of this approach is to help with problems in planning and maintaining various programs (for our purposes, educational programs) that have implications for the prevention and control of mental-health problems. A particularly frequent focus is to manage interpersonal aspects of the agency.

Caplan's framework has been modified and elaborated to make it more applicable to the schools (Meyers et al., 1979). This revised categorization provides four different approaches to mental-health consultation that are conceptualized as levels that vary in terms of the degree to which the services provided to the child are direct or indirect.

Level I is *direct service to the child*. This is a form of consultation based on the dominant techniques used today by psychologists in the schools. These include psycho–educational diagnosis and individual as well as group therapy techniques, and they all include some form of direct contact with or direct observation of the student.[2] They are only conceptualized as a part of mental-health consultation when the data gathered are used to help teachers[2] (or other school personnel) devise appropriate classroom strategies designed to promote the mental health of the child(ren).

---

[2] For the purposes of clear communication, generally the term "student" is used in place of Caplan's term "client" and the term "teacher" is used in place of Caplan's term "consultee." In schools, the student is almost always the client and the teacher is the most frequent consultee. However, it should be underscored that many other school personnel are likely consultees (e.g., administrator, speech therapist, counselor, and so on).

Level II is referred to as *indirect service to the child* and, as implied by the title, it represents a more indirect approach than Level I. When using indirect-service techniques, the consultant uses someone else to gather data about the student as a basis for defining the problem. For example, the teacher might gather the data for this type of consultation. Level II is similar to Level I, but the teacher rather than the consultant carries out the intervention derived from consultation; the primary goal is to change the child's behavior and attitudes. A frequent example of this approach is a behavior-modification plan designed to reduce disruptive behavior based on data gathered by the teacher. This is often an economical and efficient use of the consultant's time, because time spent in direct contact with the child is avoided. The reader interested in pursuing these techniques in more detail is referred to the following references: Bergan, 1977a; Meyers et al., 1979; O'Leary and O'Leary, 1972; Sulzer-Azaroff, McKinley, and Ford, 1977.

Level III is *direct service to the teacher*. Mental-health consultation conceptualizes the teacher as a central environmental factor with an important effect on the child. Because sometimes the teacher's lack of understanding or lack of confidence may interfere with effective teaching, there are occasions when the most efficient consultation strategy is to help the teacher directly. The other approaches to mental-health consultation (e.g., Level I and Level II) can also help to improve the teacher's general functioning. However, Level III (direct service to the teacher) is distinct because the primary goal is to promote change in the teacher's behavior and/or attitudes rather than the child's. Thus, Level-III consultation represents a more indirect form of service to the child, and it is consistent with a preventive orientation.

The primary methods designed to provide direct service to the teacher are derived from Caplan's consultee-centered case consultation techniques. The consultant interviews the teacher in depth concerning a school-related problem in an effort to determine whether the problem is one requiring direct service to the teacher. The reasons for using this approach include lack of knowledge, lack of skill, lack of self confidence, and lack of objectivity on the part of the teacher. Some of the intervention techniques that can be used at this level of functioning can include didactic information giving, theme interference reduction, direct confrontation, or emotional support; these techniques are considered in some detail later in this chapter. Although this approach derives initially from Caplan, it becomes apparent later in this chapter that some of the recommended techniques are inconsistent with Caplan's viewpoint.

Level IV is *service to the organization*. This approach is the most indirect form of service to the child. Anyone who has attempted to intervene in schools has experienced organizational factors that interfere with the effectiveness or even the implementation of various interventions. Frequently, the consultant's primary task must be to modify the organizational structure or climate of the school. Although it is the most indirect way of affecting the child's behavior, there are some situations for which it is the most effective consultation intervention.

For example, the author once consulted to a school in which two children died within a 1-month period. Although the staff and students throughout the school were upset and distracted by these events, cultural taboos interfered with discussion of the problem. In this atmosphere, the consultant's recommendations about specific students were to no avail because teachers were unable to focus on such specific intervention strategies. It was only after the consultant provided organizational consultation to help the school cope with bereavement that specific consultation cases could be dealt with effectively.

In addition to helping a school organization cope with specific crises such as the one just described, service to the organization often requires assessment and remediation of more generalized communication barriers. The result should be a school organization that is more successful in meeting its goals. To some extent, this approach overlaps with two categories of mental-health consultation mentioned by Caplan (program-centered and consultee-centered administrative consultation). The interested reader is referred to several sources for a detailed consideration of the techniques that may be associated with this category of consultation: Bennis, 1969; Huse, 1975; Meyers et al., 1979; Schein, 1969; Schmuck and Miles, 1971; Schmuck, Runkel, Arends, & Arends, 1977).

A Flow Chart for Implementing the Model

Mental-health consultation is a dynamic process that involves a series of stages. At the beginning, the consultant must negotiate a contract with the organization that will determine, in part, which of the four levels of consultation the consultant is sanctioned to provide. Even though this model includes four levels of consultation that should all be offered under ideal circumstances, there are many schools that will not sanction consultation at all four levels. Many school districts will not readily accept the more indirect approaches to service. For example, service to the organization (Level IV) is frequently not a sanctioned part of the school psychologist's role, whereas most districts will willingly approve direct service to the child (Level I).

In every consultation case, it is important to decide which of the four levels of consultation will be used (i.e., will the consultant use direct service to the child—Level I; indirect service to the child—Level II; direct service to the teacher—Level III, or service to the organization—Level IV—in response to a particular referral?). The preventive goal of influencing the largest possible number of children suggests that the consultant should use the most indirect approaches that promise to be effective.

Because organizational factors can interfere with any consultation intervention, service to the organization (Level IV) should be the consultant's first choice when there are system-level problems affecting the referral. If organizational

142

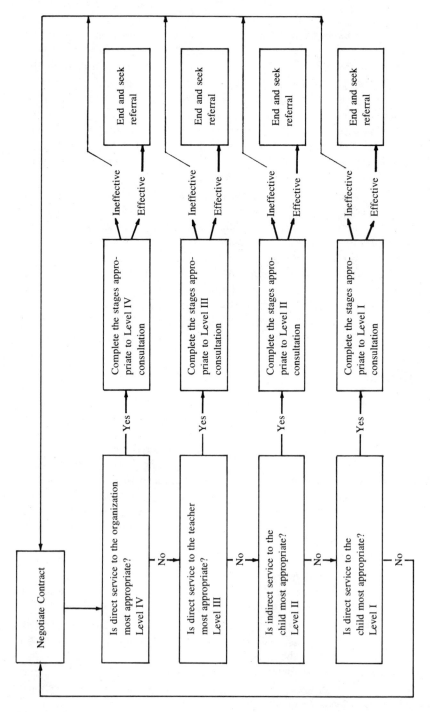

FIG. 5.1. A flow chart of the stages of consultation.[3]

factors are ruled out, then the preventive model suggests that teacher-related difficulties be considered, and direct service to the teacher (Level III) would be the consultant's next choice. If teacher-related problems can be ruled out, the most indirect intervention would be indirect service to the child (Level II). The teacher would implement intervention procedures that do not require that the consultant spend time in direct contact with the student. In those cases in which indirect service to the child cannot provide meaningful help, the consultant would use direct service to the child (Level I). Although this can be a time-consuming approach to the delivery of services to children, there are some problem situations in which the consultant needs to observe the child directly with informal observation techniques and/or formal diagnostic techniques in order to develop effective intervention procedures. The flow chart depicted in Fig. 5.1 demonstrates the integrated view of mental-health consultation that incorporates the previously discussed decision rules about the level of service.

This approach to indirect service receives some support from research and theory regarding planned change in social systems. Based on this orientation, Alpert (1977) has developed three guidelines for consultation that are consistent with the model presented in the flow chart: (1) change efforts should focus on those highest on the organizational chart who are *connected with the interaction* that is the target of change; (2) change efforts should focus on several related interactions in order to be effective in changing one interaction; (3) change efforts should emphasize the person *in the interaction* who is highest on the organizational chart.

Two points should be emphasized regarding the flow chart:

1. After negotiating a contract with a local school administration, the consultant might not receive sanction to work at some of the higher levels depicted in the chart (e.g., Level III or Level IV). In these instances, the consultant would begin by responding to referrals at the highest level sanctioned by the administration that is appropriate to the particular consultation problem. The important factor to bear in mind is that the consultant (or the consultee) always has an option to renegotiate the contract in order to gain sanction to function at higher levels. This process is demonstrated later in this section with an example. Frequently, this renegotiation can be most successful with a consultant who is valued by the school and who is willing to discuss the failure to solve a consultation problem (noted as "ineffective" on the flow chart) with the sanctioned techniques. Under these circumstances, the consultant can argue persuasively that other consultation approaches may be necessary.

2. Even though this model stresses the most indirect consultation approaches (as indicated in the flow chart), this does not preclude working at the lower levels on the chart. Even in those instances in which the consultant begins working at

---

[3]This flow chart is reproduced in its entirety from Meyers, Parsons, and Martin, 1979.

Level IV (service to the organization), after the organizational problem is solved there may still be an individual child who presents difficulties in the classroom. Under these circumstances, the consultant might use consultation techniques that are focused more specifically on the child's individual problem. For example, the consultant might attempt to resolve the child's difficulties by using Level-II techniques (indirect service to the child). The process of consultation can keep changing in this way, as the consultant may move from a high level to a lower level on the flow chart for related consultation cases.

One additional factor to clarify regarding the flow chart is that the appropriate stages must be completed regardless of the level at which the consultant chooses to intervene. These stages include negotiating an agreement with the teacher regarding the services to be provided, identifying the problem, defining the problem in detail, developing an intervention plan that is implemented by the teacher or other consultee, assessing the impact of the intervention, and concluding the relationship. Although these stages are conceptualized discretely, they do not always occur independently in practice and they do not always occur in the same order. Practicing consultants may work at more than one stage simultaneously and the process may move back and forth through the stages in a cyclical process. Nevertheless, it is useful to distinguish the stages in consultation; the interested reader is referred to other sources for more detailed treatment of this topic: Bergan, 1977a; Caplan, 1970; Meyers et al., 1979.

Issues Relevant to the Model

A key characteristic of this model is that it presents an integrated view of consultation techniques. This can be contrasted with the view of many writers who have conceptualized several separate models of consultation (Dworkin & Dworkin, 1975; Gallessich, 1974; Gibbins, 1978; Reschly, 1976; Schmuck & Schmuck, 1974). Reschly (1976), for example, presents the behavioral model, the mental-health model, and the organization-development model of consultation as three distinct models.

There has been some research comparing the relative effectiveness of different models. For example, one study found that teachers prefer nondirective approaches that use empathy, reflection, and clarification, rather than a behavioral model of consultation (Miller, 1974). Conflicting results were reported by an investigation that found behavioral change resulting from a behavioral model but not from a process model of consultation (Jason & Ferone, 1978). Research that attempts such gross comparisons may do an injustice to a helping process that is far more complex in practice. Research would be more productive if it identified specific consultation techniques and determined their effects under a variety of conditions. This sort of criticism has already been made of past research in psychotherapy, which has sought to compare general models (Bergin & Strupp,

1972). Hopefully, researchers investigating consultation will not continue to make the same mistakes that have been made previously by psychotherapy researchers. Consultation researchers should use carefully controlled investigations, with narrow and explicitly defined consultation techniques, that are assessed intensively with a variety of measurement techniques.

A particularly controversial issue is that direct service to the child is included within this model of consultation. Many writers have explicitly excluded techniques involving direct contact with the child from their definitions of consultation (e.g., Alpert, 1977; Gallessich, 1973; Reschly, 1976). These writers do not consider psycho-educational diagnosis or counseling as a part of consultation. One aspect of the argument has been that by including too many activities under the rubric of consultation the term loses meaning. Another aspect is that consultants do not have time for such direct contact with students, and that, by being restricted to indirect approaches, consultants may make more effective use of their time. Although these criticisms have some merit and should be considered carefully, they seem to ignore some important realities in the schools. The following issues need to be considered:

1. There may be some children who cannot be helped effectively without direct observation by the consultant.

2. Counseling and particularly psycho-educational assessment will continue to be part of the psychologist's role in the schools for the foreseeable future. Although one might argue the merits of this notion, this will not change the fact. Psychologists must take maximum advantage of this part of their role. It is inexcusable for a psychologist to gather information about a child (whether through testing or through counseling) and not use this information to help the child in his or her school environment.

3. If these direct-service activities are considered as part of the consultation role, then school psychologists will be in a much more realistic position to argue persuasively for a reduction in the amount of time spent on activities such as testing.

Given that the consultant's goal is to influence the largest numbers of students possible through indirect techniques, Level III and Level IV are potentially the most powerful consultation techniques. Yet, these are the two approaches to consultation that are least likely to be accepted parts of the psychologist's role. In one investigation, it was found that both teachers and psychologists were highly favorable to Level-II consultation activities (Szmuk, Docherty, & Ringness, 1979). This same study found much less support for Level-III or Level-IV consultation. This finding was particularly true for teachers and it was concluded that teachers were more comfortable conceptualizing the problem as child focused rather than considering their role in maintaining the problem. In a recent survey carried out by Division 16 (the school psychology division) of the American Psychological Association, it was found that client-centered consultation (e.g., Levels I and II) was the most prevalent approach. Specifically, 62% of the school psychologists responding to this survey indicated that they spend much or very much of their time in this form of consultation (Martin & Meyers, 1978). Although consultee-centered consultation (e.g., Level III) was not as prevalent, a surprisingly large number of respondents indicated that they use this approach much or very much of the time (i.e., 49% of the respondents). According to this sample of school psychologists, organizational consultation (e.g., Level-IV consultation) is practiced much or very much of the time by the smallest percentage of respondents (i.e., 24%). The results from these two studies indicate that although Level-II consultation (indirect service to the child) is a generally accepted part of the school psychologist's role, Level III (direct service to the teacher) and Level IV (service to the organization) will be more difficult to implement in practice. These two approaches are questioned by many school psychologists and particularly by teachers. Even though some school psychologists currently carry out these approaches to consultation, there is a need for more psychologists to implement these techniques as a regular and frequent component of their role.

Case Demonstration of the Flow Chart

An earlier section of this chapter referred briefly to a school that suffered the death of two students within a 1-month period. This example provides a good illustration of how the consultation model presented here might be implemented in practice. The case has been described previously (Meyers & Pitt, 1976). Here, the case is described with a particular effort to show how the consultant moves from one level of consultation to another.

On the occasion in question, the author served as a school psychologist consulting to a parochial school containing grades kindergarten through eight. This school was located in a small-town parish located near a large city. The school included 14 classroom teachers, three supplementary teachers, and 422 students, in addition to the psychologist who worked there 1 day per week. Many students had one or more siblings in the school and the parish had a stable population whose families had attended the same church for years. The members of this parish knew each other well.

The initial consultation contract had been negotiated informally with the school principal. Both Level I (direct service to the child) and Level II (indirect service to the child) were sanctioned consultation procedures, and it was understood that the consultant's primary activity would include indirect service to the child rather than testing. Although the consultant's eventual goal was to convince the administrator to sanction Level-III and Level-IV consultation, the initial contract was satisfactory.

During one school vacation, a sixth-grade boy died a tragic, accidental death. The school sent condolences to the family, but made no official response within the school. As a result, teachers were uncertain how to handle the situation, and discussion with students was frequently avoided at this time. Within the month, a seventh-grade boy was injured fatally in a car accident.

In a period immediately following the deaths, several new problem behaviors were observed:

1. There was an increase in discipline problems in school and on the playground. There was an increase in the number of children sent to the principal or referred to the consultant as discipline problems, and it was reported that acting out, lying, and other disruptive behavior had increased. Further, several efforts to consult with teachers about reducing their discipline problems (i.e., Level-II consultation) were unsuccessful, and the problems just mounted.

2. There was a series of bomb scares at the school with at least some connection to the deaths. The boy responsible for the last bomb scare was caught and he had been a friend of one of the deceased children. Projective testing and analysis of dream material revealed a clear emphasis on fantasies about the friend's death. Following testing, the consultant recommended counseling for the boy and a sensitive, supportive approach by the teacher (Level-I consultation). These recommendations were rejected initially. The principal indicated that the child should be expelled from school, and the teacher reported that he could not be supportive and reinforce such negative behavior.

3. There was an increase in superstitious rumors and fantasies among the students. When the kindergarten teacher reported to the consultant that her students had ''seen'' parts of the boys' bodies in the dark church basement, the consultant set up a meeting with the principal.

In this meeting, the consultant pointed out the effects the deaths were having on the children's behavior. The consultant pointed out, further, that as a result of this system-wide problem, his efforts at Level-II consultation had been unsuccessful. In other words, it was suggested that the crisis over the deaths interfered with the consultant's ability to help the teachers with classroom management. In effect, the consultant ''renegotiated'' the consultation contract so that Level-IV consultation (service to the organization) could be used to help the school deal more effectively with the bereavement process.

It was agreed that a teacher workshop on this topic would be the most effective way to help the school cope with this crisis (Level-IV consultation). Two goals were set for the workshop: (1) to help the teachers understand that the increase in disturbing behaviors might be part of the bereavement process; and (2) to help the teachers encourage students to express their feelings about death and related issues. The consultant and principal met jointly with three small groups of teachers for 1-hour sessions that were divided into four segments:

1. The general importance of allowing children to express their feelings was presented.

2. Three stages of mourning derived from Bowlby (1963) were presented and a connection was made between these stages and the behaviors that had been observed.

3. The teachers were encouraged to express their feelings about the deaths during these sessions. It was hoped that this would make some of the teachers more free to help their students discuss these feelings.

4. Finally, it was recommended that teachers provide the opportunity for students to express their feelings about the deaths.

Following this Level-IV consultation, the system was more effective in dealing with the process of bereavement. Several teachers indicated their positive experiences discussing feelings about death with their classes and there was a decrease in discipline problems.

In addition to the reduction in discipline problems, this example shows how an organizational problem (the crisis regarding bereavement) interfered with effective consultation using Level I (the bomb-scare student) and Level II (classroom management regarding discipline problems). Even though there was a reduction in discipline problems following the bereavement workshop, some teachers did continue to refer disruptive children to the consultant. In contrast with prior unsuccessful efforts to help teachers with classroom management, the consultant's efforts now met with frequent success. Thus, after the Level-IV intervention (service to the organization), Level-II efforts for classroom management were successful once again. Similarly, the Level-I (direct service to the child) consultation regarding the youngster who had made the bomb scares was now successful. Prior to the organizational consultation regarding bereavement (Level IV), the consultant was not able to convince the principal to keep this child in school and he was unsuccessful in convincing the teacher to treat the youngster in a sensitive and supportive manner. Very soon after the bereavement workshop, the principal volunteered her revised opinion that the youngster should be maintained in the school. Similarly, consultation with the teacher following the workshop resulted in his agreement that perhaps he could provide the needed support and positive relationship for this youngster. Although this Level-I consultation did not reach a successful conclusion during the system-wide crisis, the successful Level-IV consultation seemed to facilitate more effective work at Level I.

Another significant change began to occur after the organizational consultation. Teachers began to bring their own professional problems to the consultant rather than being limited to discussions of specific cases (e.g., Level-III consultation). As a result, the consultant met with the principal, indicating this general trend without revealing any teacher names. At this point, the principal was able to see the potential value of the consultant's responding to these teacher needs, and she willingly sanctioned Level-III consultation (direct service to the teacher). In one subsequent example, the consultant provided direct service to one teacher (Level-III consultation) whose concerns about death were interfering with her teaching. This teacher's sister had died when she was a child and it turned out that her feelings surrounding this earlier tragedy were interfering with her ability to be helpful to her students in the face of the current tragedy. Consultation was successful in helping this teacher to feel more comfortable talking with her students about their feelings concerning the two children who had died.

To summarize, this model of consultation can be thought of as helpful for two reasons: First, it is helpful conceptually in that several approaches to consultation, which might otherwise be thought of as independent, are integrated within one framework. Second, it is helpful because it provides practical decision rules that the consultant can use to determine the most effective technique. As noted throughout this section, the approaches vary on a continuum of indirectness and it is suggested that the consultant use the most indirect consultation technique that is judged to be appropriate.

It has been indicated previously that this chapter seeks to synthesize the theoretical/research issues in mental-health consultation while emphasizing the practical implications. It is impossible to cover thoroughly all of the consultation approaches that are integrated within this model (e.g., behavioral consultation at Level II, theme interference reduction at Level III, and organizational consultation at Level IV). Moreover, the approach that has been associated most clearly with mental-health consultation has been Level III—direct service to the teacher. Because many of the key theoretical issues regarding mental-health consultation can be presented in a discussion of Level-III consultation, the next section discusses in detail direct service to the teacher.

DIRECT SERVICE TO THE TEACHER

As indicated previously, direct service to the teacher derives primarily from Gerald Caplan's work on consultee-centered consultation. This has been selected as the level of consultation to be illustrated in some detail in this chapter because it is the approach most frequently associated with mental-health consultation, and because most of the important theoretical issues can be considered through a discussion of direct service to the teacher. This does not suggest that the other levels of consultation are less important; the interested reader has been referred to several good sources for additional detail on the consultation techniques associated with Levels I, II, and IV.

Direct service to the teacher can be conceptualized in terms of the four basic reasons teachers seek mental-health consultation, and these derive from Caplan's (1970) discussion of consultee-centered case consultation. These reasons include lack of understanding, lack of skill, lack of confidence, and lack of objectivity on the part of the teacher. Each of these reasons is defined briefly in the following sections along with a consideration of relevant consultant techniques.

Lack of Understanding

Frequently, a teacher's approach to a child is inadequate because a poor knowledge base exists. When this occurs, the consultant's job is to convey the knowledge necessary to help the teacher respond to the case with his or her typical good judgment. For example, the consultant may be called on to provide information about abnormal psychology, child development, and interpersonal behavior. This information would be communicated to the teacher in a didactic manner, and the result should be that the teacher interprets the students' behaviors more accurately in terms of the level of development or relevant environmental factors. Subsequent observations should reveal a teacher who has the freedom to try a variety of options that were not available previously.

An example occurred when the author served as a consultant to a special-education school for brain-injured children. The consultee was a competent teacher who had no training or experience working with emotionally disturbed children. One child in her class displayed a variety of autistic-like symptoms and the diagnosis included emotional disturbance. The teacher felt completely unprepared to teach this youngster, and as a result she was unable to generate a variety of strategies as she typically did. The consultant provided didactic information about autistic children, arranged to have the teacher observe such a program, and participated in several brainstorming sessions with the teacher. Once the teacher developed a conceptual understanding of this child, she was able to generate a number of productive strategies, which were implemented.

Lack of Skill

Even when the teacher understands the case, there are frequent occasions when the teacher does not possess the skill needed to implement the relevant teaching strategies. Under these circumstances, the consultant's expertise regarding observation of the classroom environment, student–teacher interaction, and student behavior can be used to develop the teacher's skills. Not only can such observation skills be trained, but the teacher can also be trained to develop classroom interventions based on these observations. To accomplish these goals, the consultant and teacher can use observation techniques derived from behavior modification (e.g., O'Leary & O'Leary, 1972), group processes (e.g., Schmuck & Schmuck, 1971, 1974), or classroom interaction systems (e.g., Flanders, 1970; Good & Brophy, 1970; Kounin, 1970; and Spaulding, 1967).

For example, a teacher who is not skilled in classroom discipline could be taught classroom management skills with Kounin's system. Initially, the consultant might observe the classroom using this system, and follow the observations with a session in which feedback is provided to the teacher. The goal would be to improve the teacher's management skills based on this system. An alternative approach could be to train the teacher to use the observation technique so that the consultant need not do all of the classroom observation.

Lack of Confidence

Teaching is a challenging responsibility. Many teachers must cope with a wide range of academic skills as well as a wide range of behaviors. Consider, for example, the second-grade class that contains children who have not mastered reading-readiness materials as well as those who are reading third-grade material in a competent manner. This classroom might also contain children who display a variety of disruptive behaviors. At the same time, teachers are often pressured by parents, administrators, teacher unions, and mass media, and they are now supposed to be responsible for emotional and interpersonal development in addition to academics. Although teachers rarely receive credit for success, the public is quick to blame teachers for any problems that appear. These challenges can threaten the self esteem of any teacher, and this is particularly true for new teachers who have not yet developed their own teaching styles.

One striking example of this type of problem was encountered in a teacher who was in her first year of teaching at a difficult inner-city elementary school. When the consultant suggested that he would try to help with any problem the teacher would like to consider, the teacher replied tearfully, "Sometimes I just don't think I teach too well." When other issues such as lack of skill, lack of knowledge, or lack of objectivity are not involved, the teacher with this sort of problem may simply need ego support. In these circumstances, the consultant's primary intervention is to listen carefully to the teacher and support the teacher's constructive ideas.

Lack of Objectivity

Caplan has devoted a great deal of attention to the notion that affective involvement with a particular case can interfere with effectiveness. Typically, this problem occurs when the teacher fails to maintain proper professional distance, and this results in clouded professional judgment on the part of the teacher. Five different reasons for lack of objectivity have been discussed (Caplan, 1970). These include direct personal involvement, simple identification, transference, theme interference, and characterological distortion. These reasons can be conceptualized on a continuum representing the degree to which the teacher loses professional distance and distorts reality.

Direct personal involvement occurs when the relationship between the teacher (consultee) and student becomes a personal relationship. When this happens, the teacher expresses personal needs in the work setting. An example could be a teacher who falls in love with a student.

Simple identification is the situation in which the teacher identifies with the student or with someone who has a close relationship to the student (e.g., mother, sibling, and so on). There is no serious distortion of reality because there is an obvious similarity that stimulates the identification. However, the identification does disturb the teacher's judgment, resulting in highly positive or negative descriptions of various persons involved in the case.

Transference is a form of identification in which there is not the obvious similarity to explain the identification, and there is a more serious distortion of reality by the teacher. The teacher actually conceptualizes problems surrounding the child's life as if they fit some aspect of his or her own life. The teacher thus transfers attitudes and feelings that derive from the past onto the present work situation.

Theme interference is described by Caplan as a minor transference reaction that occurs when an unresolved personal problem is expressed indirectly on the job. The result is often temporary ineffectiveness and emotional instability. Theme interference occurs in teachers who are characteristically effective, but who are temporarily confused or upset about something occurring in the professional situation. An additional characteristic is a rigid pattern of thinking, which Caplan suggests can be represented syllogistically as an ''inevitable link'' between two thoughts. Basically, the theme takes the form that if a particular situation occurs, then a particular outcome is rigidly and inevitably expected to occur.

Characterological distortions occur when the teacher's perception of reality is seriously disturbed and this interferes with teaching. In these instances, the teacher's personal feelings and problems pervade the work setting. These are problems that Caplan feels should be handled by supervisory staff because consultation cannot be effective.

Caplan devotes a great deal of attention to these categories of lack of objectivity and particularly to theme interference and the related intervention, which he labels theme-interference reduction. Because space does not allow a more detailed presentation of these ideas in this chapter, the reader is referred to other sources—e.g., Caplan, 1970; Meyers et al., 1979.

Caplan's work with lack of objectivity has been important for at least two reasons: First, it has clearly helped to broaden the conception of what mental-health services can be offered in the schools. Second, this is one of the few instances in the literature where a mental-health consultation technique is described in sufficient detail. Caplan's discussion of theme interference and the related techniques (i.e., theme interference reduction) is an excellent example of such detailed description.

Caplan's system has been elaborated and modified in an effort to develop an approach that is more practical for the schools (Meyers et al., 1979). This system is in the process of development and is not thought of as final or comprehensive. However, it strives to be practical by defining the reasons for mental-health consultation in objective terms that provide a clear link to direct-intervention strategies. The definitions attempt to be behavioral and stress significant environmental factors that may relate to the problem. Rather than conceptualize lack of objectivity solely in terms of the degree to which the teacher identifies with the student (or some related person), this system considers the different types of frequently occurring conflicts that contribute to the teacher's lack of objectivity. In this framework, Caplan's notion of identification is just one of the conflict areas that is considered. This revised system should provide a more practical approach to the development of consultation interventions.

Authority conflicts are a frequent source of lack of objectivity in teachers. The basic conflict is between the need to maintain control and the need to be perceived by students as a friend. Even though teachers want to establish control in the classroom, many do not want to teach in an authoritarian or undemocratic manner. This can be a particular problem for new teachers before they have established their own teaching styles. This has probably taken on increased meaning in recent years, because of the emphasis in teacher-training programs on open-classroom approaches. It can result in a debilitating effect on teachers' ability to respond effectively to rebellious or acting-out youngsters.

Dependency is a second area of teacher conflict. Some teachers frequently demonstrate a rigid approach in the classroom by demanding excessively dependent and submissive behavior from students. A further indication of this conflict can be that the teacher responds to the consultant in a dependent manner at the same time that the teacher expects this same behavior from students. Another characteristic of teachers with this conflict can be the expectation that the consultant will provide a definitive and explicit answer to the problem. Dependent teachers may be resistant to the notion that they can help develop an effective intervention strategy with the consultant.

Anger and hostility comprise the third area of teacher conflict. Any teacher will experience, at some point, a student, parent, administrator, or other staff member who generates feelings of anger or hostility. However, these feelings conflict with the concept of a good teacher held by many educators. A teacher might respond to this conflict at either end of the continuum. On the one hand, the teacher might express extreme anger, which appears unreasonable, whereas on the other hand, the teacher may refuse to acknowledge any angry/hostile feelings.

Identification is the last area of teacher conflict that has been included in this system. This conflict derives from Caplan's notion that identification with the student or a related person can interfere with the teacher's judgment and the consultant may find it useful to differentiate between direct personal involvement, simple identification, transference, and theme interference. As Caplan suggests, the category of characterological distortions is not appropriate for mental-health consultation.

Direct and Indirect Interventions

Caplan believes that indirect-confrontation techniques should be used during consultation. The model presented in this chapter contends that direct-confrontation techniques should also be used by mental-health consultants. First, let us consider Caplan's approach to indirect interventions. Although this is a general characteristic of his system, it can be demonstrated most clearly in relation to lack of objectivity where Caplan describes a number of consultation techniques that can be useful and should be considered by the consultant. The goal of these techniques is to increase the professional distance and objectivity of the teacher.

One indirect approach is to act as a role model by requesting information calmly and describing both positive and negative aspects of the case in an objective manner. This may help to calm the teacher who sees that the consultant understands the difficulty of the case but is not overwhelmed by it. It is indirect because the consultant models this behavior, and hopes the teacher will pick it up, but does not tell the teacher directly to respond to the case in a calm manner. A second indirect approach can be used in response to the teacher's overinvolvement in the case. The primary way to do this is for the consultant to describe a similar interpersonal problem that exists in the child who has been referred. This technique is indirect because the child's problem is used to communicate about the teacher rather than to discuss the teacher's problem directly. For example, if a teacher needs to be careful about being too authoritarian in the classroom, the consultant might tell the teacher about a student whose conflict is dependency. The consultant might suggest that this dependent student often stimulates highly authoritarian behavior on the part of teachers. The message would be that to discourage the student's dependent behavior, the teacher may have to be particularly careful to avoid acting in an authoritarian manner. In this way, the consultant suggests an action plan to the teacher without indicating directly the true reason underlying the recommendation.

Another indirect way to discuss the teacher's overinvolvement in the case is the "parable" (Caplan, 1970). In this technique, the consultant would discuss an anecdote that is similar to the teacher's present situation. This may be an event that actually occurred, or the consultant might invent a relevant anecdote. For example, the consultant might describe a similar problem experienced by another teacher. The idea is that this could decrease the teacher's affective involvement in the present problem and increase his or her objectivity while avoiding a direct discussion of the teacher's problem.

In addition to these indirect techniques, direct methods should be used by the mental-health consultant. Caplan's psychoanalytically based notion that direct confrontation will break down the consultee's defenses and the related notion that the short-term nature of the consultation relationship will not provide sufficient opportunity to rebuild the consultee's defenses can be questioned (Meyers et al., 1979). There are *no* data demonstrating that direct confrontation in consultation will invariably destroy the consultee's defenses. If defenses are not broken down by confrontation, then there is no need for time to rebuild defenses. On the contrary, the short-term relationship that characterizes mental-health consultation may often demand the sensitive use of direct rather than indirect confrontation. The typical consultation relationship is too short to ensure that the message underlying indirect techniques will be understood by the teacher. Direct approaches may increase the likelihood of the teacher's understanding the confrontation and changing his or her behavior.

Direct methods might be used to help the teacher resolve the four conflicts described earlier as contributing to lack of objectivity by the teacher (e.g., authority, dependence, hostility, and identification). When it is determined that one of these conflicts exists, the consultant can discuss this directly with the teacher in a supportive manner designed to help the teacher become more aware of and develop a clearer understanding of the effects this conflict has on his or her teaching. As a result of such direct discussion, the teacher and consultant generate alternative strategies for the teacher.

An example can clarify this procedure. A teacher who had difficulty with classroom control responded to one recommendation by saying, "The children would never let me get away with that." This suggested the possibility that the teacher had ambivalent feelings about being an authority figure that were interfering with her objectivity as well as with her classroom control. Further indication of this conflict was the teacher's apologetic manner in relation to her students. She would often explain or excuse her own actions to the students.

The consultation procedures included discussions that the consultant initiated by reporting his observations about the teacher's apparent conflict over being the classroom authority. Following the teacher's statement noted earlier, the consultant asked, "Did you hear what you just said? When I heard it, I thought it had particular meaning for you. What is your reaction?" This confrontation led to a discussion that focused directly on the teacher's conflict about being the authority figure in the classroom. This discussion was open ended in the sense that the consultant followed the teacher's lead after initiating the discussion. This approach helped the teacher to express her feelings of discomfort with her role in the classroom. Throughout the discussions (three sessions from 15 to 40 minutes in length), the consultant reflected and occasionally clarified what the teacher said about her feelings regarding authority. The teacher was also praised and supported for verbalizing these feelings. The result was that the teacher began to understand how her own conflict about authority may have interfered with her teaching effectiveness, and this was followed by clearly positive changes in this teacher's approach to the classroom (Meyers, 1975).

THE PROCESS OF MENTAL-HEALTH CONSULTATION

All consultation relationships involve an interpersonal process, and the interaction between the consultant and teacher can influence the outcome of consultation. Regardless of the level of consultation, the most carefully conceived recommendations are not likely to succeed if the consultation relationship is marked by difficulties. This is particularly true for direct service to the teacher because the consultant's primary focus is the teacher rather than the child. The interpersonal process is particularly important to help the consultant minimize the effects of *resistance*.

Any professional who has consulted in schools has experienced resistance to his or her interventions. Inertia regarding any form of change is a natural phenomenon. This is exacerbated in consultation (especially direct service to the teacher) because of the consultant's use of direct confrontation and because of the consultant's focus on the teacher's feelings. Even though the teacher may recognize the existence of a problem initially, frequently, the teacher will respond defensively and deny any responsibility for the situation. The teacher is likely to consider any external factor as causing the problem rather than place blame on himself/herself; this can be referred to as *externalization*. A primary goal of mental-health consultation is to help the teacher recognize and accept a responsibility for the problem. If the teacher recognizes his or her contribution, then change strategies will be available over which the teacher has maximum control. In effect, the goal is to help the teacher develop a feeling of ownership for his or her part in the problem that will result in meaningful interventions. However, blaming the teacher is not the consultant's intention.

Another factor related to this concept is that, frequently, the intense nature of the interaction between consultant and teacher creates anxiety on the part of the consultant as well as of the teacher, and as a result there are occasions when the consultant may resist helping. It is important that the consultant maintain an awareness of this possibility in order to be maximally facilitative. Consequently, mental-health consultants must consider both *consultant resistance* and *teacher resistance;* then, the process of mental-health consultation can help to minimize the effects of this resistance.

A variety of approaches exist for conceptualizing the consultation process; some of these include behavior modification, transaction analysis, social psychology, and outgrowths of Rogerian counseling. (For more detail, see Meyers et al., 1979.) There has been little research about the consultation process. This section considers the three approaches that have been researched most often (e.g., the collaborative model, derivatives of Rogerian Counseling, and the behavioral model). There is no intent to imply that these are the best approaches to the consultation process. However, they are presented here because there is a developing data base relevant to each approach. There is clearly a need for more research in this area.

The Collaborative Model of Process

One factor that is frequently considered an important part of the consultation process is the notion that consultation is a collaborative effort between two professionals (e.g., Caplan, 1970; Curtis & Anderson, 1976; Meyers, 1973). This concept derives directly from Caplan who has stated that to be effective, a consultant must conceptualize the relationship as an interchange between colleagues. This can occur if the consultant views the teacher as the person with expertise in teaching, whereas the consultant has expertise regarding mental health. According to this assumption, the goal should be for the consultant and teacher to share their expertise in a collaborative manner so that the teacher's students will benefit.

When the consultant uses this approach, (s)he does not tell the teacher what to do. Rather than present detailed recommendations to be implemented as stated, the consultant should expect the teacher to be actively involved in developing or modifying the strategy, or in developing an entirely different plan. This approach suggests that the consultant communicate clearly that the teacher has the freedom to accept or reject the consultant's recommendations.

This principle is an important part of theory about mental-health consultation and there have been a few beginning efforts at relevant research. The research to date has compared the collaborative model to various expert models for interaction between the consultant and teacher.

Curtis and Zins (1978) developed 10 video tapes simulating consultation interactions and the consultants were rated for the degree to which they used Curtis' collaborative model. They had groups of teachers and consultants observe these video tapes independent of the assessments of consultant style. The judges rated the collaborative consultants as most effective.

Ritter (1978) conducted an investigation that was not really designed to assess the consultation process, but that does relate to the present question. This longitudinal study of the impact of a collaborative model of consultation found that the consultation program was followed by a decreasing pattern of referrals over a 7-year period. Even though this study did not assess the consultants' use of collaborative style directly, the data at least suggest that a collaborative style can be effective.

One final study regarding the collaborative model was conducted by Wenger (1979) who provided consultation using "expert" and "collaborative" models of consultation. In each model, the consultant used skills related to reflection, clarification, and empathy, and invited the teacher's input. The consultant also encouraged the teachers to express their perceptions and hypotheses in both models. However, in the collaborative model, the consultant and teacher developed intervention strategies together, whereas in the expert model, the consultant developed recommendations on his own. It was found that the teachers were significantly more satisfied with the collaborative model than with the expert model. There was no overall difference in the extent to which teachers receiving each model implemented the recommendations. However, it was found that for teachers with limited experience, there was more follow-through on recommendations with collaborative consultants.

Freidman (1978) conducted an investigation that relates to this model. Three consultants were instructed to use a model similar to Curtis and Anderson's (1976) collaborative approach. Then, consultant behavior was assessed by rating consultation tapes with an adaptation of the Flanders Interaction Analysis Categories (Flanders, 1970) in order to determine the indirectness of the consultant's style. Consultants rated as indirect on this scale use techniques such as accepting feelings, praising, accepting student ideas, and asking questions, and these are similar to the collaborative model. Freidman found that two of the consultants were considerably more indirect as assessed by this scale, and these were the two consultants whose consultation relationships resulted in productive change in teacher behavior.

Taken as a whole, the data from these studies suggest that consultation will be more effective if the consultant and consultee interact in a collaborative manner. However, there are not enough data to make firm conclusions. This is a productive research area that should be pursued in the future.

Derivatives of Rogerian Counseling

Carl Rogers' ideas have had a widespread impact on applied psychology, and his proposition that several core conditions are necessary for successful psychotherapy has particular relevance for mental-health consultation. These conditions, which were defined initially by Rogers (1957), have been elaborated by others (e.g., Carkhuff, 1969a, 1969b; Egan, 1975; Gazda, Asbury, Balzer, Childers, Desselle & Walters, 1973). Operational definitions have been developed for three conditions that appear relevant to consultation (i.e., genuineness, nonpossessive warmth, and accurate empathy), and there has been ample demonstration that these are skills that can be trained (e.g., Carkhuff, 1969a; Egan, 1975; Gazda, Asbury, Balzer, Childers, Desselle, & Walters, 1973).

Genuineness occurs in a consultation relationship if the consultant is free to be himself/herself. The genuine consultant acts in an integrated, authentic fashion, in which verbal and nonverbal cues both communicate the same feelings. This does not imply that the consultant always communicates his or her feelings to the teacher, as there will be occasions when the consultant chooses freely not to express feelings during consultation. The key is that this decision should be made in light of the consultant's awareness of his or her feelings. The consultant who is genuine strives to remain nondefensive and does not retreat into a professional façade.

Nonpossessive warmth occurs when the consultant accepts the teacher without imposing conditions on the teacher for this acceptance. For example, the consultant would value the teacher as a person without evaluating him/her or imposing conditions on behavior. This does not imply unconditional approval of any teacher behavior. Instead, it suggests that regardless of the consultant's reactions to the teacher's behavior (whether positive or negative), there is always a basic sense of respect and acceptance for the teacher as a person.

Accurate empathy occurs when the consultant is able to understand the world through the teacher's eyes. The consultant experiences empathy when (s)he knows and understands the teacher's feelings and the meaning of his or her experience. A key element to this concept is that the consultant must be able to communicate this understanding to the teacher.

There has been very little research about the impact of these process variables in consultation. However, the work that has been completed is encouraging. A recent survey on consultation practice asked school psychologists to rank order several factors that are commonly thought to influence successful consultation (Martin & Meyers, 1978). Three factors clearly stood out from the others in being judged as most important. Two of these were factors related directly to Rogers' conditions. One was listening to and attempting to understand the problem from the point of view of the consultee. This relates to Rogers' notion of accurate empathy. The second was providing a warm and accepting relationship. This relates to Rogers' concept of nonpossessive warmth. This survey suggests that there is some agreement, at least among school psychologists, that two principles derived from Rogers facilitate successful consultation.

There have been a few recent efforts to examine the relationship between variables similar to the concept of empathy and consultation outcome. Schowengerdt, Fine, and Poggio (1976) measured teachers' perceptions of the consultant's facilitative characteristics (i.e., genuineness, empathy, and nonpossessive warmth) using an adaptation of the Barrett-Lennard Relationship Inventory (Barrett-Lennard, 1962). He found that the consultant's facilitativeness as measured by this scale had a highly significant positive relationship to teacher satisfaction. Wilcox (1977) studied group consultation and found that a variable measuring the understanding and empathy of the consultant had a significant relationship to consultation outcome. Meyers (1978b) also reported a relation between consultant empathy and the outcome of consultation. From transcripts of the consultation sessions of three consultation relationships, Meyers assessed empathy with Ivey's (1971) accurate-reflection-of-feelings scale and teacher resistance with a scale developed for the investigation. It was found that in the two successful (success measured by behavioral assessment of the students in the classroom) consultation relationships, accurate reflection of feelings varied as a function of resistance. In these cases, accurate reflection of feelings increased when teacher resistance increased. The one unsuccessful consultant had the lowest overall accurate-reflection-of-feelings score, and in this case accurate reflection of feelings did not vary as a function of teacher resistance. These data suggested that the relation between empathy and consultation outcome may be mediated by teacher resistance. When teacher resistance increases, the successful consultant may increase his or her use of empathy.

It should be evident that the data base related to these Rogerian variables is limited and conclusions would be premature, to say the least. However, the data can be used to develop hypotheses for future research regarding the relation between variables such as empathy and nonpossessive warmth on the outcome of consultation. This is another area that needs a great deal more research.

Behavioral Model of Process

John Bergan and his associates (Bergan, 1977a; Bergan & Tombari, 1975) have developed an approach to analyzing the consultation interaction—the Consultation Analysis Record. This scale has been developed in a manner consistent with Bergan's behavioral orientation; however, it can be applied in analyzing any consultation interaction even when a behavioral model is not used. Although behavioral consultation is not generally associated with mental-health consultation, this approach is considered here because the Consultation Analysis Record can be used to assess the process of any consultation relationship and because this has resulted in some of the best research on the consultation process to date.

The verbal elicitor is one of the process skills described by Bergan (1977a) as facilitating consultation. A verbal elicitor is a request for information and/or action from a consultee that can take the form of questions, commands, or exhortations. Evidence is emerging that suggests that elicitors can exert a controlling influence on what consultees say or do (Bergan, 1977b). A recent follow-up to this work provided evidence that: (1) a behavioral approach to the consultation process was superior to a medical-model orientation; and that (2) a task-analysis report that specifies the problem and the remediation facilitated effective consultation (Bergan, Byrnes, & Kratochwill, in press).

In one major investigation using this instrument, 11 psychologists consulting on 806 referrals were studied (Bergan & Tombari, 1976). They used the Consultation Analysis Record previously referred to to assess the consultants' interview skills with behaviors such as: (1) content focus; (2) verbal process; and (3) message control (see Bergan, 1977a; Bergan & Tomari, 1976, for more details). They found significant correlations, which ranged between .34 and .45, between the indices of consultant effectiveness and problem identification. Further, problem identification was the most important factor contributing to problem solution, as it contributed a correlation of .765 to plan implementation; 97% of the consultants who reached the plan-implementation stage achieved successful problem solution. Thus, although overall only 30% of the consultants achieved problem solution, almost every consultant who achieved problem identification was successful in solving the problem. Because it is at this early stage (i.e., problem identification) that the interview skills previously noted were found to be important (i.e., $r = .765$), this study provides support for the importance of interview skills in the process of consultation.

Transfer of Effects

As noted earlier in this chapter, a key part of the rationale for mental-health consultation is its potential for preventing future problems. This will occur only if the effects of the consultation intervention transfer to other situations. The consultant cannot be limited to helping the teacher resolve a crisis situation. In addition, the consultee must learn techniques that are used repeatedly in similar situations during the future. One of the frequent arguments supporting consultation has been that in addition to affecting one child in the present, the teacher will be more effective with many similar children in the future. Indeed, it might be argued that the transfer of effects to other situations is the most important key to successful consultation.

As with other important areas of consultation research, there has not been much completed to date. However, the few data that have been gathered present an interesting picture. Although some data have found that very specific prompting procedures are necessary to facilitate generalization, others have found generalization of effects without such specific prompting.

Generalization has recently received increased attention in the behavior-modification literature, and this is reflected in two review articles (Drabman, Hammer, & Rosenbaum, 1979; Stokes & Baer, 1977). Although there is a clear need for more research, both papers present useful schemes for conceptualizing categories of generalization as well as techniques that can be used to promote generalization. For example, it can be important to distinguish between the generalizations that can occur across time, across subjects, across behaviors, and across settings.

Stokes and Baer (1977) found that one of the most frequently used generalization procedures has been to "train and hope." They concluded that the present technology for generalization is seriously limited, and they were only able to find seven specific tactics that may be considered. Their general conclusion is that generalization should not be expected to occur without using specific procedures designed to promote such transfer effects. Consistent with this view, Bergan (1977b) has reported some initial data indicating that the generalization of the behavioral effects of recommendations will not occur without specific prompting procedures by the consultant.

There are some data that appear to conflict with these findings about the use of specific prompting procedures. Schmuck (1968) reported that, after consultation, teachers accept greater individual differences and a wider variety of student behaviors. There was no procedure reported to program specifically for this generalized effect. Similarly, Gutkin, Singer, and Brown (1980) found a generalized effect after mental-health consultation as the teacher–consultees described acting out and academic problems as less severe than a control group. Nothing was programmed systematically to stimulate this generalized effect. These findings were based solely on self-report data, which are of questionable value when they are not supplemented by observational data. However, three studies with different forms of observational data have found similar results.

One study (Ritter, 1978) examined the longitudinal effects of a consultation program and found that after 7 years, there was a significant reduction in referrals. Ritter (1978) argues that this reflected a transfer of effects. As the teachers learned more about working with problem children through the consultation program, they gradually developed less of a need to make psychological referrals.

Meyers (1975) reported an investigation that has a bearing on generalization procedures. Data were collected that indicated that a successful behavior-modification strategy recommended for one child did not have an impact on the disruptive behavior of other children in the class. This is consistent with Stokes and Baer's (1977) predictions because nothing specific was done to prompt generalization. However, later in this investigation, the consultant shifted tacts and helped the teacher explore her feelings of ambivalence regarding her role as the authority in the classroom. This later intervention was followed by impressive and widespread changes in the behavior of the rest of the class. Thus, a transfer effect occurred in this instance.

One final study reported findings that appear to be consistent with the preceding interpretation. Curtis and Watson (1980) used Bergan's (1977a) Consultation Observation Record to assess the degree to which consultants were facilitative or nonfacilitative in terms of their use of process skills. The measures of consultation outcome were derived from ratings of the teachers in neutral interviews in which they were asked to describe children who had not been discussed previously during consultation. Teachers were rated during these interviews on dimensions such as an index of content relevance, the percent of factual utterances, and the specification of current performance by the teacher. The teachers with facilitative consultants improved significantly more than the controls or the teachers with nonfacilitative consultants. Even though the collaborative consultation model did not systematically prompt such changes in the teachers' approaches to new problems, these changes were observed, suggesting a clear transfer of effects. An interesting sidelight is that they found a nonsignificant trend ($p < .1$) in which the control subjects did better than the teachers with nonfacilitative consultants, because this latter group actually declined on several measures following consultation.

Once again, the reader must be cautioned that there are not yet sufficient data to make firm conclusions. However, there are two trends that should generate productive research hypotheses. On the one hand, the work of Bergan and his associates suggests that specific verbal prompts are necessary to obtain generalized results in behavioral consultation. On the other hand, some researchers (e.g., Curtis & Watson, 1980; Meyers, 1975) have found generalized results with collaborative mental-health consultation where no specific prompting procedures were used.[4] If these opposing trends are replicated, then future hypotheses will need to make sense of *both* findings. For example, it may be that specific, case-oriented consultation problems (i.e., Level I—direct service to the teacher and Level II—indirect service to the child) require specific prompting procedures applied systematically by the consultant in order to obtain generalization. However, consultation problems focused more broadly on the teacher, the teacher's attitudes, and the teacher's feelings (i.e., Level III—direct service to the teacher) may be more likely to stimulate generalized effects without specific verbal prompting procedures. The entire issue of transfer effects is so crucial to the theory underlying mental-health consultation that it must receive considerably more research attention in the near future.

CONCLUSIONS

Mental-health consultation is a viable approach to the delivery of psychological services in the schools. It is a promising approach because it has the potential to prevent the development of problems in the future as well as to solve immediate problems. School psychology is a profession in the midst of important changes. Although there is no way to predict the outcome of these changes with certainty, school psychologists will have to do less psycho–educational assessment and spend more time trying to bring meaningful help to teachers, students, and schools in general if the profession is to survive. Because mental-health consultation is one approach that offers concrete help to school personnel, while offering the possibility of preventing or reducing future problems, it should be considered as an approach to the delivery of psychological services in the schools.

If mental-health consultation is to be implemented with reasonable frequency in the schools of the future, then training in this area for school psychologists will have to be upgraded. Even though a recent survey reported that school-based consultation was one of the training priorities of the programs surveyed (Goh, 1977), a more recent survey reported that only 43% of the programs that responded offer a course focused solely on consultation (Wurtz, Meyers, & Flanagan, 1978). In this same survey, 34% of the programs indicated that they do not even offer a course that is focused at least partially on consultation.

---

[4]In fairness to this research, it must be noted that although no specific prompting procedures were reported, it is possible that such prompting occurred without the awareness of the researchers. This is an empirical question that focuses specifically on the question of generalization in consultation.

Not only is the current consultation training insufficient, but this situation is even worse for nondoctoral school psychologists. The Thayer Conference (Cutts, 1955) concluded that consultation training should be limited to doctoral school psychologists. This position has been challenged only in recent years (Gallessich, 1974; Meyers, 1978a; Stewart & Medway, 1978), and substantially fewer nondoctoral programs currently offer training in consultation. The survey conducted by Wurtz, Meyers, and Flanagan (1978) found that although 70% of the doctoral programs offered a consultation course, only 29% of the nondoctoral programs offered such a course. If we want school psychologists to implement this role, then there must be meaningful training, and if we mean to have an impact on the general field of school psychology, then such training must occur at the nondoctoral level as well as at the doctoral level. As mental-health consultation is used in the schools with increasing frequency, there will be opportunities for more research and development of these techniques. The result might be an improved school environment that could influence all school children for the better.

REFERENCES

Alpert, J. L. Some guidelines for school consultants. *Journal of School Psychology*, 1977, *15*, 308–319.

Barrett-Lennard, G. T. Dimensions of therapist response as causal factors in therapeutic change. *Psychological Monographs*, 1962, *76*(43).

Bennis, W. G. *Organizational development: Its nature, origins, and prospects*. Reading, Mass.: Addison-Wesley, 1969.

Bergan, J. R. *Behavioral consultation*. Columbus, Ohio: Merrill, 1977. (a)

Bergan, J. R. *The control of consultee behavior in the consultation process*. Paper presented at the 85th annual meeting of the American Psychological Association, San Francisco, 1977. (b)

Bergan, J. R., Byrnes, I. M., & Kratochwill, T. R. Effects of behavioral and medical models of consultation on teacher expectancies and instruction of a hypothetical child. *Journal of School Psychology*, in press.

Bergan, J. R., & Tombari, M. L. The analysis of verbal interaction during consultation. *Journal of School Psychology*, 1975, *13*, 209–226.

Bergan, J. R., & Tombari, M. L. Consultant skill and efficiency and the implementation and outcomes of consultation. *Journal of School Psychology*, 1976, *14*, 3–14.

Bergin, A. E., & Strupp, H. H. *Changing frontiers in the science of psychotherapy*. Chicago: Aldine, 1972.

Bowlby, J. Pathological mourning and childhood mourning. *Journal of the American Psychoanalytic Association*, 1963, *11*, 500–541.

Caplan, G. Types of mental health consultation. *American Journal of Orthopsychiatry*, 1963, *3*, 470–481.

Caplan, G. *The theory and practice of mental health consultation*. New York: Basic Books, 1970.

Carkhuff, R. R. *Helping and human relations: A primer for lay and professional helpers. Volume 1: Selection and training*. New York: Holt, Rinehart, & Winston, 1969. (a)

Carkhuff, R. R. *Helping and human relations. Volume 2: Practice and research*. New York: Holt, Rinehart, & Winston, 1969. (b)

Cook, V. J., & Patterson, J. G. Psychologists in the schools of Nebraska: Professional functions. *Psychology in the Schools,* 1977, *14,* 371–376.

Curtis, M. J., & Anderson, T. *Consulting in educational settings: A collaborative approach.* Cincinnati: Faculty Resource Center, University of Cincinnati, 1976.

Curtis, M. J., & Watson, K. L. Changes in consultee problem clarification skills following consultation. *Journal of School Psychology,* 1980, *18,* 210–221.

Curtis, M. J., & Zins, J. E. *Consultative effectiveness as perceived by experts in consultation and classroom teachers.* Paper presented at the annual meetings of the National Association of School Psychologists, New York, 1978.

Cutts, N. E. (Ed.). *School psychologists at mid-century.* Washington, D.C.: American Psychological Association, 1955.

Drabman, R. S., Hammer, D., & Rosenbaum, M. S. Assessing generalization in behavior modification with children: The generalization map. *Behavioral Assessment,* 1979, *1,* 203–219.

Dworkin, A. L., & Dworkin, E. P. A conceptual overview of selected consultation models. *American Journal of Community Psychology,* 1975, *3,* 151–160.

Egan, G. *The skilled helper.* Monterey, Calif.: Brooks/Cole, 1975.

Fairchild, T. N. School psychological services: An empirical comparison of two models. *Psychology in the Schools,* 1976, *13,* 156–162.

Farling, W., & Hoedt, K. *National survey of school psychologists.* Washington, D.C.: U. S. Department of Health, Education, and Welfare, 1971.

Flanders, N. A. *Analyzing teacher behavior.* Reading, Mass.: Addison-Wesley, 1970.

Freidman, M. J. *Mental health consultation with teachers: An analysis of process variables.* Paper presented at the annual meetings of the National Association of School Psychologists, New York, 1978.

Gallessich, J. Organizational factors influencing consultation in schools. *Journal of School Psychology,* 1973, *11,* 57–65.

Gallessich, J. Training the school psychologist for consultation. *Journal of School Psychology,* 1974, *12,* 138–149.

Gazda, G. M., Asbury, F. R., Balzer, F. J., Childers, W. C., Desselle, R. E., & Walters, R. P. *Human relations development: A manual for educators.* Boston: Allyn & Bacon, 1973.

Gibbins, S. Public Law 94–142: An impetus for consultation. *School Psychology Digest,* 1978, *7,* 18–25.

Gilmore, G., & Chandy, J. Educators describe the school psychologist. *Psychology in the Schools,* 1973, *10,* 397–403.

Goh, D. S. Graduate Training in School Psychology. *Journal of School Psychology,* 1977, *15,* 207–218.

Good, T. L., & Brophy, J. E. Teacher–child dyadic interactions: A new method for classroom observation. *Journal of School Psychology,* 1970, *8,* 131–138.

Gutkin, T. B. Teacher perceptions of consultation services provided by school psychologists. *Professional Psychology,* 1980, *11,* 637–642.

Gutkin, T. B., Singer, J. H., & Brown, R. Teacher reactions to school based consultation services: A multivariate analysis. *Journal of School Psychology,* 1980, *18,* 126–134.

Hops, H. The school psychologist as a behavior management consultant in a special class setting. *Journal of School Psychology,* 1971, *9,* 473–483.

Huse, E. F. *Organization development and change.* St. Paul: West, 1975.

Ivey, A. E. *Microcounseling: Innovations in interviewing training.* Springfield, Ill.: Thomas, 1971.

Jason, L. A., & Ferone, L. Behavioral versus process consultation interventions in school settings. *American Journal of Community Psychology,* 1978, *5,* 531–543.

Kounin, J. S. *Discipline and group management in classrooms.* New York: Holt, Rinehart, & Winston, 1970.

Lambert, N., Sandoval, J., & Corder, R. Teacher perceptions of school-based consultants. *Professional Psychology,* 1975, *6,* 204–216.

Manley, T. R., & Manley, E. T. A comparison of the personal values and operative goals of school psychologists and school superintendents. *Journal of School Psychology,* 1978, *16,* 99–109.

Mannino, F., & Shore, M. The effects of consultation: A review of empirical studies. *American Journal of Community Psychology,* 1975, *3,* 1–21.

Martin, R., Duffey, J., & Fischman, R. A time analysis and evaluation of an experimental internship program in school psychology. *Journal of School Psychology,* 1973, *11,* 263–268.

Martin, R., & Meyers, J. *School psychologists and the practice of consultation: A national survey.* Division 16 Corresponding Committee on Consultation, American Psychological Association, 1978.

Medway, F. J. How effective is school consultation?: A review of recent research. *Journal of School Psychology,* 1979, *17,* 275–282.

Meyers, J. A consultation model for school psychological services. *Journal of School Psychology,* 1973, *11,* 5–15.

Meyers, J. Consultee-centered consultation as a technique in classroom management. *American Journal of Community Psychology,* 1975, *3,* 111–121.

Meyers, J. Training school psychologists for a consultation role. *School Psychology Digest,* 1978, *1,* 26–32. (a)

Meyers, J. *Resistance in teacher consultation: A relationship model.* Paper presented at the 86th annual meeting of the American Psychological Association, Toronto, 1978. (b)

Meyers, J., Freidman, M. P., & Gaughan, E. J. The effects of consultee-centered consultation on teacher behavior. *Psychology in the Schools,* 1975, *12,* 288–295.

Meyers, J., Parsons, R. D., & Martin, R. *Mental health consultation in the schools.* San Francisco: Jossey-Bass, 1979.

Meyers, J., & Pitt, N. A consultation approach to help a school cope with the bereavement process. *Professional Psychology,* 1976, *7,* 559–564.

Meyers, J., Pitt, N., Gaughan, E., & Freidman, M. A research model for consultation with teachers. *Journal of School Psychology,* 1978, *16,* 137–145.

Miller, J. N. Consumer response to theoretical role models in school psychology. *Journal of School Psychology,* 1974, *12,* 310–317.

O'Leary, K. D., & O'Leary, S. G. (Eds.). *Classroom management: The successful use of behavior modification.* Elmsford, N.Y.: Pergamon Press, 1972.

Reschly, D. J. School psychology consultation: Frenzied, faddish, or fundamental? *Journal of School Psychology,* 1976, *14,* 105–113.

Ritter, D. R. Effects of a school consultation program upon referral patterns of teachers. *Psychology in the Schools,* 1978, *15,* 239–243.

Rogers, C. R. The necessary and sufficient conditions of therapeutic change. *Journal of Consulting Psychology,* 1957, *21,* 95–103.

Ruckhaber, C. J. Four year study of a psychological consultation process. *Psychology in the Schools,* 1975, *12,* 64–70.

Schein, E. H. *Process consultation.* Reading, Mass.: Addison-Wesley, 1969.

Schmuck, R. A. Helping teachers improve classroom group processes. *Journal of Applied Behavioral Science,* 1968, *4,* 401–436.

Schmuck, R. A., & Miles, M. B. (Eds.). *Organization development in the schools.* Palo Alto, Calif.: National Press Books, 1971.

Schmuck, R. A., Runkel, P., Arends, J., & Arends, R. *The Second Handbook of Organization Development in Schools.* Palo Alto, Calif.: Mayfield, 1977.

Schmuck, R. A., & Schmuck, P. A. *Group processes in the classroom.* Dubuque, Iowa: Brown, 1971.

Schmuck, R. A., & Schmuck, P. A. *A humanistic psychology of education: Making the school everybody's house.* Palo Alto, Calif.: National Press Books, 1974.

Schowengerdt, R. V., Fine, M. J., & Poggio, J. P. An examination of some bases of teacher satisfaction with school psychological services. *Psychology in the Schools,* 1976, *13,* 269–275.

Spaulding, R. L. *An introduction to the use of the coping analysis schedule for educational settings (CASES).* Durham, N.C.: Education Improvement Program, Duke University, 1967.

Stewart, K. J., & Medway, F. J. School psychologists as consultants: Issues in training, practice and accountability. *Professional Psychology,* 1978, *9,* 711-718.

Stokes, T. F., & Baer, D. M. An implicit technology of generalization. *Journal of Applied Behavior Analysis,* 1977, *10,* 349-367.

Sulzer-Azaroff, B., McKinley, J., & Ford, L. *Field activities for educational psychology: Carrying concepts into action.* Santa Monica, Calif.: Goodyear, 1977.

Szmuk, M. I. C., Docherty, E. M., & Ringness, T. A. Behavioral objectives for psychological consultation in the school as evaluated by teachers and school psychologists. *Psychology in the Schools,* 1979, *16,* 143-148.

Waters, L. G. School psychology as perceived by school personnel: Support for a consultation model. *Journal of School Psychology,* 1973, *11,* 40-45.

Wenger, R. D. Teacher response to collaborative consultation. *Psychology in the Schools,* 1979, *16,* 127-131.

Wilcox, M. R. *Variables affecting group mental health consultation for teachers.* Paper presented at the 85th annual meeting of the American Psychological Association, San Francisco, 1977.

Wurtz, R., Meyers, J., & Flanagan, D. *A national survey of consultation training.* Division 16 Corresponding Committee on Consultation, American Psychological Association, 1978.

Ysseldyke, J. *Summary of urban representatives meeting.* National School Psychology Inservice Training Network, University of Minnesota, May 1, 1979.

6

Program Evaluation and School Psychology: Perspectives, Principles, Procedures

Charles A. Maher
Rutgers University

CHAPTER ABSTRACT

In this chapter, program evaluation is examined in relation to school psychology, from historical, conceptual, and practical perspectives, with respect to evaluation principles and procedures. Recent advances in program-evaluation thinking and technology are reviewed, the relevance of these developments for the school psychologist discussed, a problem-solving approach to school program evaluation delineated, issues in the training of school psychologists in program evaluation explicated, and future directions for program evaluation and school psychology noted. The information provided in this chapter serves heuristic and practical purposes for school psychology trainers who are interested in incorporating program evaluation into their training programs, and for school-psychology practitioners who are interested in learning about program evaluation.

INTRODUCTION

During the past decade, professional activities of the school psychologist have expanded from cognitive and personality assessment responsibilities to include classroom and school intervention (Harris & Kapche, 1978), staff training (Hunter, 1977), consultation (Kratochwill & Bergan, 1978), and educational program development (Hoover, 1978). Reasons for this expansion of role and function of the school psychologist include: (1) increased understanding that human behavior, including the behavior of children in schools, is developed and maintained by complex interactions among organismic, social, and environmental variables, requiring an ecological, systems approach to practice (Bandura, 1978; Ullman, 1977); (2) expanded standards for the practice of psychology, emphasizing systematically developed intervention procedures (APA, 1977; Pennington, 1977); (3) enactment of Public Law 94-142, which mandates the development of an appropriate, individual educational program for each handicapped child (Gotts, 1976); (4) concomitant rises in the costs of living and reductions in school budgets, necessitating effective and efficient utilization of school personnel (Barbacovi & Clelland, 1977); (5) growing public concern over quality education, including the utility of special service professionals in the schools (Maher, 1979); and (6) increased emphasis in school psychology training programs on the community context in which schools are embedded (Bardon, 1976).

One area of professional activity that is becoming recognized as a potentially important, even a required, aspect of the practice of school psychology is program evaluation (Barclay, 1978; Maher, 1979a; Schulberg & Perloff, 1979). The growing importance of program evaluation in professional psychology, in general, and school psychology, in particular, is reflected in the recent publication of special issues of *Professional Psychology* (Perloff & Perloff, 1977) and the *Journal of School Psychology* (Hoover & Maher, 1978), which have centered on program evaluation, as well as by workshops and presentations on that topic at the annual conventions of the American Psychological Association (see, for example, Maher & Barbrack, 1978; Munz, 1977).

The need for the involvement of school psychologists in program evaluation can be seen in relation to the task of the school psychology practitioner as well as to the contemporary information needs of public school districts. As practitioners, school psychologists have as their mission the prevention or remediation of the behavioral problems of a range of clients: individuals (e.g., the child, parent); groups (e.g., classrooms, teachers); and organizations (e.g., school, department of special services) (see, for example, Bardon & Bennett, 1974). Practitioners are faced with the professional responsibility of providing the ''best'' psychological service possible given the present state of knowledge, the available information about a client's behavioral assets and deficits, and the fiscal and temporal constraints of the school organization in which they practice. This mission of the practitioner derives essentially from adherence to standards for professional practice (APA, 1977; Pennington, 1977), requiring practitioners to engage in a series of interrelated tasks such as identification of the clients who are eligible for, or entitled to, school psychological and related services; assessment of psychological and educational needs of the client, in a systematic way, as a basis for program development; design and implementation of service programs geared to client needs; judgment of the impact of the program on client functioning; and dissemination of evaluative information about the program that is seen as valued by various audiences (e.g., school board, principal).

At the present time, public school districts are in need of program evaluation services (Nevo & Stufflebeam, 1976). The extrinsic press for program evaluation is also seen as due to several interrelated phenomena including reductions in public-school financial resources, requiring that decisions be made about modification or termination of existing programs (Barbacovi & Clelland, 1977); increased costs of providing educational programs as a result of the rise in the cost of living (Lynch, 1977); enactment of educational compliance legislation, such as PL 94–142, which mandates that school districts become more explicit about the nature, scope, and impact of their programs (USDHEW, 1976); and concern from legislators, parents, and the general public alike over effectiveness and efficiency of public-school education (Mellor, 1977).

The aforementioned states of affairs have required that public school administrators answer programmatic questions that require a range of information. These include: "What programs?" "Serving what pupils?" "Are providing what educational results?" "At what costs?" "Which programs should be modified, maintained, or terminated?" "In what way(s) should this be accomplished?" In order to answer these questions and related ones, school based professionals (e.g., school psychologists) are needed who can provide program-evaluation services such as needs assessment, program monitoring, outcome evaluation, cost-effectiveness analysis, and proposal writing (Maher, 1977; Taylor, 1977).

This chapter reviews recent advances in program evaluation in relation to school psychology. More specifically, it is the purpose of the chapter to: (1) provide several interrelated perspectives on program evaluation; (2) identify salient issues in program evaluation that bear on the organization and delivery of program-evaluation services in schools; (3) explicate a problem solving approach to program evaluation that addresses these issues, that is based upon advances in evaluation theory and technique, and that is particularly relevant to the practicing school psychologist; (4) discuss approaches to training school psychologists in program evaluation; and (5) offer future directions for school psychology and program evaluation. In addition, a nonexhaustive, representative, annotated bibliography on program evaluation is included as an appendix to the chapter.

PERSPECTIVES ON PROGRAM EVALUATION: A RATIONALE

It is difficult for one to obtain a thorough grasp of the nature and scope of program evaluation by trying to capsulize evaluation as a narrow, unitary concept (Merwin, 1969). Program evaluation is a term that has different meanings to different groups, focuses on various kinds and levels of programs, and is characterized by a range of methods and approaches (Baker, 1974; Pederson, 1977; Perkins, 1977). In order to understand the essence as well as the diversity of present-day program evaluation, it is helpful to view it from several perspectives: historical, parametric, conceptual, and operational.

An Historical Perspective

During the latter part of the 19th century through the 1920's, program evaluation in schools and related agencies was characterized by the use of descriptive statistical approaches (e.g., data collection on demographic characteristics of pupils), narrative case studies (e.g., descriptions of curricula), and check lists and rating scales for institutional self study (Chapin, 1947; Levine & Levine, 1975).

During the 1930's and 1940's, the emphasis of program evaluation in schools, due largely to the contributions of Ralph Tyler, was on delineation of instructional objectives, monitoring of pupil progress toward the objectives, and revision in educational programs based upon amount of progress made by the pupil (Worthen & Sanders, 1973). It was during the same time period that support was given to goal-based evaluation (Stake, 1967) and discrepancy evaluation (Provus, 1971), approaches to program evaluation that still are predominant in the public schools of today.

Program evaluation during the 1950's and 1960's began to take on more of an experimental orientation (see Campbell, 1969), especially in relation to large-scale demonstration projects (see Cooley & Lohnes, 1976; Cronbach & Suppes, 1962); community-based social programs (see Rossi, Freeman, & Wright, 1979), and individual and group applied behavioral interventions (Kazdin, 1975). During the 1970's, program evaluation in public schools, residential treatment facilities, and community mental health centers expanded from a focus on providing information for research and policy decisions at the federal and state levels to include evaluation in the service of management decision making at the local level (Demone, Schulberg, & Broskowski, 1978).

At the present time, school program evaluation has been espoused as a technology for assisting program managers (e.g., principals, directors of special education) in various ways. These purposes include assessment of client (e.g., handicapped pupils) needs as a basis for planning programs (Maher & Barbrack, 1979); development of "evaluable" programs, based upon assessed needs, as a prerequisite to process and outcome evaluation (Rutman, 1977); monitoring of program operations to detect deficiencies in program design (Freeman, 1977), and determining the extent to which program goals have been attained (Attkisson, Hargreaves, Horowitz, & Sorensen, 1978).

A Parametric Perspective

The research function has been a hallmark of psychologists. Most school psychologists have training in research, and are familiar with the nature and scope of research. However, program evaluation is not typically considered research (Freeman, 1977; Mitroff & Bonoma, 1978). In contrast to research, program evaluation is characterized by diversity of purpose, procedures, audiences, and

TABLE 6.1
A Contrast between Research and
Program Evaluation

Dimension	Research	Program Evaluation
General purpose	To establish causal relations between experimental processes and outcomes	To reduce uncertainty in program decision making by providing information about the worth of various program aspects
Unit of inquiry	Experiments and demonstration projects	Individual, group, or organizational service programs
Method of inquiry	Quantitative (e.g., experimental design)	Quantitative (e.g., time-series design) and qualitative (e.g., naturalistic inquiry)
Responsibility of the inquirer	To scientific and professional colleagues	To program managers

outcomes. Thus, in order for the school psychologist to understand the nature and scope of program evaluation, it is useful to contrast evaluation with research (see Mechanic, 1975; Rossi & Wright, 1977).

Although in practice there is some overlap between research and evaluation, especially with regard to the use of experimental design, assessment strategies, and statistical methods, program evaluation is considered more flexible in approach, contributing in a greater number of ways to school program decision making than basic or field-based research (Stufflebeam, Foley, Gephart, Guba, Hammond, Merriman, & Provus, 1971; Worthen & Sanders, 1973).

Field-based research and program evaluation can be seen in contrast to one another along several dimensions: general purpose; unit of inquiry; method of inquiry; and responsibility of the inquirer. These distinctions are summarized in Table 6.1.

General Purpose

It has been discussed widely in the program evaluation literature that the essential purpose of an evaluation study is to provide information about the worth or merit of various aspects of a program in order to allow a decision maker to make judgments about how to further develop, modify, or terminate the program (Freeman, 1977; Stufflebeam et al., 1971). The generally accepted purpose of research, however, is to establish causal relations between experimental processes and outcomes (Kaplan, 1964; Mitroff & Featheringham, 1974). Thus, program evaluation serves decision making toward program development and improvement, whereas research serves knowledge and theory development.

Program evaluation, when properly undertaken, helps reduce decision uncertainty about program aspects such as the adequacy of a program in addressing the needs of program clients; the efficiency of a program in terms of expenditure of staff effort and costs; the operations of a program relative to planned operations; the outcomes of a program relative to goals; and the impact of a program on significant others not directly involved in the program. On the other hand, research is concerned with theories, interventions related to outcomes, and the establishment of functional relations.

Unit of Inquiry

Because program evaluation is known to serve program development and improvement in organizational settings such as schools (Broskowski & Driscoll, 1978), the primary unit of inquiry for the evaluator (school psychologist) is the service program (e.g., regular education, special education, mental health programs). Research, which serves theory development, focuses on experiments and demonstration projects.

A service program, as the unit of inquiry, can be conceptualized at three distinct levels: individual programs, group programs, and organizational programs. Table 6.2 provides a definition and some examples of each kind of service program with which school psychologists typically have been involved. Researchers have usually been involved with individual and group experiments

TABLE 6.2
Examples of Service Programs at
Different Levels of Evaluation Focus[a]

Type of Service Program	Service Program
Organizational	1. Department of special education
	2. Special education school
	3. Special service team
Group	1. Title I Preschool program
	2. Remedial reading program
	3. Teacher training program
Individual	1. Individual Education Program (IEP)
	2. Behavior modification program
	3. Speech therapy program

[a] A *service program* is a configuration of human (e.g., staff), technological (e.g., methods), informational (e.g., base-line data), and financial (e.g., budget) resources that interrelate in a planned way to help a client (e.g., learning-disabled pupils) attain specified goals (e.g., improved reading comprehension).

(programs), although during the past few years, there has been increased experimentation at organizational levels (Argyris & Schon, 1978; Toronto, 1975).

Method of Inquiry

Traditionally, research has relied almost solely on the experimental paradigm, because the purpose of research is to establish causal relations between experimental processes and outcomes. Thus, experimental design and, to a lesser extent, quasiexperimental design, are the methods of choice for investigating a research hypothesis (Guba, 1978). Without these tools, it would be difficult for a researcher to rule out plausible effects, other than the programmatic variables (Campbell & Stanley, 1966; Cook & Campbell, 1979). Thus, the range of methods of inquiry for research is narrow in scope and is characterized by control and rigor, with a premium on internal validity (Campbell & Stanley, 1966).

Program evaluation, on the other hand, relies on a wide range of quantitative and qualitative methods (Guba, 1978). This is so because the purposes that program evaluation can serve are broader than research purposes. In this regard, commonly recognized program evaluation methods, discussed in more detail in a later section, are: needs assessment (Stufflebeam, 1976); evaluability assessment (Wholey, 1977); program monitoring and process evaluation (Morris & Fitzgibbon, 1978); goal attainment scaling (Kiresuk & Sherman, 1968); cost-outcome and cost-effectiveness analyses (Sorensen & Grove, 1978); and consumer-satisfaction evaluation (Morentz, 1979).

Responsibility of the Inquirer

Both program evaluation and research are types of social inquiry in that they seek answers to questions on particular units of inquiry (Mitroff & Bonoma, 1978). However, the specific responsibilities of the evaluator and researcher are different. The responsibility of the researcher is to the larger scientific community and to professional colleagues, because the contribution of the inquiry is to theory development and increased knowledge. This responsibility is usually met by publication of the experimental results in scientific and professional journals. The responsibility of the program evaluator, however, is to those individuals who commissioned the evaluation. Usually, this means the program manager, such as a superintendent, principal, or director of special services, or program funders and consumers, such as parents, board of education members, and taxpayers. This is so because the contribution of program evaluation is to program development, improvement, and modification.

A Conceptual Perspective

In order to design useful program evaluation systems and studies in schools and related agencies (e.g., day care centers), certain concepts that, to a large extent, are unique to the evaluation field must be understood by school psychologists.

This section examines three such concepts: program; program validity assumptions, and program decision types.

The Notion of Program

A fundamental, albeit often neglected, concept to understand prior to the design and conduct of a program evaluation is that of *program* (Twain, 1975). Although various definitions and ideas about a program have appeared in the program planning literature, there have been few descriptions of a program that has direct relevance to school program evaluation (Maher & Barbrack, 1979).

A school-based program (both regular education and special education programs) can be defined in relation to four program resource domains: an organized configuration of *human, technological, informational,* and *financial* resources that interrelate in a planned process to help a *client* attain one or more *goals* that are derived from the *needs* of the client (Maher, 1979c). Table 6.3 provides a definition of each kind of program resource, as well as other critical program

TABLE 6.3
Program Concepts for Program Evaluation:
Remedial Reading Program for Conduct Problem
Adolescents

Concept/Definition	Examples
Human resources: the professionals, paraprofessionals, and consultants who comprise the staff of a program	• Teachers • Behavior analysts • Evaluation consultant • Teacher aids • Counselors
Technological resources: the methods and materials that are used by the human resources in carrying out program activities	• SRA reading series (material) • Worksheets and behavioral charts (materials) • Behavioral assessment (method) • Contingency contracting (method)
Informational resources: information that is used to monitor the progress of clients toward program goals	• Base line data on frequency of correct responses • Number of positive self statements • Degree of goal attainment
Financial resources: the amount of money available to support program operation	• Staff salaries • Fixed charges (e.g., heat, electricity) • Material expenditures (e.g., costs of worksheets) • Secretarial services

concepts, and provides examples of each concept for a remedial reading program for conduct problem adolescents in a senior high school. This definition of program allows an evaluator and decision maker to focus on different aspects (e.g., resources) of a program and to obtain information to judge the worth and merit of these aspects.

Program Validity Assumptions

The definition of program, explicated in the previous section, allows for evaluation of various "program validity assumptions," which focus on different aspects of a program, and which are of concern to various program audiences (e.g., superintendent, teachers). These assumptions, which might be explicit or implicit for any particular program, are: (1) that the needs (an informational resource) of the program client have been assessed in a reliable, representative, and ecologically valid manner, which is of importance to funding agencies and governing boards; (2) that program goals (an informational resource) are valid in that they reflect the needs of the client, which is important to program planners; (3) that the program staff (human resources) is sufficient to operate the program as planned, which is of concern to program managers; (4) that program activities, methods, and materials (technological resources) are seen as valid means of facilitating goal attainment, which is important to program implementers (staff); (5) that the evaluative criteria (an informational resource) used to assess goal attainment are valid indicators of the goals, which is of importance to evaluators; (6) that the level of funding (financial resources) is sufficient to support program operations, which is of concern to program managers, planners, and implementers; (7) that the program was responsible for the client's attainment of program goals, which is of concern to evaluators, funders, and governing boards; and (8) that the program clients and significant others (e.g., parents) see the program as being beneficial (valid) in some way, which has social (substantive) significance rather than statistical significance (see Kazdin, 1977; Wolf, 1978, for thorough discussions of the social validity of a program).

Table 6.4 provides examples of evaluation questions that serve to focus program evaluation on each validity assumption relative to a Title I reading program.

Program Decision Types

Program evaluation serves (is useful in) program decision making to the extent that the evaluation information helps reduce the uncertainty of the decision maker (e.g., school superintendent, principal, director of psychological services) about various aspects of a program (e.g., needs, goals, outcomes) (Stufflebeam et al., 1971). Thus, program evaluation can be seen as closely linked to program management and, therefore, requires a close working relationship between an evaluator and a decision maker (Patton, 1978).

Program evaluation can help school decision makers with regard to three types of program decisions:

TABLE 6.4
Examples of Evaluation Questions that Relate to Program
Validity Assumptions of a Title I Reading Program

Program Validity Assumption	Evaluation Question
Appropriateness of client needs	Although children's needs have been assessed in reading and mathematics, is it worthwhile and necessary to assess needs in classroom behavior?
Relevance of program goals	Should program goals include behavioral as well as academic goals, given the needs of the program client?
Sufficiency of program staff	Are the number of teacher aides sufficient to support the reading teachers in their task of individualization of instruction?
Feasibility of program activities	Is the contingency contracting procedure seen by teachers as feasible for implementation with disruptive children?
Validity of evaluation criteria	Is the Reading Comprehension Subtest of the Iowa Test of Basic Skills a valid indicator for the reading program?
Adequacy of program funding	Is the present level of program financial support sufficient to operate the reading program for the entire school year?
Experimental validity	How confident can we be that the program's outcomes were the result of the program's processes?
Social validity	To what extent and in what ways is the reading program seen as acceptable by parents?

1. *Decisions to help with internal program operations*—providing information to an "internal decision maker" for judging the appropriateness of the program in addressing unmet needs of the program client; the evaluability of the program for process and outcome evaluation; the degree to which the program is operating as intended; and the extent to which negative side effects might be related to the program.

2. *Decisions to help meet external accountability requirements*—providing information to an "external decision maker" (e.g., U.S. Bureau of Education for the Handicapped) about the operations and efficiency of the program.

3. *Decisions about program effectiveness*—providing information to internal and external decision makers for judging the extent to which a program has been

effective—that is, the extent to which the program was responsible for program results (Rossi & Wright, 1977). In making decisions about program effectiveness in field settings (schools), however, it is problematic to determine experimental validity due to difficulties in establishing adequate experimental controls (Cook & Campbell, 1976). In school program evaluation, it is usually difficult, if not impossible, for specific findings to answer all the experimental, social, and program validity questions that could be emanated. Thus, the use of quasiexperimental methods, especially time-series evaluation methods, are particularly relevant to school psychologists in evaluation of program effectiveness (Kratochwill, 1978).

An Operational Perspective

In order to design and conduct useful school program evaluations, it is necessary for the school psychologist to identify certain operational assumptions on which evaluation is based, to become familiar with contemporary models and frameworks of evaluation, and to become knowledgeable about program evaluation services and methods. This section discusses these operational issues.

Operational Assumptions of School Program Evaluation

As discussed in a previous section of this chapter, program evaluation serves different program decisions, relative to different program units, and is intended to be of use for different program audiences. However, in order to deliver useful program evaluation services, it is necessary to explicate certain assumptions about program evaluation operations (Koocher & Broskowski, 1977; Maher, 1978; Mitroff & Bonoma, 1978; Rossi et al., 1979). These assumptions are:

1. Evaluation is a systematic process, undertaken by an evaluator with a decision maker, in order to obtain information that will enable judgments (decisions) to be made about various aspects of a program's validity. These include client needs, program goals, and evaluative criteria (planning validity); the nature, scope, and adequacy of program staff and program activities in reaching goals (theoretical validity); the manner in which the program is operating according to plan (management validity); the degree to which goals have been attained, especially as a result of program efforts (experimental validity); and the extent to which the program is seen as socially desirable by clients and other groups (social validity).

2. For evaluation to serve (be useful in) program decision making, a program evaluator must be able to accurately identify and assess the evaluation information need(s) of the decision maker, obtain consensus with the decision maker about priority needs, and seek to provide the decision maker timely, accurate, and technically adequate information that will reduce decision uncertainty, thus reducing or eliminating the information need(s).

3. For any program (individual, group, organizational), there are (can be) various decision makers who usually have diverse evaluation information needs (Nevo & Stufflebeam, 1976). For school programs, especially special service programs, these *decision making groups* and their evaluation information needs include *external agency officials* (e.g., BEH officials) who need aggregate information about program outcomes (e.g., degree of goal attainment) and program efficiency (e.g., number of pupils served relative to size of staff), with the school or school district as the program unit; *internal school district administrators* (e.g., superintendents, principals, directors of special services) who need management information about program operations (e.g., amount of service provided), program costs (e.g., costs of individual versus group counseling), and program outcome (e.g., amount of pupil progress), with the program unit ranging from the classroom level to the school-district level; *program staff* (e.g., teachers, counselors) who need information about the progress of individual pupils and small groups of pupils relative to program goals, with the program unit being the individual (e.g., IEP), small group (e.g., remedial-reading program), or classroom program; *program supporters* (e.g., parents, taxpayers) who are interested in knowing whether programs are "reaching" the "right" pupils and whether the programs are "worth it;" and *theorists, researchers, and developers* (e.g., university professors, "R & D" officials) who need cost-effective information about large scale programs that have theoretical relevance and implications for program dissemination.

4. For an evaluator to design evaluation studies that are responsive to the evaluation information needs of decision makers, the evaluator must possess skill, not only in research design and data analysis, but also knowledge and skill in organizational behavior, interpersonal relations, verbal and written communication.

5. For program evaluation to be useful to school decision making, it is important that the evaluator have an understanding of models and frameworks of evaluation and how these tools are integrated with program evaluation services.

Program Evaluation Models and Frameworks

As the field of program evaluation evolves, a range of models and frameworks for program evaluation are being developed by evaluation theorists and practitioners (Glass, 1976). Several of these approaches can be useful, in a complementary way, to the evaluation of regular education and special education programs, because each one provides a somewhat different emphasis. Each approach, because of its conceptual foundation, gives rise to a number of distinct evaluation techniques. Thus, knowledge of these models and frameworks allows for a "technically eclectic" approach to school program evaluation. In a manner not unlike a technically eclectic psychotherapeutic process (see Lazarus, 1976), a technically eclectic approach to program evaluation allows the evaluator to design program evaluation studies that are responsive to the evaluation information needs of school audiences (Davis, 1979).

Seven evaluation models, their relative emphases, and the leading proponents of each model are briefly outlined here:

Goal-Based Evaluation (Bloom, Hastings, & Madaus, 1971; Provus, 1971). This approach emphasizes the importance of evaluation of pupil progress toward program goals and the assessment of discrepancies—i.e., the needs of the pupil relative to the goals. The goal-based approach provides the decision maker (e.g., principal, teacher) with information that is useful in modifying instructional programs to meet the needs of the learner.

Decision-Oriented Evaluation (Stufflebeam et al., 1971). This approach emphasizes the program decision making process, the need to specify decision-oriented evaluation questions that, when answered, will help reduce decision uncertainty, and the importance of the interface between evaluator and decision maker. The decision-oriented approach can provide information about the context, input, process, and products of a program and, thus, is particularly useful in program planning and development activities.

Goal-Free Evaluation (Scriven, 1974, 1976). This approach emphasizes the usefulness of information about a program's positive and negative side effects, apart from criteria based on program goals. In this approach, an evaluator is unaware of a program's purposes and seeks to determine the strengths and weaknesses of the program, without knowledge of program goals. This approach can be useful when a decision maker is interested in the operations of a program and the impact of those operations on staff and other groups.

Evaluation Research (Campbell, 1969; Cooley & Lohnes, 1976; Suchman, 1967). This approach emphasizes explanation of educational effects resulting from program processes. Evaluation research is useful in determining the effects of large-scale educational programs (e.g., Head Start) and demonstration projects, especially for national dissemination purposes.

Adversarial Evaluation (Owens, 1973; Worthen & Owens, 1978). Within this conceptualization, evaluation takes on a "judicial flavor." In this approach, two opposing evaluators, in a manner much like opposing attorneys in a court of law, present the "best case" for each of two competing alternatives of a program's value (e.g., Program X is an effective program versus Program X is not an effective program). This information can be used by decision makers in making judgments about program maintenance or termination.

Transactional Evaluation (Parlett & Hamilton, 1976; Rippey, 1973). This approach to evaluation provides information about the processes of the program in relation to the value perspectives of administrators, staff, and clients who are involved in the program. In transactional evaluation, there is a reliance by the

TABLE 6.5
Examples of Program Evaluation Questions in Relation
to Program Evaluation Models

Program Evaluation Models	Program Evaluation Questions
Goal-based evaluation	To what extent have the goals of the sixth-grade career-awareness program been attained?
Decision-oriented evaluation	What are the priority needs of handicapped children in School A and how do they compare with the priority needs of handicapped children in School B?
Goal-free evaluation	What have been the positive and negative side effects of the implementation of the Mainstreaming Program in the junior high school?
Evaluation research	Which behavioral program is more effective in obesity reduction with what population of high-school pupils?
Adversarial evaluation	Is the IGE Program more effective and useful than the non-IGE Program versus is the non-IGE Program more effective and useful?
Transactional evaluation	In what ways have the classroom teachers experienced success with the new mathematics program?
Synoptic evaluation	What kinds of program-evaluation services should be provided to the department of special education during the upcoming school year?

evaluator on participant observation and other forms of naturalistic inquiry, with the information obtained being narrative and descriptive in nature.

Synoptic Evaluation (Maher, 1978). This approach emphasizes the multidimensionality of program evaluation in which evaluation is seen as an information gathering and reporting process useful in program development, program implementation, and in making judgments about program outcome. A synoptic approach to evaluation provides a framework for organizing the delivery of a range of program evaluation services in various school settings.

Table 6.5 outlines examples of program evaluation questions and provides examples of the particular evaluation models that can be applied as an overall strategy for addressing the questions.

Program Evaluation Services and Methods

Program evaluation services are those helping activities provided by the evaluator to the decision maker. In providing program evaluation service to a decision maker, an evaluator employs particular program evaluation methods to help answer particular evaluation questions seen as pertinent by the decision maker. These methods, which are not unique to any one particular evaluation model previously discussed, but which overlap among them, can be categorized into four types of methods: needs assessment, evaluability assessment, process evaluation, and outcome evaluation. These general types of program evaluation methods are discussed here:

Needs Assessment. This is a program evaluation method that is used to provide evaluation information to a decision maker about discrepancies between a present state of functioning of a particular client group in a particular area (e.g., fourth-grade pupils in mathematics) and a more desired state. In essence, the process of needs assessment involves obtaining information about client needs as a basis for the development of individual and group programs. In addition, an assessment of service delivery-system needs can be undertaken with needs-assessment methods—e.g., assessment of the capability of a department of special education to provide behavior management programs (Maher, 1979b; Roth, 1977).

Table 6.6 provides examples of needs assessment domains, and variables within each domain, when the needs assessment concern is with groups of

TABLE 6.6
Examples of Needs Assessment Domains and
Assessment Variables for Groups of Pupils

Behavioral Domain
- Classroom behavior (e.g., working style at desk, attentiveness, rate of completion of assignments)
- School behavior (e.g., truancy, extracurricular involvement)
- Motor behavior (e.g., gross-motor and fine-motor behavior)

Affective Domain
- Classroom related affect (e.g., happiness, sadness, temperament)
- Out-of-classroom related affect (e.g., emotional conduct, temperament)

Sensory/Perceptual Domain
- Sensory (e.g., visual and auditory acuity)
- Perceptual (e.g., visual perception, auditory perception)

Cognitive Domain
- Verbal communication skills (e.g., articulation, use of syntax)
- Written communication skills (e.g., correct use of grammar, spelling)
- Computational skills (e.g., knowledge of math concepts, application of facts)
- Problem solving (e.g., belief systems, self-efficacy)

Interpersonal Domain
- Peer relations (e.g., in-classroom cooperation, out of classroom)
- Relations with school staff (e.g., compliance with teacher requests)
- Relations with adults in community (e.g., cooperation with shopkeepers)

Physical Domain
- Dental health (e.g., condition of teeth)
- Nutritional health (e.g., nutritional status)
- Skeletal/muscular adequacy (e.g., orthopedic conditions)
- Cardiovascular function (e.g., hypertension)

pupils. Table 6.7 provides examples of needs assessment domains, and variables within each domain, when the concern is with a special service delivery system as an organizational program. Table 6.8 provides examples of techniques and instruments that can be used by pupil personnel service practitioners in conducting needs assessments (see Maher, 1979b, for a detailed description of a systems-oriented needs assessment framework for special services that integrates the assessment of pupils with the assessment of the service delivery system).

Evaluability Assessment.   This program evaluation method is used when a program manager, funding agency official, or program evaluator wishes to learn about the parameters of a program and whether the program is "evaluable" (Wholey, 1977). Evaluability information allows a determination to be made about the extent to which the program is capable of being evaluated by process and outcome evaluation methods (discussed later in this chapter). Evaluability assessment, which was developed by Wholey and his colleagues for the evaluation of federal social action programs (see Wholey, Nay, Scanlon, & Schmidt, 1975), involves a good deal of interaction between an evaluator and decision maker. In engaging in evaluability assessment, the evaluator must have a definition of what an evaluable program is, including criteria for an evaluable program. Table 6.9 provides one set of criteria for an evaluable program that has been used in evaluability assessments with individual, group, and organizational programs (see Maher, 1979e, 1979).

In engaging in evaluability assessment, an evaluator can use two methods: (1) *reviews* of programmatic documents such as written descriptions of activities and goals, which might be available; and (2) *interviews* with program managers,

TABLE 6.7
Examples of Needs Assessment Domains
and Assessment Variables for a
Special Service Delivery System

Human Resources Domain
- Staff size (e.g., number of professionals, paraprofessionals)
- Level of staff education/training (e.g., knowledge of behavioral principles)
- Staff availability (e.g., amount of time available for teacher consultation)

Technological Resources Domain
- Scope of present special service programs (e.g., number of group counseling programs)
- Methods and materials used by staff (e.g., contingency contracting)
- Innovative programs or pilot projects (e.g., alternate school programs)

Informational Resources Domain
- Program evaluation capability (e.g., specificity of goals and goal indicators)
- Program evaluability (e.g., number of evaluable program designs)
- Information processing (e.g., practices for monitoring pupil progress relative to the IEP)

Financial Resources Domains
- Funding sources (e.g., local, state, federal)
- Accounting systems (e.g., budgeting format, cost-finding procedures)

TABLE 6.8
Needs Assessment Matrix for Pupil Personnel Practitioners

Area of Needs Assessment	How: Methods and Techniques[a]	To Whom: Which Levels of Intervention[b]	By Whom: Which Pupil-Service Workers[c]
Pupil achievement	7, 8, 13, 16, 17, 1, 2	I, G, SS, SYST	PSYCH., L.C., COUNS., S.T.
Pupil overt behavior (e.g., talking out in class)	9, 1, 2, 15, 17, 3, 10, 11, 12	I, G	PSYCH., L.C., S.W., S.T., SP., NRS.
Psycho–motor/physical status of pupil	1, 2, 3, 8, 9, 13, 14	I, G, SS	PSYCH., NRS., S.W., AT., SP., L.C.
Teacher satisfaction/ expectations	1, 4, 9, 10	I, G, SS, SYST	PSYCH., S.W., COUNS.
Parental views	3, 6, 12	I, G, SS, SYST	S.W., COUNS., PSYCH, AT., NRS.

[a] (1) Teacher interview; (2) pupil interview; (3) parent interview; (4) teacher questionnaire; (5) pupil questionnaire; (6) parent questionnaire; (7) group standardized tests; (8) individually administered tests; (9) classroom observations; (10) teacher logs; (11) pupil logs; (12) parent logs; (13) cumulative file; (14) health file; (15) main-office data (attendance, discipline); (16) grades; (17) criterion referenced data.
[b] I = individual; G = group level; SS = subsystem level; SYST = system level.
[c] PSYCH. = psychologist; S.W. = social worker; L.C. = learning consultant; COUNS. = counselor; NRS. = nurse; S.T. = special-education teachers; SP. = speech therapist; AT. = attendance counselor.

TABLE 6.9
Criteria for an Evaluable Program[a]

Criterion Number	Category	Description
1.	Pupil data base:	written information on the assets and deficits (needs) of the child, organized according to the behavioral, affective, sensory/perceptual, academic, and physical domains
2.	Goal structure:	written goals and objectives, categorized by psycho–educational domain, that relate to the information in the pupil data base
3.	Goal indicators:	evaluative criteria, which are observable and measureable, and which are attached to goal statements
4.	Special-service program structure:	a list of the special education and related service programs (e.g., counseling) to be provided the child, organized according to the goal(s) addressed by the program
5.	Evaluation procedures:	a list of the methods and measures used in evaluation of goal attainment, including the time period(s) when measurement will occur.
6.	Regular-education participation:	a written description of the extent to which the child will participate in the regular education program.
7.	Annual review:	a specific date and time for the yearly review of the program, including the persons who will participate in the review

[a] A more detailed description of the criteria is available from the author.

executives, and staff to obtain information on program goals, activities, and to identify the assumed causal links between goals and activities. These interviews are conducted with individuals and in a group format, and include the use of structured interviewing devices such as check lists or rating scales.

The outcome of an evaluability assessment is an "Evaluable Program Design." This Program Design is a written document that is presented to the program manager, and that serves as the basis for the development of a program evaluation contract between the evaluator and manager. The written Program Design explicates information about the following programmatic elements: (1) client population; (2) client needs; (3) program goals and goal indicators; (4) programmatic resources, including staff and activities; (5) assumptions linking activities to goals; (6) program budget; and (7) evaluation design. This document can be used by the evaluator to measure the extent to which the program is operating as intended and to determine the impact of the program on the client.

Process Evaluation.   This program evaluation method is used when information is sought about the extent to which a program, as designed, has actually occurred (Freeman, 1977). Process evaluation is considered critical to program management because, without knowledge of the degree of program implementation, it will be difficult to relate any programmatic outcomes to the program, because it will not be clear what program processes have occurred (Rutman, 1977). Process evaluation centers on two evaluative questions: "To what extent has the program been implemented? and Have any negative side effects occurred as a result of program implementation?" Table 6.10 provides reasons for, and examples of, the use of process evaluation with public-school programs and examples of specific process evaluation questions that apply to particular programs.

Two methods can be used to answer process evaluation questions: retrospective monitoring and naturalistic monitoring (see Riecken & Boruch, 1974, for a detailed treatment of specific process evaluation methods).

Retrospective monitoring involves obtaining self-report information from program managers and staff about the manner in which the program has been operationalized. The kind of information that is obtained, however, is subject to some degree of bias because the evaluators must rely on the interviewee's memory of what transpired during the program. In retrospective monitoring, the evaluator conducts a series of individual or small-group interviews. During these meetings, information is sought on program process variables such as the frequency of program sessions held relative to number of sessions planned, the range of methods and materials used in the sessions, and any negative side effects that might be seen as related to the program, such as attrition from the program or unrest with staff or parents. As a supplement to the interviews or conferences, the

TABLE 6.10
Some Purposes and Evaluation Questions
of Program Process Evaluation

Purpose	Evaluation Question
To measure degree of implementation for program documentation or program monitoring	What procedures were prescribed for the teachers to follow and did they follow through on the procedures according to plan?
To determine a program's critical characteristics	In what activities were students engaged and were these activities part of the program design?
To determine the amount of variation in a program	To what extent are the six compensatory-education reading programs different with respect to program activities?

evaluator can engage in a retrospective and unobtrusive review of program-permanent products, such as a sample of written assignments or staff activity logs.

Naturalistic monitoring is characterized by the evaluator's direct observation of programmatic activities. The naturalistic approach, however, is known to produce a reactive effect (Webb, Campbell, Schwartz, & Sechrest, 1966). Moreover, the approach can be an expensive one, and the evaluator can observe only a small sample of activities. In naturalistic monitoring, the evaluator employs check lists and rating scales to obtain information on the nature and scope of the activities being provided, and for comparison of that information in relation to the kinds of programmatic activities specified in the evaluable program design. Naturalistic monitoring complements the retrospective monitoring approach by obtaining specific information on those aspects of the program that retrospective monitoring indicated have not been implemented completely.

The outcome of the program process evaluation is a written report that provides detailed information about the degree to which the program has been implemented, as well as the specific ways in which the program has deviated from the program design.

Outcome Evaluation.   This program evaluation method is used when information is required about goal attainment (Kiresuk & Sherman, 1968), cost effectiveness (Sorensen & Grove, 1978), experimental validity (Cook & Campbell, 1976, 1979), and social validity (Kazdin, 1977; Wolf, 1978). However, the specific kind of outcome evaluation methods to be employed depends on the nature of the program and the type of evaluation design that can be used, given the nature of the program.

The confidence that can be placed in any particular program outcome evaluation statement is directly related to such factors as the evaluability of the program, the amount of information available on the nature of the implemented school-based program as obtained by process evaluation methods, and the number of threats to internal and external validity that can be ruled out, which is contingent upon the kind of evaluation design (e.g., experimental, quasiexperimental, case study) utilized by the evaluator. Evaluation of programs in field settings is difficult, because the controls necessary to rule out most threats to internal as well as external validity (e.g., random assignment to groups) are difficult to establish (see, e.g., Boruch & Gomez, 1977; Campbell, 1969). In many situations, therefore, a program must be evaluated in relation to its program goals without any comparison or control groups, much like the case study (nonexperimental) designs that are detailed in Campbell and Stanley (1966).

In the evaluation of school-based, behavioral intervention programs, such as classroom behavior management programs and educational programs directed toward improving academic performance, there are outcome evaluation design problems, not common to laboratory settings, that require particular methodological approaches (Cook & Campbell, 1979). In behavioral intervention programs, which are service oriented rather than research oriented in nature, the primary goal is to change specific behaviors of specific pupils, either as part of an individual or a group program (Kazdin, 1975). In this context, the outcome evaluation design is aimed at demonstrating that the program, in fact, had the desired effect on pupil behavior(s). Thus, the issue of control of possible outside influences (factors) that might have been responsible for the observed changes but that were not detected is of paramount importance in behavioral outcome evaluation (Werts & Linn, 1971). This is the case especially with school behavioral intervention programs, where it is extremely difficult for school psychologists and other special service professionals to impose full experimental controls, as can be done in the laboratory setting (Kratochwill, 1977; Taylor & Kratochwill, 1978).

Behavioral time-series designs are very useful, practical strategies for estimating, with some degree of confidence, the extent to which a behavioral program has produced behavior change (see, e.g., Hersen & Barlow, 1976; Kratochwill, 1978). Time-series methodology, and the evaluation of time-series data, are characterized by systematic, periodic measurement of an individual or group relative to specific behaviors (e.g., class cutting, frequency of correct responses in reading); introduction of the behavioral program into the series of measurements; and continued, systematic, periodic measurement of the behavioral data following the intervention. If, by means of visual inspection of the data, there is a noticeable change in level and slope of the data (i.e., there is a discontinuity in measurement), then the behavioral program can be "weakly accepted" as the cause. If, however, visual analysis reveals no perceptible change in the data, then the use of statistical analysis can be performed by the evaluator. (For thorough treatments of issues in time-series design and evaluation, including issues in visual and statistical data analyses, the reader is referred to Hersen & Barlow, 1976; Kazdin, 1976; Kazdin & Wilson, 1978; Kratochwill, 1978.)

The amount of progress program clients make toward program goals also can be evaluated by a goal-based approach. In this method, the program evaluator uses goals and goal indicators outlined in the program design. Then, in a systematic manner, the evaluator collects base line data on the goal indicators; documents that the programmatic activities that are assumed to lead to goal attainment have occurred; collects progress data on goal attainment on a periodic basis; and makes evaluative judgments at specific time intervals about the degree of goal attainment.

Another kind of outcome evaluation that can be undertaken is consumer satisfaction. This enables an evaluator to obtain information on the perceptions of program participants about the program. The evaluation questions on which consumer satisfaction evaluation information can be obtained are: "In what ways and to what extent are you (i.e., the program participant) satisfied with the program?" and "In what ways can the program be made more worthwhile for you?"

The end product of outcome evaluation is a report that provides a range of evaluation information. This information, which is presented to a program manager in a meaningful format, addresses itself to the following issues: (1) the degree to which the program has been successful in fulfilling its purposes; (2) the extent to which the program is "internally valid"—i.e., the confidence that one can attribute program outcomes to program process; (3) the extent to which the program is "externally valid"—i.e., the extent to which an evaluator can generalize about the program to other clients and settings; (4) specific recommendations, based upon the evaluation information, about how the program manager can improve upon the design of the program for the ensuing school year.

ISSUES IN THE CONDUCT OF PROGRAM EVALUATION IN SCHOOLS

A range of issues are apparent when evaluating school programs. These issues must be recognized and appreciated by the evaluator if (s)he is to design and conduct a responsive program evaluation. Thus, in this section, several salient issues are discussed: (1) delineating decision makers, programs, and evaluation purposes; (2) designing responsive program evaluations; (3) delivering evaluation services; (4) communicating evaluation information; (5) evaluating an evaluation; (6) organizing for program-evaluation services; and (7) the propriety of program evaluation.

Delineating Decision Makers, Programs, and Evaluation Purposes

The program evaluation process usually begins with a request for evaluation service from one or more individuals who are either internal (e.g., a program director) or external (e.g., a government agency official) to the program. The nature of the evaluation request (e.g., information for program improvement, renewed funding) helps in determining whether the program evaluator will be internal (e.g., a program staff supervisor) or external (e.g., a federal official) to the organization (Horst, Nay, Scanlon, & Wholey, 1974; Wildavsky, 1972). Following the request for evaluation, the program evaluator must identify the decision maker, as well as specify the particular aspects of the program on which evaluation activity will focus.

A decision maker is defined as any individual who has authority or responsibility for overseeing or administering a program. For example, when a day care center is conceptualized as the program, the decision makers might be the board of directors, if the agency is private, or the state department of human services, if it is publicly operated. Within this facility, however, there are a number of other decision makers who have responsibility for administering particular programs. These professionals might be a director of social work services who has management responsibility for counseling and parent education programs, a director of education with responsibilities for academic and recreational training programs, and a teacher who can be seen as a "learning manager" relative to the individual education programs of the youngsters in a particular activity group. Within a community-based day care center, decision makers include a citizen advisory board, the center director, or a state department of human services planner.

In the preceding case, decision makers can be seen as having different evaluation (information) needs because their programs differ in nature and scope. The failure to delineate the decision maker in relation to a particular program unit has been shown to reduce the likelihood that an evaluation will address relevant decision making needs, as well as the chances that the evaluation will contribute to decision making (see, e.g., Hawkins, Roffman, & Osborne, 1978; Patton, 1978). The evaluator, therefore, must relate to these needs within the program context.

Once a decision maker and program have been delineated, the task is to define the specific purpose of the evaluation, although, in most instances, a global or overall evaluation purpose is known before this stage is reached. Thus, specification of evaluation purpose requires that consideration be given to the origin of the request for evaluation and the purposes (e.g., program design, outcome evaluation) toward which program evaluation can be directed (Alkin, Daillak, & White, 1979).

Designing Program Evaluations

Once the purpose and questions of the evaluation have been delineated, it is then possible to design an evaluation study in concert with the decision maker. The evaluation study should focus on the evaluation questions in order that relevant information can be obtained to answer the questions.

A program evaluation study is a strategy that consists of various people (e.g., evaluator, data collectors, decision maker) engaged in certain evaluative activities (e.g., generation of evaluation questions, data collection and analysis), using particular evaluation methods (e.g., interviewing, hypothesis testing) and materials (e.g., interview forms, data-processing equipment), in order to answer specific evaluation questions.

Once the evaluation study is designed, it is important that agreement be obtained between the evaluator and decision maker about the nature and scope of the study. This agreement can be set forth in an evaluation contract that outlines the evaluation questions to be addressed, the methods used to obtain the information to answer the questions, the procedures for data analysis, and the manner in which the evaluation information will be reported to the decision maker.

Delivering Program Evaluation Services

Evaluation services are the specific evaluation activities undertaken by the evaluator and are derived from the evaluation design. These services allow for the acquisition, analysis, and interpretation of the data derived from the evaluation so that the evaluation questions can be answered and the evaluation purpose met. At this stage, the evaluator is concerned with delivering a well designed evaluation study through the implementation of the evaluation services set forth in the evaluation design.

In providing program evaluation services, it is important to ensure quality control of the data by using procedures that allow for obtaining data that are valid, reliable, and representative; analyzing data according to appropriate data-analysis procedures (e.g., the use of appropriate statistical tests), and making interpretations that are accurate and credible and that are warranted by the data.

Communicating Evaluation Information

The primary purpose of program evaluation is to provide information useful in program decision making. To date, however, the actual usefulness of evaluation information for facilitating program decision making in human service settings has been less than encouraging (Davis & Salasin, 1975). Reasons given for the apparent low level utilization of evaluation information include the findings that evaluation information does not reflect the needs of decision makers (Cox,

1978), evaluation information is too technical and unclear (Brown, Braskamp, & Newman, 1978), and the evaluation information arrived too late to be used in decision making (Weiss, 1973).

In order to communicate evaluation information useful to program decision making, three factors need to be considered by the evaluator:

1. It is necessary to involve administrators and program staff, as well as decision makers, in determining the purpose of the evaluation and in designing the evaluation strategy (Rossi, 1972). This involvement increases the possibility that the evaluation information to be obtained reflects the information needs of the decision maker, as well as the other information audiences who might use the information.

2. An emphasis must be placed on using a range of methods—such as verbal presentations, graphic displays, and narrative reports (Stufflebeam, 1976)—for presentation of evaluation information. In disseminating evaluation information to decision makers, the evaluator must always be aware of the information-processing capabilities of the individuals who will receive the information (Janis & Mann, 1977). For example, in some schools, the level of technical sophistication might be such that a highly detailed statistical report would confuse the school's board and staff and, thus, prevent the use of the evaluation in decision making. The importance of presenting evaluation information to agency decision makers in a form that is understandable to them has been demonstrated by Hawkins, Roffman, and Osborne (1978) and Bigelow (1975).

3. The evaluation strategy must include procedures for ensuring that the evaluative information is provided to the decision makers in a timely manner so that the information can be used prior to the time when the decision(s) must be made (Weiss, 1972).

Evaluating an Evaluation

In order to develop program evaluations that contribute to program decision making, it is important to determine the degree to which each evaluation has been helpful in making the decisions. This "evaluation of evaluation," or metaevaluation, has been seen as crucial for the continued growth of evaluation for program management purposes (Cook & Gruder, 1978).

The metaevaluation of school program evaluation studies is enhanced if the evaluator and decision maker agree upon the elements of a useful program evaluation (Stufflebeam, 1976). In this regard, three standards can serve to guide the metaevaluation process: (1) the evaluation should provide information to the decision maker prior to the time when the decision must be made; (2) the information provided should be perceived by the decision maker as answering the evaluation questions; and (3) the decision maker must acknowledge that the evaluation was worth the cost (i.e., money, effort) relative to the product (i.e., evaluation report) and the product's contribution to decision making.

The area of metaevaluation, albeit an important aspect of program evaluation activity, is largely an underdeveloped one.

Organizing for Program Evaluation Services

In order to deliver appropriate program evaluation services in schools, it is necessary to look at the issue of organizing for evaluation. In developing mechanisms and procedures for designing and delivering program evaluation studies, attention must be given to a range of factors, several of which are outlined here in the form of principles:

1. The evaluation information to be provided must directly relate to the needs of the special education decision maker. For example, a special education teacher is desirous of information on the progress of each child relative to the IEP goals, whereas a special education administrator needs goal-attainment information on all pupils in the class in a more aggregate form. The program evaluator (e.g., school psychologist) must adhere to this principle when deciding upon an evaluation strategy.

2. Professional personnel (e.g., school psychologists) who are competent to design and deliver a range of program evaluation services to various evaluation units must be available. Moreover, ability to communicate the information to a range of audiences (e.g., teachers, parents, administrators) in written and verbal form is needed.

3. The organizational unit from which program evaluation services are delivered needs to be designated. Essentially, there are two alternative approaches to organizing for program evaluation. One approach, in school districts of relatively large size (e.g., urban districts), is the development of an evaluation division within the department of special education, or a department of planning and evaluation. In smaller school districts, especially in those districts that do not have a history of program evaluation in the schools, the assignment of responsibility to one or more professionals (e.g., school psychologists) who have competence in program evaluation may be more feasible.

The Propriety of Program Evaluation

An important issue in the conduct of a program evaluation is that of propriety. The propriety of program evaluation refers to the professional responsibility of the evaluator to ensure that an evaluation is conducted legally and ethically, and with due regard for the welfare of those involved in the evaluation or affected by its results. In this regard, several important points must be considered in the design and conduct of an evaluation and the dissemination of evaluation results:

1. It is useful to develop a written evaluation contract or agreement, thereby ensuring that the evaluation and decision maker understand what will and what will not be included in an evaluation. If a disagreement arises over the nature and scope of the evaluation, this should be dealt with openly and honestly, prior to the initiation of the evaluation.

2. The evaluator must design the program evaluation with an understanding of the rights of human subjects who are involved in the evaluation, as well as the right of certain audiences to be informed about the nature, process, and outcomes of an evaluation.

3. The evaluator should strive to present the evaluation information in a manner that is fair in terms of the strengths and weaknesses of the program.

4. The financial resources allocated for an evaluation should reflect only what is necessary to conduct the evaluation.

A PROBLEM SOLVING APPROACH
TO PROBLEM EVALUATION

Fundamental to the task of the school psychologist is problem solving, a systematic approach to helping school clients improve their functioning (Bardon & Bennett, 1974). The generic problem solving process, considered as the hallmark of applied professional psychology (see, e.g., Peterson, 1976), consists of a series of interrelated activities. These include defining the problem, developing a plan that addresses the problem and that attempts to resolve it, implementing the plan in the form of a program, evaluating the extent to which the program has helped resolve the problem, and communicating information to others about the extent to which the problem was resolved.

In a psychological sense, problem solving can be seen as behavior, involving cognitive and skill aspects (Miller, Galanter, & Pribram, 1960). Thus, given each step of the problem solving process, the "problem solving behavior" of school psychologists can be studied—that is, it can be assessed and modified in order to improve upon it.

Program evaluation, in and of itself, also can be conceived of as a form of problem solving. Three advantages of viewing the program evaluation process as a problem solving process can be noted. First, program evaluation has been recognized as an activity that is useful in helping a client (e.g., program manager) reduce decision uncertainty (i.e., solve a problem of program management). Second, in order for program evaluators to provide useful evaluation information, they must work with decision makers (clients) in an explicit, systematic way. Finally, in order to improve upon future program evaluation efforts, evaluators must possess a way of examining how they have designed and conducted particular evaluations.

It is possible that, by viewing program evaluation as problem solving, the school psychologist qua program evaluator will be provided with a familiar perspective on the program evaluation process, which will be helpful in generating alternative ways of providing evaluation assistance to schools and school districts. Moreover, it also is conceivable that school psychologists and other school professionals will be able to develop more effective and efficient evaluation methods and techniques.

This section of the chapter delineates a problem solving approach to program evaluation considered as having heuristic and practical value for school psychologists interested in program evaluation in the schools. This approach appears to address the evaluation issues discussed in the previous section of the chapter. It has been used by the author in his own evaluation practice, as well as in the training of school psychologists, counselors, and administrators in program evaluation. Five interdependent steps characterize the problem solving approach to program evaluation. These steps, portrayed visually in Fig. 6.1, are: (1) clarification of the evaluation problem; (2) design of the program evaluation; (3) implementation of the program evaluation; (4) dissemination of the evaluation information; and (5) Metaevaluation. In this section, each step is discussed with regard to the nature, scope, and purpose of the step, evaluation questions that focus the evaluation activities of each step, and informational outcomes emanating from each step.

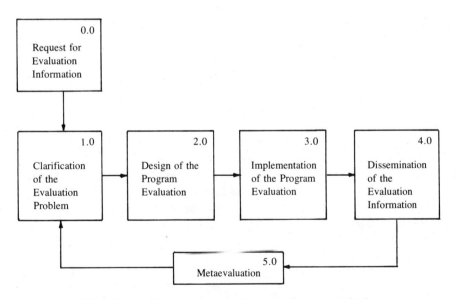

FIG. 6.1. A problem solving approach to school program evaluation.

Clarification of the Evaluation Problem

The initial task of the program evaluator is to clarify the evaluation problem and to obtain agreement with the decision maker on this problem conception. An evaluation problem situation is defined as some unsatisfactory state of affairs, perceived by a program decision maker for specific reasons, which relates to the need for evaluation information about one or more aspects of a program. For example, evaluation information may be desired by a board of education about the priority needs and goals of a district's special education program as a basis for allocation of funds; by a school superintendent on the cost of this program in relation to program outcomes as a basis for deciding about program expansion; and by the director of special education on the operations of the program relative to the way it was planned as a basis for helping to decide how a program should be revised.

In clarifying an evaluation problem, a series of interrelated questions are used by the evaluator in concert with the decision maker. These questions and some brief comments follow:

Who is (are) the client(s) of the evaluation? The primary evaluation client is the decision maker who requested the evaluation. Other secondary, but important, evaluation clients are those individuals or groups who have interest or involvement in the program, but who do not have direct decision making authority. For any school program, evaluation clients might be the board of education, school superintendent, principal, regular and special education teachers, parents, and state department of education officials.

What are the evaluation information needs of the client(s)? A need is defined as a discrepancy between a present state of affairs perceived as undesirable and a more desired state of affairs (Kaufman, 1977). An evaluation information need of a program decision maker (client) involves a discrepancy between lack of information about the worth or merit of some aspect of a program (an unsatisfactory state of affairs) and the availability of timely, technically adequate, and useful information about that aspect (a more desirable state of affairs).

The task of the evaluator in this first step is to specify the evaluation-information needs of the client(s) as a basis for the design of a program evaluation. Evaluation information needs are divided into three categories: (1) the need for evaluation information helpful in the planning and development of a program; (2) the need for evaluation information helpful in deciding how to implement a program or modify the operations of a program already implemented; and (3) the need for evaluation information helpful in judging the effectiveness of a program and the extent, if any, to which the program should be continued or expanded (disseminated).

What is the program unit on which the evaluation will focus? As discussed in a previous section, school programs can be conceptualized at three levels: individual, group, and organizational programs. The task of the evaluator, relative to this question, is to obtain agreement with the decision maker about the parameters of the program, including agreement about issues such as location(s) of the program, program population(s), program goals, and the policies and procedures of the program.

What are the evaluation questions that, when answered, will alleviate evaluation information needs? Evaluation questions serve to focus an evaluation and should relate to the evaluation information needs of a decision maker. Thus, the evaluator must elicit from the decision maker specific questions and obtain agreement from the decision maker on these questions. For example, if the evaluation information is needed about how to plan and develop a resource room program, typical evaluation questions include: "What populations of pupils should receive the resource-room program?" "What are the priority psycho-educational needs of these populations?" "What are the goals of the program and from what needs were they derived?" When evaluation information is needed about how to modify the operations of a secondary-school remedial-reading program, evaluation questions might be: "Is the program staff applying methods and materials as planned?" "To what extent are pupils being reinforced socially by the teachers for correct responses?" "Have the teachers reported any high rates of absenteeism from the program or any other negative side effects?" When evaluation information is needed about the effectiveness of a new career-education program, evaluation questions may be: "Is the new program more cost effective than the traditional program?" "Are program participants satisfied with their participation in the program?" "To what extent should the program be disseminated to other schools?"

An evaluation problem is clarified to the extent that the preceding four questions have been answered by the evaluator. The outcome of this step of the problem solving program-evaluation process is information about the client(s), the client evaluation information needs, the program unit of interest, and the evaluation questions that are derived from the needs.

Design of the Program Evaluation

A program evaluation, in and of itself, can be seen as a program. In this sense, a "program evaluation program" can be defined as any other program: an organized configuration of human, technological, informational, and financial resources that interrelate toward a particular purpose to help a client alleviate evaluation-information needs. This programmatic conception of a program evaluation (program) serves as the basis for planning and developing an evaluation (program) that is in response to a clarified evaluation problem. The following questions are used by the evaluator toward the design of a responsive program-evaluation program:

Is there consensus between evaluator and evaluation client about the purpose of the evaluation? The purpose of the evaluation derives from the evaluation-information needs of the client and the evaluation questions. Ultimately, an evaluation should provide the decision maker (client) timely, technically adequate, and useful information that will help alleviate the needs. Thus, prior to the design of an evaluation, it is important that the evaluator and decision maker obtain consensus on the nature, scope, and purpose of the evaluation.

What resources are required to design a responsive program evaluation? A responsive program evaluation is one that answers the evaluation questions that are derived from the evaluation information needs of the decision maker. In order to design such an evaluation, it is necessary to identify necessary evaluation program resources and to determine whether these resources exist in sufficient amounts to design and implement the evaluation. This task involves generating alternate resources and considering the advantages and disadvantages of each alternative and combinations of alternatives. In order to design a program evaluation, it is necessary to address the following issues:

1. What *human resources* are necessary to conduct the evaluation (e.g., consultants, statistical analyists, data collectors)?

2. What *technological resources* must be brought to bear in order to answer the evaluation questions (e.g., administration of questionnaires or rating scales, use of time-series designs)?

3. What kinds of *informational resources* must be collected (e.g., criterion-referenced data on pupil progress) and over what period of time (e.g., daily, weekly) in order to answer the evaluation questions?

4. What *financial resources* (e.g., evaluation-staff salaries, funds for data processing) must be expanded to support the implementation of the evaluation?

What are the evaluation activities to be carried out as part of the evaluation? Given that available evaluation resources have been identified and considered by the evaluator, it is necessary to delineate specific evaluation activities to be carried out. In this regard, five questions must be answered: (1) What particular human resources (2) will utilize what technological resources (3) to obtain what informational resources over what period of time (4) on what populations (e.g., pupils, teachers) (5) relative to what program? Table 6.11 provides an example of evaluation activities for the outcome evaluation of a behavioral group counseling program.

Is there agreement between the evaluator and evaluation client on the program evaluation to be implemented? Prior to the implementation of the evaluation, it is necessary to obtain agreement between evaluator and client on the nature and scope of the evaluation. Unless this agreement is forthcoming, it is not feasible to implement the evaluation. In this regard, a written contractual agreement can help clarify the design and facilitate the evaluation.

The outcome of this step of the problem-solving–program-evaluation process is written information, usually in the form of a contract, which details the human,

TABLE 6.11
Evaluation Resources and Activities for an Outcome Evaluation
of a Behavioral Group Counseling Program

Human Resources (Evaluation Personnel)

- School psychologist (evaluator)
- School psychology intern (evaluation assistant)

Technological Resources (Evaluation Methods)

- Times-series design and analysis for entire group
- Single-subject design for a representative sample of subjects
- Gotman's Integrated Moving Average Statistical Program

Informational Resources (Data to be Collected)

- Class truancy
- Teacher compliance
- School grades

Population and Program

- All pupils who have participated in the group-counseling program during the entire school year

---

technological, informational, and financial resources to be used in the evaluation.

Implementation of the Program Evaluation

As with any programmatic effort, it is paramount that the program evaluation be implemented according to plan. To properly implement a program evaluation, the evaluator must be concerned with whether the evaluation activities are being carried out and whether any negative effects result that suggest revision in the evaluation design. Two questions that are of importance in this regard are:

1. *Is the program evaluation staff carrying out evaluation activities?* The specific evaluation activities of a program evaluation will vary as a function of the evaluation questions and program unit. The evaluator, however, must make certain that permission has been obtained from the appropriate authorities to collect the data, that testers and data collectors have been properly trained and are carrying through in the manner prescribed, that subjects have been sampled appropriately, and that data have been appropriately analyzed.

2. *Are there any negative side effects related to implementation of the program evaluation?* Program evaluation occurs in a political arena (Weiss, 1973). The evaluator should recognize that evaluation information is fraught with politi-

cal implications. Moreover, numerous organizational factors (e.g., the location and type of school) and the view of evaluation in the administrative hierarchy of the school district will influence the extent to which staff participate in the evaluation process. Thus, it is important for the evaluator to seek to determine any negative effects that might be related to the evaluation, such as resistance of teachers to collect data, grievances to teachers' unions, or parental concerns over evaluation activities and use of evaluation data. If detected, this kind of information may suggest revision in the evaluation design.

The outcome of this step is information that enables the evaluator to determine the extent to which the program evaluation has been implemented according to plan (design).

Dissemination of Evaluation Information

Dissemination of evaluation information is a critical aspect of the problem solving approach to program evaluation. Dissemination of evaluation information, useful for decision making purposes, requires that the evaluator consider the following questions:

1. Has appropriate information been obtained to answer the evaluative questions?
2. Who are the audiences for the evaluation information (e.g., teachers, principals) and with what reporting formats (e.g., pupil profile, narrative reports, verbal presentations) can the evaluation information best be disseminated to them?
3. Is the evaluation information presented to the audiences at the proper time (e.g., prior to budget development)?
4. To what extent has confidentiality of the data been guaranteed in the reporting process (e.g., what written assurances are available)?

The outcome from this step is a written and/or verbal report that clearly communicates appropriate information to the decision makers.

Metaevaluation

The probability of "pay off" from an evaluation can be increased if there is emphasis on quality rather than quantity, and if some time is devoted to evaluating the program evaluation program. Metaevaluation (i.e., evaluation of evaluation) enhances the prospects for the development and application of useful evaluation procedures, and is known to promote greater effectiveness and efficiency in program evaluation (Cook & Gruder, 1978). Thus, metaevaluation is particularly important to a problem solving approach to program evaluation.

Several questions can guide the process of metaevaluation:

1. Did the program evaluation provide valid, reliable, and representative information to the evaluation client(s)?
2. Was the information presented to the evaluation client(s) in a timely manner and in a meaningful format?
3. Was the evaluation cost effective relative to the goals (i.e., desired benefits) of the evaluation in terms of time, money, and personnel allotted to the evaluation?

In determining levels of evidence for judging whether an evaluation has been appropriate, two general strategies are available: a metaevaluation conducted by an "internal" evaluator and a metaevaluation conducted by an "outside" evaluator who is not part of the program. Evidence appropriate to the internal program evaluator includes the opinion of the evaluator that the program manager was satisfied with the evaluation information, the opinion of the evaluator that the manager acted upon the information, and written documentation by the manager that the information was useful and acted upon. Evidence appropriate to an outside evaluator includes the documented opinion of the program manager that the evaluative information was useful, measurement of satisfaction of the manager through comparison of evaluation (information) needs prior to and following the evaluation, and documentation of action taken by the manager to maintain, modify, or terminate the program based upon program-evaluation findings.

The information from metaevaluation is used by the program evaluators and program manager to modify existing evaluation practices as well as to expand or maintain already existing ones.

TRAINING SCHOOL PSYCHOLOGISTS IN PROGRAM EVALUATION

During the past decade, human service organizations have been required to become more accountable for the effectiveness and efficiency of their programs (Broskowski & Driscoll, 1978). As a result of this increased emphasis on program accountability, it has become apparent that human service professionals must engage in a range of program planning and evaluation activities such as goal setting, writing program guides, assessing goal attainment, and communicating evaluation information to decision makers (Schulberg & Perloff, 1979). Public school systems, as one type of human service organization, are no exception to this recent phenomenon (Sanders, 1978). Federal legislation, such as the Education for All Handicapped Children Act (USDHEW, 1976), had necessitated that public school professionals (e.g., school psychologists, principals, curriculum supervisors) develop skills in the planning and evaluation of educational programs (Maher, 1978; Nevo & Stufflebeam, 1976).

The acquisition of skills in program planning and evaluation by school personnel is seen as important to the successful management of public-school systems (organizations). Unless educational programs can be designed in evaluable formats, it will be difficult, if not impossible, to measure the extent to which the programs have been implemented or to determine the degree to which program goals have been attained (see Wholey, 1977). Thus, in order to improve upon a school district's program planning and evaluation capability, the training of school professionals in program planning and evaluation has been seen as desirable (Nietzel, Winett, MacDonald, & Davidson, 1977).

This section of the chapter discusses several issues in the training of school psychologists in program evaluation: goals of training, methods of training, and evaluation of training experiences. The material presented is based on the author's experiences in program evaluation training at the Rutgers School Psychology Program and the Rutgers School Planning and Evaluation Center.

Goals of Training

In developing training procedures and programs in evaluation, it is necessary that trainers of school psychologists, school psychological administrators, and practitioners ask two questions: "Which school psychologists are to be given training in program evaluation?" and "What should be the scope of the training?"

The extent to which training in program evaluation will be given priority in university and field settings is seen as a function of several factors including available information about the perceived need for such training, which could be compiled on a national, state, or local level; the commitment by university-based professionals to integrate program evaluation into their training curricula; the desire of practitioners to learn about program evaluation; information about effective training methods and materials; and availability of financial and human resources to conduct such training. Thus, the kinds of program evaluation training goals that are viewed as important depend, in part, on the priority needs of practitioners and school districts as well as on the conception of program evaluation to which one subscribes. Increasingly, program evaluation is being seen as a process, closely linked to program planning, and an integral part of a comprehensive approach to professional practice (Attkisson & Broskowski, 1978; Maher, 1978). Thus, the goals of program evaluation training can be classified into one of four domains: cognitive; affective; service (behavioral), and interpersonal. Each domain, a rationale, and examples of possible priority goals for each domain are shown in Table 6.12.

TABLE 6.12
Goals for Program Evaluation Training
by Content Domain

Cognitive Domain

Rationale: In order to design and conduct a useful program evaluation, the practitioner must have a clear understanding of the nature and scope of program evaluation, including how evaluation is distinct from research.

Goals

• Knowledge of the parameters of program evaluation (e.g., being able to distinguish between service-oriented and research-oriented program evaluation).

• Knowledge of the school as an organization (e.g., being aware of the social, political, and systemic factors that influence organizational behavior).

• Knowledge of the units for program evaluation (e.g., individual, group, and organizational programs).

Affective Domain

Rationale: In order to engage actively in program evaluation, the practitioner must have an appreciation for the importance of evaluative activity.

Goals

• Awareness of the professional responsibility for evaluation of school psychological service programs, and the evaluation of school district educational programs.

• Commitment to engage in program evaluation activity as a routine part of professional practice.

Service (Behavioral) Domain

Rationale: Closely allied with a knowledge of program evaluation, and an appreciation for program evaluation activity, are particular skills a practitioner must possess.

Goals

• Clarification of the evaluation problem.
• Design of a program evaluation study.
• Administration of a program evaluation.
• Data analysis and interpretation.
• Communication of evaluation information.
• Evaluation of the utility of an evaluation.

Interpersonal Domain

Rationale: In order to conduct an evaluation that is useful to decision makers, it is necessary that the practitioner develop a close working relationship with the program manager.

Goals

• Competence in entry into the evaluation problem situation.
• Development of an evaluation contract.
• Competence in program evaluation consultation.

Methods of Training

Various methods and materials can be used for training school psychologists in program evaluation. These include: (1) conceptual frameworks and models; (2) courses, projects, and simulation exercises; and (3) a service center.

Conceptual Frameworks and Models

The utilization of conceptual frameworks and models allows for an understanding of the parameters of the program evaluation process (cognitive goals), and helps develop an appreciation for the state of the art of program evaluation (affective goal). Program evaluation training can be based in a particular conceptual framework (e.g., the Synoptic Evaluation Framework, Maher, 1978). In addition, the strengths and weaknesses of various program evaluation models, such as goal-oriented evaluation (Provus, 1971), decision oriented evaluation (Scriven, 1974), evaluation research (Cooley & Lohnes, 1976), and adversarial evaluation (Owens, 1973), can be discussed.

Courses, Projects, and Simulation Exercises

Formal graduate courses ensure that program evaluation is integrated into school psychology curricula. These courses might be year-long, semester, or minicourses, and can combine didactic and experiential activities. Two courses can complement each other relative to training in program evaluation: a course in program evaluation, which provides didactic and experiential activities and focuses on cognitive, service, and affective goals, and a course in consultation, which emphasizes interpersonal goals (see Table 6.12).

Program evaluation projects and simulation exercises have been found useful in program evaluation training in courses and institutes (Weller, Bartlett, & Northman, 1978). For example, at Rutgers, students in the program-planning and evaluation course are required to design and conduct a program evaluation in a school setting, and to evaluate the usefulness of the evaluation for decision making. In this course, as well as in a consultation course, a range of simulation exercises that bear directly on the development of program evaluation competencies are undertaken by students during class sessions.

Program Evaluation Service Center

In order to provide advanced training in program evaluation to students who request such training, it may be desirable to develop a unit or center that provides consultative and technical assistance to schools, and that can serve as a vehicle for the training. At Rutgers, the School Planning and Evaluation Center (SPEC) was developed by this author for this purpose.

The mission of SPEC is to assist school systems in the planning and evaluation of special service programs for children and youth with learning, emotional, and behavioral difficulties. This aim is accomplished through research, development, service, and dissemination activities, within a systems perspective of human behavior. SPEC, which is codirected by the present author, employs field-based practitioners and advanced doctoral students to engage in activities relative to the mission of the Center. In this regard, the activities of the Center staff include: (1) testing program planning and evaluation theory in a range of school settings; (2) developing methods and materials for the design, implementation, and evaluation of special service programs; (3) training school-psychology students, practitioners, and related special service personnel (e.g., counselors, social workers) in principles of and procedures for program evaluation; (4) providing technical assistance to schools in the measurement (e.g., needs assessment) and documentation (e.g., outcome evaluation) of special service programs; and (5) disseminating written information on its activities, in the form of occasional conceptual and technical papers, to interested audiences.

Evaluation of Training Experiences

The evaluation of professional training programs is a relatively underdeveloped area of activity, and evaluation of training programs in program evaluation is no exception (Grant & Anderson, 1977). However, comprehensive evaluation of training programs in evaluation, to determine their quality and effect, is essential if such programs are to be relevant to practice, and if school psychology is to contribute to programmatic decision making.

Evaluation of training in program evaluation must be concerned not only with the validity of the effect of particular programs, but also with the need to modify programs as a result of measurement of effect, changes in school psychological practice, and public-school evaluation needs. Three types of program evaluation methods can be used in evaluation of training: (1) goal-based evaluation of student performance in courses, based upon judgment of the quality of projects and products of simulations, using a defined set of criteria or the use of goal-attainment scaling methods (Kiresuk & Sherman, 1968); (2) student satisfaction with the program evaluation training, using informal feedback and course-evaluation forms; and (3) consumer satisfaction evaluation of professionals in public schools who have been recipients of program evaluation services provided by students, using informal verbal feedback.

FUTURE DIRECTIONS AND SUGGESTIONS: PROGRAM EVALUATION AND SCHOOL PSYCHOLOGY

The recent enactment of Public Law 94-142, rapidly diminishing school budgets, rising costs of living, increased public interest in quality education, and more explicit standards for professional practice (APA, 1977) have necessitated that school psychologists develop knowledge about, skill in, and methods for program planning and evaluation.

Directions

At the present time, it appears that *systems* of program evaluation must be developed as well as personnel to consult on and provide program evaluation studies. In this regard, it is posited that school psychologists can have a large part to play in the evaluation of school educational programs.

In a general sense, school psychologists are trained in skills that are useful in program evaluation: research design; measurement; data analysis and interpretation, and report writing. These skills, combined with competence in consultation, provide the school psychologist with a solid background for providing technical assistance on program-evaluation studies. Furthermore, knowledge in organizational theory and systems theory, areas that, increasingly, are becoming a part of school psychology training programs, provide an additional basis for the psychologist to help in the development of program evaluation systems at all levels of the school organization.

Specifically, it is possible that school psychologists can contribute to program evaluation as consultants to regular and special educators on the design of program-evaluation systems and studies, as directors of departments (units) of research, planning, and evaluation in schools and school districts, and as trainers of regular educators and special educators in methods and techniques of program evaluation, especially with regard to the IEP and classroom and school behavioral-intervention programs.

Suggestions

During the past several years, it has been this author's impressions, supported by empirical evidence (Maher, 1979d), that school psychologists are engaging in program evaluation. At the present time, however, in order to develop a knowledge base about actual and potential relationships between the field of program evaluation and the professional specialty of school psychology, the following kinds of activities are suggested:

1. The implementation by school psychology trainers of surveys of representative samples of school psychologists to determine the extent to which school psychologists are engaging in program evaluation; the kinds of program-evaluation activities in which they are engaging; and specific areas of, and skills in, program evaluation in which they believe training may be helpful.

2. Research investigations that focus on the impact that training school psychologists in program evaluation has on public school districts.

3. Research investigations that compare different procedures for training school psychologists and other school professionals in program evaluation (see Maher, 1979d and 1979e, for examples of these kinds of investigations).

4. Surveys of public school districts to determine the extent to which program evaluation is an integral aspect of the district; the nature and scope of the

evaluation information presently being collected; the number and kinds of professionals who engage in program evaluation; and the perceptions of school administrators and staff about the necessity and value of program evaluation.

5. Development of a network on "Program Evaluation and School Psychology" that would serve as a forum for trainers and practitioners on conceptual, technical, and practical matters relating to program evaluation and school psychology.

APPENDIX A: ANNOTATED BIBLIOGRAPHY OF REFERENCES ON PROGRAM EVALUATION (FOR SCHOOL PSYCHOLOGISTS)

The field of program evaluation is in a formative stage of development. The awareness of the need for evaluative activity in human service settings, including schools, became clear during the early 1960's with concern over the accountability of federal programs. During the past several years, with an increased emphasis on "fiscal responsibility" and educational compliance, school-program administrators, consumers, legislators, and the general public alike are requesting evaluative information on the nature, scope, and quality of special-service programs in schools. Clearly, this concern with accountability involves evaluation of special-service programs, such as the Individual Education Program (IEP), as well as group programs and service delivery systems. Given these contemporary circumstances, a need is apparent for special service program evaluation as well as for professionals who can conduct relevant program evaluation studies.

At the present time, program evaluation is characterized by varied definitions, conflicting terminologies, and an array of evaluative methods. In order to increase understanding of the nature of program evaluation and, the present "state of the art" of this field of endeavor, the school psychologist might benefit from a list of references on evaluation. Toward this end, a representative, nonexhaustive, annotated reference list is delineated here. This list provides informational resources on a range of important conceptual, methodological, technical, and practical issues in special service program evaluation. They are listed in alphabetical order by the name of the first author. A more detailed list of references is available from the present author upon request: Department of School Psychology, Graduate School of Applied and Professional Psychology, Rutgers University, New Brunswick, New Jersey 08903.

Abt, C. C. (Ed.). *The evaluation of social programs.* Beverly Hills: Sage Publications, 1977.

This book provides viewpoints of program evaluation research conducted in social settings. Included are discussions of the impact of evaluation research on policy decisions and emerging evaluation strategies.

Anderson, S. B., Ball, S., Murphy, R. T., & Associates. *Encyclopedia of educational evaluation.* San Francisco: Jossey-Bass, 1975.

This encyclopedia provides summary articles of key topics in terms that are useful in educational program evaluation. Categories in which articles are grouped include evaluation models, measurement approaches, analysis and interpretation, planning and design, and systems technologies.

Attkisson, C., Hargreaves, W. A., Horowitz, M. J., & Sorensen, J. E. *Evaluation of human service programs.* New York: Academic Press, 1978.

This book, which is designed for the graduate student and practitioner, provides information on major topics pertinent to program evaluation. Among the areas covered are: analysis of roles of the program evaluator and functions of evaluation; assessment of need for services; evaluation of program quality and outcome; and future directions for program evaluation.

Campbell, D. T., & Stanley, J. C. *Experimental and quasi-experimental designs for research.* Chicago: Rand McNally, 1966.

This seminal work provides information on, and examples of, experimental designs and nonexperimental approaches to conducting a range of field-based investigations including program-evaluation studies.

Cook, T. J., & Campbell, D. T. *Quasi-experimentation: Design and analysis issues for field studies.* Chicago: Rand McNally, 1979.

This book summarizes the work of Campbell and Stanley (1966) extends and elaborates their work, emphasizes statistical conclusion and construct validity, and outlines a number of quasiexperimental designs useful for program evaluation in organizational settings such as special-education day and residential schools.

Cooley, W. W., & Lohnes, P. R. *Evaluation research in education: Theory, principles and practice.* New York: Halstead Press, 1976.

Examples of evaluation research in educational settings, including data-analytic methods used in various evaluation studies, are presented in this book. Interpretation of results for decision making is also stressed.

Davidson, P. O., Clark, F. W., & Hamerlynck, L. A. *Evaluation of behavioral programs in community, residential and school settings.* Champaign, Ill.: Research Press, 1974.

An outgrowth of the Fifth Banff International Conference on Behavior Modification, this volume provides a range of articles describing conceptual issues and methodological problems in program evaluation in school and related settings. Various program evaluation technologies (e.g. cost–benefit analysis, system analysis) are offered.

Demone, H. W., & Harshbarger, D. (Eds.). *A handbook of human service organizations*. New York: Behavioral Publications, 1974.

This volume examines human-service organizations as complex, open systems. It is written with an emphasis for professionals who are involved, directly and indirectly, in the management and "study" of programs delivered to groups of various characteristics.

Guttentag, M., & Struening, E. L. (Eds.). *Handbook of evaluation research* (Vol. 2). Beverly Hills: Sage Publications, 1975.

This volume, which complements Struening and Guttentag, contains articles that focus on pragmatic aspects of evaluation, as well as examples of program-evaluation studies in selected content areas.

Hammer, R. J., Landsberg, G., & Neighber, W. (Eds.). *Program evaluation in community mental health centers*. Available from Maimonides Community Mental Health Center, Brooklyn, New York.

This work provides a section on conceptual and practical issues and a section offering a range of abstracts on program evaluation studies that have been conducted in a range of school-related settings.

Hargreaves, W. A., Attkisson, C. C., & Sorensen, J. E. (Eds.). *Resource materials for community mental health program evaluation (2nd ed.)*. Rockville, Md.: National Institute of Mental Health, 1977.

This is a volume of a range of documents designed to help community mental-health professionals with compliance to federal legislation. It includes articles focusing on a range of program evaluation methods including needs assessment and planning, management information systems, and outcome/effectiveness evaluation.

Isaac, S., & Michael, W. B. *Handbook in research and evaluation*. San Diego: Edits Publishers, 1975.

This book provides a collection of principles, methods, and strategies useful in the planning, design, and evaluation of systems, programs, and services in education and the behavioral sciences.

Kratochwill, T. R. (Ed.). *Single subject research: Strategies for evaluating change*. New York: Academic Press, 1978.

This edited book is written for psychologists involved in the evaluation of research and service programs that focus on the individual client. The book presents a comprehensive, yet concise, overview of issues in single-subject research and evaluation, and contrasts single-subject approaches with group approaches. Besides discussion of research-design issues, a variety of statistical issues and data-analytic procedures are explicated.

Rutman, L. (Ed.). *Evaluation research methods: A basic guide*. Beverly Hills: Sage Publications, 1977.

This book explains, in a clear and concise manner, the essential procedures for planning and conducting program evaluation studies. Case studies, examples, and illustrations are used to concretize the fundamental problems and issues involved in the conduct of program evaluation in human service settings.

Struening, E. L., & Guttentag, M. (Eds.). *Handbook of evaluation research* (Vol. 1). Beverly Hills: Sage Publications, 1975.

This volume, a companion to Guttentag and Struening (Vol. 2), provides a range of conceptual articles on evaluation design, methodology, analysis, and utilization. It also includes a comprehensive bibliography on program evaluation.

Weiss, C. H. *Evaluation research. Methods of assessing program effectiveness*. Englewood Cliffs, N.J.: Prentice-Hall, 1972.

This book examines a range of evaluative methods in relation to program outcome evaluation within the context of the sociopolitical arena in which most evaluation takes place.

Zusman, J., & Wurster, C. R. (Eds.). *Program evaluation: alcohol, drug abuse, and mental health services*. Lexington, Mass.: Lexington Books, 1975.

This book provides a theoretical overview of program evaluation in human service settings, provides examples of field-based program evaluation studies, discusses evaluation at the federal level, and deals with political issues in evaluation and the training of evaluators.

REFERENCES

Alkin, M. C., Daillak, R., & White, P. *Using evaluations—does evaluation make a difference?* Beverly Hills: Sage Publications, 1979.

American Psychological Association. Standards for providers of psychological services. *American Psychologist*, 1977, *32*, 495–505.

Argyris, C., & Schon, D. A. *Organizational learning: A theory of action perspective*. Reading, Mass.: Addison-Wesley, 1978.

Attkisson, C. C., & Broskowski, A. Evaluation and the emerging human service concept. In C. C. Attkisson, W. A. Hargreaves, M. J. Horowitz, & J. J. Sorenson (Eds.). *Evaluation of Human Service Programs*. New York: Academic Press, 1978.

Attkisson, C. C., Hargreaves, W. A., Horowitz, M. J., & Sorensen, J. E. Evaluation: Current strengths and future directions. In C. C. Attkisson, W. A. Hargreaves, M. J. Horowitz, & J. E. Sorensen (Eds.), *Evaluation of human service programs*. New York: Academic Press, 1978.

Attkisson, C. C., McIntyre, H. H., Hargreaves, W. A., Harris, M. R., & Ochberg, M. A. A working model for mental health program evaluation. *American Journal of Orthopsychiatry,* 1974, *44,* 741–753.

Baker, F. The living human service organization: Applications of general systems theory and research. In H. W. Demone & D. Harshbarger (Eds.), *A handbook of human service organizations.* New York: Behavioral Publications, 1974.

Bandura, A. The self-system in reciprocal determinism. *American Psychologist,* 1978, *33,* 344–358.

Barbacovi, D. R., & Clelland, R. W. *Public Law 94–142. Special education in transition.* Arlington, Va.: American Association of School Administrators, 1977.

Barclay, A. G. In M. Wertheimer, A. G. Barclay, S. W. Cook, C. A. Kiesler, S. Koch, K. Riegel, L. G. Rores, V. L. Senders, M. B. Smith, & S. E. Sperling. Psychology and the future. *American Psychologist,* 1978, *33,* 631–647.

Bardon, J. I. The state of the art (and science) of school psychology. *American Psychologist,* 1976, *32,* 785–791.

Bardon, J. I., & Bennett, V. C. *School psychology.* Englewood Cliffs, N.J.: Prentice-Hall, 1974.

Bigelow, D. A. The impact of therapeutic effectiveness data on community mental health center management: The systems evaluation project. *Community Mental Health Journal,* 1975, *11,* 64–73.

Bloom, B. S., Hastings, J. T., & Madaus, G. F. *Handbook on formative and summative evaluation of student learning.* New York: McGraw-Hill, 1971.

Boruch, R. F., & Gomez, H. Sensitivity, bias, and theory in impact evaluations. *Professional Psychology,* 1977, *8,* 411–434.

Broskowski, A., & Driscoll, J. The organizational context of program evaluation. In C. C. Attkisson, W. A. Hargreaves, M. J. Horowitz, & J. E. Sorensen (Eds.), *Evaluation of human service programs.* New York: Academic Press, 1978.

Brown, R. D., Braskamp, L. A., & Newman, D. L. Evaluator credibility as a function of report style. *Evaluation Quarterly,* 1978, *2,* 331–341.

Campbell, D. T. Reforms as experiments. *American Psychologist,* 1969, *24,* 409–429.

Campbell, D. T., & Stanley, J. C. *Experimental and quasi-experimental designs for research.* Chicago: Rand McNally, 1966.

Chapin, F. S. *Experimental designs in sociological research.* New York: Harper, 1947.

Cook, T. J., & Campbell, D. T. The design and conduct of quasi-experiments and true experiments in field settings. In M. D. Dunnette (Ed.), *Handbook of industrial and organizational psychology.* Chicago: Rand McNally, 1976.

Cook, T. J., & Campbell, D. T. *Quasi-experimentation: Design and analysis issues for field settings.* Chicago: Rand McNally, 1979.

Cook, T. J., & Gruder, C. L. Metaevaluation research. *Evaluation Quarterly,* 1978, *2,* 5–50.

Cooley, W. W., & Lohnes, P. R. *Evaluation research in education: Theory, principles, and practice.* New York: Halstead Press, 1976.

Cox, G. B. Managerial style: Implications for the utilization of program evaluation information. *Evaluation Quarterly,* 1978, *1,* 449–508.

Cronbach, L. J., & Suppes, P. (Eds.). *Research for tomorrow's schools: Disciplined inquiry for education.* New York: Macmillan, 1962.

Davis, B. G. *System evaluation: Principles and procedures for school psychologists.* Paper presented at the 87th annual convention of the American Psychological Association, New York, September 1979.

Davis, J. R., & Salasin, S. E. The utilization of evaluation. In E. L. Struening & M. Guttentag (Eds.), *Handbook of evaluation research* (Vol. 1). Beverly Hills: Sage Publications, 1975.

Demone, H. W., Schulberg, H. C., & Broskowski, A. Evaluation in the context of developments in human services. In C. C. Attkisson, W. A. Hargreaves, M. J. Horowitz, & J. E. Sorensen (Eds.), *Evaluation of human service programs.* New York: Academic Press, 1978.

Fredericksen, N. Proficiency tests for training evaluation. In R. Glasser (Ed.), *Training in research and evaluation.* Pittsburgh: University of Pittsburgh Press, 1962.

Freeman, H. E. The present status of evaluation research. In M. Guttentag (Ed.), *Evaluation studies review annual* (Vol. 2). Beverly Hills: Sage Publications, 1977.

Glass, G. V. Introduction. In G. Class (Ed.), *Evaluation studies review annual* (Vol. 1). Beverly Hills: Sage Publications, 1976.

Gotts, E. A. The individualized educational program: Potential change agent for special education. *Conference summary of Public Law 94-142*. Washington, D. C.: Roy Littlejohn Associates, 1976.

Grant, D. L., & Anderson, S. B. Issues in the evaluation of training. *Professional Psychology*, 1977, *16*, 659-673.

Guba, E. G. *Toward a methodology of naturalistic inquiry in educational evaluation*. CSE Monograph Series In Evaluation (No. 8). Los Angeles: Center For the Study of Evaluation, University of California, 1978.

Harris, A., & Kapche, R. Behavior modification in schools: Ethical issues and suggested guidelines. *Journal of School Psychology*, 1978, *16*, 25-33.

Hawkins, J. D., Roffman, R. A., & Osborne, P. Decision makers' judgements: The influence of role, evaluative criteria, and information access. *Evaluation Quarterly*, 1978, *2*, 435-454.

Hersen, M. H., & Barlow, D. G. *Single-case experimental designs: Strategies for studying behavioral change*. New York: Pergamon Press, 1976.

Hoover, J. G. The school psychologist in evaluating educational programs. *Journal of School Psychology*, 1978, *16*, 312-321.

Hoover, J. G., & Maher, C. A. (Eds.). Program evaluation and school psychology. Special issue of *Journal of School Psychology*, 1978, *16*(4).

Horst, P., Nay, J., Scanlon, J. W., & Wholey, J. S. Program management and the federal evaluator. *Public Administration Review*, 1974, *34*, 300-308.

Hunter, C. P. Classroom observation instruments and teacher inservice training by school psychologists. *School Psychology Monograph*, 1977, *3*, 45-88.

Janis, I. L., & Mann, L. *Decision making. A psychological analysis of conflict, choice, and commitment*. New York: Free Press, 1977.

Kaplan, A. *The conduct of inquiry. Methodology for behavioral science*. Scranton, Pa.: Chandler, 1964.

Kaufman, R. A. A possible taxonomy of needs assessments. *Educational Technology*, 1977, *19*, 60-64.

Kazdin, A. E. Methodological and assessment considerations in evaluating reinforcement programs in applied settings. *Journal of Applied Behavioral Analysis*, 1973, *6*, 517-531.

Kazdin, A. E. *Behavior modification in applied settings*. Homewood, Ill.: Dorsey Press, 1975.

Kazdin, A. E. Statistical analysis for single case experimental designs. In M. Hersen & D. Barlow (Eds.), *Single case experimental designs: strategies for studying behavioral change*. New York: Pergamon Press, 1976.

Kazdin, A. E. Assessing the clinical or applied importance of behavior change through social validation. *Behavior Modification*, 1977, *1*, 427-452.

Kazdin, A. E., & Wilson, G. T. *Evaluation of behavior therapy: Issues, evidence, and research strategies*. Cambridge, Mass.: Ballinger, 1978.

Kiresuk, T. J., & Sherman, R. E. Goal attainment scaling: A general method for evaluating comprehensive community mental health programs. *Community Mental Health Journal*, 1968, *4*, 443-453.

Koocher, G. B., & Broskowski, A. Issues in the evaluation of mental health services for children. *Professional Psychology*, 1977, *8*, 583-592.

Kratochwill, T. R. N = 1: An alternative research strategy for school psychologists. *Journal of School Psychology*, 1977, *15*, 239-249.

Kratochwill, T. R. (Ed.). *Single subject research: Strategies for evaluating change*. New York: Academic Press, 1978.

Kratochwill, T., & Bergan, J. Training school psychologists: Some perspectives on a competence-based behavioral consultation model. *Professional Psychology*, 1978, *9*, 71–82.

Lazarus, A. A. *Multimodal therapy*. New York: Springer Press, 1976.

Levine, A., & Levine, M. Evaluation research in mental health: Lessons from history. In J. Zusman & C. R. Wurster (Eds.), *Program evaluation: Alcohol, drug abuse, and mental health programs.* Lexington, Mass.: Lexington Books, 1975.

Lynch, W. W. Training educational personnel under the new law: Prospects and problems. *Viewpoints*, 1977, *53*, 78–87.

Maher, C. A. *Evaluation needs of special education program personnel: A survey.* Unpublished manuscript, June 1977. (Available from author: Department of School Psychology, GSAPP, Rutgers University, New Brunswick, N.J. 08903.)

Maher, C. A. A synoptic framework for school program evaluation. *Journal of School Psychology,* 1978, *16*, 322–333.

Maher, C. A. School psychology and special education program evaluation: Contributions and considerations. *Psychology in the Schools*, 1979, *16*, 240–245. (a)

Maher, C. A. *A systems-oriented needs assessment framework for special service program planning.* Paper presented at the 87th annual convention of the American Psychological Association, New York, September 1979. (b)

Maher, C. A. Systems thinking for pupil personnel services. *Journal of the International Association of Pupil Personnel Workers*, 1979, *23*, 97–102. (c)

Maher, C. A. *Training school supervisors in program evaluation: A comparison of two procedures.* Manuscript submitted for publication, 1979. (d)

Maher, C. A. *Training special service teams to develop evaluable IEPs: Three procedures.* Manuscript submitted for publication, 1979. (e)

Maher, C. A. Implementation and evaluation of a behavioral, school-based special service delivery system. *Child Behavior Therapy*, 1979, *1*, 337–346.

Maher, C. A., & Barbrack, C. R. *Perspective and principles for the evaluation of special service programs.* Workshop conducted at the 86th annual convention of the American Psychological Association, Toronto, August 1978.

Maher, C. A., & Barbrack, C. R. Special service program evaluation: Perspective and principles. *Journal of Special Education*, 1979, *16*, 16–23.

Mason, E. On putting psychology back into school psychology. *School Psychologist*, 1978, *32*, 2 & 10.

Mechanic, D. Evaluation in alcohol, drug abuse, and mental health programs: Problems and prospects. In J. Zusman & C. R. Wurster (Eds.), *Program evaluation: Alcohol, drug abuse, and mental health programs.* Lexington, Mass.: Lexington Books, 1975.

Mellor, W. L. Dynamic information systems in an educational environment. *Educational Administrative Quarterly*, 1977, *13*, 92–107.

Merwin, J. C. Historical review of changing concepts of evaluation. In R. W. Tyler (Ed.), *Educational evaluation: New roles, new means. The Sixty-Eighth Yearbook of the National Society for the Study of Education, Part 2.* Chicago: University of Chicago Press, 1969.

Miller, G. A., Galanter, E., & Pribram, K. H. *Plans and the structure of human behavior.* New York: Holt, Rinehart, & Winston, 1960.

Mitroff, I., & Bonoma, T. V. Psychological assumptions, experimentation, and real world problems: A critique and an alternative approach to evaluation. *Evaluation Quarterly*, 1978, *2*, 235–257.

Mitroff, I. I., & Featheringham, T. R. On systematic problem solving and the error of the third kind. *Behavioral Science*, 1974, *19*, 383–393.

Morentz, P. E. A citizen-conducted evaluation of acceptability: The Ronah school evaluation committee. In G. Landsberg, W. D. Neigher, R. J. Hammer, C. Windle, & J. R. Woy (Eds.), *Evaluation in practice.* Rockville, Md.: National Institute of Mental Health, 1979.

Morris, L. L., & Fitzgibbon, C. T. *How to measure program implementation.* Beverly Hills: Sage Publications, 1978.

Munz, D. *Evaluative–applied psychology: A new career alternative.* Paper presented at the 85th annual convention of the American Psychological Association, San Francisco, August 1977.

Nevo, D., & Stufflebeam, D. The availability and importance of evaluative information within the school. *Studies in Educational Evaluation,* 1976, *21,* 203–209.

Nietzel, M. T., Winett, R. A., MacDonald, M. L., & Davidson, W. S. *Behavioral approaches to community psychology.* New York: Pergamon Press, 1977.

Owens, T. R. Educational evaluation by adversary proceedings. In E. R. House (Ed.), *School evaluation: The politics and process.* Berkeley: McCutchan, 1973.

Parlett, M., & Hamilton, D. Evaluation as illumination: A new approach to the study of innovatory programs. In G. V. Glass (Ed.), *Evaluation studies review annual* (Vol. 1). Beverly Hills, Calif.: Sage Publications, 1976.

Patton, M. Q. *Utilization-focused evaluation.* Beverly Hills: Sage Publications, 1978.

Pederson, K. M. A proposal model for evaluation studies. *Administrative Science Quarterly,* 1977, *22,* 306–317.

Pennington, L. W. Provision of school psychological services. *School Psychology Digest,* 1977, *6,* 50–70.

Perkins, D. T. Evaluating social interventions. *Evaluation Quarterly,* 1977, *1,* 639–656.

Perloff, R., & Perloff, E. (Eds.). Evaluation of psychological service delivery programs. Special issue of *Professional Psychology,* 1977, *8*(4).

Peterson, D. Need for the doctor of psychology degree in professional psychology. *American Psychologist,* 1976, *31,* 792–798.

Provus, M. M. *Discrepancy evaluation.* Berkeley: McCutchan, 1971.

Riecken, H. W., & Boruch, R. F. *Social experimentation: A method for planning and evaluating social intervention.* New York: Academic Press, 1974.

Rippey, R. M. (Ed.). *Studies in transactional evaluation.* Berkeley: McCutchan, 1973.

Rossi, P. H. Testing for success and failure in social action. In P. H. Rossi & W. Williams (Eds.), *Evaluating social programs.* New York: Seminar Press, 1972.

Rossi, P. H., Freeman, H. E., & Wright, S. R. *Evaluation: A systematic approach.* Beverly Hills: Sage, 1979.

Rossi, P. H., & Wright, S. R. Evaluation research: An assessment of theory, practice and politics. *Evaluation Quarterly,* 1977, *1,* 5–52.

Roth, J. Needs and the needs assessment process. *Evaluation News,* 1977, *5,* 15–17.

Rutman, L. Planning an evaluation study. In L. Rutman (Ed.), *Evaluation research methods: A basic guide.* Beverly Hills: Sage Publications, 1977.

Sanders, J. R. School professionals and the evaluation function. *Journal of School Psychology,* 1978, *16,* 301–311.

Schulberg, H. C., & Perloff, R. Academia and the training of human service delivery program evaluators. *American Psychologist,* 1979, *34,* 247–254.

Scriven, M. Pros and cons about goal-free evaluation. In W. J. Popham (Ed.), *Evaluation in education: Current applications.* Berkeley: McCutchan, 1974.

Scriven, M. Maximizing the power of causal investigations: The modus operandi approach. In G. V. Glass (Ed.), *Evaluation studies review annual* (Vol. 1). Beverly Hills: Sage Publications, 1976.

Sorensen, J. E., & Grove, H. D. Using cost-outcome and cost-effectiveness analyses for improved program management and accountability. In C. C. Attkisson, W. A. Hargreaves, M. J. Horowitz, & J. E. Sorensen (Eds.), *Evaluation of human service programs.* New York: Academic Press, 1978.

Stake, R. E. The countenance of educational evaluation. *Teachers College Record,* 1967, *68,* 523–540.

Stufflebeam, D. L. *Meta-evaluation* (Occasional Paper No. 3). Kalamazoo: Evaluation Center, Western Michigan University, 1976.

Stufflebeam, D. L., Foley, W. J., Gephart, W. J., Guba, E. G., Hammond, R. L., Merriman, H. O., & Provus, M. M. *Educational evaluation and decision making.* Itasca, Ill.: Peacock, 1971.

Suchman, E. A. *Evaluative research.* New York: Russel Sage, 1967.

Taylor, J. P. *An administrator's perspective of evaluation.* Occasional paper series #2 (available from the Evaluation Center, Western Michigan University, Kalamazoo, Michigan), 1977.

Taylor, M. J., & Kratochwill, T. R. Modification of preschool children's bathroom behaviors by contingent teacher attention. *Journal of School Psychology,* 1978, *16,* 64–71.

Toronto, R. S. A general systems model for the analysis of organizational change. *Behavioral Science,* 1975, *20,* 145–156.

Twain, D. Developing and implementing a research strategy. In E. L. Struening & M. Guttentag (Eds.), *Handbook of evaluation research* (Vol. 1). Beverly Hills: Sage Publications, 1975.

Ullman, L. P. Behavioral community psychology. Implications, opportunities and responsibilities. Foreword in M. T. Nietzel, R. A. Winett, M. L. MacDonald, & W. S. Davidson (Eds.), *Behavioral community psychology.* New York: Pergamon Press, 1977.

U. S. Department of Health, Education & Welfare. Education of Handicapped children and incentive grants program. *Federal Register,* December 30, 1976, 56966–56998.

Webb, E. J., Campbell, D. T., Schwartz, R. D., & Sechrest, L. *Unobtrusive measures: Nonreactive research in the social sciences.* Chicago: Rand McNally, 1966.

Weiss, C. H. *Evaluation research. Methods of assessing program effectiveness.* Englewood Cliffs, N.J.: Prentice-Hall, 1972.

Weiss, C. H. Between the cup and the lip. *Evaluation,* 1973, *1,* 49–55.

Weller, B. S., Bartlett, D. P., & Northman, J. E. Simulation as a method for teaching program evaluation. *Evaluation and Program Planning,* 1978, *2,* 221–228.

Werts, C. E., & Linn, R. L. Problems with inferring treatment effects from repeated measures. *Educational and Psychological Measurement,* 1971, *31,* 857–866.

Wholey, J. S. Evaluability assessment. In L. Rutman (Ed.), *Evaluation research methods: A basic guide.* Beverly Hills: Sage Publications, 1977.

Wholey, J. S., Nay, J. N., Scanlon, J. W., & Schmidt, R. E. Evaluation: When is it really needed? *Evaluation,* 1975, *2,* 89–93.

Wildavsky, A. The self-evaluating organization. *Public Administration Review,* 1972, *32,* 509–520.

Windle, C., & Ochberg, F. M. Enhancing program evaluation in the community mental health centers program. *Evaluation,* 1975, *2,* 30–36.

Wolf, M. Social validity: The case for subjective measurement or how applied behavior analysis is finding its heart. *Journal of Applied Behavior Analysis,* 1978, *11,* 203–214.

Worthen, B. R., & Owens, T. R. Adversarial evaluation and the school psychologist. *Journal of School Psychology,* 1978, *16,* 334–345.

Worthen, B. R., & Sanders, J. *Educational evaluation: Theory and practice.* Worthington, Ohio: Charles A. Jones, 1973.

7

Advances in Criterion-Referenced Assessment

Anthony A. Cancelli
Thomas R. Kratochwill
University of Arizona

INTRODUCTION

The development of criterion-referenced testing in psychology and education has provided a new and necessary dimension to assessment over the last decade. Initially spurred by a need arising from objective-based instructional programs, this measurement procedure has since been popularized for a variety of uses. In addition to tracking a student's progress through objective-based instructional programs, criterion-referenced tests (CRTs), among other things, have been useful in evaluating educational and social-action programs, assessing competencies on certification and licensing examinations, and, of most importance to practicing school psychologists, diagnosing learning deficiences (Hambleton, Swaminathan, Algina, & Coulson, 1978). The popularity of CRTs has also given rise to a decade of debate regarding their advantages and disadvantages in contrast to norm-referenced tests (NRTs).

In addition to finding their own niche as a useful assessment strategy, CRTs have also gone through continual refinements, and, yet, as Popham (1978a) points out, "the measurement strategy is far from polished [p. 8]." Contributions to their continuing development have come from several sources. The purpose of this chapter is to review some of these contributions and to presage developments anticipated from present trends. However, before beginning, we need to briefly discuss what is meant by criterion-referenced assessment.

CRITERION-REFERENCED ASSESSMENT DEFINED

The term "criterion referenced," first coined by Glaser and Klaus in 1962, refers to a strategy for measuring students' skills in absolute rather than relative terms.

The importance of this distinction was elaborated upon a year later by Glaser (1963) in an article in the *American Psychologist*. Glaser pointed out that there are basically two kinds of information that can be obtained from an achievement test. One kind provides information concerning a student's performance relative to others who have taken the test; this was labeled by Glaser as "norm referenced." It was further pointed out that most attention had been given traditionally to designing and interpreting achievement tests from a norm-referenced perspective. The second kind of information provided by an achievement test relates to whether a student's performance has met criterion—that is, when compared to an absolute standard, can the student be judged as having satisfactorily mastered the skill purported to be reflected in the test? This kind of information was identified as criterion referenced and is most readily accessible through the use of CRTs.

As the distinctions between CRTs and NRTs grew, it became apparent that a new technology was necessary for the proper design and use of CRTs. With continued evolution came an additional need for a more precise definition of CRTs (Livingston, 1977). Several definitions have been offered in recent years. Popham and Husek (1969), for example, in a now classic article entitled "Implications of Criterion-Referenced Measurement" define criterion-referenced measures as: "... those which are used to ascertain an individual's status with respect to some criterion, i.e., performance standard. It is because the individual is compared with some established criterion, rather than with other individuals, that these measures can be described as criterion-referenced [p. 2]." Similarly, Glaser and Nitko (1971) define a CRT as: "... one that is deliberately constructed to yield measurements that are directly interpretable in terms of specified performance standards ... [p. 653]."

Alkin (1974) suggests that the similarity in most definitions of CRTs is that they emphasize two characteristics: (1) the organization of the test around behavioral objectives; and (2) assessment in terms of predefined performance criterion.

With respect to the former, continued developments in the design of CRTs brought a growing appreciation for the need to adequately delineate the content of the behavioral domains specified in the behavioral objectives defining the content of the curriculum. Work in this area has resulted in strategies for more clearly identifying the potential items that can be drawn from the behavioral domain represented by an objective. The use of amplified objectives (Popham, 1974b), domain specifications (Popham, 1975, 1978c), item form analysis (Hively, Maxwell, Rabehl, Sension, & Lundin, 1973), facet analysis (Berk, 1978), and algorithms (Scandura, 1977) have all been proposed as an intermediate step between writing objective and sampling items for a CRT. The major purpose of this step is to define the content of a behavioral domain to the extent that qualified judges can agree on whether or not a test item is included in the definition (Cronbach, Glaser, Nanda, & Rajaratnam, 1972). This advancement has prompted some writers to suggest a change in the name of this measurement strategy from "criterion referenced" to "domain referenced" (e.g., Hively, 1974; Millman, 1974). Recently, Hambleton et al. (1978) recommended that we continue to use the term criterion-referenced assessment instead of switching to domain-referenced testing for two reasons. First, they argue that it has been implicit from the outset that the word criterion was intended to refer to a domain of behavior. Recently developed procedures for specifying domain content has only made possible what had been conceptually clear all along. Second, because CRTs had become popularized and have gained wide acceptance, a change in the name would only serve to confuse work in the area. Hambleton et al. (1978), however, do suggest that a distinction be made between CRTs and what they refer to as objective-referenced tests. The latter are those tests that still use objectives as the basis for generating test items. These are referred to by Popham (1974a) as "cloud-referenced" tests.

CONTRIBUTIONS TO CRITERION-REFERENCED ASSESSMENT

As previously mentioned, the contributions to the development of CRTs have come from several areas, three of which are identified for our present discussion: (1) instructional psychology; (2) psychometric theory; and (3) behavior therapy. Two criteria were used for selecting these areas for review. The first relates to the unique contributions made by each in the *conceptualization, design,* and *use* of CRTs. The second involves the potential usefulness of these contributions in the delivery of school-psychological services.

In the area of instructional psychology, research related to an analysis of learning tasks has been influential in advancing our *conceptualization* of domains of knowledge and the hierarchical relations among the domains in the curricula for which CRTs are developed. In the area of psychometric theory, researchers have largely focused on *design* questions related to the construction of CRTs and have advanced our understanding of the special psychometric issues related to criterion-referenced testing. The third area identified, behavior therapy, has advanced our understanding of the *use* of CRTs as an important component in a package of academic-assessment strategies in delivering services to the individual learner. A discussion of the contribution in each of these areas is included in this section.

Instructional Psychology

The investigation of instructional processes as a legitimate enterprise in psychology is attested to by the growing number of researchers who have turned their attention to it in recent years (Glaser & Resnick, 1972). In an analysis of what it is that encompasses the study of instructional processes, Glaser and Resnick (1972) identified five characteristics: (1) analysis of the task properties of a knowledge domain; (2) diagnosis of the characteristics of the learner; (3) design of the instructional environment; (4) assessment of specific instructional effects; and (5) evaluation of generalized learning outcomes. The contribution of instructional psychology in the area of analyzing learning tasks has provided the greatest impact on the development of thought associated with CRTs and is the focus of this section.

Gagné's Theory

One theory of instruction that has emphasized the analysis of learning tasks as an essential component of effective instruction is that proposed by Gagné (1977). Gagné contends that a highly important factor to consider in designing an instructional program for facilitating learning is an understanding of the previously learned capabilities that the learner brings with him/her to the learning environment. Among the most important of these capabilities is one that rests at the heart of Gagné's theory—"intellectual skill." According to Gagné, intellectual skills are those skills that enable an individual to interact with his/her environment through the use of symbols. Five major classes of intellectual skills are identified (Gagné, 1977); (1) basic forms of learning (including associations and chains); (2) discriminations; (3) concepts; (4) rules; and (5) higher-order rules.

All intellectual skills are hypothesized to vary in their level of complexity from the most simple (i.e., associations) to the most complex (i.e., higher-order rules). Gagné (1977) contends that intellectual skills are prerequisitely ordered on this dimension of complexity such that the learning of more complex skills requires the previous acquisition of the less complex skills that are considered its components. For example, a child performing a simple addition problem is believed to possess prerequisite knowledge necessary for the satisfactory resolution of the problem. Included in this list of prerequisites would be tasks such as understanding the operation implied by the plus sign and knowing, for example, that the numeral 5 represents five units. These skills would then be components of the addition task, which can be identified as the superordinate task. Although experimental evidence to date supports Gagné's assumption of the existence of prerequisite skills, evidence that they optimize or facilitate learning is not yet available (Cotton, Gallagher, & Marshall, 1977).

The psychological organization of a set of intellectual skills is referred to by Gagné as a learning hierarchy. One way suggested by Gagné (1968) for identifying hierarchical sequences of intellectual skills is through the use of task-analysis procedures. Task analysis first emerged in the 1950's and 1960's in military job training as a systematic procedure for identification of skills prerequisite to performing tasks such as keypunching (Bernard, 1975). Although historically, task-analysis designs have included an analysis of a wide variety of internal conditions necessary for learning to occur (e.g., attention), procedures recommended by Gagné are geared toward identifying prerequisite intellectual skills. A learning hierarchy from Gagné's perspective includes only intellectual skills, and, as a result, specifically includes those prerequisites that are minimally essential for advanced learning to occur. Previously learned cognitive strategies or motor skills, although necessary in a complete learning analysis, are not considered.

Basically, task analysis is a "rational" process in that it involves an analysis of the subject-matter structure as understood by masters or experts. Gagné's (1968) procedures for conducting task analysis simply requires the person analyzing a complex task to ask the question: "What (skill) should the learner already know how to do and be able to recall when faced with the task of learning the new rule, the absence of which would make it impossible for him to learn the new rule?" One can next ask the same question about each of the components thus derived to further break down the task. This process would continue until, for all practical purposes, the components become simple enough for their intended use.

The foregoing task-analysis procedure reflects the importance Gagné attributes to the rule as an intellectual skill. Most school behavior, according to Gagné, can be viewed as rule governed—that is, involving the application of rules. Thus, in his procedure, the analysis of rules is an essential feature. However, it should be understood that tasks involving less complex intellectual skills (e.g., discriminations and concepts) are task analyzed in the same manner. In Gagné's procedure, the word "skill" or "intellectual skill" can be substituted for the word "rule" where appropriate.

Another popular task-analysis procedure is one designed by Resnick, Wang, and Kaplan (1973). In this procedure, the difference between a component and a prerequisite skill is emphasized. A component skill is a skill that is part of the superordinate skill in the sense that the person performing the superordinate task either covertly or overtly exhibits the skill. A prerequisite skill, on the other hand, is not actually performed as a part of the superordinate task, yet its mastery facilitates learning the more complex superordinate task. Presumably, prerequisite skills are skills that are initially learned in a hierarchy and then drop out and are not performed as part of the superordinate task.

The preceding discussion has emphasized Gagné's conceptualization of intellectual skills and the hierarchical arrangement of these skills. It is these conceptualizations that have contributed to an understanding of the structure of the content of curricula for which CRTs are designed.

Intellectual Skills and CRTs

The design of any CRT first starts with an analysis of the curriculum validating its existence. As mentioned earlier, before test items can be drawn for inclusion in a CRT, objectives need to be defined and a clear specification of the potential items comprising the domain of behaviors encompassed by the objective needs to be detailed. In providing a framework for the development of CRT's, Shoemaker (1975) has suggested conceptualizing all potential test items that can be drawn from a performance objective as an "item universe" and labeling those specific collections of items sampled from an item universe as an item domain. Yet, despite a variety of efforts made in designing procedures for specifying the content of item domains, little attention has been paid to the preliminary analysis of the scope of behaviors to be included in each objective.

A common approach for the design of an item domain starts with an expert or team of experts designing objectives for a specified curriculum content. No rules governing the size of the objectives are usually identified. This decision is generally left to the experts to be made on "intuitive" grounds. Hambleton and Eignor (1979b) suggest that the size of the domain representing an objective should in part be governed by the purpose for which the CRT is to be used. When constructing a CRT for assessing mastery of a large amount of information, they suggest that domains large in scope should be designed. This would allow for tests of reasonable length. However, Cancelli (1978) has suggested that the scope of a domain should be decided on after a consideration of factors related to the acquisition of the items in the domain and not solely on intuitive grounds or for practical reasons. It is to this end that Gagné's conceptualization of an intellectual skill, especially his concept of a rule, has a significant contribution to make. Learned behaviors are not conceived of by Gagné (1977) as the acquisition of discrete behaviors, but rather as the acquisition of classes of responses. The acquisition of a response class is considered to be mediated by an intellectual skill. Consequently, if behavioral objectives are designed around intellectual skills so that each objective represents a single response class, a framework for deciding on the scope of an objective and consequent item domain is provided.

The idea of a homogeneous set of items (i.e., a response class), in structuring item domains such that if one is answered correctly all are capable of being answered correctly, is not restricted to Gagné's writings. In discussing the concept of item domains, most investigators either directly state or imply the existence of such response classes. Hively (1974), for example, suggests that the best form for an item domain is one in which all the items form a single response class. Popham and Husek (1969) have suggested that an ideal CRT is one in which the items sampled from the item population are homogeneous in nature. Macready and Merwin (1973) have pointed out that the design of a good diagnostic test depends on the relations among test items within diagnostic categories.

From an assessment perspective, a distinct advantage is gained through the use of intellectual skills in defining the scope of an objective (Cancelli, 1978). To demonstrate this advantage, let us now take a look at the limitations encountered when objectives are structured around heterogeneous sets of items comprising more than a single response class. As an example, let us assume that the following typical behavioral objective not designed to reflect a single response class has been identified as part of the curriculum content:

Given two four-digit numbers with one or more zeros in the minuend, a child will be able to compute their difference 90% of the time when regrouping is required.

Using an appropriate domain statement and item-sampling procedure, a sample of items can be drawn for assessment purposes. Two examples of such items are:

$$
\begin{array}{cc}
3400 & 4430 \\
-2372 & -3851 \\
\hline
\end{array}
$$

Let us now suppose a 10-item test so constructed is administered to a child who answers 60% of the items in this domain correctly. What can be said about the child's mastery of all the items in this domain and, more importantly, what instructional plan does such performance imply? In response to the first question, much can be said about the child's mastery of the content. The procedures used to identify the items allow for comfortable inferences concerning the percent mastery of all items within the item domain (i.e., 60%).

The answer to the second question is more nebulous. The performance of our hypothetical child suggests that continued instruction on items sampled from the item domain is still necessary. Even though this is probably the case, ambiguity regarding those items not yet mastered within the item domain still exists. If there is no relation between the items within the defined item domain and all represent discrete behavioral capabilities, then the structure of the item domain becomes relatively unimportant and the grouping of items is just as well justified on the grounds of convenience. Under this circumstance, the ability to respond correctly to one item would be unrelated to the ability to respond to another item successfully. However, if we hypothesize that there are classes of responses such that a specified number of items are capable of being correctly answered if one item is answered correctly, then ambiguity in the identification of items yet to be mastered within the item domain will exist if the structure of the item domain is not designed around these response classes. Thus, under this conceptualization, the 60% of the items answered by our hypothetical child are difficult to interpret using heterogeneous item domains. They could, for example, represent complete mastery of one of several response classes within the item domain. If such were the case, any continued instruction on those items requiring responses within a mastered response class would be redundant. The point of the matter is, then, that if these hypothesized response classes do exist, domain structures not designed congruently with items forming a response class result in ambiguous test findings that are difficult to correctly interpret and use to design efficient instructional plans.

Hierarchies and CRT's

The second and more obvious contribution made by instructional psychology to the design of CRTs has been in the hierarchical sequencing of learning tasks.

As Gray (1978) points out, even though many of the earlier writings on criterion-referenced measurement implicitly suggested that individual performance is based on a knowledge continuum (i.e., learning hierarchy), most workers in the area have concentrated their efforts exclusively on the design and structure of individual item domains.

The value of the concept of learning hierarchies underlying domains in a CRT stems from its recognized potential value in treatment-oriented assessment. This advantage relates to the problem of adapting instruction to the needs of individual learners. First, CRTs may be developed to individualize the placement of learners in an instructional sequence (Glaser & Nitko, 1971; Nitko & Hsu, 1974; Resnick et al., 1973). Second, CRTs based on hierarchies may be used in the initial phases of instruction to determine the point in an instructional sequence that will enable a learner to encounter readily attainable goals and at the same time to avoid activities related to objectives that have already been mastered. Third, CRTs may also be used at the end of a sequence to determine what has been learned and thereby to establish what should be taught next (Nitko & Hsu, 1974).

In addition to their application in testing linked to specific curriculum sequences, hierarchies may be useful in the development of assessment devices used by school psychologists working with instructional personnel to facilitate the academic progress of students manifesting learning difficulties (Bergan, 1977). It may happen that a learner will fail to develop prerequisite skills necessary for the mastery of superordinate skills of immediate concern in instruction and that this failure will not be readily apparent. Under these conditions, a CRT comprised of relevant, hierarchically related skills may be useful in diagnosing the source of learning problems (Bergan, 1977; Bergan, Byrnes, & Kratochwill, 1979).

As previously implied, because it is the instructional content that justifies the existence of CRTs, attention to the design of CRTs around the concept of learning hierarchies should not be an afterthought, but rather should be essential to their existence. Such thinking prompted Gray (1978) to recently offer the following definition for CRTs: "Criterion-referenced tests are those designed to produce measurement directly interpretable in terms of specified performance standards where the standards form a continuum of knowledge that is dependent on the prerequisite relations among the various levels of the continuum [p. 227]."

Empirical Validation of Item Domains and Learning Hierarchies

Although the concepts of intellectual skills and learning hierarchies have had some influence on the design of CRTs, the impact appears to be, at best, indirect. One apparent reason for their failure to have a greater impact on CRTs than they have had is that, until recently, there has been no adequate empirical validation

procedures for structuring homogeneous item domains and hierarchical sequences that could be used by test developers. With respect to domain validation,
for example, White (1974) discussed the need to determine statistically the extent
to which different items assessed the same skill, but was forced to conclude that
there were no available statistical procedures for making such a determination. In
the area of validating learning hierarchies, during the period since Gagné (1962)
introduced his model, there have been several studies attempting to validate
isolated hierarchical sequences (cf. White & Gagné, 1974). However, early investigations on hierarchies were marred by serious methodological flaws (White,
1973). White (1973, 1974) suggested modifications in hierarchy-validation techniques. Despite these advances, adequate hierarchy validation has been slow in
coming, probably as a result of the time-consuming nature of the procedures,
which makes them unsuitable for broad-scale application. Consequently, test
developers who wish to design their CRTs around the concept of intellectual
skills and learning hierarchies have been forced to use rational task-analysis
procedures to identify response classes and their prerequisite relations.

Most recently, however, practical procedures suitable for the empirical validation of item domains and learning hierarchies have been made available. These
procedures described in detail by Bergan (1980a) make use of latent structure
analysis combined with related procedures for scaling response patterns (Goodman, 1974, 1975). The use of these procedures has provided new impetus to
domain and hierarchy validation research. Recent studies designed to test
hypotheses germaine to the development of our understanding of intellectual
skills and learning hierarchies have been conducted making use of the these
procedures with promising results (Bergan, in press, 1980b; Bergan, Cancelli, &
Karp, 1979; Cancelli, Bergan, & Jones, 1979; Cancelli, Bergan, & Taber,
1980). The advent of these procedures has resulted in a new form of assessment
proposed by Bergan (see Bergan's chapter in this volume), which he identifies as
path-referenced assessment.

Psychometric Theory

While work in the area of instructional psychology has provided advances in our
thinking about CRTs involving the scope and sequence of the structure of knowledge, researchers involved in psychometric theory have been studying issues
primarily related to test construction and score interpretation. Much emphasis has
been placed on the design of domain statements, procedures for generating test
items, and issues related to reliability, validity, and the selection of performance
standards. Following is a brief discussion of each of these issues. The purpose of
this section is not to be exhaustive with respect to some of the highly technical
developments, but rather to provide the reader with an overview of some of the
problems now being addressed.

Domain Statements

The purpose of a domain statement is to more clearly identify those items to be included as part of the domain. It is an elaboration of the content implied by a behavioral objective. Whereas those involved in the instructional-psychology movement have been most concerned with the scope of behaviors in a domain, those involved in the psychometric movement have turned their attention to methods for clearly specifying the content of a domain. Those involved in the latter movement usually perceive homogeneous item domains as desirable, but not essential, to the design of an acceptable CRT (Cancelli, 1978).

As previously mentioned, Shoemaker (1975) conceptualizes all potential items that can be included in a domain as an "item universe" and those that are clearly identified as part of the domain as an "item domain." The necessity for specifying the content of item domains should not be underestimated. The results of a CRT drawn from item domains are often used to make inferences concerning an individual's mastery of the domain. The validity of such inferences are to a large extent determined by an accurate specification of the behavioral domain (Traub, 1975).

Traub (1975) distinguishes between two types of domain statements. The first type involves procedures for specifying the *parameters* of an item universe. The specific items forming the item domain are only *implicitly* identified through the statement of these parameters. When implicit domain statements are used, Shoemaker (1975) suggests the "pooling" or "banking" of items to define the item domain. Basically, these procedures involve generating items through the use of the implicit domain statement and storing them for use at a later date. The collection of the items would then be the operational definition of the domain. Included among those procedures for implicitly defining a domain are amplified objectives (Popham, 1974b) and domain specifications (Popham, 1975, 1978a).

The least specific of the implicit domain statements is the amplified objective (Popham, 1974b). An amplified objective, according to Millman (1974), "is an expanded statement of an educational goal which provides boundary specifications regarding testing situations, response alternatives and criterion of correctness [p. 335]." An example of an amplified objective is presented in Fig. 7.1. As can be seen in the Fig., an amplified objective provides similar information as that provided in a standard behavioral objective. The difference is that the amplified objective is more detailed.

Popham (1975) has also presented a domain statement procedure, identified as "domain specifications," which is more specific than an amplified objective. Hambleton and Eignor (1979b) view a domain specification as a logical extension of an amplified objective. An example of a "domain specification" is presented in Fig. 7.2. As can be seen in this Fig., the degree of detail in the domain specification is greater than that in the amplified objective. However, the type of information is similar. In addition to a detailed description of stimulus

Amplified Objective:

Testing Situation

1. The student will be given three sentences and will identify their proper sequence on the basis of verb tenses and signal words.
2. Three sentences containing signal words and/or changes in verb tense will be provided.
3. Vocabulary will be familiar to the third grader.

Response Alternatives

1. Three possible orderings of the sentence will be given.
2. At least one distractor should *not* consist of a random ordering. It should maintain the first event as first, varying only the second and third events.
3. The other distractor may be any other incorrect ordering of the events.

Criterion of Correctness. The correct answer will be the order that can be determined on the basis of one of the following:

1. Words that signify sequence, e.g., afterwards, finally, then, before, during, now, next, lastly, later, earlier, meanwhile, long ago, once.
2. Verb tense (future, past, present).

FIG. 7.1   An example of an amplified objective. (Source: Popham, 1978b. Reproduced by permission.)

and response attributes to be included in the items, the domain specification also includes a sample item.

The second type of domain statement identified by Traub (1975) involves procedures that are *explicit* in their identification of all items making up the domain. Item-form analysis (Hively et al., 1973) and facet analysis (Berk, 1978) are two examples of explicit domain statements. With such a domain statement, there is no need to "pool" or "bank" items and the item universe and item domain become the same thing.

The most highly detailed procedure for specifying the boundaries and content of a domain is the item form (Hively et al., 1973). An example of an item form is presented in Fig. 7.3. Whereas amplified objectives and domain-specification procedures provide general rules to be followed in constructing an item, as previously mentioned, the item-form approach identifies all the stimulus elements that can possibly be included in constructing an item. A description of how these stimulus elements are to be sampled from the specified set of stimulus elements is also provided in the item form.

Item Selection

Once the task of specifying the domain content has been accomplished, the next step is to select the items to be included in the test. Item-selection strategies are designed so that a representative sample of items can be selected from the item domain. Random-sampling and stratified-sampling procedures are those

An illustrative set of criterion-referenced test specifications:
applying concepts of United States foreign policy.

GENERAL DESCRIPTION

Given a description of a fictitious international situation in which the United States may wish to act, and the name of an American foreign-policy document or pronouncement, the students will select from a list of alternatives the course of action that would most likely follow from the given document or pronouncement.

SAMPLE ITEM

Directions: Read each fictitious example below. Decide what action the United States would most likely take based on the given foreign-policy document. Write the letter of the action on your answer sheet.

Some Russian agents have become members of the Christian Democratic Party in Chile. The party attacked the President's house and arrested him. The Russian agents set themselves up as President and Vice-President of Chile. Chile then asked to become an "affiliated republic" of the USSR.
Based on the Monroe Doctrine, what will the United States do?

a. Ignore the new status of Chile.
b. Warn Russia that its influence is to be withdrawn from Chile.
c. Refuse to recognize the new government of Chile because it came to power illegally.
d. Send arms to all groups in the country that swear to oppose communism.

STIMULUS ATTRIBUTES

1. The fictitious passage will consist of 500 words or less followed by the name of a foreign-policy pronouncement or document inserted into the question, "Based on the _____, what will the United States do?"
2. The policy named in the stimulus passage will be a document or pronouncement selected from the specification supplement.
3. Each passage will consist of two parts: (a) a background description of an action taken by a foreign nation and (b) a statement of the action to which the foreign-policy document or pronouncement is to be applied.
   a. The background statement will be analogous to an historical situation that either proceeded the issuance of the cited document or pronouncement or for which the document or pronouncement was used. For example, the Monroe Doctrine was drawn up in response to European designs on American nations that were attempting to establish independence. An analogous case today might describe a European country attempting to encroach on the sovereignty of an American country.
   b. The statement of an action will describe an action taken by a real foreign nation that conforms to one of the following categories:
      (1) Initiation of an international conflict.
      (2) Initiation of a civil conflict. This may include coups, revolutions, riots, protest marches, civil war, or a parliamentary crisis.
      (3) Initiation of an international relationship. This may include trade negotiations, friendship pacts, military alliances, and all classes of treaties.
      (4) Appeal for foreign aid to meet economic or military needs.
      (5) Development and stockpiling of military weapons.

4. All statements in the passage will refer to specific nations and events. Descriptions such as "A nation is at war with another country" are not acceptable.

5. When the document or pronouncement mentioned in the stimulus passage is tied to a particular geographical region, countries named in the passage must belong to that region.

6. Passages will be written at no higher than the seventh-grade reading level.

RESPONSE ATTRIBUTES

1. Students will be asked to mark the letter of one of four given response alternatives consisting of the correct response and three distractors. Each alternative will possess the following characteristics:

   a. Describe a specific course of action that refers to the people, nations, and actions in the stimulus passage.

   b. Be brief phrases written to complete the understood subject, "The United States will . . ."

2. Distractors (wrong answers) will be written to meet these additional criterion:

   a. Each distractor will describe an action derived from a different document or pronouncement selected from the specification supplement.

   b. Documents or pronouncements from which identical courses of action may be derived will not be used.

   c. The decision for the United States not to act may be used as a course of action when it is based on a document or pronouncement.

3. The correct response will be the course of action that is governed by the principles described in the document or pronouncement named in the stimulus passage.

SPECIFICATION SUPPLEMENT: ELIGIBLE POLICY DOCUMENTS AND
PRONOUNCEMENTS

1. The Declaration of Independence
2. The Monroe Doctrine
3. Open Door in China
4. The Fourteen Points
5. The Truman Doctrine
6. The Marshall Plan
7. The North Atlantic Treaty
8. American–Japanese Defense Pact

FIG. 7.2   An example of a domain specification. (Source: Popham, 1978a, pp. 129 to the top of 131, with the exception of the domain specification supplement. Reproduced by permission.)

most commonly used for this purpose. With explicitly defined domains, a random-sampling procedure can be used whereas a stratified random sample is more appropriate with implicitly defined domains (Hambleton & Eignor, 1979b). However, as Subkoviak and Baker (1977) stress, such sampling procedures should only be preliminary to piloting the items so that flaws can be eliminated. Unintended cues and ambiguities should be the focus of the analysis and, if necessary, either the items or domain statement should be restructured according to the findings. Procedures utilizing the feedback of the test takers (Millman, 1974), content specialists (Rovinelli & Hambleton, 1977), and empirical

ITEM FORM 1
   Solving Algebraic Problems Involving *Term Transposition.*
GENERAL DESCRIPTION
   The individual is given an algebraic equation involving three or four letters and is asked to solve for an unknown X, by isolating that unknown, on either side of the equation.
STIMULUS AND RESPONSE CHARACTERISTICS
Constant for all Cells
   Algebraic problems are presented in written form. A written response is required.
Distinguishing Among Cells
   Type of term transposition:
(1) addition or subtraction (one step); (2) multiplication or division (one step); (3) addition or subtraction (two steps); (4) multiplication or division (two steps).
Varying Within Cells
   Type of problem presented and letters used to represent variables.
CELL MATRIX   Set

	Set
addition or subtraction (one step)	1
multiplication or division (one step)	2
addition or subtraction (two steps)	3
multiplication or division (two steps)	4

ITEM FORM SHELL
Materials
Pencil
Problem sheet with space for responses

Directions to Experimenter	Script
Place materials in front of individual.	"Here is a sheet of problems. Solve for X in each problem. Try to do all of the problems. You will have as much time as you need.

SCORING SPECIFICATIONS
   All items will be scored dichotomously (0 for incorrect response, 1 for correct response).
REPLACEMENT SCHEME
   Use any of the problems from the replacement sets. Any letter of the alphabet may be substituted for another, except for X. Choose one from each of the following sets:
Replacements Sets

Set 1:
$$X + A = B$$
$$X - A = B$$
$$A - X = B$$
$$A + X = B$$

Set 2:
$$X/A = B$$
$$AX = B$$

Set 3:
$$X + A - B = C$$
$$X + A + B = C$$
$$X - A + B = C$$
$$X - A - B = C$$

Set 4:
$$BX/A = C$$
$$ABX = C$$
$$X/A/B = C$$

FIG. 7.3   An example of an item form. (Source: Bergan, Cancelli, & Towstopiat, 1979.)

230

methods of analysis, such as comparing the deviance of response pattern, have been proposed for this purpose.

Reliability

Reliability is a measure of the consistency of a test. It is just as important to establish the reliability of CRTs as it is for NRTs. Given the different assumptions governing the design of CRTs when compared to NRTs, however, the use of traditional test-theory approaches to establish CRT reliability is not altogether appropriate. Such difficulties have led to a reconceptualization of reliability consistent with the underlying assumptions of CRTs. A brief review of some of the main issues and simpler methods for calculating reliability are presented here. For in-depth discussions of recent advances in this area, the reader is referred to reviews by Hambleton et al. (1978) and Subkoviak and Baker (1977).

Traditional estimates of norm-referenced reliability involve the use of correlational analyses. In order for such an analysis to be effective, the data must contain response variance. Reduced response variance reduces the correlation and suggests reduced reliability. Because response variability is an essential characteristic of NRTs (i.e., items are designed so that they optimally have a .5 discrimination index), the assumptions of reduced reliability as suggested in a low correlation is justifiable. However, with CRTs, variability is not always found in performance on items within a domain. Although such variability is often the case, it is not essential. There are three reasons why variability would occur in responses to items measuring a domain in a CRT. The most obvious is the result of measurement error. The second reason is that the domain as specified may possess several response classes, some of which are within the behavioral repertoire of the individual and others that are not. Consequently, scores for domains consisting of multiple response classes may reflect mastery of only a proportion of the response classes. Third, a portion of the sample may be in transition (Bergan, in press). A "transition person" is one who is in the process of mastering a response class. In such a case, the transition person would respond correctly to some of the items in a single response class and incorrectly to others. All three of the forementioned reasons, however, may or may not be reflected in a domain score and the quality of the CRT is not influenced adversely by their occurrence.

If variability is available in the population sampled, then traditional correlational procedures can possibly be used (Haladyna, 1974) for establishing reliability. The standard error of measurement can be computed and a confidence level established for any single administration of the test. Alternative estimates of reliability more consistent with the assumptions of CRTs have also been proposed. As Hambleton et al. (1978) point out, two additional general approaches have been taken. The first approach involves establishing the reliability of the domain-score estimate whereas the second examines the consistency of correctly classifying the examinee as a master or nonmaster of the domain measured. Both approaches are similar in that they examine variations about a cut-off score in their analysis rather than around a mean (i.e., the classical test-theory approach). In the former approach, the standard error of measurement can be computed and confidence bands set up around the domain score estimate. The latter approach argues that differences between domain score and cut-off score is not as important as determining if an examinee falls on the same side of the cut-off score upon retesting (Hambleton & Novick, 1973). A variety of statistical procedures have been advanced for establishing the reliability of both a domain-score estimate (e.g., the index of dependability) and mastery-classification decisions (e.g., coefficient K).

One simple procedure for establishing the reliability of mastery-classification decisions is offered by Popham (1978a). Basically, this procedure, identified as estimating the "percentage of decision-consistency" involves first establishing a cut-off score that will be used to define mastery for the domain. The consistency of placing individuals in the mastery and nonmastery categories over separate administrations of the test can then be estimated by identifying the percentage of students who are classified the same over repeated test administrations. If one wishes to compute a statistic to test for differences between the decisions made after the first and second administrations of the same test, a chi-square analysis can be performed.

The same procedure for estimating reliability may also be used to establish the reliability of equivalent forms of a test designed to measure the same domains. Whereas the procedure described in the preceding paragraph was equivalent to classical stability measures, this procedure is directly comparable to classical methods for establishing the reliability of parallel forms.

The number of items necessary to obtain an acceptable reliable estimate of an examinee's domain score has also been an issue receiving much attention in the measurement literature. Suffice it to say that several approaches for determining test length have been advanced and their efficacy is currently being examined. Some of the more prominent approaches identified by Hambleton et al. (1978) include the Bayesian approach of Novick and Lewis (1974) and the approaches of Millman (1973), Fhaner (1974), and Wilcox (1976). Out of the work of Novick and Lewis (1974) and Millman (1973) have come tables relating test length to the reliability of the measure. These tables have proven useful to test developers deciding on how many items from each domain they need to include in their CRTs to achieve an acceptable reliability figure for their purpose. The most useful way to establish the reliability of CRTs has not yet been decided in the psychometric literature. However, advances to date have provided a sound foundation for the technical developments yet to come (Hambleton et al., 1978).

Validity

The validity of CRTs, as with traditional NRTs, refers to whether the test is actually measuring what it purports to measure. However, although three types of validity are commonly recognized as important to consider in examining

NRTs (i.e., *content, construct,* and *criterion related*), common practice has been to offer only *content validity* in evidence of the overall validity of a CRT. Because the major purpose of a CRT is to measure specific behaviors operationally defining the domain statements from which the test was drawn, it has been commonly accepted that in order to establish validity, one only needs to demonstrate that the items are representative of the domain statement. Because little inference is made from the results of the tests, the need for construct or criterion-related validity has not been considered highly important.

In general, strategies for establishing *content validity* in NRTs have not been exemplary (Popham, 1978a). Likewise, neither have those involving CRTs. Two types of strategies can be identified. The first involves the use of expert judges who subjectively appraise the legitimacy of the domain statement and items drawn from the domain statement to determine its *content validity*. The second type involves an empirical analysis for establishing *content validity*. Cronbach (1971) suggests an empirical method in which two tests are drawn from a domain statement and are administered to the same group. Performance on the two tests can then be statistically analyzed to determine congruence in the examinees' performance. If performance is similar, an argument for the *content validity* of both tests can be made.

One type of *content validity* specific to the needs of CRTs is described by Traub (1975) as *domain sampling validity*. *Domain sampling validity* addresses the concern of the adequacy of the items contained in a test in representing an entire item universe. Traub (1975) further delineates two types of *domain sampling validity—strong* and *weak. Strong domain sampling validity* occurs when one has explicitly defined domain statements and *weak domain sampling validity* occurs with implicitly defined domain statements. *Strong domain sampling validity* allows for strong inferences to be made concerning the legitimacy of the items as representatives of the item universe whereas *weak domain sampling validity* allows for somewhat weaker inferences.

As previously mentioned, even though it has been common practice to ignore types of validity other than *content validity* for CRTs, several measurement specialists have objected to this approach as inadequate (Cronbach, 1971; Messick, 1975). Messick (1975), for example, points out that in order to establish the validity of any test, it is necessary to validate the interpretations that are made with the test scores. *Content validity,* it is argued, is a characteristic of the test and speaks only indirectly to the validity of how the test is used. Consequently, any inferences made concerning the meaning of the test score (e.g., as it relates to learning new tasks) need to be validated. Hambleton et al. (1978) conclude their review of this problem by suggesting that although *content validity* is essential during the development stage of a CRT, construct validation studies including correlational and experimental methods are vital to establishing the overall psychometric validity of a CRT.

Popham (1978a) suggests that the different types of validity used to verify the legitimacy of NRTs are not appropriate for CRTs. He identifies three types of validity that should be established for CRTs—namely, *descriptive validity, functional validity,* and *domain-selection validity.* The first, *descriptive validity,* is similar to the traditional notion of *content validity* in that it describes a validation strategy that focuses on establishing the relevance of a test in measuring desired content. However, Popham argues that CRTs are often designed to deal with measuring psychomotor and affective skills—skills not customarily handled in traditional notions of *content validity.* He therefore recommends the use of the more general notion of *descriptive validity.*

The second type of validity is identified as *functional validity.* An argument similar to that of Messick's (1975) discussed above is used to substantiate the importance of functional validity. Popham (1978a) writes:

> While we may say that a test's results are accurately descriptive of the domain of behaviors it is supposed to measure, it is quite another thing to say that the function to which you wish to put a descriptively valid test is appropriate. The accuracy with which a criterion-referenced test satisfies the purpose to which it is being put can be described as its functional validity [p. 159].

The counterpart of *functional validity* in the NRT literature is *criterion-related validity.* Popham argues that the more general term functional is needed when speaking of CRTs because CRTs may function as useful instruments in situations other than those involving a criterion. Exactly what type of situation he is referring to is not clearly identified.

One point Popham (1978a) makes in his description of *functional validity* should not go unmentioned. He reminds us that the value and distinctive characteristic of a CRT is that it provides relevant information concerning what an examinee knows and does not know with respect to some defined content. Consequently, the *descriptive validity* of the test is of extreme importance. Increasing the predictive power of a CRT at the cost of reducing its *descriptive validity* is defeating the purpose of the test. Thus, even though movement toward establishing the *functional validity* of a CRT is considered highly important by Popham, test developers should remain wary of some of the traditional psychometric procedures that guide the development of NRTs toward more powerful *predictive validity* at the expense of *content validity.*

The third type of validity identified by Popham (1978a) is *domain-selection validity.* He suggests that at times there will be judgments that need to be made concerning which of several item domains purported to measure the same item universe under consideration should be chosen. As an example, suppose four domain statements are available to measure the ability of an examinee to construct a short story. The domain statements may vary, for example, in response requirements. Popham indicates that in order to increase the validity of the test, the domain statement that demonstrates the most generalization to the items drawn from the competing domain statements should be used. He calls this type of validity *domain-selection validity*. One problem presently identified arising from this type of validity concerns itself with the homogeneity of the items within a domain. Although Popham, as well as others, have encouraged the design of item domains consisting of homogeneous sets of items, the procedure he recommends for establishing *domain-selection validity* may result in the selection of item domains that are most heterogeneous in nature. It would seem that item domains with the greatest generalizability may also be those with the most heterogeneous items. More work on clarifying both the value of renaming the types of validity and the legitimacy of the concept of domain-selection validity as presented by Popham is still needed.

Performance Standards

CRTs can be used for several purposes. When such tests are used simply to describe the performance of a class of examinees in a particular content area, it is not necessary to make a decision as to what test-performance standard should be set to determine, for example, mastery or nonmastery within each domain. However, if a CRT is to be used for such decision making, a cut-off score for discriminating degree of mastery needs to be identified. For example, when making a decision as to whether a student should move on to instruction in superordinate domains or whether remedial exercises should be prescribed in the measured domain, a cut-off score has to be established. Despite the understood importance for setting cut-off scores, Glass (1978) was recently very critical of measurement specialists for not paying enough attention to this fundamental issue.

A variety of possible methods have been proposed (approximately 25) that can be used to establish cut-off points. Most of them are arbitrary in the sense that they require some judgment in its determination (Hambleton & Eignor, 1979b). Although the arbitrariness of these procedures have made some measurement specialists uneasy, the legitimacy of continuing to investigate the viability of these procedures, despite their arbitrariness, has been supported by Glass (1978) and Popham (1978c). Glass (1978) writes "arbitrariness is no bogeyman, and one ought not to shrink from a necessary task because it involves arbitrary decisions [p. 42]." For interested readers, a thorough review of the issues related to cut-off scores has been conducted by Meskauskas (1976) and Millman (1973).

An important decision that must be addressed by those responsible for establishing cut-off points is what method should be adopted. Jaeger (1976) points out that all methods have potential drawbacks and the method chosen needs to be made only after careful consideration of the merits of each. To date, relatively few sets of guidelines are available to help in applying these methods. Guidelines for the use of a few of the more popular methods, however, has been provided by Zieky and Livingston (1977).

One of the most fundamental differences between the models proposed to date is related to the underlying assumption made concerning how the content of the skill or skills within a domain are acquired. Two basic models have been proposed drawing on this difference. The first is the continuum model, which assumes that the acquisition of the items within a domain is continuous in nature. In other words, a learner progresses in a continuous manner through mastery of the items in a domain. Most of the models proposed in the measurement literature have made this assumption. Hambleton and Eignor (1979a) have organized these models into three categories, which they label judgmental, empirical, and combined (see Table 7.1). Judgmental models utilize judges to determine the presence of variables such as guessing which may effect the determination of a cut-off score. Experimental methods use examinee responses to aid in the standard-setting process whereas combination methods use both judgmental and empirical methods for setting cut-off scores (Hambleton & Eignor, 1979a). It should be noted that even those models employing empirical methods involve some arbitrary decisions.

The second proposed model is the *state model,* which views mastery of items within a domain as categorical. Most of the work in this area has viewed mastery as an all-or-none proposition. That is, an examinee falls into one of the two categories—he/she is either a master or nonmaster (Macready & Dayton, 1977). Bergan (1980b) has advanced a state model that includes three latent classes. In addition to the mastery and nonmastery categories, a third category of examinees

TABLE 7.1[a]
A Clarification of Methods for Setting Standards

Judgmental Methods	Empirical Models[b]	Combination Models	
Item Content	*Data-Criterion Measure*	*Judgmental– Empirical*	*Educational Consequences*
Nedelsky (1954)			
Angoff (1971)	Livingston (1975)	Contrasting Groups	Block (1972)
Modified Angoff	Livingston (1976)	(Zieky and Livingston,	
(ETS, 1976)	Van der Linden and	1977)	
	Mellenbergh (1977)	Borderline Groups	
		(Zieky and Livingston,	
Ebel (1972)		1977)	
Jaeger (1978)	*Decision-Theoretic[c]*	Criterion Groups	
		(Berk, 1976)	
Guessing	Hambleton and		
Millman (1973)	Novick (1973)	*Bayesian Methods*	
		Hambleton and Novick (1973)	
		Schoon, Gullion, and Ferrara	
		(1978)	

[a]Source: Hambleton, 1980. Reproduced by permission.
[b]Involve the use of examinee response data.
[c]In addition, there are a number of decision–theoretic models that deal with test-length considerations. These are also applicable to cut-off score determination (see, for example, Millman, 1974).

identified as transition learners is proposed. The nature of the transition learner and the implications this class has for instruction has yet to be identified.

One additional feature of the state models proposed by Macready and Dayton (1977) and Bergan (in press) that distinguishes them from the continuous models should be pointed out. The analysis of test responses using the Macready and Dayton (1977) and Bergan (1980b) state-models structures item domains into homogeneous sets of items. Such an advantage allows for these psychometric strategies to complement the advances reported in the previous section on instructional psychology.

Behavior Therapy

Criterion-referenced testing has found favor among many behavior therapists who assess academic problems in applied settings. Because a primary purpose of CRTs is to identify cognitive skills without normative comparisons, such test results have frequently served as a measure of baseline performance in an academic area. Such assessment has also extended over treatment phases to help validate behavior change in academic skills. However, despite the conceptual similarities of CRTs to many of the goals of behavioral assessment and therapy, there have been relatively few discussions in the behavioral literature of this specific assessment procedure relative to other assessment techniques (but, see Bijou, 1976; Kratochwill, 1981; Livingston, 1977). Neither has there been discussion of the contributions behavioral thought has made in advancing our appreciation of one appropriate use for CRTs—namely, in determining effective behavioral-intervention programs. In this section, we review some of the issues involved in using CRTs from the behavioral perspective in assessment and delivering services to individual learners. To help understand the use of CRTs within behavior therapy and assessment, we present an overview of the use of CRTs within behavior therapy and assessment and present an overview of the differences between traditional and behavioral assessment approaches. This is because many of our perspectives on academic assessment are still defined by the uses of NRTs.

Traditional and Behavioral Assessment

Contemporary behavior therapy is characterized by a great deal of diversity in treatment approaches and assessment methods (Kazdin, 1979a). It is generally recognized that there are four major areas of models of behavior therapy (cf. Kazdin & Wilson, 1978), including (1) applied behavior analysis; (2) a neobehavioristic mediational S–R model; (3) cognitive behavior modification; and (4) social learning theory. Assessment varies among these models based on what is included as behavior. For example, both cognitive behavior modification and social learning-theory approaches would promote the assessment of cognitive processes (thoughts, images, feelings), whereas applied behavior-analysis

methods would focus almost exclusively on observable behavior and avoid inferred internal states of "behaviors." All of these models of behavior therapy
tend to be unified by five general characteristics (Kazdin, 1978). These include:
(1) a focus on current rather than historical determinants of behavior; (2) an
emphasis on overt behavior changes as the main criterion by which treatment
should be evaluated; (3) a specification of treatment in objective terms so as to

TABLE 7.2[a]
Differences Between Behavioral and Traditional Approaches to Assessment

	Behavioral	*Traditional*
I. Assumptions		
1. Conception of personality	Personality constructs mainly employed to summarize specific behavior patterns, if at all	Personality as a reflection of enduring underlying states or traits
2. Causes of behavior	Maintaining conditions sought in current environment	Intrapsychic or within the individual
II. Implications		
1. Role of behavior	Important as a sample of person's repertoire in specific situation	Behavior assumes importance only insofar as it indexes underlying causes
2. Role of history	Relatively unimportant, except, for example, to provide a retrospective base line	Crucial in that present conditions seen as a product of the past
3. Consistency of behavior	Behavior thought to be specific to the situation	Behavior expected to be consistent across time and settings
III. Uses of data	To describe target behaviors and maintaining conditions	To describe personality functioning and etiology
	To select the appropriate treatment	To diagnose or classify
	To evaluate and revise treatment	To make prognosis; to predict
IV. Other characteristics		
1. Level of inferences	Low	Medium to high
2. Comparisons	More emphasis on intraindividual or idiographic	More emphasis on interindividual or nomothetic
3. Methods of assessment	More emphasis on direct methods (e.g., observations of behavior in natural environment)	More emphasis on indirect methods (e.g., interviews and self-report)
4. Timing of assessment	More ongoing; prior, during, and after treatment	Pre- and perhaps posttreatment, or strictly to diagnose
5. Scope of assessment	Specific measures and of more variables (e.g., of target behaviors in various situations, of side effects, context, strengths as well as deficiencies)	More global measures (e.g., of cure or improvement) but only of the individual

[a] Source: Hartmann et al., 1979. Reproduced by permission.

make replication possible; (4) a reliance on basic research in psychology as a source of hypotheses about treatment and specific therapy techniques; (5) specificity in defining, treating, and measuring the target problems in treatment (Kazdin, 1978).

Behavioral assessment tends to be characterized by as much diversity as behavior therapy. Discussions of behavior assessment (e.g., Goldfried, 1979; Goldfried & Kent, 1972; Hartmann, Roper, & Bradford, 1979; Haynes, 1979; Jones, 1979; Kanfer, 1979; Kratochwill, 1981; Mash, 1979; Nelson & Hayes, 1979; O'Leary, 1979; Wiggins, 1973) suggest that the area is rapidly evolving. The major differences between behavior assessment and other (more traditional) approaches to assessment have recently been nicely summarized by Hartmann et al. (1979). Table 7.2 summarizes some features that help distinguish the two approaches to assessment. Within the context of these dimensions, the use of criterion-referenced assessment approaches in behavior therapy is discussed. Some of the differences presented here also characterize the differences between CRTs and NRTs in general.

In discussing the use of CRTs within behavioral psychology, it is useful to present how performance is characterized within the behavioral analysis perspective. It is the characterization of performance within this perspective that has enhanced our understanding of the use of CRTs in the overall design of individual intervention programs. Bijou (1976) noted that performance on a CRT is a function of the immediate test situation and the previous interactions that comprise the history of the child (see Fig. 7.4). This formulation further assists in drawing contrasts between CRTs in behavioral assessment and other traditional testing practices, such as intelligence testing.

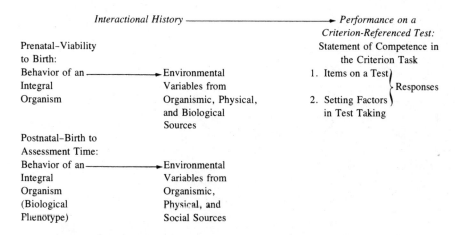

FIG. 7.4.   Behavioral concept of competence: Analysis of performance on a criterion-referenced test. (Source: Bijou, 1976. Reproduced by permission.)

Assumptions

Traditional perspectives on academic and social disorders have long been based on intraorganismic variables or constructs to account for the observed problems (Nelson & Hayes, 1979). Assessment within these approaches has focused primarily on identification of traits, states, or processes that account for the observed academic problems. Within criterion-referenced behavioral assessment, it is not necessary to posit an underlying state or trait to account for academic performance. However, the use of constructs such as "domain" or "response class" have been used to summarize behaviors within this behavioral approach. As noted in the previous section of this chapter, these constructs are employed to help operationalize certain items that should be included in the test. As would be true in other areas of behavioral assessment, a major concern would be with the content validity of such tests. As mentioned in the previous section, content validity refers to how well the items included on the test represent the domain being assessed. For example, in developing a CRT of fraction skills, from a behavioral perspective one would need to know all the tasks comprising the response class being considered (Resnick & Ford, 1978). The notion of a response class in behavioral assessment is theoretically consistent with the concept of homogeneous item domains reviewed earlier in the section on instructional psychology. In behavioral terms, however, the problem is often conceptualized as an issue related to the phenomenon of generalization.

Within behavioral assessment, it is also recognized that the assessor is interested in describing the client's behavior in a particular set of circumstances (cf. Kazdin, 1979b; Mischel, 1968). Thus, within behavioral criterion-referenced assessment, the assessor would be interested in knowing how well the circumstances under which the client's responses (behavior) were actually observed during the testing represent those circumstances in which the intervention will occur (Livingston, 1977). This validity concern typically makes the behavioral approach to CRT different from its use in other models. The situation in which the client takes the test (and the various factors operating in that situation) is important in drawing conclusions about performance. For example, the child's performance in an isolated room may differ from his/her performance on those same items in the regular classroom. Thus, it is important to remember that the child's performance is due to test items and setting factors (see Fig. 7.4). As Bijou (1976) has noted, "... the momentary power of a contingent stimulus is dependent upon the prevailing setting factor [p. 8]." Within the behavioral assessment approach, it follows that the causes of behavior or performance on the test are generally related to maintaining conditions in the current environment, rather than to traits or states within the client.

Implications

Hartmann et al. (1979) identified three implications that emerge from the differences between behavioral and traditional assessment approaches—namely, the role of behavior, the role of history, and consistency of behavior. Within the criterion-referenced behavioral approach, it is deemed important to sample a client's repertoire (behavior) in specific situations. Again, the concept of domain or response class emerges as important, as does the situation in which these are assessed.

The role of history within criterion-referenced assessment is given *reduced emphasis* relative to the emphasis on current maintaining conditions and the content of the test. Yet, history is considered more than some general construct to be dismissed. As Fig. 7.4 shows, the behavior of an individual is said to be a function of environmental variables from organismic, physical, and social sources. Thus, in the use of a CRT, one would take into account the child's interactional history in the design of instructional programs. Historical factors play a role in as much as they relate to the interactional history of the person with the items and situational context.

Within the behavioral approach, behavior is regarded as specific to a particular situation rather than as consistent across time and settings. Mischel (1968, 1971, 1979) noted that many response characteristics that were traditionally viewed as personality traits (honesty, aggression) are not consistent across situations and over time. Yet, the situation-specific nature of behavior may pose special problems in behavioral assessment. The results of a CRT obtained under a restricted range of assessment conditions (i.e., individual testing by the school psychologist) may be specific to this narrow set of conditions. Kazdin (1979b) noted:

> The situational specificity problem for behavioral assessment is that behavior changes demonstrated under restricted assessment conditions may not reflect changes under naturalistic conditions outside of the laboratory or clinic setting where several stimulus conditions vary. If behavior is specific to a variety of stimulus conditions, claims that the benefits of treatment extend to the client's ordinary environment become particularly tenuous, unless direct supporting data are available [p. 65].

This concern raised by Kazdin is especially problematic when CRTs are used over time to measure therapeutic changes in specific academic skill areas. When such monitoring of therapeutic effectiveness occurs in very specific settings (e.g., an isolated treatment room in the school, clinic office, university lab), one cannot assume that the therapeutic benefits extend beyond these settings in the absence of empirical data.

Kazdin (1979b) made three recommendations to help resolve the situational-specificity problem that have implications for the conduct of criterion-referenced assessment. First, behavior should be sampled directly in situations in the natural environment. When testing occurs in the situation of interest, situational specificity may not be as problematic. Criterion-referenced assessment conducted in the classroom where the academic problem occurs will help overcome some of the problems of situational specificity. For example, individual assessment by the school psychologist should be replicated by the regular class teacher (or other teachers) involved with the child. Second, individuals in the natural environment (e.g., teachers, parents) can serve as "informants" to provide information about performance under the conditions of primary interest. Such individuals, according to Kazdin (1979b), "may provide unobtrusive measures because their presence need not serve as a cue that assessment is being conducted [p. 86]." Teachers may administer academic assessments under natural conditions because this is a typical event in classroom settings. However, using "informants" may result in practical problems, such as when teachers are not able to integrate such testing into their classroom schedules. Teachers may also have difficulty with such assessment unless trained in giving certain tests. Nevertheless, when these problems are resolved, the information on the child's performance will be quite valuable.

A third option to help solve the situational-specificity problem relates to establishing criterion-related validity for the criterion-referenced measure. When it can be demonstrated that measures of various skills on the test correlate highly with performance on the main criterion of interest (i.e., demonstration of the skills in the classroom, home, or community setting), the situation-specific nature of performance will not be especially worrisome. Of course, this will be a matter of degree because correlations will probably be less than perfect.

Validity concerns can be evaluated in two ways. Each of these involves empirical research on the CRT: First, a comparison of testing performance in a clinic or individual setting with those in the treatment (e.g., classroom) setting should be conducted. Such *concurrent validity* measures will be important to establish the base-line level of performance on skills sampled. Likewise, *predictive validity* could be useful, such as in determining how much assessment will predict future performance in a specific skill area.

Uses of Data

Behavioral-assessment approaches have typically been used to describe target behaviors (and maintaining conditions), to select an appropriate treatment, and to evaluate and revise treatment. Each of these factors are readily applied to the use of CRTs within behavior therapy (Bijou, 1976). A description of target behaviors essentially involves a diagnosis of the skill problems. The test would provide an inventory of the child's repertoire, but would not necessarily lead to a traditional diagnosis such as "learning disability." Within this chapter, we have repeatedly stressed that this assessment must involve a careful analysis of the skill domain of concern. Once the domain is identified and the hierarchy of prerequisite skills established, a diagnosis of the skill-deficit problem has begun. Further assessment must, of course, focus on conditions that will facilitate the acquisition of the missing skills. These include a range of environmental factors as well as cognitive strategies that relate to learning academic material. It may be determined that the child will acquire missing skills through a program radically different from regular classroom instruction.

Selecting an appropriate treatment program will extend assessment in determining how the child best learns new information (Kratochwill, 1977). Increasingly, package programs consisting of many variables may be necessary (Azrin, 1977). Such components as reinforcement, feedback, modeling, and rehearsal can be packaged to maximize skill acquisition of academic tasks. Assessment of specific skills *and* factors that maximize the acquisition of these skills are essential in the behavioral approach.

The third use of data in criterion-referenced behavioral assessment is one of monitoring performance and assessing progress in some educational program (Bijou, 1976). In monitoring learning, CRTs are used primarily in individualized programs in which the materials are graded in difficulty and in which the teaching procedures are modified on the basis of observations or findings from systematic evaluations of the child's responses. This approach emphasizes both the monitoring of skill acquisition and the teaching procedures used to help the child acquire the skills. Teaching procedures are modified depending on the child's performance during the teaching trials.

An example of this use in applied settings would occur when a teacher employs a CRT to assess entry skills prior to beginning a unit on the use of fractions. The child would first be assessed on various operations in fractions and then be taught the missing skills. Testing would then determine if the skills taught have been mastered. Such a sequence of test–teach–test would be repeated until the unit of academic material were completed to some specified criterion level.

Other Characteristics

Hartmann et al. (1979) listed five characteristics of behavioral assessment that are not easily classified under the previous headings presented. Each of these five characteristics has a role in the application of CRTs within behavior therapy.

Levels of Inference.   Behavioral and traditional assessment differ in the levels of inference used to assess personality or behavior (Goldfried, 1976, 1977). Whereas in behavioral assessment, predictions about nontested behavior are made from other representative samples of the behavior of interest, traditional assessment tends to employ constructs or traits as the basis of inferring behavior in nontest situations. In the criterion-referenced approach, testing is based on the careful analysis and sampling of items from domains in some area (e.g., addition, subtraction). The test items are used as samples from the domains of items in the academic area of concern. This approach contrasts directly with a traditional approach, in which an ability trait is presumed to underlie performance in the test setting and is then used to explain performance in a nontest setting (e.g., the classroom). IQ tests provide a typical example of this latter approach. Nevertheless, both CRTs and all behavioral-assessment approaches involve making *predictions* about performance. The use of a domain in CRT represents an intermediate level construct because the sample (items) is presumed to relate to the domain. Empirical work specifying the relation between the test items and the domain greatly reduce the mystery associated with CRTs.

Comparisons.   Because traditional-assessment approaches have typically been associated with prediction and classification, they have tended to emphasize differences among individuals. Normative data are built into test development so that an individual's score can be compared to a norm group. The behavioral approach has focused on intraindividual comparisons with normative data typically deemphasized. In this context, the behavioral approach bears similarity to criterion-referenced assessment where the comparisons are within individual performance. This standard of reference (i.e., group or individual) has been a major feature distinguishing norm-referenced and criterion-referenced approaches (e.g., Drew, 1973; Glaser, 1963; Hambleton & Novick, 1973; Livingston, 1972, 1977; Popham & Husek, 1969). However, as we have stressed, the normative data characteristic is not the only difference that distinguishes the two assessment approaches. Such factors as the criteria for items selection, reliability, and validity issues must also be considered.

The major advantage that has been realized throughout the evolution in criterion-referenced measurement have been the tighter linking between assessment and curriculum content. However, refinements in this linkage notwithstanding, the use of CRTs has not replaced traditional NRT devices for making many placement decisions, such as in special-education classes. Two general reasons for the continued use of NRTs for such purposes can be noted.

The first involves the use of preintervention achievement testing for the identification of global deficits in a child's academic functioning and the production of global achievement. As Popham (1978a) noted, traditional achievement tests are general tests in that they gather data pertinent to amorphous "cloudy objectives." The items in such tests are not related to specific performance objectives; instead, general groupings of items are banded together and purported to measure global areas of functioning, such as comprehension in reading or measurement in math. Such information addresses the pervasiveness or scope of the deficit and, given such instrumentation with established predictive utility, it allows for discussions concerning a child's overall performance and what can be expected of him or her without intervention.

The second and more obvious reason presently identified for maintaining use of traditional NRTs is the information they provide in comparing children's performances. Information concerning achievement needed for placement decision making must provide a comparison of a child's performance against some relative standard. That traditional relative standard is the performance of other children. Significant deviation from the norm is generally sought for placement in many special-education classes and NRTs are commonly used for that goal. Grade equivalencies, percentile rankings, standard scores, and the like all speak to this need.

Among behavior therapists, there has been a renewed interest in the norm-criterion issue, with a definite trend toward stressing the positive features of norm-based assessment (e.g., Evans & Nelson, 1977; Hartmann et al., 1979). Hartmann et al. (1979) listed nine potential useful purposes for norms:

1. Normative comparisons can serve a screening function to help identify deficient or otherwise problematic performance.

2. Norms can assist in determining both the target person and optimum treatment strategies.

3. Norms can assist in the decisions as to whether to treat an identified problem.

4. By helping to identify skilled and inept performances, normative ratings can assist indirectly in discovering the sometimes subtle but critical skill components that produce superior ratings. These skill components then can be incorporated into intervention programs for remediating the behavior of inept performers.

5. Norms can be helpful in establishing performance levels that represent realistic treatment goals.

6. Norms can be useful for grouping clients into relatively homogeneous treatment groups.

7. Normative data can supplement other sources of descriptive information for purposes of defining subject samples in a manner that promotes comparisons between samples.

8. When normative data are available in a variety of dimensions, one can examine the degree of convergence between alternative measurement procedures.

9. Normative data can be used to evaluate the clinical significance of social validity of treatment outcomes [pp. 9–19].

It must be stressed that we do not believe that normative assessment should replace criterion-referenced assessment, or vice versa. Rather, both types of assessment paradigms can be used to help in client assessment and treatment. The use of normative data in behavioral assessment does not presume that a NRT (e.g., IQ) is or should be used. Normative data can be gathered through rating scales, checklists, and direct observation.

The use of social-validation data provides one example of this type of normative data that could supplement criterion-referenced assessment. Social validation has been proposed as a procedure for evaluating whether behavior changes achieved during treatment are clinically important (Kazdin, 1977; Wolf, 1978). Wolf (1978) suggests that social validation occurs on three levels: "the social significance of the *goals,* the social appropriateness of the *procedures,* and the social importance of the *effects* [p. 207]." Social validation procedures can be used in research and practice. Based on Kazdin's (1977) analysis, social validation can be used in two ways when a CRT is implemented to monitor client progress in a specific skill domain. First, the child's performance can be compared to that of his/her peers who do not have the skill-deficit problem. Second, subjective evaluations of the child's performance by individuals in the natural environment (e.g., classroom teacher) can be solicited. The clinical importance of the behavior change is determined by examining the client's skills performance against the range of socially established levels. Such levels represent normative data obtained by others' judgments of the client's behavior or rating qualitative improvement.

Methods of Assessment.   The use of behavior-assessment strategies is premised on the belief that a direct sampling of the behavior of interest will provide the most useful treatment information. The "directness" of the assessment method relates to the degree to which the problem is actually observed in its natural setting. Just as behavioral and traditional methods differ in the directness of their respective assessment procedures, techniques *within* the general behavioral-assessment rubric also can be categorized on a dimension of directness (Cone, 1977). Specifically, behavioral-assessment methods can be preordered along a continuum of directness representing the extent to which they (1) measure the behavior of clinical relevance; and (2) measure it at the time and place of its natural occurrence.

Criterion-referenced behavioral assessment measures the behavior of clinical relevance vis-a-vis a direct sample of the academic skills targeted for intervention. In reading problems, assessment would focus on a specific set of skills (e.g., work recognition, phonetics, comprehension). This would contrast an approach that focuses on correlated processes of reading disabilities that might be determined by performance on subtests of the Wechsler Intelligence Scale for Children—Revised or the Illinois Test of Psycholinguistic Abilities. The latter method of assessment is less direct and involves more inference in what accounts for the learning problems. Moreover, with such approaches, there is typically little concern with sampling specific skills in settings in which the problem is occurring. Because underlying processes are presumed to be consistent causes of the disability, sampling in natural situations (e.g., classroom) is of less importance.

Measuring the behavior at the time and place of its natural occurrence involves several issues. When a teacher administers a CRT of academic skills to a child in the setting in which academic instruction is occurring, this represents a relatively direct sampling of the target behaviors. However, if the child is assessed outside of this setting, such as, for example, in a clinic by a psychologist, the assessment is best considered an analogue. In this sense, the sample is less direct because behavior (academic skills) is/are not assessed in the setting in which the problem occurs. School psychologists using CRTs in settings removed from the environment in which the problem is occurring must consider that the assessment is an analogue and should, therefore, address reliability and validity concerns associated with their methods (cf. Kratochwill, 1981; Nay, 1977; see also earlier discussion of situation specificity).

Timing of Assessment.   The repeated measurement of behavior over time has been one of the hallmarks of the behavior-assessment approach (Bijou, Peterson,

& Ault, 1968; Bijou, Peterson, Harris, Allen, & Johnson, 1969; Hersen & Barlow, 1976; Kratochwill, 1978). The usual repeated-measurement strategy is typically implemented through one of the direct measurement strategies (i.e., self monitoring, analogue testing, observation in the natural environment). Criterion-referenced assessment can also be used in an ongoing fashion over various phases of behavior therapy. Bijou (1976) presents one example of the ongoing nature of this approach:

> . . . in using remedial writing programmed instructional material, the teacher tests the child at the beginning of each unit to see whether he has the prerequisite behavior to succeed in that unit (can he discriminate the numbers from one to six?), and again at the end of each unit to see whether he has achieved all the objectives in that unit (can he name the numbers and recite them in serial order?). Testing for monitoring purposes may proceed along the lines of the instructional plan [p. 99].

Assessment of the specific skills through repeated criterion-referenced testing represents one dimension of the ongoing nature of assessment. Other aspects of the child's performance (e.g., social performance) should be assessed as well. Such ongoing social assessment helps provide the analysis of conditions affecting the child's behavior on the academic task, other than the specific skill acquisition per se. Essentially, this involves a functional analysis of learning.

Scope of Assessment. In this section of the chapter, we have been focusing on the use of criterion-referenced assessment of specific skill problems in academic areas. This is certainly in keeping with the behavioral framework in which specific measures are operationalized and targeted for change. However, rarely are learning problems related to only a specific skill deficiency. The clinician must always expand the scope of assessment within the particular domain identified. The merging of criterion- and path-referenced assessment approaches (see Bergan, this volume) have pointed to the importance of an extended perspective on assessment in this area.

As part of the expanded nature of assessment, the behavior therapist typically focuses on social behaviors in addition to the specific skills in academic areas. Moreover, there is an increased recognition that side effects of the assessment and treatment should be examined (Haynes, 1978), as well as the maintenance and generalization of therapeutic effects (Stokes & Baer, 1977).

SUMMARY AND CONCLUSIONS

This chapter identified several of the advances made in criterion-referenced assessment that hold present utility and future promise for the practice of school psychology. Three areas that have made unique contributions to this end were identified. In the area of instructional psychology, the work of Gagné related to the analysis of learning tasks was reviewed. The contributions of intellectual skills and learning hierarchies to the conceptualization of curriculum content and consequently of CRTs was assessed. As reported, work in this area has had only an indirect impact on the design of CRTs because of the only recent development of practical methods for empirically validating the scope and sequence of skills making up a learning hierarchy. Yet, despite the only indirect influence of instructional psychology in the formal assessment of academic achievement through the use of CRTs, informal procedures governed by the concepts of intellectual skills and learning hierarchies appear to be influencing the behavior of school psychologists. The use of task-analysis procedures, for example, has been incorporated by many school psychologists into their treatment-oriented assessment with resultant findings used to help in the development of individualized educational programs. The potential usefulness of empirical procedures recently developed for the validation of homogeneous item domains in learning hierarchies appears to hold much promise for the near future. The evolving technology necessary for what Bergan (this volume) identifies as path-referenced assessment appears to have direct impact for the practice of school psychology.

In the area of psychometric theory, those developments most relevant to the design of CRTs were examined. Advances in detailing the content of an item domain through the use of domain statements were reviewed. Issues related to the selection of items, reliability, validity, and selection of performance standards were also examined. All things considered, out of the areas just mentioned to which psychometric theory has contributed over the last decade, establishing the validity of CRTs has received the least attention. However, CRT validity notwithstanding, significant advances have been made in our understanding of the underlying assumptions governing the construction of CRTs. It appears that the next major contribution to be made by psychometric theory to the advancement of CRTs is in the area of technical application. A technology for the adequate design and interpretation of CRTs that can be easily digested and practically implemented by test developers is sorely needed. Attempts to provide such guidelines have been undertaken by several writers and the outlook for continued contribution in this area looks promising (Hambleton et al., 1978). Hopefully, advances in our understanding of the structure of curriculum content made by researchers in the area of instructional psychology will influence these contributions.

In the area of behavior therapy, advances in our understanding of how CRTs can be used in delivering services to individual learners was examined. One of the major contributions in this area has been the demonstration of the importance of setting factors and situation-specific influences in the acquisition of behaviors represented on a CRT. An emphasis of these factors has helped sensitize CRT users to the necessity for considering the setting in which the assessment occurs and for assessing other than content-related variables in developing sound intervention programs.

In addition, behavioral psychology has viewed assessment as an ongoing process that terminates only after success of treatment is demonstrated. This has influenced our perspective on assessment and has pointed to the value of using CRTs throughout treatment and as an essential component for instructional evaluation. The compatibility between the underlying assessment assumptions for both criterion-referenced testing and more readily identifiable forms of direct behavioral assessment (e.g., direct observation) is still to be completely appreciated. Continued exploration of the congruence between criterion-referenced measurement and other methods of behavioral assessment will only help to further advance our understanding of the potential usefulness of CRTs.

ACKNOWLEDGMENTS

The authors wish to express thanks to Ronald Hambleton and Michael Subkoviak for their comments on earlier versions of this chapter.

REFERENCES

Alkin, M. C. "Criterion-referenced measurement" and other such terms. In C. W. Harris, M. C. Alkin, & W. J. Popham (Eds.), *Problems in criterion-referenced measurement* (CSE Monograph Services in Evaluation No. 3). Los Angeles: Center for the Study of Evaluation, University of California at Los Angeles, 1974.

Angoff, W. H. Scales, norms, and equivalent scores. In R. L. Throndike (Ed.), *Educational measurement*. Washington, D.C.: American Council on Education, 1971.

Azrin, N. H. A strategy for applied research: Learning based but outcome oriented. *American Psychologist,* 1977, *32,* 140–149.

Bergan, J. R. *Behavioral consultation.* Columbus, Ohio: Merrill, 1977.

Bergan, J. R. The structural analysis of behavior: An alternative to the learning hierarchy model. *Review of Educational Research,* 1980, *50,* 625–646. (a)

Bergan, J. R. Mastery assessment with latent class and quasiindependence models representing homogeneous item domains. *Journal of Educational Statistics,* 1980, *5,* 65–81. (b)

Bergan, J. R. Models of the structure of some rule-governed mathematical behaviors. *Contemporary Educational Psychology,* in press.

Bergan, J. R., Byrnes, I. M., & Kratochwill, T. R. Effects of behavioral and medical models of consultation on teacher expectancies and instruction of a hypothetical child. *Journal of School Psychology,* 1979, *17,* 307–316.

Bergan, J. R., Cancelli, A. A., & Karp, C. Replacement and component rules in hierarchically ordered mathematics rule learning tasks. Unpublished manuscript, University of Arizona, 1979.

Bergan, J., Cancelli, A. A., & Towstopiat, O. *A structural approach to the validation of hierarchical training sequences* (Task 1 Tech. Report). Arizona Center for Educational Research and Development, University of Arizona, December 1979.

Berk, R. A. Determination of optimal cutting scores in criterion-referenced measurement. *Journal of Experimental Education,* 1976, *45,* 4–9.

Berk, R. A. The application of structural facet theory to achievement test construction. *Educational Research Quarterly,* 1978, *3,* 62–72.

Bernard, M. E. *Task analysis in instructional program development.* Theoretical Paper No. 52. Madison, Wis.: Wisconsin Research and Development Center for Cognitive Learning, University of Wisconsin, May 1975.

Bijou, S. W. *Child development: The basic stage of early childhood.* Englewood Cliffs, N.J.: Prentice-Hall, 1976.

Bijou, S. W., Peterson, R. F., & Ault, M. H. A method to integrate descriptive and experimental field studies at the level of data and empirical concepts. *Journal of Applied Behavior Analysis,* 1968, *1,* 175–191.

Bijou, S. W., Peterson, R. F., Harris, F. R., Allen, K. E., & Johnston, M.S. Methodology for experimental studies of young children in natural settings. *Psychological Record,* 1969, *19,* 177–120.

Block, J. H. Student learning and the setting of mastery performance standards. *Educational Horizons,* 1972, *50,* 183–190.

Cancelli, A. Behavioral assessment: The structure of domains in psychoeducational assessment. In J. R. Bergan (Chair), *Behavioral approaches to psychoeducational assessment.* Symposium presented at the meeting of the American Psychological Association, Toronto, August 1978.

Cancelli, A., Bergan, J., & Jones, S. Hierarchical and instructional sequences in the teaching of elementary subtraction skills. Unpublished manuscript, University of Arizona, 1979.

Cancelli, A., Bergan, J., & Taber, D. The relationship of complexity to hierarchical sequencing. *Journal of Educational Psychology,* 1980, *72,* 331–337.

Cone, J. D. The relevance of reliability and validity for behavioral assessment. *Behavior Therapy,* 1977, *8,* 411–426.

Cotton, J. W., Gallagher, J. P., & Marshall, S. P. The identification and decomposition of hierarchical tasks. *American Educational Research Journal,* 1977, *14,* 189–212.

Cronbach, L. F. Test validation. In R. L. Thorndike (Ed.), *Educational measurement* (2nd ed.). Washington, D.C.: American Council on Education, 1971.

Cronbach, L. F., Glaser, G. C., Nanda, H., & Rajaratnam, N. *The dependability of behavioral measurements: Theory of generalizability for scores and profiles.* New York: Wiley, 1972.

Drew, C. J. Criterion-referenced and norm-referenced assessment of minority group children. *Journal of School Psychology,* 1973, *11,* 323–329.

Ebel, R. L. *Essentials of educational measurement.* Englewood Cliffs, N.J.: Prentice-Hall, 1972.

Educational Testing Service. *Report on a study of the use of the National Teachers' Examination by the state of South Carolina.* Princeton, N.J.: Educational Testing Service, 1976.

Evans, I. M., & Nelson, R. O. Assessment of child behavior problems. In A. R. Ciminero, K. S. Calhoun, & H. E. Adams (Eds.), *Handbook of behavioral assessment.* New York: Wiley, 1977.

Fhaner, S. Item sampling and decision making in achievement testing. *British Journal of Mathematical and Statistical Psychology,* 1974, *27,* 172–175.

Gagné, R. M. The acquisition of knowledge. *Psychological Review,* 1962, *69,* 355–365.

Gagné, R. M. Learning hierarchies. *Educational Psychologist,* 1968, *6,* 1–9.

Gagné, R. M. *The conditions of learning* (3rd ed.). New York: Holt, Rinehart, & Winston, 1977.

Glaser, R. Instructional technology and the measurement of learning outcomes. *American Psychologist,* 1963, *18,* 519–521.

Glaser, R. A criterion-referenced test. In W. J. Popham (Ed.), *Criterion-referenced measurement: An introduction.* Englewood Cliffs, N.J.: Educational Technology Publications, 1971.

Glaser, R., & Klaus, D. J. Proficiency measurement: Assessing human performance. In R. M. Gagné (Ed.), *Psychological principles in system development.* New York: Holt, Rinehart, & Winston, 1962.

Glaser, R., & Nitko, A. J. Measurement in learning and instruction. In R. L. Thorndike (Ed.), *Educational measurement* (2nd ed.). Washington, D.C.: American Council of Education, 1971.

Glaser, R., & Resnick, L. B. Instructional psychology. *Annual Review of Psychology,* 1972, *23,* 207–276.

Glass, G. V. Standards and criteria. *Journal of Educational Measurement,* 1978, *15,* 237–261.

Goldfried, M. R. Behavioral assessment. In I. B. Weiner (Ed.), *Clinical methods in psychology.* New York: Wiley, 1976.

Goldfried, M. R. Behavioral assessment in perspective. In J. D. Cone & R. P. Hawkins (Eds.), *Behavioral assessment: New directions in clinical psychology.* New York: Brunner/Mazel, 1977.

Goldfried, M. R. Behavioral assessment: Where do we go from here? *Behavioral Assessment,* 1979, *1,* 19–22.

Goldfried, M. R., & Kent, R. N. Traditional versus behavioral personality assessment: A comparison of methodological and theoretical assumptions. *Psychological Bulletin,* 1972, *77,* 409–420.

Goodman, L. A. The analysis of systems of quantitative variables when some of the variables are unobservable. Part 1—a modified latent structure approach. *American Journal of Sociology,* 1974, *79,* 1179–1259.

Goodman, L. A. A new model for scaling response patterns: An application of the quasi-independence concept. *Journal of the American Statistical Association,* 1975, *70,* 755–768.

Gray, W. M. A comparison of Piagetian theory and criterion-referenced measurement. *Review of Educational Research,* 1978, *48,* 223–249.

Haladyna, T. M. Effects of different samples on item and test characteristics of criterion-referenced tests. *Journal of Educational Measurement,* 1974, *11,* 93–99.

Hambleton, R. Test score validity and standard setting methods. In R. Berk (Ed.), *Criterion-referenced measurement: State of the art.* Baltimore: Johns Hopkins Press, 1980.

Hambleton, R. K., & Eignor, D. R. Competency test development, validation and standard setting. In R. Jaeger & C. K. Tittle (Eds.), *Minimum competency achievement testing.* Berkeley: McCutchan, 1979. (a)

Hambleton, R. K., & Eignor, D. R. *Criterion-referenced test development and validation-methods.* Material from workshop presented at the American Educational Research Association, San Francisco, April 1979. (b)

Hambleton, R. K., & Novick, M. R. Toward an integration of theory and method for criterion-referenced tests. *Journal of Educational Measurement,* 1973, *10,* 159–170.

Hambleton, R. K., Swaminathan, H., Algina, J., & Coulson, D. B. Criterion-referenced testing and measurement: A review of technical issues and developments. *Review of Educational Research,* 1978, *48,* 1–47.

Hartmann, D. P., Roper, B. L., & Bradford, D. C. Some relationships between behavioral and traditional assessment. *Journal of Behavioral Assessment,* 1979, *1,* 3–21.

Haynes, S. N. *Principles of behavioral assessment.* New York: Gardner Press, 1978.

Haynes, S. N. Behavioral variance, individual differences, and trait theory in behavioral construct system: A reappraisal. *Behavioral Assessment,* 1979, *1,* 41–49.

Hersen, M., & Barlow, D. H. *Single case experimental designs: Strategies for studying behavior change.* New York: Pergamon, 1976.

Hively, W. Introduction to domain-referenced testing. In W. Hively (Ed.), *Domain-referenced testing.* Englewood Cliffs, N.J.: Educational Technology Publications, 1974.

Hively, W., Maxwell, G., Rabehl, G., Sension, D., & Lundin, S. *Domain referenced curriculum evaluation: A technical handbook and a case study from the Minnemast Project* (CSE Monograph Series in Evaluation No. 1). Los Angeles: Center for the Study of Evaluation, University of California at Los Angeles, 1973.

Jaeger, R. M. Measurement consequences of selected standard-setting models. *Florida Journal of Educational Research,* 1976, *18,* 22–27.

Jaeger, R. M. *A proposal for setting a standard on the North Carolina High School Competency Test.* Paper presented at the 1978 spring meeting of the North Carolina Association for Research in Education, Chapel Hill, 1978.

Jones, R. R. Program evaluation design issues. *Behavioral Assessment,* 1979, *1,* 51–56.

Kanfer, F. H. A few comments on the current status of behavioral assessment. *Behavioral Assessment,* 1979, *1,* 37–39.

Kazdin, A. E. Assessing the clinical or applied importance of behavior change through social validation. *Behavior Modification,* 1977, *1,* 427–452.

Kazdin, A. E. *History of behavior modification.* Baltimore: University Park Press, 1978.

Kazdin, A. E. Fictions, factions, and functions of behavior therapy. *Behavior Therapy,* 1979, *10,* 629–654. (a)

Kazdin, A. E. Situational specificity: The two-edged sword of behavioral assessment. *Behavioral Assessment,* 1979, *1,* 57–75. (b)

Kazdin, A. E., & Wilson, G. T. *Evaluation of behavior therapy: Issues, evidence and research strategies.* Cambridge, Mass.: Ballinger, 1978.

Kratochwill, T. R. The movement of psychological extras into ability assessment. *Journal of Special Education,* 1977, *11,* 299–311.

Kratochwill, T. R. *Single subject research: Strategies for evaluating change.* New York: Academic Press, 1978.

Kratochwill, T. R. Advances in behavioral assessment. In C. R. Reynolds and T. B. Gutkin (Eds.) *Handbook of School Psychology.* New York: Wiley, 1981.

Kratochwill, T. R., Alper, S., & Cancelli, A. A. Nondiscriminatory assessment in psychology and education. In L. Mann & D. A. Sabatino (Eds.), *Fourth Review of Special Education.* New York: Grune & Stratton, in press.

Livingston, S. A. Criterion-referenced applications of classical test theory. *Journal of Educational Measurement,* 1972, *9,* 13–26.

Livingston, S. A. *A utility-based approach to the evaluation of pass/fail testing decision procedures* (Report No. COPA-75-01). Princeton, N.J.: Center for Occupational and Professional Assessment, Educational Testing Service, 1975.

Livingston, S. A. *Choosing minimum passing scores by stochastic approximation techniques* (Report No. COPA-76-02). Princeton, N.J.: Center for Occupational and Professional Assessment, Educational Testing Service, 1976.

Livingston, S. A. Psychometric techniques for criterion-referenced testing and behavioral assessment. In J. D. Cone & R. P. Hawkins (Eds.), *Behavioral assessment: New directions in clinical psychology.* New York: Brunner/Mazel, 1977.

Macready, G. B., & Dayton, C. M. The use of probabilistic models in the assessment of mastery. *Journal of Educational Statistics,* 1977, *2,* 99–120.

Macready, G. B., & Merwin, J. C. Homogeneity within item forms in domain-referenced testing. *Educational and Psychological Measurement,* 1973, *33,* 351–360.

Mash, E. J. What is behavioral assessment? *Behavioral Assessment,* 1979, *1,* 23–29.

Meskauskas, J. A. Evaluation models for criterion-referenced testing: Views regarding mastery and standard-setting. *Review of Educational Research,* 1976, *46,* 133–158.

Messick, S. A. The standard problem: Meaning and values in measurement and evaluation. *American Psychologist,* 1975, *30,* 955–966.

Millman, J. Passing scores and test lengths for domain-referenced measures. *Review of Educational Research,* 1973, *43,* 205–216.

Millman, J. Criterion-referenced measurement. In W. J. Popham (Ed.), *Evaluation in education: Current applications.* Berkeley: McCutchan, 1974.

Mischel, W. *Personality and assessment.* New York: Wiley, 1968.

Mischel, W. *Introduction to personality.* New York: Holt, Rinehart, & Winston, 1971.

Mischel, W. On the interface of cognition and personality: Beyond the person–situation debate. *American Psychologist,* 1979, *34,* 740–754.

Nay, W. R. Analogue measures. In A. R. Ciminero, K. S. Calhoun, & H. E. Adams (Eds.), *Handbook of behavioral assessment.* New York: Wiley, 1977.

Nedelsky, L. Absolute grading standards for objective tests. *Educational and Psychological Measurement,* 1954, *14,* 3–19.

Nelson, R. O., & Hayes, S. C. Some current dimensions of behavioral assessment. *Behavioral Assessment*, 1979, *1*, 1-16.

Nitko, A. J., & Hsu, T. Using domain-referenced tests for student placement, diagnosis and attainment in a system of adaptive, individualized instruction. In W. Hively (Ed.), *Domain-referenced testing*. Englewood Cliffs, N.J.: Educational Technology Publications, 1974.

Novick, M. R., & Lewis, C. Prescribing test length for criterion-referenced measurement. In C. W. Harris, M. C. Alkin, & W. J. Popham (Eds.), *Problems in criterion-referenced measurement* (CSE Monograph Series in Evaluation No. 3). Los Angeles: Center for the Study of Evaluation, University of California at Los Angeles, 1974.

O'Leary, K. D. Behavioral assessment. *Behavioral Assessment*, 1979, *1*, 31-36.

Popham, W. J. An approaching peril: Cloud-referenced tests. *Phi Delta Kappan*, 1974, *56*, 614-615. (a)

Popham, W. J. Selecting objectives and generating test items for objective-based tests. In C. W. Harris, M. C. Alkin, & W. J. Popham (Eds.), *Problems in criterion-referenced measurement* (CSE Monograph Series in Evaluation No. 3). Los Angeles: Center for the Study of Evaluation, University of California at Los Angeles, 1974. (b)

Popham, W. J. *Educational evaluation*. Engelwood Cliffs, N.J.: Prentice-Hall, 1975.

Popham, W. J. *Criterion-referenced measurement*. Englewood Cliffs, N.J.: Prentice-Hall, 1978. (a)

Popham, W. J. *A lasso for runaway test items*. Paper presented at the First Annual Johns Hopkins University National Symposium on Educational Research, "Criterion-referenced measurement: The state of the art," Washington, D.C., October 1978. (b)

Popham, W. J. *Setting performance standards*. Los Angeles: Instructional Objectives Exchange, 1978. (c)

Popham, W. J., & Husek, T. R. Implications of criterion-referenced measurement. *Journal of Educational Measurement*, 1969, *6*, 1-9.

Resnick, L. B., & Ford, W. W. The analysis of tasks for instruction: An information-processing approach. In A. C. Catania & T. A. Brigham (Eds.), *Handbook of applied behavior analysis: Social and instructional processes*. New York: Irvington, 1978.

Resnick, L. B., Wang, M. C., & Kaplan, J. Task analyses in curriculum design: A hierarchically sequenced introductory mathematics curriculum. *Journal of Applied Behavioral Analysis*, 1973, *7*, 679-710.

Rovinelli, R. J., & Hambleton, R. K. On the use of content specialists in the assessment of criterion-referenced test item validity. *Dutch Journal for Educational Research*, 1977, *2*, 49-60.

Scandura, J. B. *Problem solving: A structural process approach with educational implications*. New York: Academic Press, 1977.

Schoon, C. B., Gullion, C. M., & Ferrara, P. *Credentialing examinations, Bayesian statistics, and the determination of passing points*. Paper presented at the annual meeting of American Psychological Association, Toronto, 1978.

Shoemaker, D. M. Toward a framework for achievement testing. *Review of Educational Research*, 1975, *45*, 127-147.

Stokes, T. F., and Baer, D. M. An implicit technology of generalization. *Journal of Applied Behavior Analysis*, 1977, *10*, 349-367.

Subkoviak, M. J., & Baker, F. B. Test theory. In L. S. Shulman (Ed.), *Review of Research in Education*. Itasca, Ill.: Peacock, 1977.

Traub, R. E. *Stirring muddy water: Another perspective on criterion-referenced measurement* (mimeo). Ontario: Ontario Institute for Studies in Education, 1975.

Van der Linden, W. J., & Mellenbergh, G. J. Optimal cutting scores using a linear loss function. *Applied Psychological Measurement*, 1977, *1*, 593-599.

White, R. T. Learning hierarchies. *Review of Educational Research*, 1973, *43*, 361-375.

White, R. T. The validation of a learning hierarchy. *American Educational Research Journal*, 1974, *11*, 121-136.

White, R. T., & Gagné, R. M. Past and future research on learning hierarchies. *Educational Psychologist*, 1974, *11*, 19–28.

Wiggins, J. S. *Personality and prediction: Principles of personality assessment.* Reading, Mass.: Addison-Wesley, 1973.

Wilcox, R. R. A note on test length and passing score of a mastery test. *Journal of Educational Statistics*, 1976, *1*, 359–364.

Wolf, M. M. Social validity: The case for subjective measurement or how applied behavior analysis is finding its heart. *Journal of Applied Behavior Analysis*, 1978, *11*, 203–214.

Zieky, M. J., & Livingston, S. A. *Manual for setting standards on the Basic Skills Assessment Tests.* Princeton, N.J.: Educational Testing Service, 1977.

8 Path-Referenced Assessment in School Psychology

John R. Bergan
University of Arizona

INTRODUCTION

Assessment activities in school psychology serve a number of functions: One has to do with the classification of students for purposes of educational placement. Another involves diagnosis aimed at identifying specific learning and adjustment problems and the causes of those problems. School psychologists rely heavily on norm-referenced tests in conducting both classificatory and diagnostic assessment. These tests describe individual test performance by specifying examinee position in a suitable norm group. Norm-referenced tests have been used widely in classifying students from the early part of the 20th century until the present. Moreover, notwithstanding widespread criticisms (e.g., Popham, 1978b), other forms of assessment have posed no serious challenge to the norm-referenced strategy in student classification.

Even though a norm-referenced approach has been relatively successful for purposes of classification, its diagnostic utility has been seriously questioned. Major criticisms of the norm-referenced approach to diagnosis have come from advocates of criterion-referenced assessment. For example, proponents of the criterion-referenced approach point out that norm-referenced instruments aimed at diagnosing learning difficulties do not indicate the specific competencies that are present or lacking in students (Popham, 1978b). Accordingly, norm-referenced tests are not effective in determining what should be taught in remediating learning difficulties. Advocates of criterion-referenced assessment have taken the position that diagnostic tests should indicate the specific competencies that students manifesting learning problems have failed to achieve. When missing competencies have been precisely identified, instruction can be targeted at the development of those competencies.

Proponents of criterion-referenced testing have recognized not only that diagnostic testing could be enhanced by focusing assessment on what students can and cannot do, but also they have long been sensitive to the possibility that behavioral capabilities may be structured in important ways. For example, intellectual skills may be arranged in a hierarchical structure such that subordinate capabilities affect the acquisition of superordinate capabilities (Gagné, 1977).

Although proponents of criterion-referenced assessment have long recognized the potential value of structural analyses of behavioral capabilities for diagnostic assessment, models capable of representing the structure of behavioral competencies in a form amenable to empirical validation have been lacking. However, in recent years, new mathematical techniques have begun to evolve that can be applied to the task of representing behavioral structures of importance in learning and adjustment. These procedures provide the foundation for a new kind of assessment, which I call path-referenced assessment, that can be used to identify the interrelationships among capabilities including the effects of subordinate capabilities on superordinate competencies.

PATH-REFERENCED ASSESSMENT AND THE STRUCTURAL ANALYSIS OF BEHAVIOR

Path-referenced assessment refers to the strategy of describing test performance by indicating examinee position in a structural model (Duncan, 1975; Goodman, 1978) specifying relations among classes of behavior. For example, such a model could represent a hierarchically ordered learning sequence. If this were the case, a path-referenced test would specify examinee position in the sequence. This could be done by describing examinee placement in a path diagram indicating causal relations among behaviors in the hierarchical sequence (Duncan, 1975; Goodman, 1978). For example, suppose that performance on learning task A affected performance on task B and that task B in turn influenced performance on task C. A path diagram for such a sequence would contain an arrow from A to B and an arrow from B to C. If a child had mastered A and B but not C, his/her performance would be described by placing him/her at B in the diagram. This placement would show not only what skills (s)he had acquired, but what (s)he would need to learn next to progress in the sequence.

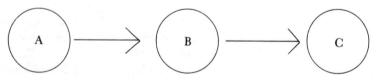

FIG. 8.1.   A path diagram showing the effect of task A on task B and task B on task C.

The development of path-referenced tests requires a structural analysis of behavior (Bergan, 1980c); that is, it necessitates the construction and empirical validation of mathematical models representing the structure of sets of interrelated behavioral classes. For example, suppose that a procedure such as task analysis were used to develop an hypothesized structure showing relations among intellectual skills assessed by a set of learning tasks. The construction of a path-referenced test for such a structure would require the development of mathematical models that could represent the structure and that could be tested empirically. Empirical testing would involve determining the extent to which behavioral patterns predicted under the models accurately matched observed performance.

Two types of structural analyses occur in the development of path-referenced tests. One has to do with the scaling of behaviors assessed by test items. The other involves the establishment of causal relations among behaviors assessed by items.

Scale Structure

The analysis of structure in path-referenced assessment begins with a determination of the extent to which items assessing behavioral patterns of interest are ordered, or at least partially ordered, to form a scale. The first step in the scaling process is to group test items into item domains. Scaling is then carried out by establishing relations among domains.

Item Domains.   A path-referenced test is composed of a group of item sets, each of which represents a well-defined domain or class of behaviors. Procedures for determining well-defined behavior domains have been elaborated by a number of authors (e.g., Shoemaker, 1975). At the heart of domain definition is the linking of each domain to an objective specifying in a precise way the categories of behavior included in the domain.

Item domains may be homogeneous or heterogeneous in nature. A homogeneous item domain is defined by the fact that examinees tend to respond in the same fashion to all items in the domain (Macready & Merwin, 1973). Establishing a homogeneous item domain requires demonstration of an equivalence relation among items representing the domain. Equivalence exists for a given set of items when examinees perform at a consistent level of competency for all items in the set. For example, equivalence is shown when examinees who pass one item pass the other items in the set, and examinees who fail one item also fail the other items in the set.

Homogeneous item domains are useful in path-referenced assessment. For example, consider the case in which two subordinate capabilities are assumed to have a beneficial effect on the learning of a third superordinate competency. In a situation such as this, each subordinate capability will generally be presumed to encompass a class of behaviors emitted in the presence of a class stimuli. The items used to assess each capability may be thought of as exemplars of a class, any member of which could be used in the assessment of the competency in question.

In the absence of empirical evidence validating the existence of a homogenous item domain, a number of disquieting questions may arise concerning the categorization of behavioral capabilities assessed by items in the domain. For instance, in the preceding example, there would be no way to determine whether each of the subordinate capabilities actually represented a separate competency. It could happen that the two would be measures of the same skill. The test items used to measure competencies presumed to be discrete are often suspiciously similar. Accordingly, there may be many cases in which items purported to assess discrete skills are really measuring the same thing.

In recent years, substantial advances have been made in the development of procedures for determining whether or not an item set forms a homogeneous domain. For example, Macready and Dayton (1977) have proposed models that describe examinee performance for homogeneous item domains in terms of two classes, one representing domain mastery, the other representing nonmastery. Bergan (in press)   has suggested a number of three-class models that include mastery and nonmastery classes such as those proposed by Macready and Dayton and in addition a third class reflecting a transition state between nonmastery and mastery. The Bergan models assume that in the process of learning, an individual will progress from a state of complete nonmastery to a state of transition in which mastery has not been completely achieved. Following transition, the learner attains mastery and is capable of responding correctly to all items assessing the behavior of interest.

Macready and Dayton (1977) have developed procedures for classifying examinees as belonging in the mastery or nonmastery classes depicted under their models. Bergan, Cancelli, and Luiten (1980) have extended the Macready and Dayton procedures to cover a broad range of additional models including three-class models involving nonmastery, transitional, and mastery classes.

Although it is often useful to establish homogeneous item domains, there may be instances in which it is preferable to construct heterogeneous domains—that is, domains that do not require an equivalence relation among items. For example, it may be convenient for instructional purposes to group elements of factual knowledge into a single item domain. In such a case, there may be no reason to expect an equivalence relation among the items in the domain.

Great strides have been made within the criterion-referenced testing tradition in the development of technology for constructing heterogeneous item domains. Procedures have been established for estimating domain scores indicating the proportion of a domain mastered by a learner. Techniques are also available for categorizing a learner as a master or nonmaster of a domain. Moreover, procedures have been developed for determining the reliability of domain scores and of mastery classification scores. These techniques have been detailed by Hambleton, Swaminathan, Algina, and Coulson (1978) in an excellent review of criterion-referenced assessment technology. The techniques described by Hambleton and his colleagues can be used in the construction of heterogeneous item domains for path-referenced tests.

Domain Ordering.   After items have been assigned to domains, they may be ordered to form an hypothesized structure. This ordering requires empirical validation of a number of possible relations that may exist among domains. First of all, it is necessary to determine whether or not equivalence relations exist between any of the domains. For example, it could happen that two homogeneous item domains turn out to be equivalent to each other. In a case such as this, the domains should be merged into one.

After the equivalence of domains has been assessed, ordered relations among the domains are examined. The most important type of relation considered in the ordering process is the ordered implication. An implication relation occurs when mastery of one domain implies that another domain has been mastered. For example, the ability to work subtraction problems involving borrowing may be assumed to imply the ability to work similar problems that do not require borrowing. Note that the implication relation includes the case in which two domains are mastered at the same time. This is awkward, because inclusion of simultaneous mastery makes it impossible to distinguish between an equivalence relation and an implication. Equivalence is a special case of the implication that occurs when two skills are mastered simultaneously. The notion of an ordered implication is introduced here to make the equivalence relation separable from other forms of implication. The distinguishing feature of an ordered implication is that significant numbers of individuals have mastered a subordinate capability without having acquired the related superordinate competency.

The ordered implication is similar to Gagné's prerequisite relation, which asserts that mastery of a subordinate skill is essential to mastery of a superordinate skill. However, there are important differences between the prerequisite relation and the ordered implication. One of these is that the prerequisite relation includes simultaneous skill mastery. The basic criterion employed in judging whether one skill, A, is prerequisite to another, B, is that no one should display mastery of B without having mastered A (e.g., Gagné, 1962, 1977). White and Clark (1973) have developed a test of inclusion that is based on this criterion and that is widely used in the validation of hypothesized prerequisite relations. The White-and-Clark test cannot distinguish between prerequisite and equivalence relations because an equivalence relation might well occur for two skills, A and B, such that the number of individuals who mastered B without also having mastered A would not differ significantly from zero. Indeed, in the ideal equivalence case, the number of such individuals would be exactly zero.

The ordered implication also differs from the prerequisite relation in that it includes implication relations not covered in the prerequisite category. For example, an ordered implication of importance in path-referenced assessment asserts that current mastery of a superordinate capability implies current mastery of a subordiante competency. This type of implication can be assumed to indicate that the subordinate capability is prerequisite to the superordinate competency. However, the converse does not follow. That is, a subordinate competency may be prerequisite to a superordinate competency when the current presence of the superordinate competency does not imply the current presence of the subordinate competency. For example, a subordinate capability may facilitate the learning of a superordinate capability and then drop out of a learner's repertoire of skills (White, 1973).

For assessment purposes, it may be useful to determine that current mastery of a superordinate skill implies mastery of a related subordinate skill when it is not useful or practical to establish a prerequisite relation for the two skills. The central advantage to the current-presence type of implication is that it may be determined by testing individuals at a single point in time. By contrast, the establishment of a prerequisite relation requires assessment of students across time during skill learning. Obviously, an important savings in time and expense may be effected when implication relations are established by testing at a single point in time rather than during the course of skill learning. For example, suppose that a test constructor were faced with the problem of developing a path-referenced test assessing basic arithmetic skills. A variety of ordered relations could occur in arithmetic. For instance, subtraction problems without borrowing may be assumed to be subordinate to subtraction problems that require borrowing (Bergan, 1980b). To demonstrate an ordered implication for borrowing and nonborrowing problems, a test constructor could include both types of problems in a test administered to a random sample of children who might be expected because of age and grade level to vary in subtraction skills. Statistical procedures described later in this chapter would then be used to determine whether or not the data supported the assumption of an ordered relation between borrowing and nonborrowing problems. This would be a much more efficient approach than that of having the test constructor attempt to determine the relationship between the two types of problems by directly observing the learning of children who could not initially solve either type of problem correctly.

Despite the advantage of employing the current-presence relation in the analysis of structure, until recently the use of this type of implication was not advocated (White, 1973). The central reservation expressed in this regard had to do with the possibility that skills might be forgotten in a different order than the order in which they were learned. This different-order assumption received support in an early study of hierarchical learning and retention by Gagné and Bassler (1963). However, the Gagné and Bassler study suffered from methodological problems. First of all, the items used to measure retention differed from those used to assess learning. Thus, differences in the ordering of skills during learning and retention could have occurred because the items were assessing different skills. A second problem was that adequate techniques for validating hierarchical relations were not available at the time of the Gagné and Bassler study. Thus, it is not certain that the ordering assumed for either the learning or retention items was accurate. White (1976) and White and Gagné (1978) have provided new evidence that does not support the differential forgetting hypothesis. Accordingly, Gagné has changed his early views on the usefulness of the current-presence implication.

The position taken in the present chapter is that for reasons of efficiency current-presence implications should be used in the development of path-referenced tests. However, validity studies should be conducted for samples of items aimed at assessing the extent to which the ordering of competencies assessed at a single point in time matches the ordering of competencies assessed during learning.

Two other types of relations that may be encountered in the analysis of scale structure are the conjunctive relation linked to an implication and the disjunctive relation linked to an implication. These two types of relations make it possible to represent nonlinear orderings of behaviors. The conjunctive type is illustrated by the situation in which mastery of a superordinate capability implies that two subordinate capabilities have also been passed. The disjunctive type occurs when mastery of a superordinate competency implies that either of two subordinate capabilities has also been mastered. The conjunctive type is well represented in the literature on learning hierarchies (e.g., Resnick, Wang, & Kaplan, 1973). By contrast, reports of disjunctive relations in research on the ordering of behaviors are lacking.

Validation of Scale-Structure Models

In recent years, a number of mathematical techniques have been developed that make it possible to represent hypothesized scale relations of the type described in the preceding section (Bergan, 1980c). These techniques can be used to test statistically the extent to which a model representing hypothesized relations adequately describes the observed behavior of individuals. The capability of testing models statistically and of representing a range of different types of relations sets the currently available techniques apart from procedures such as scalogram analysis (Guttman, 1944) and the ordering theoretic method (e.g., Bart & Krus, 1973), which have been widely used in the research on learning hierarchies (Bergan, 1980c).

One type of model that has recently been suggested for use in the analysis of scale relations is the quasiindependence model (Goodman, 1975). Quasiindependence models test the hypothesis that the probability of a particular response on any given item will be independent of the probability of a particular response on any other item after selected response patterns are ruled out of consideration. The data presented in Table 8.1, taken from a study by Bergan (in press), illustrate the quasiindependence type of model. These data describe the performance of 283 children on a set of four items assessing skill in identifying fractions. The four items are composed of two identical pairs. For the two items

TABLE 8.1
Children's Performance on Two
Pairs of Fraction-Identification
Tasks[a]

		1/5	1	1	2	2
		1/5	1	2	1	2
1/5	1/5					
1	1	157	7	6	1
1	2	6	3	1	3
2	1	4	1	6	4
2	2	5	3	8	68

[a] The four items represented in this Table required the identification of one-fifth of a set of five objects. One pair, denoted by 1/5, involved identifying one-fifth of five circles. In the other pairs, 1/5 required identification of one-fifth of five objects that varied in shape. A 1 signifies a passing response and a 2, a failing response.

in the first pair, the children were asked to put an X on one-fifth of a set of five circles. The other pair required putting an X on one-fifth of a set of five objects that varied in shape. The ones and twos describing the item patterns indicate passing and failing responses, respectively.

It was assumed that performance on these four items would support the hypothesis that the items formed a homogeneous domain. More specifically, children who passed one item were expected to pass all four items; children who failed one item were expected to fail all four items. It was also assumed that there would be some youngsters who had not yet mastered the skill of identifying a fractional part of a set, but who were in a transitional state between mastery and nonmastery. The performance of these children was expected to be inconsistent. The probability that they would respond correctly to one item was assumed to be independent of the probability that they would respond correctly to any other item in the set.

The quasiindependence model used to test the preceding assumption includes three categories of individuals: individuals who pass all items and may be described as masters of the item domain; individuals who fail all items and are considered to be nonmasters, and transition individuals. The model of quasiindependence tests the hypothesis that the probability of a correct response on one item will be independent of the probability of a correct response on any other item when the response patterns for masters and nonmasters are ruled out of consideration. In other words, the model assumes independence for individuals in the transition category. In addition, the probability of a correct response for masters is assumed to be one, whereas for nonmasters it is assumed to be zero.

Fay and Goodman (1973) have developed a computer program called ECTA

(Everyman's Contingency Table Analyzer), which was used with the fraction data to generate maximum likelihood estimates of expected cell frequencies under the model of quasiindependence. The chi-squared likelihood ratio statistic was then used to assess the correspondence between observed frequencies and estimates of expected cell frequencies generated under the model. In testing the hypothesis of quasiindependence, the two response patterns reflecting mastery and nonmastery were ruled out. This was accomplished by making the observed and expected frequency for these patterns equal. Because the observed and expected frequencies were made equal, the mastery and nonmastery cells contributed nothing to the value obtained for the chi-squared test.

When the correspondence between expected and observed frequencies is close, the model being tested is said to provide an acceptable fit for the data. The test of the model of quasiindependence for the fraction data yielded an X^2 of 14.58 ($df = 9$, $p < .25$). Note that the p value is well above the frequently used rejection level of .05. High p values indicate an acceptable fit. Thus, the model of quasiindependence did provide an acceptable fit for the fraction data set.

The second type of model that may be used in assessing scale relations is the latent class model (Goodman, 1974a, 1974b). Latent class models assume that the relationship among a set of items can be explained by one or more latent (i.e., unobserved) variables, each of which contains a set of latent (unobserved) classes. For example, Macready and Dayton (1977) have suggested a model for a homogeneous item domain that attempts to explain the association among a set of items in terms of latent variables containing two latent classes, a mastery class and a nonmastery class.

Latent class models define the probability of occurrence of each possible response pattern for a set of items by estimating for each pattern the joint probability of each latent class and the response pattern. These probabilities are then summed across latent classes. For example, if the joint probability of getting all items in a set correct and mastery were .85, and the corresponding joint probability and nonmastery were .05, the probability of all items correct would be .90. The maximum likelihood estimate of the expected cell frequency for the cell representing all items correct would be .90 times sample size. Thus, if 100 subjects were tested, the estimated expected cell frequency would be 90. The joint probability for each latent class and response pattern are generated by an iterative procedure described by Goodman (1974b). Clogg (1977) has developed a computer program for carrying out the iterative process. The Clogg program was used to test the fit of the Macready and Dayton two-class model to the data for the four fraction-identification items described earlier. The X^2 obtained for this model was 29.49 ($df = 12$, p < .01), which indicates that the Macready and Dayton model does not afford an acceptable model–data fit for this particular data set.

Various kinds of restrictions can be imposed on latent class models. For example, the probability of a correct response can be restricted to be equal for all items in a given latent class. Likewise, probability can be set to a specific value, such as one or zero. The quasiindependence model described earlier illustrates latent class restrictions. Quasiindependence models can be conceived of as latent class models. The quasiindependence equivalence model previously described is a latent class model with three latent classes—a mastery class, a nonmastery class, and a transition class. The probability of a correct response in the mastery class is restricted to one. In the nonmastery class, it is restricted to zero. No restrictions are imposed on the transition class.

An important advantage of the latent class type of model is that it permits the testing of models containing a wide range of different restrictions. For example, consider the following variation on the quasiindependence model: Suppose that the nonmastery and transitional classes are identical to those in the quasiindependence model. However, the probability of a correct response is not constrained to be one in the mastery class. Rather, the probability of a correct response is restricted to be equal across items. This model was tested for the fraction items and yielded an X^2 of 6.59 ($df = 8$, $p < .75$). This model fits the data very well indeed.

The foregoing examples illustrate models for the equivalence relation. Latent class and quasiindependence models for assessing other relations are also available. For example, suppose that the identification of one-fifth of five circles was thought to be necessary to identification of one-fifth of five objects of varying shapes. A quasiindependence model for this assumption would include four classes—masters, nonmasters, transition individuals, and individuals who had mastered the circle task but not the varied-shapes task. The model would be tested using the chi-squared statistic in exactly the same way as the equivalence quasiindependence model.

Causal Structure

Given that the analysis of scale structure has revealed ordered implications among domains, it is useful to establish a causal structure for the domains. The determination of causal structure requires the construction and empirical validation of a structural model indicating the effects of subordinate domain mastery on superordinate domain mastery.

Three conditions are necessary for establishing causal relations (Heise, 1975). One is an appropriate theory asserting causal hypotheses. The second has to do with temporal relations among variables of interest, and the third involves empirical testing of causal hypotheses.

Theory. Determining causal relations among variables requires a plausible theory that indicates hypothesized relations between explanatory (i.e., causal) variables and response variables. A number of theoretical frameworks are available for justifying the assumption that intellectual competencies are structurally related and that intellectual operations acquired during the early phases of learning may have a causal influence on the acquisition of more complex capabilities. Robert Gagné's (1977) learning-hierarchy model represents the dominant structural viewpoint at the current time. However, other theoretical perspectives are also emerging. For example, Brown and Burton (1978) have developed a structural theory focusing on systematic errors that interfere with the mastery of academic tasks. The learning of subtraction skills can be used to illustrate the Brown and Burton position. Before learning to borrow in solving simple subtraction problems, a child may adopt the misguided strategy of subtracting the smaller number from the larger number even when the smaller number is on top. Mastery of borrowing may require disabusing the child of his or her views about subtracting smaller numbers from larger numbers (Brown & Burton, 1978).

Temporal Relations. The second criterion necessary for establishing a causal relation is that explanatory (i.e., causal) variables occur either simultaneously with or prior to response variables. When applied to path-referenced assessment, this condition implies the need for a temporal ordering of domains. More specifically, when causal relations are presumed, it must be reasonable to assume that behaviors represented by subordinate domains are acquired either simultaneously with or prior to related behaviors represented by superordinate domains. The analysis of scale structure provides one source of justification for this assumption. The presence of an ordered implication revealed in scale-structure analysis indicates a significant number of individuals who have mastered the subordinate capability without acquiring a related superordinate competency. At the same time, the low probability of subordinate mastery prior to superordinate mastery supports the view that the subordinate competency is not learned in advance of the superordinate capability.

The use of scale-structure analysis makes it possible to assess hypothesized causal relations on the basis of data collected at a single point in time. The result is a substantial temporal and financial savings having a markedly beneficial influence on the feasibility of developing path-referenced tests within reasonable cost and time limitations. Despite its advantages, testing during a single time period should not be the only strategy for determining causal relations in path-referenced assessment. Direct tests of causal hypotheses are needed to enhance the validity of causal models based on tests administered at a single point in time.

The assumption that mastery of a subordinate domain will have an effect on acquisition of a superordinate domain may be tested directly by means of transfer of training studies (White & Gagné, 1974). For example, consider the case of two skills forming an ordered-implication relation. To assess the effects of subordinate skill mastery on superordinate skill acquisition, a sample of subjects would be selected possessing all relevant subordinate skills except for the two being tested. The subjects would be assigned at random to an experimental and a control condition. The subjects in the experimental condition would receive instruction in the subordinate skill whereas those in the control condition would not. Then both groups would receive instruction in the superordinate skill and their performance on the superordinate skill would be compared statistically. An hypothesized causal effect would be supported by the data if superordinate skill performance in the experimental group was significantly superior to performance in the control group.

The transfer of training approach to validating causal hypotheses would be considerably more expensive than single time-period testing. It would not be practical from the standpoint of cost to employ the transfer of training strategy to validate all causal hypotheses in a path-referenced test. However, transfer of training studies could be used for subsets of hypothesized causal relations to enhance the validity of models based on single time-period testing.

Another strategy that could be employed to validate causal hypotheses in path-referenced assessment would be to employ time-series designs (Kratochwill, 1978). For example, suppose that a school was using a path-referenced test to identify the source of a child's reading difficulties and that path-referenced assessment revealed that the child was missing subordinate competencies underlying the skills currently being taught. In a case of this kind, base-line data could be collected for instruction on superordinate skills. During a subsequent intervention period, instruction could be provided in subordinate skills. An increase in superordinate skill performance associated with subordinate skill intervention would indicate a subordinate skill effect on superordinate skill acquisition. This example illustrates an extremely simple application of time-series methodology. The variety of available time-series designs that could be employed in the validation of causal models is almost unlimited. For a thorough discussion of available designs and the factors influencing design selection, see Kratochwill (1978).

Validation of Causal Models

The third condition necessary for establishing a causal relation is an empirical test of the relation. A variety of techniques are available for testing causal models. When dependent variables are measured on an interval scale, structural equation procedures derived from Wright's (1921) pioneering work in path analysis can be used in model testing. These procedures employ techniques based on regression (Duncan, 1975; Heise, 1975) and regression and factor analysis (Jöreskog & Sörbom, 1979).

In most instances, path-referenced test scores will involve dichotomous or polytomous measures rather than interval scale measures. Goodman (1972, 1973a, 1973b) has developed causal models for use with dichotomous and polytomous measures based on path analysis (Goldberger & Duncan, 1973). These models can be used to assess the effects of subordinate domain mastery on the odds of superordinate domain mastery. For example, Goodman's techniques could be used to test a model asserting that mastery of two subordinate domains influenced the odds of acquisition of a third superordinate domain. The Goodman models generate maximum likelihood estimates of expected cell frequencies representing response patterns for a set of domain scores. The ECTA computer program described earlier is used to generate the maximum likelihood estimates. As in the case of scale-structure analysis, the extent to which estimated cell frequencies correspond to observed frequencies is determined by use of the chi-square technique.

Results of a structural analysis using Goodman's techniques can be summarized in a path diagram like the one in Fig. 8.2. The letters in the diagram indicate domains. The curved arrow between A and B indicates a noncausal relation between these two domains. The arrows from A and B joined at the small circle indicate that A and B interact in affecting C. That is, the effect of A on C depends on the level of B. Of course, one could also say that the effect of B on C depends on the level of A. For example, the odds of mastering C given mastery of A might be markedly higher for mastery of B than for nonmastery of B. By contrast, given nonmastery of A, mastery of B might have little effect on mastery of C. The straight arrow from C to D indicates a direct effect of C on D. This effect (assuming that it is positive) indicates that the odds of mastery of D are markedly higher for mastery of C than for nonmastery of C.

Path diagrams indicating causal structure specify relations among domains in a concise way. In addition, they afford a useful tool for describing examinee performance on path-referenced tests. As indicated earlier, referencing examinee performance to position in a causal model indicates in a precise way what the examinee has learned and what he or she needs to learn to progress further.

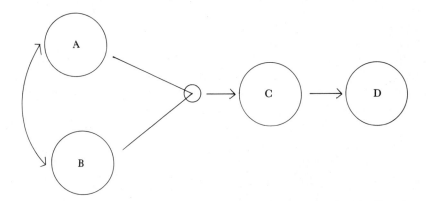

FIG. 8.2.   Path diagram for four hypothetical domains in a path-referenced test. Letters indicate domains. The curved arrow indicates a noncausal relation. The arrows from A and B joined at the small circle indicate that A and B interact in affecting C. The straight arrow shows a direct effect of C on D.

PATH-REFERENCED PSYCHOMETRICS

In order for path-referenced tests to be useful in educational settings, their psychometric properties must be established. For example, questions of validity and reliability arise with respect to path-referenced assessment just as they do in other forms of assessment. However, path-referenced assessment procedures used to establish reliability and validity differ from the techniques employed in other forms of assessment.

Reliability

Consistency in performance is an important issue in path-referenced assessment, as it is in other forms of assessment. Reliability or consistency in performance on a path-referenced test is best determined in relation to the domains established through scale-structure analysis. The domain-reliability question of major concern has to do with consistency in assigning individuals to mastery states. For instance, it is important to determine whether or not an individual classified as a master of a given domain on one administration of a test would be categorized as a master on a subsequent administration of the same test.

Swaminathan, Hambleton, and Algina (1974) have suggested that reliability of mastery classification be established for parallel forms of the same test or for two administrations of the same test. They suggest the use of Cohen's (1960) kappa for this purpose. Huynh (in press) has recently evaluated the use of kappa for establishing reliability based on a single test administration. Kappa has the advantage of providing a measure of agreement that takes into account spurious agreement caused by chance factors. However, one problem with the kappa coefficient is that it does not have a directly interpretable meaning. For example, a kappa coefficient of .90 does not have a precise meaning. Bergan (1980a) has developed a quasiindependence measure of agreement that can be used in path-referenced assessment. The Bergan coefficient gives the probability of agreement under a model hypothesizing independence among response patterns reflecting disagreement. The Bergan procedure can be used only in cases in which examinees are assigned to three or more mastery states. However, Bergan (1980d) recently has extended his procedure to cover cases involving dichotomous classifications such as master, nonmaster.

Validity

The principal means by which validity is established in path-referenced assessment is through the use of scale-structure analysis and the analysis of causal structure. The structural models used in path-referenced assessment express hypotheses about relationships among item domains. Model testing using the techniques described previously in this chapter affords evidence concerning model validity. For example, a transfer of training study assessing the effects of subordinate skill mastery on superordinate skill acquisition provides evidence as to the validity of the hypothesis that the subordinate skill has a causal influence on the acquisition of the superordinate capability.

Norms

Hambleton and Eignor (1979) have pointed out that it may be useful to establish norms for criterion-referenced tests. This is the case whenever it is important to know examinee position in a suitable reference group. Hambleton and Eignor's views apply in the case of path-referenced assessment. Norms can be useful in path-referenced assessment and the well-known procedures for establishing norms can be applied with path-referenced instruments.

Norms could be particularly useful in path-referenced tests that might be employed in school psychology. School psychologists use norms in making placement decisions. Thus, the inclusion of norms in path-referenced instruments could enhance the value of such instruments for placement purposes.

Popham (1976) points out that one danger associated with the inclusion of norms in criterion-referenced tests is that test users may rely on norms exclusively in decision making based on test results. This point also applies in the case of path-referenced assessment. For example, school psychologists historically have relied heavily on norms in making placement decisions. As is discussed later in this chapter, path-referenced tests can provide information aside from norm-referenced scores that may be useful in determining placement. In order to make this information play a role in placement, steps would have to be taken to ensure that test users did not overlook the benefits to be gained from considering information beyond norm-referenced scores.

TEST BIAS IN PATH-REFERENCED ASSESSMENT

One of the most difficult problems in assessment is that of developing testing practices that are not biased against (i.e., unfair to) one or more of the many ethnic groups that make up our pluralistic society. The possibility of bias or unfair use of tests may arise when group differences appear in test performance. Cleary, Humphreys, Kendrick, and Wesman (1975) recognize this point in their review of the educational uses of tests with disadvantaged students prepared for the American Psychological Association Board of Scientific Affairs. They write: "A test is considered fair for a particular use if the inference drawn from the test score is made with the smallest feasible random error and if there is no constant error in the inference as a function of membership in a particular group [p. 25]."

Tests that discriminate among groups rather than only among individuals provide the potential for bias to occur. Because they differentiate among groups, they will almost invariably be discriminatory. That is, they will favor differential treatment by group. This is not to say that discriminatory treatment will in all cases be unfair treatment. All that is being asserted is that group discrimination can be a precursor to bias associated with the use of tests.

The large body of literature on bias has focused exclusively on unfair test use arising from test discrimination among groups. For example, potential bias in IQ tests is made possible by the fact that the mean level of performance on such tests is different for different ethnic groups (e.g., Blacks and Whites). Bias or unfair use may also occur when a test fails to discriminate group differences. For example, if test results describe a child's learning inaccurately because of a failure to discriminate cultural differences in learning patterns, then the test is being used unfairly.

Structural Congruence

Bias arising from a failure to discriminate group differences may arise in path-referenced assessment when a path-referenced test fails to identify ethnically related differences in the structural patterning of behavior. Different scale structures and/or causal structures may exist for different ethnic groups. Bergan and Henderson (1979) report an anecdote relating to Mexican–American children illustrating how this could occur. They indicate that Mexican–American children who are taught basic math skills by their parents may learn arithmetic operations in ways that differ markedly from those typically employed by Anglo children. For instance, in carrying out subtraction problems that would require borrowing for an Anglo child, Mexican–American children may make appropriate alterations in the bottom row of a subtraction problem rather than borrowing on the top row. Procedural differences of this kind could produce ethnically related differences in scale and causal structure on a path-referenced test assessing arithmetic skills.

Lack of congruence across ethnic groups in scale structure or causal structure could eventuate in unfair test use. For instance, if scale structure differed for Mexican–American and Anglo students and if structure were established without regard for ethnic differences by testing a predominantly Anglo sample, information provided by the test for Mexican–American children would be misleading and thereby could have an adverse effect on the academic progress of Mexican–American examinees.

Because of the possibility of ethnically related differences in scale and causal structures, it is essential in path-referenced test development to establish structural congruity for the various ethnic groups who may make use of the test. Mathematical models are available for determining structural congruence. For example, suppose that a quasiindependence model were used to assess a scale structure. As indicated earlier, such a model would assert independence among items after selected response patterns were ruled out of consideration. A model investigating structural congruence across ethnic groups would examine structure within each ethnic group of interest. It would test the hypothesis of conditional quasiindependence. That is, it would test the hypothesis of quasiindependence within each ethnic group. If the hypothesized model did not fit the data for one or more groups, the model of conditional quasiindependence would be rejected. This would indicate the need to assume a different structure for different ethnic groups. A model asserting this kind of assumption could be tested and appropriate alterations in the path-referenced model being developed could be made on the basis of results of the test.

Ethnicity and Domain Achievement

The age or grade at which a given domain is mastered may differ by ethnic group. When path-referenced tests assess basic academic skills and are used with diverse ethnic groups, age- or grade-related differences in domain achievement may well occur. Path-referenced tests revealing such differences are discriminatory. Thus, they could eventuate in bias against certain groups.

When a path-referenced test is shown to discriminate among ethnic groups with respect to achievement, it may be useful to examine the item content of the test for bias. Some items may be heavily loaded with content that reflects cultural background (Oakland & Matuszek, 1977). Such items will produce ethnically related differences in performance. Although it is probably not possible to eliminate cultural item bias entirely (Kratochwill, Alper, & Cancelli, in press), it may be feasible to substitute items that minimize bias for items that are heavily weighted in favor of a particular ethnic group.

In some cases, examination of internal content may reveal that test items are assessing behavior of importance across ethnic groups even though the items discriminate among ethnic categories. In such cases, it becomes important to determine the source of ethnic differences. An enormous amount of effort has gone into the task of determining the genetic and environmental factors that produce ethnically related differences on norm-referenced tests (Bergan & Henderson, 1979). It is far beyond the scope of this chapter to address the vast literature that has accumulated on genetic and environmental influences. However, it should be pointed out that the question of genetic and environmental determination of test performance can be raised in the study of path-referenced assessment as it has been in norm-referenced assessment. Nonetheless, there are fundamental differences between path-referenced assessment and norm-referenced tests that may influence the kinds of questions that are asked with respect to genetic and environmental effects and the kinds of research carried out to answer those questions. For example, path-referenced tests are designed to identify behavioral domains and the structural relationships among those domains. Often, the domains of interest are learned skills. In the event that ethnic-group differences are observed in performance on a path-referenced test assessing skill mastery, a question of immediate import would be that of determining whether or not there are also differences in skill learning across groups. For instance, Bergan and Parra (1979) found that preschool Mexican–American and Anglo children differed in achievement on a letter-learning task. However, the Mexican–American children caught up to their Anglo counterparts when instruction was provided to both groups. The Mexican–American children apparently had had very little prior exposure to the task.

As the preceding example shows, the investigation of learning can be useful in determining the source of ethnically related differences that might arise in path-referenced assessment. By contrast, the question of the influence of learning on test performance is not easy to deal with in norm-referenced assessment because behavior domains are not specified operationally in norm-referenced tests. A researcher interested in examining the effects of learning on norm-referenced test performance would probably have to face the charge that he or she was teaching students to perform on the test rather than teaching them the ability underlying that performance. When behavior domains are not defined, it is difficult to successfully defend against that charge.

Ethnicity, Prediction, and Effects on Criterion Performance.   Bias resulting from the use of tests in predicting criterion behavior has been an issue of major concern in the test-bias literature (see, for example, Hunter & Schmidt, 1976). For instance, in school psychology, norm-referenced IQ tests are used to predict academic performance. Decisions with respect to placement in special-education programs are based in part on assumptions regarding the predictive accuracy of norm-referenced instruments. Ethnic-group differences in scores on norm-referenced IQ tests have eventuated in the placement of inordinately large numbers of minority group children in special-education programs (Mercer, 1973). Not surprisingly, the issue of possible test bias associated with educational placement has been hotly debated. Recently, a federal judge has ruled that IQ tests used in the placement of Black children in classes for the mentally retarded in the state of California are biased and therefore cannot be used for that purpose in the future (Bersoff, in press).

Path-referenced tests can be used to predict such criterion as school performance. For example, a regression equation could be constructed for a path-referenced test using domain scores as predictor variables and total test score on a standard achievement test as the criterion variable. A minimum level of acceptable performance could be established for each grade level on the criterion test. Cut-off scores could then be determined for the domains. These could be used in special-education placement. If this strategy were adopted, the problem of test bias relating to prediction of criterion variables would be handled in the same way that it would be addressed in norm-referenced assessment (see Kratochwill et al., in press).

An alternative to this approach would be to construct a structural equation model (Duncan, 1975; Jöreskog & Sörbom, 1979), treating the domains and ethnicity as explanatory variables and the achievement test as the dependent variable. In the structural-equation approach, domain mastery and ethnic-group membership would be treated as having a causal influence on achievement.

Cut-off scores could be established and used for placement purposes as in the predictive approach. In addition, specific recommendations could be made for educational programs. For example, if it were found that a particular set of domains had not been mastered and that mastery of those domains had a large effect on overall achievement level, it would be useful to recommend focusing instruction on those domains.

The problem of test bias could be addressed in two ways under the structural equation approach. First of all, the extent to which ethnicity was observed to have a causal influence on achievement could be used as a sign of possible test bias. To illustrate the signaling function of ethnicity, suppose that ethnicity were the only explanatory variable in a structural equation identifying influences on school achievement. In this case, variations in achievement associated with variation in ethnicity could occur in part because of unidentified skills linked to both achievement and ethnicity. If some subset of these skills were subsequently identified, measured, and added as explanatory variables in the structural equation, variations in achievement that had previously been attributed to ethnicity could now be identified as variation attributable to a set of learned skills. Because not all of the skills were identified, some of the remaining variation attributed to ethnicity could be variation that should have been linked to specific skills. To the extent that the test had not identified all ethnically related skills, unfair use would result. For example, it would not be possible to recommend needed instruction for skills that had not been identified. This would be unfair to the particular group most lacking in those skills. Not all achievement variations associated with ethnicity would necessarily be linked to learned skills. Other factors could also play a part in producing ethnicity effects on achievement. However, unless those factors were satisfactorily identified, the possibility of skill effects could not be ruled out.

The second way of addressing bias in the structural approach involves ethnically related changes in achievement related to domain mastery. The structural approach asserts that domains affect achievement. This assumption implies that as domains are mastered achievement levels should rise. Moreover, increases in achievement accompanying domain mastery should not be related to ethnicity. Failure of achievement levels to increase with increases in domain mastery would indicate overall invalidity in the structural model. Ethnically related increases in achievement associated with increases in domain mastery would indicate possible bias. The possible implication would be that important domains related to ethnicity and achievement had not been identified.

Uses of Path-Referenced Assessment in School-Psychology Practice

Path-referenced tests can be used in a variety of different ways in the practice of school psychology. One relates to screening assessment undertaken to identify previously undetected problems manifested by learners. A second has to do with classification, and a third relates to diagnosis.

Screening. Path-referenced tests can be used in screening children for the purpose of identifying learning and adjustment problems not previously detected in the classroom or in the home. The central advantage of the path-referenced approach to screening relates to the fact that path-referenced tests focus attention on specific behaviorally defined domains rather than on constructs such as traits, aptitudes, and abilities that are generally not conceptualized in a way that clearly identifies a specific class or set of classes of examinee behavior. This advantage derives from the criterion-referenced assessment approach to domain definition (Shoemaker, 1975), which is used in path-referenced assessment.

Focus on behaviorally defined domains in screening makes it possible to link test behavior to behavior in the natural environment. For example, if a child were observed on a path-referenced screening test to lack a particular set of academic skills, it would be essential to determine whether or not the child evidenced similar skill deficits in the classroom setting. Behaviorists have pointed out that behavior emitted in a structured testing situation may not be the same as behavior emitted in the natural environment (Haynes, 1978; Kazdin, 1978). A fundamental premise underlying the use of screening devices is that screening may serve as a vehicle for identifying problems that teachers, parents, and other socializing agents may have overlooked. Insofar as it does identify overlooked problems, it serves as a useful addition to the customary referral process in which teachers or parents are confronted with a specific learning or adjustment difficulty that causes them to seek services. However, it is also possible that some problems observed in structured testing situations are not identified in the natural environment because they simply do not occur in the natural setting. When this is the case, the screening device may create a pseudoproblem that, at the very least, will waste the time of socializing agents and that could have a damaging effect on the child.

When the focus of screening is on specifically defined behavioral domains, conditions can be arranged to determine the extent to which behavior deficits identified during structured testing actually occur in the natural environment. For example, arrangements can be made to assess skill deficits in the classroom. In the event that classroom assessment reveals the same skill deficits as those identified in structured testing, the value of screening has been confirmed. On the other hand, should classroom assessment reveal a lack of congruence with structured test findings, creation of a pseudoproblem can be avoided.

Placement.   Path-referenced assessment can be used by school psychologists in determining program placement as well as in the identification of undetected learning and adjustment difficulties. As indicated earlier, it is possible to develop norms for path-referenced tests. Path-referenced tests can be used to determine an individual's position in a suitable norm group. This information can be employed in making placement decisions.

Information on the structure of domains and on a student's position in a structural model may also be useful in determining placement. A path-referenced test indicates the behaviors that are in a student's repertoire and the sequential ordering of those behaviors. A number of authors have pointed out the potential usefulness of information on position in a behavioral sequence for placement purposes (e.g., Gagné & Briggs, 1974; Glaser & Nitko, 1971). Given that accurate information were available specifying objectives and the sequencing of objectives for instructional programs, it would be possible to base placement in part on the match between domain mastery and the character of available instruction in various educational programs. For example, Public Law 94–142 mandates that individualized educational plans (IEPs) be established for all children receiving special-education services. These plans must specify objectives articulated directly to the instructional needs of the individual child. Path-referenced tests could be used to assist in the development of IEPs for individual children. These IEPs would indicate position in each learning sequence. Information on position would be used in selecting a program capable of accommodating the child's current position. In addition, it would be used to determine the appropriate starting point for each instructional sequence provided to the child.

Diagnostic Testing.   The potential value of diagnostic tests capable of identifying skill deficits in a structure specifying sequential relationships among skills is well recognized in the literature (Gagné & Briggs, 1974). Learners may fail to master complex objectives because they lack subordinate competencies. Diagnostic tests capable of identifying missing competencies can serve a useful function in directing instruction toward skills that might otherwise be overlooked. For example, Bergan, Byrnes, and Kratochwill (1979) found that a substantial majority of teachers faced with the task of identifying the source of a learning problem in a hypothetical child were unable to identify a subordinate capability that the child lacked unless they were given specific diagnostic information detailing the missing subordinate competency.

Although the value of diagnostic tests indicating the structure of behavioral capabilities has long been recognized, tests linked to empirically validated behavioral structures have been lacking (White & Gagné, 1974). Educators and psychologists have relied heavily on hypothesized learning sequences constructed on the basis of task analysis. Task analyses breaking complex instructional objectives into components provide hypotheses about the structure of behavior but do not afford a way to validate structures empirically. Clearly, tests based on task analysis alone do not provide an acceptable substitute for tests based on empirical validation of scale structures and causal structures. One of the principal advantages of path-referenced assessment is that it provides a way to validate hypothesized scale structures and causal structures empirically.

A second advantage of path-referenced assessment in diagnostic testing is that path-referenced tests afford information on the magnitude of effects of subordinate domain mastery on superordinate domain learning. For example, a path-referenced test can provide information on the odds of acquiring mastery of a superordinate domain for learners who have acquired a subordinate domain and on the odds of superordinate domain acquisition for learners who have not mastered the prerequisites. The ratio of these two odds can give direct and easily interpreted information on skill effects to another person. For example, a school psychologist communicating test results to a teacher might say, *"George does not know how to borrow. The odds of a student responding correctly to problems like the ones in his workbook are 40 times higher for children who know how to borrow than they are for children who have not mastered borrowing."*

Program Evaluation.   School psychologists are assuming new and important roles in the broad-scale evaluation of instructional programs. For example, school psychologists may serve as consultants to administrators and school faculty in the development of instructional objectives, in the design of procedures for evaluating program effectiveness, and in determining the extent to which instructional objectives have been attained (Kratochwill & Bergan, 1978). Path-referenced assessment can be useful to the school psychologist in the evaluation process. Path-referenced tests identify empirically validated behavioral domains that can be linked directly to instructional objectives. Thus, path-referenced tests provide a vehicle for assessing the extent to which program objectives have been achieved. In addition, the mathematical models used in path-referenced assessment can be employed in assessing program effects on instructional outcomes. For example, instructional variations may be included in structural models hypothesizing causal relations between instruction and educational outcomes. Moreover, structural models may be constructed that assess the separate and interactive influences of instructional variations and mastery of subordinate capabilities on superordinate competencies.

The use of path-referenced assessment in program evaluation may require tests that are tailor-made to educational programs. As Popham (1978a) has pointed out, the tradition of local control of American education fosters diverse curricula in different school districts. In discussing the role of criterion-referenced testing in educational evaluation, Popham suggests that adequate development for instructional evaluation may require assistance from consulting firms capable of tailor-making tests to the needs of individual districts. The use of path-referenced assessment in program evaluation would be facilitated by an arrangement of this kind.

PATH-REFERENCED TEST DEVELOPMENT AND SCHOOL-PSYCHOLOGY PRACTICE

Whether or not path-referenced assessment will find a significant place in the practice of school psychology will depend in part on the availability of path-referenced tests. Availability can be expected to be influenced by theory, technology, and need.

Gagné's (1962, 1970, 1977) pioneering work on learning hierarchies has provided a theoretical framework that has encouraged psychologists and educators to advance hypotheses about structural relationships among behaviors in a variety of academic areas. As indicated earlier in the chapter, other theoretical perspectives (e.g., Brown & Burton, 1978) are also emerging that provide potentially useful ways to conceptualize structural relationships among behaviors. These new theoretical positions can be expected to encourage further thinking about structure by psychologists and educators in the years ahead.

The many hypotheses that have already been developed about structure in specific academic content areas provide a strong foundation for guiding the development of path-referenced tests. For example, many school districts have conducted task analyses identifying hypothesized learning sequences in a large variety of curriculum areas. Sequentially ordered objectives derived from task analyses could serve as a basis for establishing the content for path-referenced tests assessing academic skills.

School psychologists are already attempting to incorporate assessment of structure into their evaluation activities (Bergan, 1977). Task-analysis procedures are being used to generate hypotheses about structure. Informal assessment devices are being constructed on the basis of such analyses and results of structural assessment are being employed in educational programming (Bergan, 1977). The rapid advances that have occurred in the development of mathematical models capable of empirically validating scale and causal structures provide the needed techniques to make path-referenced tests a reality. The need for putting available techniques to use is apparent in the efforts of psychologists and educators to assess structure even in the absence of appropriate tests for carrying out such assessment. The combination of appropriate theory, apparent need, and available technology suggests that conditions may be right for spawning path-referenced assessment as a new form of assessment for use in school psychology.

REFERENCES

Bart, W. M., & Krus, D. J. An ordering–theoretic method to determine hierarchies among items. *Educational and Psychological Measurement*, 1973, *33*, 291–300.

Bergan, J. R. *Behavioral consultation*. Columbus, Ohio: Charles E. Merrill, 1977.

Bergan, J. R. Measuring observer agreement using the quasi-independence concept. *Journal of Educational Measurement*, 1980, *17*, 59–69. (a)

Bergan, J. R. Preferred model selection in the validation of scales involving hierarchical dependencies among learning tasks. *Contemporary Educational Psychology*, 1980, *5*, 232-240. (b)

Bergan, J. R. The structural analysis of behavior: An alternative to the learning hierarchy model. *Review of Educational Research*, 1980, *50*, 625-646. (c)

Bergan, J. R. A quasi-equiprobability model for measuring observer agreement. *Journal of Educational Statistics*, 1980, *5*, 363-376. (d)

Bergan, J. R. Models of the structure of some rule-governed mathematical behaviors. *Contemporary Educational Psychology*, in press.

Bergan, J. R., Byrnes, I. M., & Kratochwill, T. R. Effects of behavioral and medical models of consultation on teacher expectancies and instruction of a hypothetical child. *Journal of School Psychology*, 1979, *17*, 307-316.

Bergan, J. R., Cancelli, A. A., & Luiten, J. Mastery assessment with latent class and quasi-independence models representing homogeneous item domains. *Journal of Educational Statistics*, 1980, *9*, 65-81.

Bergan, J. R., & Henderson, R. W. *Child development*. Columbus, Ohio: Charles E. Merrill, 1979.

Bergan, J. R., & Parra, E. Variations in IQ testing and instruction and the letter learning and achievement of Anglo and bilingual Mexican-American children. *Journal of Educational Psychology*, 1979, *71*, 819-826.

Bersoff, D. N. Legal issues in school psychology. In J. R. Bergan (Ed.), *Contemporary school psychology*. Columbus, Ohio: Charles E. Merrill, in press.

Brown, J. S., & Burton, R. R. Diagnostic models for procedural bugs in basic mathematical skills. *Cognitive Science*, 1978, *2*, 155-192.

Cleary, T. A., Humphreys, L. G., Kendrick, S. A., & Wesman, A. Educational uses of tests with disadvantaged students. *American Psychologist*, 1975, *30*, 15-41.

Clogg, C. C. *Unrestricted and restricted maximum likelihood latent structure analysis: A manual for users* (Working Paper No. 1977-09). Unpublished manuscript, Pennsylvania State University, 1977.

Cohen, J. A. A co-efficient of agreement for nominal scales. *Educational and Psychological Measurement*, 1960, *20*, 27-36.

Duncan, O. D. *Introduction to structural equation models*. New York: Academic Press, 1975.

Fay, R., & Goodman, L. A. *ECTA program description for users*. Unpublished program description, July 1973. (Available from Dr. Goodman, Department of Sociology, University of Chicago, Chicago, Illinois.)

Gagné, R. M. The acquisition of knowledge. *Psychological Review*, 1962, *69*, 355-365.

Gagné, R. M. *The conditions of learning* (2nd ed.). New York: Holt, Rinehart & Winston, 1970.

Gagné, R. M. *The conditions of learning* (3rd ed.). New York: Holt, Rinehart, & Winston, 1977.

Gagné, R. M., & Bassler, O. C. Study of retention of some topics of elementary nonmetric geometry. *Journal of Educational Psychology*, 1963, *54*, 123-131.

Gagné, R. M., & Briggs, L. J. *Principles of instructional design*. New York: Holt, Rinehart, & Winston, 1974.

Glaser, R., & Nitko, A. J. Measurement in learning and instruction. In R. L. Thorndike (Ed.), *Educational measurement* (2nd ed.). Washington, D.C.: American Council on Education, 1971.

Goldberger, A. S., & Duncan, O. D. (Eds.). *Structural equation models in the social sciences*. New York: Seminar Press, 1973.

Goodman, L. A. A general model for the analysis of surveys. *American Journal of Sociology*, 1972, *77*, 1035-1085.

Goodman, L. A. The analysis of multidimensional contingency tables when some variables are posterior to others: A modified path analysis approach. *Biometrika*, 1973, *60*, 179-192. (a)

Goodman, L. A. Causal analysis of data from panel studies and other kinds of surveys. *American Journal of Sociology*, 1973, *78*, 1135-1191. (b)

Goodman, L. A. The analysis of systems of quantitative variables when some of the variables are unobservable. Part 1—A modified latent structure approach. *American Journal of Sociology,* 1974, *79,* 1179–1259. (a)

Goodman, L. A. Exploratory latent structure analysis using both identifiable and unidentifiable models. *Biometrika,* 1974, *61,* 215–231. (b)

Goodman, L. A. A new model for scaling response patterns: An application of the quasi-independence concept. *Journal of the American Statistical Association,* 1975, *70,* 755–768.

Goodman, L. A. *Analyzing qualitative/categorical data.* Cambridge, Mass.: ABT Associates, 1978.

Guttman, L. A basis for scaling qualitative data. *American Sociological Review,* 1944, *9,* 139–150.

Hambleton, R. K., & Eignor, D. R. *A practitioner's guide to criterion-referenced test development validation and test score usage* (2nd ed.) (Laboratory of Psychometric and Evaluation Research, Report No. 70). Amherst, Mass.: School of Education, University of Massachusetts, March 1979.

Hambleton, R. K., Swaminathan, H., Algina, J., & Coulson, D. B. Criterion-referenced testing and measurement: A review of technical issues and developments. *Review of Educational Research,* 1978, *48,* 1–47.

Haynes, S. N. *Principles of behavioral assessment.* New York: Gardner Press, 1978.

Heise, D. R. *Causal analysis.* New York: Wiley, 1975.

Hunter, J. E., & Schmidt, F. L. Critical analysis of the statistical and ethical implications of various definitions of test bias. *Psychological Bulletin,* 1976, *83,* 1053–1071.

Huynh, H. Reliability of decisions in domain-referenced testing. *Journal of Educational Measurement,* in press.

Jöreskog, K. G., & Sörbom, D. *Advances in factor analysis and structural equation models.* Cambridge, Mass.: ABT Associates, 1979.

Kazdin, A. E. *History of behavior modification: Experimental foundations of contemporary research.* Baltimore: University Park Press, 1978.

Kratochwill, T. R. *Single-subject research: Strategies for evaluating change.* New York: Academic Press, 1978.

Kratochwill, T. R., Alper, S., & Cancelli, A. A. Non-discriminatory measures in special education. In L. Mann & D. Sabatino (Eds.), *Fourth review of special education.* New York: Gardner Press, in press.

Kratochwill, T. R., & Bergan, J. R. Evaluating programs in applied settings through behavioral consultation. *Journal of School Psychology,* 1978, *16,* 375–386.

Macready, G. B., & Dayton, C. M. The use of probabilistic models in the assessment of mastery. *Journal of Educational Statistics,* 1977, *2,* 88–120.

Macready, G. B., & Merwin, J. C. Homogeneity within item forms in domain referenced testing. *Educational and Psychological Measurement,* 1973, *33,* 351–360.

Mercer, J. R. *Labeling the mentally retarded.* Berkeley: University of California Press, 1973.

Oakland, T., & Matuszek, P. Using tests in non-discriminatory assessment. In T. Oakland (Ed.), *Psychological and educational assessment of minority children.* New York: Brunner/Mazel, 1977.

Popham, W. J. Normative data for criterion-referenced tests. *Phi Delta Kappan,* 1976, *5,* 593–594.

Popham, W. J. *Criterion-referenced measurement.* Englewood Cliffs, N.J.: Prentice-Hall, 1978. (a)

Popham, W. J. The case for criterion-referenced measurements. *Educational Researcher,* 1978, *7,* 6–10. (b)

Resnick, L. B., Wang, M. C., & Kaplan, J. Task analysis in curriculum design: A hierarchically sequenced introductory mathematics curriculum. *Journal of Applied Behavioral Analysis,* 1973, *7,* 679–710.

Shoemaker, D. M. Toward a framework for achievement testing. *Review of Educational Research,* 1975, *45,* 127–148.

Swaminathan, H., Hambleton, R. K., & Algina, J. Reliability of criterion-referenced tests: A decision theoretic formulation. *Journal of Educational Measurement*, 1974, *11*, 263–268.

White, R. T. Learning hierarchies. *Review of Educational Research*, 1973, *43*, 361–375.

White, R. T. Effects of guidance sequences and attribute treatment interactions on learning, retention, and transfer of hierarchically ordered skills. *Instructional Science*, 1976, *5*, 133–152.

White, R. T., & Clark, R. M. A test of inclusion which allows for errors of measurement. *Psychometrika*, 1973, *38*, 77–86.

White, R. T., & Gagné, R. M. Past and future research on learning hierarchies. *Educational Psychologist*, 1974, *11*, 19–28.

White, R. T., & Gagné, R. M. Summative evaluation applied to a learning hierarchy. *Contemporary Educational Psychology*, 1978, *3*, 87–94.

Wright, S. Correlation and causation. *Journal of Agricultural Research*, 1921, *20*, 557–585.

9 Naturalistic Observation in Design and Evaluation of Special-Education Programs

Gene P. Sackett
Sharon Landesman-Dwyer
Victor N. Morin
*Child Development and Mental Retardation Center,
and Regional Primate Research Center,
University of Washington*

INTRODUCTION

The relocation of retarded people from institutions to community residences, and legislation requiring "education for all" (PL 94–142), have raised important educational problems. Free education for retarded children is now a basic right, and school systems must provide appropriate and meaningful programs. Solutions to resulting economic, political, and ethical issues are proceeding largely through litigation. Educational responses to these issues have mainly involved demonstration projects to develop models for educating retarded children and training teachers to apply model methods in community schools (e.g., Hayden & Haring, 1977). This chapter addresses reasons why it is necessary to measure the impact of such educational programs on the everyday lives of retarded people. We review problems concerning maintenance and generalization of training, provide an overview of methodology used in naturalistic observation of behavior, and describe an applied example concerning observation of retarded people in a training and residential setting.

For intellectually normal children, casual observation reveals that basic skills learned in school are usually generalized to a variety of situations. Most normal children who learn to read and count use these skills away from school. However, for retarded children and others at high risk of school failure, classroom learning may be less likely to be used in other settings. The purpose of this chapter is to illustrate the need for behavioral observation to assess the effects of schooling on everyday behavior. Such information is important for evaluating any educational program, but is critical for measuring the success of efforts with intellectually deficient individuals. Simply demonstrating that a skill can be learned is not sufficient; rather, the acquired skill must be used appropriately outside the training setting.

TRANSFER AND MAINTENANCE OF LEARNING IN RETARDED PEOPLE

Educational programs for retarded people usually involve teaching skills and information related to self-care, vocational, and interpersonal behavior. Such programs attempt to increase adaptive abilities and to mesh behavior with the needs and expectations of the social environment in which the retarded person lives. Philosophically, the results of training are expected to increase the individual's quality of life and independence of action and choice. Practically, it is expected that trained behaviors will be maintained over a long time and will be used in appropriate situations. If such learning does not transfer across situations, the training has failed.

Learning theory identifies two basic forms of transfer (Osgood, 1949). *Stimulus generalization* involves performing a learned response when the stimulus array differs from that present during original learning. For educational programs, this array involves more than specific items, such as words or pictures, used during learning. It also includes persons such as teachers, parents, or classmates, settings such as classrooms, homes, or play areas, and even differences in time of day within the same setting. *Response generalization* refers to changes in behaviors other than those specifically learned. In training specific skills, this typically applies to behaviors that are functionally related to the learned response (Skinner, 1953), or that have motor components similar to the learned response (Garcia, Baer, & Firestone, 1971).

However, in addition to teaching new behaviors, programs for retarded people often focus on eliminating maladaptive or idiosyncratic behaviors such as physical aggression or stereotyped motor actions. Response generalization here has a somewhat different meaning. When undesirable behavior forms a large portion of an individual's behavioral repertoire, some other activities must necessarily replace the behavioral time occupied by the eliminated actions. A major generalization issue in training retarded people concerns these replacement behaviors, which too often appear as either total inactivity or some other undesirable behavior taking the place of an extinguished action. Too few studies on the retarded have been concerned with such generalized changes in the behavioral repertoire following either training for skill acquisition or extinction of maladaptive behavior.

During the past 20 years, major advances have been made in training methodology for the retarded (Kazdin, 1973). These relate to increased understanding of discrimination and memory abilities (e.g., Zeaman & House, 1963) and to developments in applied behavior analysis (e.g., Baer, Wolf, & Risley, 1968). Trained primarily by operant methods, even the most profoundly retarded people have learned a variety of motor, cognitive, and language skills (Cleland, Swartz, & Talkington, 1976; Cleland & Talkington, 1975). These studies demonstrate that most retarded people can benefit from training, but almost none assess whether this training transfers to independent aspects of the person's life. The few exceptions demonstrate that learning in retarded populations usually fails to generalize *unless* systematic training is extended into the transfer settings (Baer & Stokes, 1977; Baer et al., 1968; Kazdin & Bootzin, 1972). This poses a major problem for public education, as these studies lead to the prediction that successful transfer will occur only when parents or other caregivers are part of the training program.

Guess, Sailor, and Baer (1978) described a remedial language-training program for nonverbal, profoundly retarded children. Their procedures emphasized the extension of newly learned skills to the child's natural environment. Their major goal was to specifically train generalization of language skills to many persons and different situations. To do this, significant individuals in the child's everyday environment were included in the generalization procedures. Even with specific generalization programming, transfer to new settings was not often observed and many children overgeneralized, using their new skills indiscriminately even when the context was not appropriate. A similar set of problems involving inappropriate generalization were discussed by Cuvo (1979). Stokes and Baer (1976) described a potential approach to the generalization problem in which children who learned a language skill acted as tutors for other students. In effect, the tutors served as discriminative stimuli for transfering skills over time and across settings. Of equal importance, this example of successful generalization suggests that peers, family members, or significant other individuals may be the key to generalization problems with retarded people.

The transfer environment for retarded children may be a group home, temporary foster home, nursing home, or institution. Accordingly, school programs need to involve the parents or staff responsible for a child's everyday care. Sometimes, parents may be retarded or undereducated and themselves require extensive training in order to implement an interactive program with school personnel. Continuity of the program may also be disrupted by high staff turnover in group homes (Bell, 1976). These problems in developing a transfer program are not unique to retarded populations. In programs designed to maintain cognitive and social skills among nonretarded populations at high risk of school failure, education and involvement of parents are the key to success (Heber, Garber, Harrington, Hoffman, & Felender, 1972). To evaluate the degree of success, the very least a program should do is obtain direct and objective measures of training effects in significant transfer environments.

Drabman, Hammer, and Rosenbaum (1979) present a comprehensive model for assessing transfer effects that could be useful in both designing and evaluating education programs. Four distinct types of generalization were identified from a review of the child behavior-modification literature. These include generalization across time, settings, behaviors, and students. Alternatively, these might be labeled: (1) response maintenance; (2) transfer effects; (3) influences of training on the student's entire behavioral repertoire; and (4) effects of a student's training target behavior on the behavior of peers and other people. The model describes how multiple base-line measures could be used to permit assessment of each type of generalization and the interactions among all combinations of these dimensions. Along with this paper, Kazdin's (1973) analysis of similar issues, the procedures detailed by Guess et al. (1978), and work by Stokes and Baer (1977) provide experimental design models for studying generalization using naturalistic observation across a number of settings.

An example of the need to measure generalization is seen in the influential work of Hayden and Haring (1977) on training children with Down's syndrome. In 1969, these investigators began one of the first model programs for training young retarded children. Their curriculum and assessment techniques were later incorporated in primary-level public-school classes for children with Down's syndrome, thus fulfilling one major objective of a demonstration program. Compared with expectations for this population, rather spectacular progress was reported. Many students attained nearly normal developmental levels on intelligence tests and on a specially devised developmental rating scale. These data show that Down's-syndrome children can acquire normal scholastic behaviors in classroom conditions. Unfortunately, no objective data are available to measure how, and to what degree, these near-normal skills are exercised and maintained longitudinally outside the school setting. Thus, an important aspect of the success of this excellent model program remains untested.

In contrast to school programs, vocational training programs have demonstrated success in altering specific behaviors of retarded teenagers and adults across settings and time. Two programs have shown that profoundly retarded people are capable of learning assembly techniques and can earn an independent living with their skills (Bellamy, Peterson, & Close, 1975; Gold, 1972). Their methodology is based on systematic programming for skill acquisition coupled with specific training for transfer across tasks, persons, and settings. This involves careful measurement of both trained and untrained behavior, and long-term follow-up observation. Individuals with IQs below 50, who were classified as "unemployable," have been successfully trained for food-industry jobs (Moss, 1980). Success for most of these people depended on continued observation and feedback by a trainer in the job setting.

These successful vocational programs contrast with a number of unsuccessful attempts to modify basic personal, social, and cognitive behaviors of severely and profoundly retarded people. Several attempts have been made to train language skills (Garcia et al., 1971; Guess & Baer, 1973; Hamilton, 1966; McClure, 1968). Training was conducted in a special test room, and transfer was not specifically trained. Transfer was not found when behavior was assessed in other settings. Garcia (1974) trained language skills in nonverbal retarded people and did obtain generalization across experimenters and settings when target behaviors were reinforced by each experimenter in each setting. Maintenance and generalized use of other learned behaviors such as self-help skills (O'Brien & Azrin, 1972; Page, Iwata, & Neef, 1976), elimination of self-injurious behavior (Corte, Wolf, & Locke, 1971; Lovaas & Simmons, 1969), and social interactions (Mayhew, Enyart, & Anderson, 1978; Stokes, Baer, & Jackson, 1974; Whitman, Mercurio, & Caponigri, 1970) were all found to depend on continued training in each transfer setting.

A major feature of these studies is that direct behavioral observations were made in both the original training environment and in each transfer setting. Such observations are critical for evaluating the program results, yet most demonstration projects ignore this step. One reason is undoubtedly the expense and time involved in gathering behavioral data in nonschool settings. A second reason relates to the lack of training in *quantitative* behavioral observation in many areas of behavioral science including education. A third reason, illustrated by the methodology of most model education programs, is the historical use of test instruments designed to measure conceptual attributes of behavior or subjective reports or ratings, rather than the actual responses of individuals going about their everyday affairs.

OVERVIEW OF QUANTITATIVE OBSERVATIONAL METHODS

In quantitative behavioral observation, human perceptual and judgmental abilities are used to measure the onsets and offsets of overt responses by subjects behaving individually or in groups. This contrasts with conventional experimental techniques employing mechanical and electrical devices to index behavioral events, and with standardized test instruments or rating scales. These latter methods generally restrict the range of responses possible in the research setting, and purposely direct the subject's attention toward a relatively small set of stimuli or stimulus dimensions. For research addressing questions about the existence or degree of specific behaviors or abilities, such methods do, of course, generate appropriate data. However, many aspects of behavior, such as social interaction, cannot be detected by automated devices, or such devices may be prohibitively expensive. Standardized tests of skills and abilities gather information about what a person is capable of doing, but do not reveal what that person actually does with these skills in real-life situations. Thus, the main purposes of direct observation as an alternative measurement method are to collect objective data when automated devices are unavailable or when the research questions concern what a person actually does, unhampered by the constraints of an arbitrary or restrictive test situation.

In recent years, direct observation of behavior has become a major research tool in a number of behavior sciences, especially those dealing with child development. Many observational studies are truly naturalistic, being conducted in real-life environments (e.g., Landesman-Dwyer & Sackett, 1978; Sykes, 1977). Other research has proceeded under more standardized and controlled conditions. For example, Gottman, Markham, and Notarius (1977) used quantitative observation to measure interaction patterns of married couples undergoing counseling or therapy. In many studies, early parent–child interaction has been observed in both hospital and home settings (Parke & O'Leary, 1976; Thoman, Becker, & Freese, 1978). Recently, even cognitive development has been studied under natural conditions. Charlesworth (1978) developed observational techniques for measuring intelligent behaviors by normal and retarded children during their daily lives at home and at play. Quantitative observation has also been used in classroom situations to study behavior patterns of both teachers and students. Herbert and Attridge (1975) discuss specific behavior items that might be measured in the school, whereas Rosenshine and Furst (1973) and Parsonson, Baer, and Baer (1974) provide examples of studies directed toward teacher behaviors. Wang (1976) also describes how direct observation can be used to evaluate different methods of instruction.

Regardless of the degree of environmental naturalness, a number of issues and problems are common in all observational research. These include: (1) deciding what to observe; (2) devising an appropriate sampling strategy; (3) demonstrating that the data generated are reliable and accurate; and (4) identifying valid statistical procedures for description of results and for hypothesis testing.

What to Observe

A behavioral taxonomy consists of descriptive labels and operational definitions describing the activities to be observed. These definitions identify the categories into which observers will score behavior. Depending on the research purpose, these categories can be relatively molar, labeling a large number of specific actions by their presumed functional or motivational properties. Examples include categories such as play and fear, as well as care-giving and care-demanding activity. For other purposes, more molecular behaviors identified with specific motor and vocal actions may be scored. Examples vary from extent and direction of movement by specific body parts to eye contact between interacting partners.

In some studies, only selected behavioral categories are measured. In other studies, great effort is taken to devise mutually exclusive and exhaustive category sets in which no time can pass during the observation without the presence of a scorable behavior. This latter approach is essential for research problems concerning response generalization, especially when the problem concerns the activities appearing in an individual's repertoire after a major behavior class has been eliminated through training. Kaufman and Rosenblum (1966) present an excellent example of an exhaustive taxonomy system used in studying nonhuman primate individual, maternal, and social behavior.

The Kaufman–Rosenblum system used either the mother or her infant as a focal individual, whose personal behaviors and interactions with others were scored sequentially with paper and pencil. The major categories of the system included nonsocial behaviors (e.g., sleeping, doing nothing, exploring, or playing with parts of the inanimate environment), self-directed activities (e.g., digital sucking, grooming, clasping parts of the body), maternal care-giving acts (nursing, grooming, holding, punishment, rejection), positive social interactions with others (e.g., play, grooming, nonaggressive physical contact), negative social behaviors (threat, attack, fear, withdrawal), and sexual activities. Over 200 individual behaviors were defined on the bases of motor-action pattern or initiation versus reception of a response by others, and any combination of these activities could be scored in describing the ongoing activity. The data generated by this category system measure the occurrences of all individual behaviors, as well as the types of social interactions that happen, who is involved in the interactions, and who initiates, receives, or reciprocates social behavior.

General issues in devising such behavioral categories are also described by Sackett (1978) and by Rosenblum (1978). The design of molecular coding schemes is illustrated in an important work by Stern (1974) on measurement of mother–infant interaction patterns.

The choice of behavioral categories and molecularity of measurement affects the physical method used to collect the observations. Molecular coding of more than a few specific responses almost always demands film, audio, or video taping of behavior. This has the advantage of using stop-motion editing equipment and of being able to view the behaviors many times, thus ensuring reliability and enabling the coding of various aspects having short durations. It has the disadvantage of requiring expensive equipment and much time to score the behaviors. The alternative is to code behavior as it happens, using any one of a variety of paper–pencil or digital electronic techniques. It is likely that real-time direct observation of behavior as it is happening will be the most practical method in educational research. These issues and methods are discussed by Holm (1978), Sykes (1977), and by Sackett, Stephenson, and Ruppenthal (1973), with examples of video methods illustrated by Strayer and Strayer (1976) and Bench and Wilson (1976).

Sampling Strategies

In addition to choosing appropriate categories, the method of sampling behavior during observational sessions requires careful thought. Behavior can be observed, filmed, or taped on a *continuous* basis. In this case, frequency, sequences of actions, and duration of behavior can all be measured from the raw data. The "stream of behavior" is measured by entering codes into an electronic device that marks the exact time into a scoring session when each codable behavior occurred. The number of occurrences and the total time spent in each behavior can be extracted from this record. If the category scheme is one in which no time can pass without scoring a behavior, this record also allows calculation of percentage of total test time spent in each behavior and the probability (relative frequency) of each behavior out of the total number of behavior changes occurring in the session. Continuous data also preserve the exact sequence in which behaviors occur, yielding a record from which the probability of various acts preceding and following each other can be extracted.

In fact, most observational studies have not collected continuous real-time information, but have used various time-sampling methods. The most frequently used technique, modified frequency counts, measures the number of time intervals during a session in which each behavior occurs at least once. These time intervals may vary from a few seconds to minutes or hours. For example, a teacher might wish to measure (1) attending to a task; (2) disruptive activities; (3) interaction with other children; and (4) sitting doing nothing during a class period. These four activities could be listed in the rows of a check sheet, with columns indicating successive 1-minute periods since the start of class. Each student being observed would receive a check in the row for a given behavior and column for the elapsed time if that behavior occurred in that 60-second period. Only one occurrence would be noted, even if several bouts of the activity actually happened. The modified-frequency score for each behavior would then be the number of 1-minute periods in which the behavior had a check, or the percentage of 1-minute intervals checked out of the total intervals observed. Modified-frequency counts do not directly measure either the actual frequency or the actual duration of any given behavior, unless the sampling interval is very short, so it is usually not possible to know whether the count reflects the number of occurrences of the behavior or the amount of time spent in it.

A second basic technique is point sampling. Behaviors occurring at specific elapsed times into a session are scored regardless of what occurred between time points. The score generated by these techniques is the number or percent of time points at which the behavior was seen. Such techniques are insensitive to short-duration behaviors and are unlikely to score behaviors that have relatively low rates of occurrence.

Generally, the use of a time-sampling procedure rather than continuous data collection is dictated by the complexity of the coding system and the number of behaviors that can occur in a short time. When pencil and paper recording is used and many behaviors occur rapidly, time sampling may be the only way to collect and generate reliable data. These and other issues are described by Altmann (1974) and by Sackett (1978).

Reliability

Methodologically, the only difference between direct observation and switches or electronic devices for measuring behavior involves the accuracy and consistency of noting the onsets and offsets of the responses. This problem, termed reliability, concerns errors made within and between observers. These are of two types: omission errors, in which the observer does not see a behavior, and commission errors, in which the observer sees the behavior but codes it in the wrong category. Considerable advances have been made recently in measuring these types of error, in understanding and correcting their causes, and in maintaining reliable data over long time periods. These are described by Johnson and Bolstad (1973) in an especially important paper, and by Hollenbeck (1978), Sykes (1978), and Reid (1970).

Statistical Analysis

Observational research often generates a large mass of data, requiring considerable care and sophistication for appropriate statistical description and inferential analyses. The most important problem is that the behavioral categories are almost never uncorrelated. Some of this lack of independence is inherent in almost all behavioral taxonomies. For example, consider an exhaustive category scheme measuring both social and nonsocial behavior of nursery-school children (e.g., Bijou, Peterson, Harris, Allen, & Johnston, 1969). Suppose that under base-line conditions, a child spends only 5% of his or her observational time engaged in social activities. Following a period of training to interact positively with other children, social-behavior time increases to 30%. Because of the nature of the coding system, there must be a resulting drop of 25% in nonsocial-activity time. Independent statistical analyses of both social and nonsocial behavior would thus be unwarranted and inappropriate because of the reciprocal nature of these behavioral dimensions. Likewise, some behaviors represent high activity levels whereas others represent low levels. An individual exhibiting a great deal of active behavior will, by definition, score relatively low on inactive behaviors. For such problems, analyzing each separate behavior for effects of relevant study variables will capitalize on chance due to the large number of comparisons that are often made, and may also contain a spuriously large number of significant effects due to the high degree of correlation among the behaviors. Multivariate analysis techniques are required here, but these have rarely been used in observational work. Sackett (1978) discusses these problems, and Gottman (1978) illustrates some methods for solving them. Chamove, Eysenck, and Harlow (1972) provide an interesting example using factor analysis to define behavioral profiles from observational dependent variables.

Although analyses of nonsequential data require careful methodology, sequential analysis poses the additional problem of identifying serial correlations among behaviors. Such analyses concern measurement of sequences and patterns in the temporal flow of behavior by single individuals, and patterns of bidirectional influence among behaviors of interacting partners. A recent flurry of activity in this area has produced a number of alternative methods for description and analysis of sequential dependency and cyclicity of observed behaviors

(Bakeman, 1978; Bakeman & Brown, 1977; Gottman, 1978; Gottman & Notarius, 1978; Sackett, 1979). Some of these techniques may be useful in school research studying teacher–student and student–student interactions, as well as transfer of social skills learned in school to other settings.

Applying Observation in Educating Retarded People

Our approach to evaluating the effectiveness of programs for educating retarded people requires two steps, one presumably simple and the second more complex. First, training goals should include an analysis of the settings and social conditions to which transfer of the trained behaviors is desired or expected. Second, an observational study measuring appropriate dimensions of social and nonsocial behavior should be conducted in these transfer settings to determine whether the trained skills or behaviors actually occur. If little or no evidence can be found for transfer, the program should be changed toward producing transfer. According to the literature previously discussed, such changes would involve specific training by personnel in the school and in the transfer situations.

At first glance, such an observational study may seem overwhelming and impossible to conduct. However, the results of a model study suggest that this task is neither impossible nor prohibitively expensive. We studied the behavior of over 350 retarded subjects, ranging from young children to aged persons, living in 26 group homes scattered throughout the state of Washington (Landesman-Dwyer, Stein, & Sackett, 1976, 1978). Each subject was observed once every 15 minutes during several 24-hour days. The results yielded behavioral profiles of everyday behavior as a function of age, level of retardation, type of group home, geographic location, time previously spent in institutions, and a number of other dimensions.

Some of the results failed to confirm several common assumptions underlying the movement toward deinstitutionalization. For example, smaller homes and frequent visits by parents did not yield more normal and adaptive social and emotional behavior. Other findings suggested that we knew little about how to manage the placement of retarded individuals in community residences. This information was used by state agencies in designing their current plan for community placement. It also had the benefit of slowing down implementation of the prior plan, which had been hastily conceived as a response to political and economic pressure.

The methodology for the study presented next was a direct outgrowth of this initial project. The behavior categories that had been developed were reliable and appeared to be reasonably valid in describing the way retarded people spent their days in a residential setting. We used these categories to study a large number of profoundly retarded adults who were to be moved from a conventional state institution to small home-like residences. Our purpose was to measure changes in behavior after moving, and attempt to predict from premove behavior those individuals who would be successful in adapting to the homes. A number of these people were involved in an educational training program. Here, we present their data in order to see if training-setting behaviors generalized to behavior in the institutional setting.

TRAINING OBJECT-FOCUSED BEHAVIOR: BASE-LINE BEHAVIOR CORRELATES AND IMPACT ON EXTRACURRICULAR ACTIVITIES

Subjects

The data reported here are part of a study measuring the effects of residence changes on the behavior of 165 severely and profoundly retarded adults in an institution. A subset of 39 subjects (26 females and 13 males) were studied. They ranged from 22 to 64 years of age ($\bar{x} = 33.6$, S.D. $= 9.5$ years), and had an average AAMD developmental age of 3.7 years (S.D. $= 1.6$). All but five were in generally good health, although 10 subjects had a recent history of physical social aggression.

Training

Each subject participated in an education/training program for an average of 30 hours each week. Although the actual study was not designed to assess effectiveness of this training program, these 39 subjects had a complete set of observational data for their first 5 months into training. For most, this was their first exposure to any adult education. *We emphasize that the data presented here are being used merely to illustrate potential uses of observational data for program assessment.* The study was not actually designed to assess the training program of these people.

The training objectives included increasing the time spent in performing specific focused tasks, such as object sorting. Object-focused activities are a prerequuisite for any type of vocational training, but are often lacking in the natural repertoire of people with very low IQs. In addition, subjects were encouraged to follow group instructions and to respond appropriately to peers. The trainers did identify short-term goals for individual people. However, no overall consistent program was applied, nor were systematic assessments made by the training staff to evaluate program progress.

Observational Methods

Subjects were observed on a regular basis in two settings: one of 11 ward residences in the institution (the *unstructured* setting), and the training program (the *structured* setting). Each person was observed for at least six sessions every 2 weeks over a 5-month period. At least four observation sessions were conducted in the unstructured setting and two in the structured environment.

Each observation session lasted 3 minutes. The focal subject's activities were sampled and coded six times, once every 30 seconds, during each session. The measurement system sampled the following behavioral dimensions: (1) the *major* ongoing *activity;* (2) type of *vocalizations,* if any; (3) *direction,* in terms

TABLE 9.1
Names, Definitions, and Overall Percentage of Occurrence for the
Classification of Nine Mutually Exclusive, Exhaustive,
Major-Activity Categories

Major-Activity Category	Definition	Overall % Occurrence
Inactive	Subject is not engaged in any focused interaction with the social or inanimate environment, is not receiving direct input from others, is not locomoting, and is perceived as "doing nothing."	45.5
Physical activity	Subject is locomoting or participating in a nonsocial gross-motor activity.	14.8
Self-care activity	Subject is eating, dressing, grooming, toileting, or attending to other aspects of personal care.	4.2
TV, radio, stereo	Subject is actively watching and/or listening to TV, radio, record player or other media communication.	6.6
Object-focused activities	Subject is behaving in a focused and appropriate manner, involved in fine-motor and craft activities, academic-oriented work, household chores, and tasks set up specifically to train such behaviors.	6.2
Undesirable, idiosyncratic, asocial activities	Subject is behaving in an inappropriate, abnormal, or unacceptable manner that does not directly involve others. Behaviors include destroying property, self abuse, stereotypy, loss of temper, mimicking, bizarre postures, and other idiosyncratic patterns.	4.5
Positive social behavior	Subject is interacting with or receiving input from others. Subject initiates, receives, or mutually engages with at least one other person in any of the following: planning, supervising, teaching, care giving, offering affection, consoling, praising or rewarding, assisting, sharing resources, participating in a game or recreational activity, or other positive interactions (specified in the observer's notes).	13.0
Negative social behavior	Subject imitates, receives, or mutually engages in any of the following with at least one other person: physical or verbal agression, scolding or punishing, annoying, obstructing, teasing, or actively disobeying.	0.8
Other	Subject leaves premises or is unobservable because in a private area or cannot be found.	4.5

of whether the subject initiated, received, or reciprocated the major activity; (4) the *other people* involved in the subject's social activities; and (5) the occurrence of *stereotyped* motor behavior.

Here, we present data only for the major activities. The original codes had 56 independent activities. For our purposes, these were combined into nine mutually exclusive and exhaustive categories, yielding a profile of all activities engaged in by the subject. Table 9.1 presents definitions for each category. Reliability measures of agreement between several different observers coding the same subjects at the same time average 75% over all original 56 categories. Product–moment correlations between observers for total occurrences per session of each of the nine categories reported here were all above $r = +.90$. Reliability was thus high, indicating that different observers gave the same names to the actions they saw and heard, and their session summary measures were about the same.

During the first 2.5-month "base-line" period of data collection in the unstructured setting, 45% of all behavior was categorized as inactivity (Table 9.1). Inactivity, physically moving about from place to place, watching television or listening to the radio, and negative or undesirable behavior occurred in over 70% of the observations. Engaging in any type of object-focused activities accounted for only 6.2% of all observations.

These base-line behavioral profiles set the basic goals for our data analyses. We wished to determine if the degree of object-focused and undesirable activities in the unstructured setting would be related to behavior in the structured situation. We also wished to see if individuals showing relatively large increases in object-focused behavior in the training situation would show any correlated behavior changes (potential transfer effects) in the unstructured condition. To approach these goals, we compared behavior of various subject groupings in the structured and unstructured settings during the first and second halves of the 5-month observation period.

Results

Base-Line Object-Focused Behavior.   The 39 subjects were classified in three groups of 13 individuals on the basis of their rank order of object-focused behavior during the first 2.5-month period in the structured setting. Fig. 9.1 plots the distribution of each category for these low, medium, and high object-focused individuals in each situation during each period. The object-focused percentage is shown in the bar graphs on the right in each panel, with the distribution of the other nine categories shown by the curves on the left. It should be noted that in these behavior profiles, the sum of all categories equals 1.00, thus representing the total behavior repertoire of the individuals in each grouping. Further, if a large group difference appears in one or more categories, there must be a corresponding trade-off in terms of a reciprocal group difference on some other category(ies).

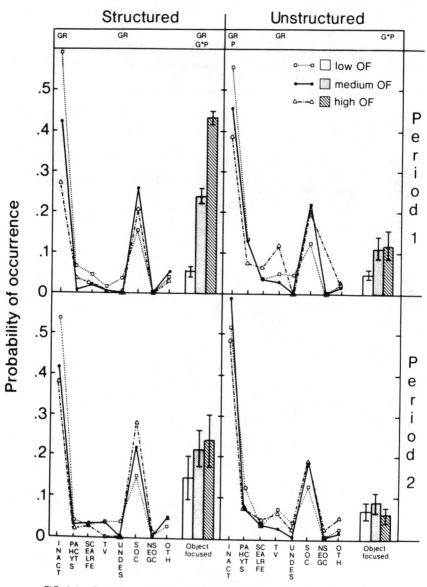

FIG. 9.1. Behavior profiles for subjects having low, medium, and high levels of object-focused behavior during period 1 in the training setting. Probabilities for the target, object-focused activities are shown by bar graphs for each setting and period. Curves show probabilities for the other eight major activities. Letters at the top of each column indicate significant ($p < .01$) effects from repeated measure analyses of variance for each category. Groups (GR) were the uncorrelated variable and Periods (P) the repeated measure. Note that the bar graphs in the upper left panel simply summarize the data defining each group in terms of position of subjects in thirds of the object-focused rank ordering. Category abbreviations: INACT = inactivity; PHYS ACT = physical activity; UNDES = undesirable behavior; SOC = positive social behavior; NEG SOC = negative social behavior; OTH = other activity.

The upper left panel of Fig. 9.1 shows the object-focused behavior levels that defined each group (the histogram comparisons). The trade-off between group differences in the target behavior and other behaviors occurred at statistically acceptable levels only for inactivity. High object-focused individuals had the lowest inactivity, whereas low object-focused individuals had the highest inactivity. The upper right panel shows some correspondence between the structured and unstructured settings. The low object-focused group was also low in their residential unit, but the medium and high subjects did not differ in that setting. The behavioral profiles were similar in both settings, except that: (1) the overall level of object-focused activity per 3-minute test interval was lower in the ward than in the training setting for the medium and high groups; (2) inactivity was higher on the ward than in the training settings; and (3) high object-focused subjects watched more television during period 1 on the ward than did the other groups (all $p < .01$).

During period 2 in the structured setting, object-focused behavior did not differ reliably between groups. However, a significant decrease did occur for individuals that were high during period 1 and an increase occurred for those low in object-focused behavior during period 1 (both $p < .01$). The only major change in behavioral profiles in the training setting was an increase during period 2 ($p < .025$) in both inactivity and social behavior by individuals who had been high in object-focused activity during period 1.

During period 2 in the unstructured setting, there were no group differences in object-focused behavior, and the profiles for each group were all but identical. Taken as a whole, these data suggest that: (1) during initial training, behavior in the structured setting was essentially the same as that in the ward; (2) training decreased the level of object-focused behavior for those initially showing higher amounts; and (3) no general transfer effects were seen in object-focused or other behaviors from the structured to the ward setting.

Change in Object-Focused Behavior During Training.   Fig. 9.2 shows behavior in each setting and period for subjects who increased, did not change, or decreased their rank ordering of object-focused activity between periods 1 and 2 in the training situation. Subjects who decreased to a lower third of the rank ordering ($n = 10$) had the highest object-focused activity in period 1, but the lowest in period 2 in the structured setting (left panels). Subjects who stayed in the same third of relative rankings ($n = 13$) or who increased to a higher third of the rankings ($n = 14$) had relatively low levels of object-focused behavior during period 1, and did not differ reliably from each other during period 2. During period 1, the structured setting profiles were essentially identical for all groups, with an inverse relation between object-focused and inactivity behaviors. During period 2, subjects who decreased object-focused behavior showed a marked increase in inactivity and positive social behavior ($p < .01$).

In the unstructured setting, the behavioral profiles were essentially identical for all three change groups. The sole effect of 2.5 months of experience in the

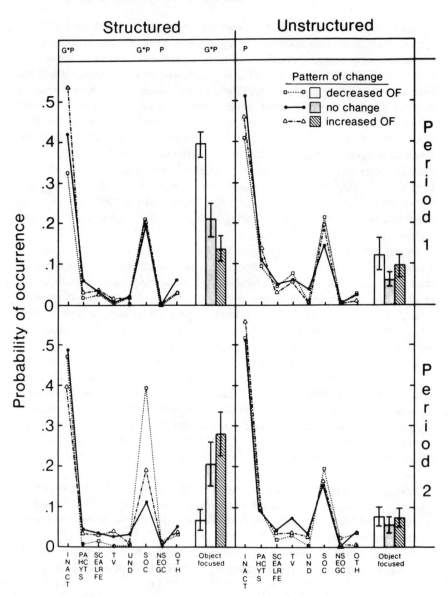

FIG. 9.2. Behavioral profiles for subjects who decreased, did not change, and increased their positions in thirds of the object-focused rank ordering between periods 1 and 2 in the structured setting. To increase, the ranking third in period 2 was either one- or two-thirds higher than that attained in period 1. To decrease, the ranking third in period 2 was either one- or two-thirds lower than that of period 1. As in Fig. 9.1, significant effects of GR × P analyses of variance for each category are shown at the top of each column and the same abbreviations identify the categories.

training situation was a correlated increase in the amount of inactivity in the home ward as training progressed. In sum, there were no apparent transfer effects of changes in the trained behaviors other than a possible increase in the amount of doing nothing. Further, for subjects who were initially high in the target behavior, further training reduced this behavior and increased the amount of social behavior and inactivity.

Specific Patterns of Change in Object-Focused Behavior.   Change patterns were broken down further to assess interactions between initial level of object-focused activities and the direction of change. Fig. 9.3 illustrates the results for nine groups based on their third of the rank order in periods 1 and 2. For most groups, the behavior profiles within and between periods were remarkably similar and stable. All but two groups simply showed a trade-off between inactivity and social behavior as object-focused behavior was relatively high or low. However, one exception concerned subjects who were in the lowest third of the rankings in both periods (upper left panel). They had the highest inactivity levels in both periods and were the lowest of any group in social behavior (both p < .01). They also had reliably higher undesirable behavior than members of the other groups (p < .01). A second exception was the two subjects who went from the lowest to the highest third of the ranking (upper right panel). They achieved the highest object-focused behavior of any group during period 2, but did so by not only decreasing inactivity, but also by markedly decreasing positive social behavior.

Fig. 9.4 shows behavior for these nine groups in the unstructured setting. As already seen in Fig. 9.1, people who had high or medium object-focused behavior in the training setting during period 1 were also high in this behavior on the home ward during period 1. During period 2 in the ward setting, none of the groups differed in object-focused activity except the two subjects who had changed from low to high in the structured situation (upper right panel). Their data reveal a complete lack of transfer! Although they had the highest target behavior of any group in the period-2 training environment, they had zero scores on these activities in their ward. Unstructured-situation behavior profiles were essentially identical for periods 1 and 2 within each group, except for a general increase in inactivity by those who were initially high or medium in object-focused behavior in the training situation.

Undesirable Behavior.   Undesirable behaviors are characteristic of many individuals in retarded populations such as those studied here. We conducted a final analysis to see how these negative activities related to object-focused and other behavior. Two groups were formed based on those individuals exhibiting no undesirable behavior (n = 25) and those with some amount (n = 14) during period 1 in the unstructured setting. As seen in Fig. 9.5 (bargraphs), subjects who initially had undesirable behavior also exceeded the other group in these

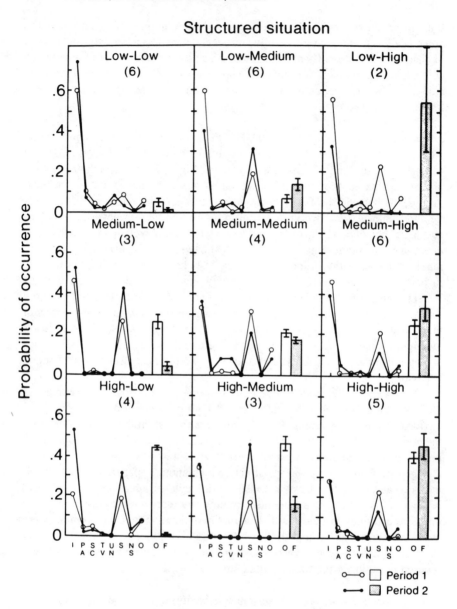

FIG. 9.3. Structured-setting behavior profiles for nine subject groupings formed by third of object-focused rank order in the structured setting attained in both periods 1 and 2. For example, the upper left panel shows profiles for subjects who were in the bottom third of object-focused behavior in *both* periods. Sample sizes for each group are given in parentheses. Category Abbreviations: I = inactive; PA = physical activity; SC = self care; UN = undesirable; S = positive social; NS = negative social; O = other; OF = object-focused.

Unstructured situation

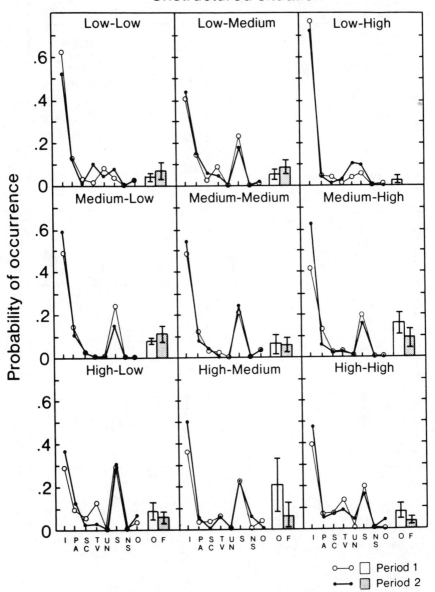

FIG. 9.4.   Behavior profiles for the same nine subject groupings shown in Fig. 9.3, but depicting activities in the *unstructured* ward setting. Sample sizes and category abbreviations are the same as in Fig. 3.

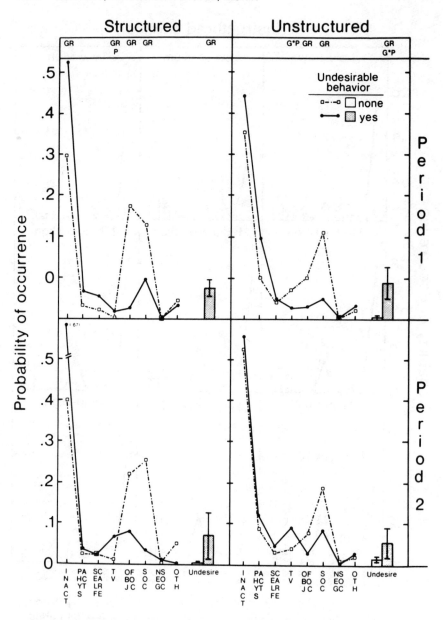

FIG. 9.5. Behavior profiles for individuals with no undesirable behavior during period 1 on the home ward, compared with people showing undesirable behavior on the home ward. Significant effects from GR × P analyses of variance for each category are shown at the top. Category abbreviations are the same as in Fig. 9.1.

activities in the other setting and periods. In the training situation during both periods, the undesirable behavior group was more inactive and had lower object-focused and social behavior. Lower levels of object-focused and social behavior were also seen in the unstructured setting during both periods for subjects in the undesirable behavior group. However, in the home ward, both groups had high, and not reliably different, levels of inactivity.

DISCUSSION AND CONCLUSIONS

These data suggest that the current training program for these retarded people is ineffective. Subjects with initially high levels of the target training dimension—an aspect of behavior essential for almost any kind of vocational training and employment—generally deteriorated as training progressed. There was also no evidence of positive transfer to another situation, even for individuals showing an apparent benefit of training. This is, of course, expected for programs having no formal component attempting to train target activities in other environments.

Our major finding was that behavior profiles were remarkably constant over the 5-month period in, and between, each of the settings. One finding with positive implications for training concerned people who showed undesirable behavior. They also exhibited a correlated low level of object-focused activity in both the training and home-ward settings. This suggests that training to eliminate undesirable behavior from the repertoire—either at home or at "school"—may be a prerequisite for training more positive activities.

This preliminary study supports our contention that behavior can be quantitatively measured in retarded people both at "school" and during their daily lives at home. The data also reinforce the findings of others (e.g., Stokes & Baer, 1977) that for retarded adults unsystematic attempts to train important behaviors are ineffective and also fail to affect any important aspect of behavior outside the training situation. On the other hand, some of the results would seem to be useful in generating hypotheses about what might be done to train retarded adults (e.g., the relation between undesirable and object-focused behavior).

The results of this study, and of our prior efforts (Landesman-Dwyer et al., 1978), suggest that behavioral observations are necessary at the stage of program design as well as program evaluation. A principle of science is that observation and description of basic phenomena must be done before attempting studies aimed at prediction or explanation. In the study of animal behavior, and recently of child development (e.g., Strayer & Strayer, 1976), this step involves the formation of *ethograms*. These are quantitative descriptions of the daily activities of populations behaving in one or more of their naturally occurring environments. The ethogram includes measurement of basic categories of adaptive behavior and an ecological description of the environmental resources correlated with variation in adaptive behaviors exhibited by different populations (Bekoff, 1979).

Ethograms for special populations of humans at risk of learning failures are all but nonexistent. In fact, formal ethograms are not available for human families that are not at risk of educational failure. The type of problem raised by lack of normative data on everyday human behavior is illustrated by our prior work in group homes. Activities judged to involve teaching and learning behaviors occupied less than 1% of the 24-hour day for retarded people ranging in age from 10 through 70 years. However, this finding was difficult to interpret. There are no data on the amount of teaching–learning activities in middle-class homes or even special populations such as juvenile offenders, mentally ill, or physically handicapped living in group homes.

Logically, the successful education of special populations would seem to depend on knowledge of the typical behavioral repertoires exhibited by these individuals during their ordinary lives—namely, ethograms of both students and significant others in their environment. These could identify important target behaviors requiring extinction in order to substitute more desirable activities, potential social and environmental contingencies that might support behavior changes, and patterns of social and personal behavior to be expected in an educational setting. Of equal importance, such ethograms serve as a valid base line for judging transfer of formal training. Our studies show that ethogram data can be collected for human populations. The data have been useful in understanding the impact of environments and training on retarded people. We believe that this natural observation methodology can aid both identification of fundamental principles underlying behavior change in special populations and assessment of programs designed to effect such changes.

The observational methods and generalization issues described in this chapter are also basic to the study of the "ecology" of education. Bronfenbrenner (1976, 1977) has stressed the idea that formal education is part of a system of environmental influences, including both social components and environmental resources, that shape an individual's development. Successful educational components of such a system must have ecological validity—relevance to both the skills and abilities of the students, but also to their needs and behaviors outside of the educational setting (e.g., Brooks & Baumeister, 1977; Gibbs, 1979). Ecological validity implies that what is learned is useful—and used—in adapting to everyday life. The study of ecological validity requires measurement in natural situations to determine whether adaptive behaviors generalize across settings and persons.

Applications of these ideas to school settings are straightforward theoretically, but practically difficult. School psychologists and special educators must be trained to measure behavior both at school and in homes and other locations. With intellectually handicapped populations, parents, group-home managers and staff, and even staff at institutions must be part of the total effort. Along with the issues concerning generalization and transfer previously discussed, behavioral contrast problems must be recognized and managed. Behavioral contrast concerns situations in which suppression of behavior in one setting leads to an increase in that behavior in other settings. For example, Walker, Hyman, and Johnson (1975) suppressed deviant behavior of retarded children in a classroom using behavior-modification techniques. Unfortunately, children who decreased in classroom deviancy increased these same behaviors in their homes. Naturalistic observation can also be of use to school personnel in determining whether a particular program is actually being implemented as planned (Hall & Loucks, 1977). For example, teachers may be trained to behave in specific ways to coach, reward, or punish various behaviors. Observational methods can be employed to measure the extent to which the teachers actually behave according to the program protocol. Finally, it seems clear that school personnel must know more about the actual and potential behavior repertoires of handicapped students if effective educational programs are to be designed. The cornerstone of such information is measuring what these people actually do while engaged in their everyday affairs.

ACKNOWLEDGMENTS

This research was supported by NICHD grant HD11551. Preparation of the manuscript was facilitated by NICHD grant HD08633 and NIH grant RR00166.

REFERENCES

Altmann, J. Observational study of behavior: Sampling methods. *Behaviour*, 1974, *49*, 227–265.

Bakeman, R. Untangling streams of behavior: Sequential analysis of observational data. In G. P. Sackett (Ed.), *Observing behavior* (Vol. 1). Baltimore: University Park Press, 1978.

Bakeman, R., & Brown, J. V. Behavioral dialogues: An approach to the assessment of mother–infant interaction, *Child Development*, 1977, *48*, 195–203.

Baer, D. M., & Stokes, T. F. Discriminating a generalization technology: Recommendations for research in mental retardation. In P. Mittler (Ed.), *Research to practice in mental retardation* (Vol. 2). Baltimore: University Park Press, 1977.

Baer, D. M., Wolf, M. M., & Risley, T. R. Some current dimensions of applied behavior analysis. *Journal of Applied Behavior Analysis*, 1968, *1*, 91–97.

Bekoff, M. Behavioral acts: Description, classification, ethogram analysis, and measurement. In R. B. Cairns (Ed.), *The analysis of social interactions: Methods, issues, and illustrations*. Hillsdale, N.J.: Lawrence Erlbaum Associates, 1979.

Bell, C. W. *We share our lives*. Seattle: Washington State Association of Group Homes, 1976.

Bellamy, T., Peterson, L., & Close, D. Habilitation of the severely and profoundly retarded: Illustrations of competence. *Education and Training of the Mentally Retarded*, 1975, *10*, 174–186.

Bench, J., & Wilson, I. A comparison of live and videorecord viewing of infant behavior under sound stimulation. III. Six-month-old babies. *Developmental Psychobiology*, 1976, *9*, 297–303.

Bijou, S. W., Peterson, R. F., Harris, F. R., Allen, K. E., & Johnston, M. S. Methodology for experimental studies of young children in natural settings. *Psychological Record*, 1969, *19*, 177–210.

Bronfenbrenner, U. The experimental ecology of education. *Educational Researcher*, 1976, *5*, 5–15.

Bronfenbrenner, U. Toward an experimental ecology of human development. *American Psychologist*, 1977, *32*, 513–531.

Brooks, P. H., & Baumeister, A. A. A plea for consideration of ecological validity in the experimental psychology of mental retardation. *American Journal of Mental Deficiency*, 1977, *81*, 407–416.

Chamove, A. S., Eysenck, H. J., & Harlow, H. F. Personality in monkeys: Factor analysis of rhesus social behavior. *Quarterly Journal of Experimental Psychology*, 1972, *24*, 496–504.

Charlesworth, W. R. Ethology: Its relevance for observational studies of human adaptation. In G. P. Sackett (Ed.), *Observing behavior* (Vol. 1). Baltimore: University Park Press, 1978.

Cleland, C. C., Swartz, J. D., & Talkington, L. W. (Eds.). *The profoundly mentally retarded* (2nd conference proceedings). Western Research Conference and Hogg Foundation, 1976.

Cleland, C. C., & Talkington, L. W. (Eds.). *Research with profoundly retarded* (a conference proceeding). Western Research Conference and the Brown Schools, 1975.

Corte, H. E., Wolf, M. M., & Locke, B. J. A comparison of procedures for eliminating self-injurious behavior of retarded adolescents. *Journal of Applied Behavior Analysis*, 1971, *4*, 201–213.

Cuvo, A. J. Multiple-baseline design in instructional research: Pitfalls of measurement and procedural advantage. *American Journal of Mental Deficiency*, 1979, *84*, 219–228.

Drabman, R. S., Hammer, D., & Rosenbaum, M. S. Assessing generalization in behavior modification with children: The generalization map. *Behavioral Assessment*, 1979, *1*, 203–219.

Garcia, E. The training and generalization of a conversational speech form in nonverbal retardates. *Journal of Applied Behavior Analysis*, 1974, *7*, 137–149.

Garcia, E., Baer, D. M., & Firestone, I. The development of generalized imitation within topographically determined boundaries. *Journal of Applied Behavior Analysis*, 1971, *4*, 101–112.

Gibbs, J. C. The meaning of ecologically oriented inquiry in contemporary psychology. *American Psychologist*, 1979, *34*, 127–140.

Gold, M. W. Stimulus factors in skill training of the retarded on a complex assembly task: Acquisition, transfer, and retention. *American Journal of Mental Deficiency*, 1972, *76*, 517–526.

Gottman, J. M. Nonsequential data analysis techniques in observational research. In G. P. Sackett (Ed.), *Observing behavior* (Vol. 2). Baltimore: University Park Press, 1978.

Gottman, J. M., Markham, H., & Notarius, C. The topography of marital conflict: A sequential analysis of verbal and nonverbal behavior. *Journal of Marriage and the Family*, 1977, *39*, 461–477.

Gottman, J. M., & Notarius, C. Sequential analysis of observational data using markov chains. In T. Kratochwill (Ed.), *Strategies to evaluate change in single subject research*. New York: Academic Press, 1978.

Guess, D., & Baer, D. M. An analysis of individual differences in generalization between receptive and productive language in retarded children. *Journal of Applied Behavior Analysis*, 1973, *6*, 311–329.

Guess, D., Sailor, W., & Baer, D. M. Children with limited language. In R. L. Schiefelbush (Ed.), *Language intervention strategies* (Vol. 2). Baltimore: University Park Press, 1978.

Hall, G. E., & Loucks, S. F. A developmental model for determining whether treatment is actually implemented. *American Educational Research Journal*, 1977, *14*, 263–276.

Hamilton, J. Learning of a generalized response class in mentally retarded individuals. *American Journal of Mental Deficiency*, 1966, *71*, 100–108.

Hayden, A. H., & Haring, N. G. The acceleration and maintenance of developmental gains in Down's syndrome school-age children. In P. Mittler (Ed.), *Research to practice in mental retardation* (Vol. 1). Baltimore: University Park Press, 1977.

Heber, R., Garber, H., Harrington, S., Hoffman, C., & Felender, C. *Rehabilitation of families at risk for mental retardation.* Madison: University of Wisconsin Press, 1972.

Herbert, J., & Attridge, C. A guide for developers and users of observation systems and manuals. *American Educational Research Journal,* 1975, *12,* 1–20.

Hollenbeck, A. R. Problems of reliability in observational research. In G. P. Sackett (Ed.), *Observing behavior* (Vol. 2). Baltimore: University Park Press, 1978.

Holm, R. A. Techniques of recording observational data. In G. P. Sackett (Ed.), *Observing behavior* (Vol. 2). Baltimore: University Park Press, 1978.

Johnson, S. M., & Bolstad, O. D. Methodological issues in naturalistic observation: Some problems and solutions for field research. In L. A. Hamerlynck, L. C. Handy, & E. J. Mash (Eds.), *Behavior change: Methodology, concepts, and practice.* Champaign, Ill.: Research Press, 1973.

Kaufman, I. C., & Rosenblum, L. A. A behavioral taxonomy for *M. nemestrina* and *M. radiata:* Based on longitudinal observation of family groups in the laboratory. *Primates,* 1966, *7,* 205–258.

Kazdin, A. E. *Behavior modification in applied settings.* Homewood, Ill.: Dorsey Press, 1973.

Kazdin, A. E., & Bootzin, R. R. The token economy: An evaluative review. *Journal of Applied Behavior Analysis,* 1972, *5,* 343–372.

Landesman-Dwyer, S., & Sackett, G. P. Behavioral changes in nonambulatory mentally retarded individuals. In C. E. Meyers (Ed.), *Quality of life in severely and profoundly mentally retarded people: Research foundations for improvement* (Monographs of American Association on Mental Deficiency). Washington: AAMD, 1978.

Landesman-Dwyer, S., Stein, J. G., & Sackett, G. P. *Group homes for the retarded: An ecological and behavioral study* (Tech. Rep.). Olympia, Wash.: Department of Social and Health Services, 1976.

Landesman-Dwyer, S., Stein, J. G., & Sackett, G. P. A behavioral and ecological study of group homes. In G. P. Sackett (Ed.), *Observing behavior* (Vol. 1). Baltimore: University Park Press, 1978.

Lovaas, O. I., & Simmons, J. Q. Manipulation of self-destruction in three retarded children. *Journal of Applied Behavior Analysis,* 1969, *2,* 143–157.

Mayhew, G. L., Enyart, P., & Anderson, J. Social reinforcement and the naturally occurring social responses of severely and profoundly retarded adolescents. *American Journal of Mental Deficiency,* 1978, *83,* 164–170.

McClure, R. F. Reinforcement of verbal social behaviors in moderately retarded children. *Psychological Reports,* 1968, *23,* 371–376.

Moss, J. W. *Postsecondary vocational education for mentally retarded adults* (Tech. Rep.). Washington, D.C.: Division of Developmental Disabilities, HEW, 1980.

O'Brien, F., & Azrin, N. H. Developing proper mealtime behaviors of the institutionalized retarded. *Journal of Applied Behavior Analysis,* 1972, *5,* 389–399.

Osgood, C. E. The similarity paradox in human learning: A resolution. *Psychological Review,* 1949, *56,* 132–143.

Page, T. J., Iwata, B. A., & Neef, N. A. Teaching pedestrian skills to retarded persons: Generalization from the classroom to the natural environment. *Journal of Applied Behavior Analysis,* 1976, *9,* 433–444.

Parke, R. D., & O'Leary, S. E. Father–mother–infant interaction in the newborn period: Some findings, some observations, and some unresolved issues. In K. Riegel & J. Meacham (Eds.), *The developing individual in a changing world.* The Hague: Mouton, 1976.

Parsonson, B. S., Baer, A. M., & Baer, D. M. The application of generalized correct social contingencies: An evaluation of a training program. *Journal of Applied Behavior Analysis,* 1974, *7,* 427–437.

Reid, J. B. Reliability assessment of observation data: A possible methodological problem. *Child Development,* 1970, *41,* 1143–1150.

Rosenblum, L. A. The creation of a behavioral taxonomy. In G. P. Sackett (Ed.), *Observing behavior* (Vol. 2). Baltimore: University Park Press, 1978.

Rosenshine, B., & Furst, N. The use of direct observation to study teaching. In R. M. W. Travers (Ed.), *Second handbook of research on teaching*. Chicago: Rand McNally, 1973.

Sackett, G. P. (Ed.). *Observing behavior* (Vol. 1): *Theory and applications in mental retardation; Observing behavior* (Vol. 2): *Data collection and analysis methods*. Baltimore: University Park Press, 1978.

Sackett, G. P. The lag sequential analysis of contingency and cyclicity in behavioral interaction research. In J. D. Osofsky (Ed.), *The handbook of infant development*. New York: Wiley, 1979.

Sackett, G. P., Stephenson, E., & Ruppenthal, G. C. Digital data acquisition systems for observing behavior in laboratory and field settings. *Behavior Research Methods and Instrumentation,* 1973, *5,* 344–348.

Skinner, B. F. *Science and human behavior*. New York: Free Press, 1953.

Stern, D. N. Mother and infant at play: The dyadic interaction involving facial, vocal, and gaze behaviors. In M. Lewis & L. A. Rosenblum (Eds.), *The effect of the infant on its caregiver*. New York: Wiley, 1974.

Stokes, T. F., & Baer, D. M. Preschool peers as mutual generalization-facilitating agents. *Behavior Therapy,* 1976, *7,* 549–556.

Stokes, T. F., & Baer, D. M. An implicit technology of generalization. *Journal of Applied Behavior Analysis,* 1977, *10,* 349–367.

Stokes, T. F., Baer, D. M., & Jackson, R. L. Programming the generalization of a greeting response in four retarded children. *Journal of Applied Behavior Analysis,* 1974, *7,* 599–610.

Strayer, F. F., & Strayer, J. An ethological analysis of social agonism and dominance relations among preschool children. *Child Development,* 1976, *47,* 980–989.

Sykes, R. E. Techniques of data collection and reduction in systematic field observation. *Behavior Research Methods and Instrumentation,* 1977, *9,* 407–417.

Sykes, R. E. Toward a theory of observer effect in systematic field observation. *Human Organization,* 1978, *37,* 148–156.

Thoman, E. B., Becker, P. T., & Freese, M. P. Contingency interaction between mothers and their developmentally delayed infants. In G. P. Sackett (Ed.), *Observing behavior* (Vol. 1). Baltimore: University Park Press, 1978.

Walker, H. M., Hyman, H., & Johnson, S. M. Generalization and maintenance of classroom treatment effects. *Behavior Therapy,* 1975, *6,* 188–200.

Wang, M. C. The use of direct observational data for formative evaluation of an instructional model. *Instructional Science,* 1976, *5,* 365–389.

Whitman, T. L., Mercurio, J. R., & Caponigri, V. Development of social responses in two severely retarded children. *Journal of Applied Behavior Analysis,* 1970, *3,* 133–138.

Zeaman, D., & House, B. J. The role of attention in retardate discrimination learning. In N. R. Ellis (Ed.), *Handbook of mental deficiency*. New York: McGraw-Hill, 1963.

10 Treatment of Hyperactive, Aggressive, and Antisocial Children

Mark A. Stewart, M.D.
Howard B. Ashby, M.D.
University of Iowa College of Medicine

INTRODUCTION

Our understanding of children's behavior problems has progressed during the past decade and new ways of treating them have been developed. However, these advances have established beachheads rather than secure regions of new knowledge. This chapter is, therefore, somewhat tentative. The authors describe new approaches that are supported by the present evidence, by theory, or by their own clinical experiences.

The terms hyperactive, aggressive, and antisocial are broad and they mean different things to different people. Often, these terms are understood as referring to syndromes of behavior, rather than being taken literally. The authors therefore start by discussing current ideas on what these terms denote. In the sections that follow, they discuss the nature of these problems, possible limits to the results of treatment, and the actual methods.

TERMINOLOGY

Hyperactivity is usually taken to mean a pattern of behavior in which the dominant features are a high activity level, difficulty staying on task, impulsivity, impatience, low tolerance for frustration, and disorders of conduct such as aggressiveness, noncompliance, and disruptiveness. Some clinicians and researchers, particularly those who use the term minimal brain dysfunction as synonymous with hyperactivity, include still other kinds of behavior, ranging from specific reading disability to generalized clumsiness, inability to experience pleasure, and bedwetting.

Researchers in Great Britain have consistently taken a more conservative view of this syndrome. In their studies, hyperkinesis is a rather rare disorder that is associated with severe retardation or definite brain damage and that is defined by extreme overactivity and an attention span limited to seconds (Ingram, 1956; Ounsted, 1955; Rutter, Graham, & Yule, 1970). What is called hyperactivity in this country is considered a conduct disorder in Britain and solid evidence for this point of view has been reported (Sandberg, Rutter, & Taylor, 1978; Shaffer, McNamara, & Pincus, 1974).

A flaw in research on hyperactivity in the United States and Canada has been that investigators have compared hyperactive children to normal children rather than to other children attending a clinic. The evidence, therefore, does not serve to establish a specific syndrome; it shows that the so-called hyperactive children differ from average children, but not that they differ from deviant children in general. Recent studies in North America suggest that hyperactivity is a confusing diagnostic label (Schuckit, Petrich, & Chiles, 1978), and that it is not a valid syndrome (Offord, Sullivan, Allen, & Abrams, 1979; Stewart, Cummings, Singer, & deBlois, 1981; Stewart, deBlois & Cummings, 1980; Stewart, deBlois & Singer, 1979). Furthermore, the follow-up studies of Loney, Langhorne, and Paternite (1978) and Milich and Loney (1979) have shown that for hyperactive boys, aggression predicts clinical outcome in adolescence, whereas the level of activity is only a rather weak predictor of school achievement.

Conduct disorder is a term that covers any childhood behavior that goes against the rules of society. It is a more formal name for the common expression "behavior problem." In clinical practice, most children who are brought to a clinic for conduct disorder are troublesome to adults because they are aggressive as well as disobedient. Hewitt and Jenkins (1946) were the first to define this pattern of behavior on an empirical basis. Using early correlational techniques, they found a group of children among 500 admissions to a child-psychiatry clinic who presented the combination of resistance to discipline, frequent fighting, destructiveness, and meanness. Surprisingly, there has been virtually no follow-up of their work and to this day the existence of this syndrome is not established. We need a more detailed description of the syndrome, validation of the clinical description through direct observations and standardized tests, long-term follow-up studies, evidence on the origins of the syndrome, and the discovery of biologic or psychologic markers in order to establish this pattern of behavior as a legitimate syndrome.

Antisocial children are those who are involved in specific behaviors such as lying, stealing at home, stealing from neighbors or stores, cheating, playing hookey, running away from home, cruelty to little children and animals, fire setting, and vandalism. A great deal is known about antisocial or delinquent adolescents, but little about children who behave in this way. Work by Stewart, deBlois, Meardon, and Cummings (1980) suggests that at least half of the children involved in antisocial behavior are also aggressive and noncompliant.

The characteristics of the children who are antisocial but do not have aggressive conduct disorder are simply not known.

In this outline of the three syndromes, the authors have not mentioned the many studies in which factor analysis has been applied to the behavioral symptoms of problem children. These studies, which have culminated in the elegant work of Achenbach (1978) and Achenbach and Edelbrock (1979), give us vital insights into the dimensions of behavior present in problem children, but they do not tell us how the several behaviors cluster together in actual individuals. The dimensional approach is a powerful one in research, but a categorical approach lends itself more to clinical practice.

The remainder of this chapter focuses on children with aggressive conduct disorder because this is the most common problem facing clinicians, whether they work in schools or clinics. In other words, the focus is on "behavior-problem" or chronically disruptive children.

NATURE OF THE PROBLEM

If we knew the general nature of conduct disorder, we might be able to design treatments that fitted the problem and set realistic goals. For example, knowing that social learning was the basis of the misbehavior (i.e., that children defied their parents and attacked their siblings because such behavior got them the attention they needed and because it put a stop to parental nagging), we could reasonably expect that a program to change interactions in the family from negative to positive would improve the children's behavior. However, we do not know that this is a complete explanation of conduct disorder, nor can we be sure that other explanations, biologic or psychologic, are either necessary or sufficient. We also lack the data on long-term results of cognitive, behavioral, and social learning treatments that would tell us the extent to which conduct disorder is tractable. Given our ignorance, it seems wise to be somewhat skeptical about all treatments. Those who feel a surge of enthusiasm over the results of early studies on impulse control or social-skills training should remember the adage about repeating history if one does not learn from it. Delinquency has proven intractable, either to treatment or prevention. Successive waves of clinicians and researchers have tackled this problem filled with optimism, only to be frustrated (e.g., Byles & Maurice, 1979; McCord, 1978). Children with conduct disorder, especially those who are antisocial (Moore, Chamberlain, & Mukai, 1979), may be equally hard to treat. With these cautions, it is still worth taking stock of the clues we have to the nature of conduct disorder and reviewing treatment.

Putting aside the issue of what causes the problem, we have strong hints that its signs appear early in a child's life and are quite stable over time. Kagan and Moss (1962) reported that aggressive tendencies and an associated resistance to discipline appear by age 3 and are relatively stable, at least in boys, into early

adult life. Bronson's studies (1966a, 1966b) on central orientations in the growing child, which are based on data collected in the *Berkeley Growth Study,* show
the same trends. Among the more stable and central traits that Bronson uncovered were those she termed "resistive-compliant" and "passive-domineering."
Gersten, Langner, Eisenberg, Simcha-Fagan, and McCarthy (1976) found that
conflict with parents, fighting with peers, and antisocial behavior were relatively
stable through the years 6 to 16, each cluster of behaviors following a specific
pattern of stability or change. In follow-up studies of patients, conduct disorder
has regularly been found to persist, in marked contrast to emotional or neurotic
disorder (Graham & Rutter, 1973; Morris, Escoll, & Wexler, 1956; Robins,
1966).

The unfortunate persistence of these traits or deviant patterns of behavior may
be due to the children's growing up in stably pathologic homes. In fact, this
association is well documented (Morris et al., 1956; Robins, 1966; Rutter, 1971;
Stewart et al., 1979; Stewart & Leone, 1978). It is also possible that these traits
that emerge early in life and persist through childhood and adolescence are
aspects of an inborn temperament, determined genetically or by external biologic
factors (e.g., perinatal stress) affecting the child in utero or as an infant. Thomas,
Chess, and Birch (1968) and Thomas and Chess (1977) have followed 110
children from birth, observing their behavior and the parents' interactions with
them; they found that difficult traits such as irritability, overreactivity, and lack
of adaptability in the first 4 years of life predicted the later development of
behavior disorders. These researchers, working primarily with the families of
professionals, observed that one-third of the parents of difficult children were
able to adjust successfully to the children's special needs and prevent the onset of
problems. In the remaining two-thirds of families, the children's behavior tended
to worsen in the face of parents' impatience, frustration, or sense of helplessness.
Several other researchers have found that difficult babies elicit avoidance or other
negative behavior from their parents, a commonplace to pediatricians who recognize a syndrome known as the "mother-killer." Als, Tronick, Adamson, and
Brazelton (1976), Osofsky and Danzger (1974), Shaw (1977), and others have
reported evidence of such interactions between a baby's temperament and the
parents' behavior. This field is, therefore, quite well established and promises to
broaden our understanding of children's psychological problems in general. The
connection between early events and aggressive conduct disorder in 10-year-old
boys is still tenuous, however, for want of convincing data that this problem
starts in the first few years of life. Nevertheless, the recognition that young
children shape their parents' behavior as much as the parents shape theirs, and
that deviant trends may appear in infancy, puts a different light on the common
observation that children with conduct disorder have often been disliked or
rejected by their parents from the start. It is now reasonable to ask which came
first, the rejection or the misbehavior, whereas this question was rank heresy 15

to 20 years ago, when psychoanalytic explanations of children's behavior held most clinicians in thrall.

Is there specific evidence that biologic factors, environmental or genetic, contribute to the origin of conduct disorder? A variety of relatively common insults to the brain, from perinatal stress to lead poisoning, have been put forward as significant causes of behavior problems. In fact, the data show that some of these lead to lowering of intelligence (see the review by Stewart & Gath, 1978), but there is no clear-cut evidence that they produce conduct disorder. Rutter et al., (1970) surveyed the 2100 10- and 11-year-old children from a community in England and found that those who had definite signs of brain dysfunction, such as cerebral palsy or epilepsy, were more likely to have neurotic or conduct disorders than were healthy children. However, one can calculate from this work and the survey of the whole population of children in this age group (Rutter, Tizard, & Whitmore, 1970) that brain damage only accounts for a small proportion, about 1%, of all children with conduct disorder.

Whether genetic factors predispose children to be more or less aggressive, hard to discipline, and self centered is an open question. The results of studies of twins (e.g., Christiansen, 1977) and "cross-fostered" children (Crowe, 1974; Hutchings & Mednick, 1977) make it seem quite likely that genes contribute to antisocial behavior in adults. The evidence that the same is true in children is scanty. Cadoret and Gath (1980) found that behavior problems in children adopted early in life were associated with alcoholism or antisocial behavior in the biologic fathers. Bohman (1971) found no such association in a much larger sample of adoptees, but his method of finding whether a child had behavior problems was limited and insensitive. A number of studies have shown that hyperactivity tends to run in families (Cantwell, 1972; Morrison & Stewart, 1971) and that this probably reflects genetic as well as social transmission (Cantwell, 1975; Morrison & Stewart, 1973). These studies may well have been describing the correlates of conduct disorder rather than hyperactivity because the definition of the latter is so broad. More recent evidence suggests that it is conduct disorder in boys, not hyperactivity, that is associated with psychopathology in the parents, in particular alcoholism and antisocial behavior in the boys' natural fathers (Stewart, deBlois, & Cummings, 1980; Stewart & Leone, 1978). In short, there is a possibility that genes are a cause of aggressive and antisocial behavior in children, but the evidence is far from convincing.

Another intriguing clue that biologic factors play a part lies in Waldrop, Bell, and Goering's (1976) finding that boys who are overactive and aggressive tend to have more than the usual number of minor congenital anomalies (wide-spaced eyes, low-set ears, simian palmar creases, and so on). This association suggests that some boys have behavior problems because they are carrying a subtle chromosomal anomaly or because they experienced an insult in the first 3 months of their intrauterine development.

LIMITS TO BEHAVIOR THERAPY

The authors wrote this long preamble, emphasizing physical determinants of behavior problems, because they want to raise the possibility that there are biologic limits to the changes a therapist can effect in a child's behavior. The psychological restraints of the child's motivation and that of his or her parents are well recognized. For example, the most common reason for failure in the alarm treatment of bedwetting is the lack of will in the child to get up to pass water when the alarm goes off, or in the parents to get up and see that this is done. Biologic limits have not been defined, but they may well exist. We believe that genes may determine a "reaction range" for the level of aggressiveness in an individual, whereas experience determines the actual level. This would be analogous to a widely accepted model for gene–social interactions determining an individual's IQ. Events that may illustrate this idea were reported by Patterson, Littman, and Bricker (1967). These investigators tracked aggressive incidents in two nursery schools over a year. They observed that a small number of children in each school were responsible for most of the incidents. A majority of the other children learned to fight back after being attacked, but a few never learned. This seems analogous to the progress of bright, average, and dull students in a demanding academic curriculum. An implication is that one probably should not expect to make an impulsive, aggressive child into a deliberate, quiet one, or vice versa, through any psychological treatment. Dog breeders have accepted temperament as a fact for centuries and researchers have begun to study it scientifically. Dykman, Murphree, and Reese (1979) have bred two strains of a specific type of hunting dog, one energetic and outgoing, the other fearful of people and too high strung to hunt. Cross fostering has made no difference in the behavior of puppies, which follows the temperament of the natural parents. Behavioral treatment for the human phobia of the nervous dogs has failed. It is as though the desired behaviors were not in these dogs' repertoire and therefore could not be elicited and reinforced. Anyone who has done psychotherapy with a very passive patient is familiar with this problem.

TYPES OF TREATMENT

Fortunately, children with aggressive conduct disorder do not lack either the motivation to change or the tendency to prosocial behavior. The authors have had the good fortune to see more than 100 boys and girls with this problem show their assets as well as their liabilities on a psychiatric ward run on behavioral lines. In a warm and structured environment, these children tend to be happy, concerned for others, and eager to win the approval of adults. They do not fight with their peers, nor do they abuse adults, but they are still extremely competitive, need a great deal of attention, and test limits. They tend to be impulsive, inattentive, loud, and restless. Most obvious is their lack of skill in interacting with other children and their inability to behave reasonably in a group of peers.

The main goal of treatment is to help such children learn to regulate and channel their energy and drive in ways that are acceptable to others. They also have to learn to accept rules and directions. As they learn to control their own behavior rather than reacting to others, they gain self confidence and win back the love of their families. They begin to make and keep friends and they shed the image of the crazy kid.

Approaches that are useful in working with most children who have aggressive conduct disorder include the following:

1. Training in self awareness and in monitoring one's own behavior.
2. Coaching in specific social skills.
3. Training in normal assertiveness.
4. Training in impulse control and problem solving.
5. Wilderness-survival training.

Helping the child to build up his or her healthy, prosocial behavior and to govern difficult behavior is the first priority. These alterations in the child seem most likely to last, whereas the good effects of external control (e.g., a contingency management plan used by parents) are likely to disappear when the control is no longer enforced. However it is important to try to change the child's environment, particularly for younger children. Parents, siblings, and teachers need to understand the target child's behavior and see how their own attitudes and responses tend to maintain the child's bad behavior. The adults need to practice effective ways of setting limits, and know how to give children meaningful rewards for their good behavior or punishment for bad. Personal problems in the parents and conflict between them have to be attended to. The mother who is depressed will probably not be able to put into practice a new way of disciplining her child. Parents who are at war with each other tend not to have the energy or interest to change their bad habits and they will not be able to work together. "Multiple-problem families," in which the father has a personality disorder or is an alcoholic, the mother is dull and depressed, whose finances are precarious, and whose household is chaotic need intensive case work and psychiatric help before the child's problems can be tackled effectively.

Treatment Directed at the Child

Self Awareness and Self Monitoring. In their classic description of the mechanisms involved in psychotherapy, Dollard and Miller (1950) gave an important place to the therapist's teaching the patient to label his or her behavior. Active understanding developed as the patient learned to identify motives, meanings, and effects of the problematic patterns of behavior. With understanding came the ability to see and practice healthier behavior. This link between naming and self regulation was also the center of Luria's (1961) theory as to how children learned to control processes such as attention, planning, and the handling of frustration. His work inspired the development of methods for treating impulsive children, which is discussed later in this chapter.

It seems only common sense that aggressive and antisocial children should be coached to label their problems because they are unable to control themselves. In fact, there are reasons to believe that these children are handicapped by poor language skills (Camp, 1977). The authors do not know of any studies that show specifically that the problem children are not able to label their behavior adequately, or that teaching this skill reduces deviant behavior. Nevertheless, this approach seems to be helpful. Commonly used techniques are transactional analysis, talking over social situations shown on cards ("consequence cards," "sensitivity cards"), and immediate discussion of incidents with other children ("life-space interviews").

The role of self awareness in adults' social behavior has been thoughtfully reviewed by Wicklund (1979). To quote him: "the person who becomes self-aware is more likely to act consistently, be faithful to societal norms, and give accurate reports about himself [p. 187]." This statement was based on a considerable body of date. Here, we only cite two studies that are clearly related to the present topic. Diener and Wallbom (1976) found that subjects who were made more aware of themselves by seating them in front of a mirror and playing their tape-recorded voices back to them were less likely to cheat on a test than controls. Seventy-one per cent of the latter cheated, 7% of the former. Scheier, Fenigstein, and Buss (1974) reported an experiment in which male subjects used an aggression machine on female victims. The presence of a mirror in front of the subject or of an audience with whom he had eye contact both inhibited aggression.

Some of the ways in which one can foster self awareness in children have been mentioned already. Playing back video tapes of their natural behavior or of role playing are methods that have a strong impact on children, especially when the tapes are discussed with a teacher or a nurse with whom children have close relationships. For older children, the tapes can be used as the focus for group discussions and problem solving.

Requiring a child to rate his or her own behavior on a simple form during the school day and having the child determine the reinforcement (e.g., points per period) is another technique that is used widely now. The belief is growing that children should be made responsible for carrying out their own behavior modification whenever possible and as early as possible. One advantage is that the child has to practice self awareness. Another common method is to require the child to keep a detailed diary of each day's progress on the problem behaviors. For example, the authors have had boys who are being trained in assertiveness record all the angry feelings they have had each day and how they have handled them.

Ability to Appreciate the Feelings and Ideas of Others. Attention to these skills follows naturally from work on self awareness. In role playing and role rehearsal, and in coaching children in specific social skills, the two functions go together. In this case, however, there is experimental evidence that antisocial adolescents lack the ability to take the perspective of another and that training may reduce antisocial behavior. Chandler (1973) found that delinquents were not able to tell a story presented in cartoons as a bystander in the cartoon series would have seen it. Their scores on a measure of egocentrism were significantly greater than those of controls. After a 10-week treatment program, which consisted of filming skits in which each subject had to play a variety of roles, delinquents' egocentrism scores were markedly reduced. More impressive was the finding that the number of offenses committed by the experimental group over the next 18 months was significantly lower than corresponding numbers for a placebo group and a control group. In a second study, Chandler, Greenspan, and Barenboim (1974) applied the same test of ability to take roles and a test of ability to communicate complex information to a large group of children with severe behavior problems. The children did less well than normal peers on these tests. Following specific training, an experimental group improved considerably more than an untreated group. Clinicians caring for these children were asked to rate their behavior before and after treatment, but the reliability of the ratings was poor and it was therefore not clear whether treatment had any effect on the children's actual problems.

These approaches seem sensible and promising. Furthermore, Chandler has established some relatively simple tests with which one can measure a child's skills and follow the effects of treatment. A set of closely related tests have been described by Clark and Delia (1976), who studied the ability of normal children of different ages to persuade an adult to do specific favors for them.

Coaching in Social Skills. One general theory of deviant behavior is that it represents a deficiency of normal social behavior. There is not a disease; there is not a syndrome of bad behavior. Rather, there is an absence of healthy social behavior. Whatever one thinks of the theory, the practical treatment that flows from it has been widely applied to patients with chronic psychiatric disorders, and has proven effective (Trower, Bryant, & Argyle, 1978). Goldstein, Sherman, Gershaw, Sprafkin, and Glick (1978) have discussed the techniques needed in applying such treatment to aggressive adolescents and the reader will find their suggestions wise.

Oden and Asher (1977) have reported encouraging results from a relatively brief period of training given to socially isolated children, a group that probably included a high proportion of aggressive and antisocial children. The target children were chosen on the basis of their sociometric scores and these were later used as the criterion for effects of treatment. The coaching consisted of verbal instruction in social skills, practicing the skills in playing with a peer, and a review session after the play. The specific skills taught were how to take part in a game, how to take turns, share, and so on; how to talk with and listen to another, and how to help or give attention to another child. The three treatment conditions were coaching, playing with a peer without coaching, and control. Thirty-three isolated children were recruited from third- and fourth-grade classes in a middle-class community. Six treatment sessions, each lasting about 25 minutes, were given over a period of a month. A second set of sociometric ratings showed that the coached children made significantly greater gains as "someone I'd like to play with" than the two comparison groups. The children were rated again a year later and the coached group had continued to gain in popularity. At this point, the once-isolated children who had been coached were only slightly below the mean for their classes, whereas the other two groups remained about 1 S.D. below the mean.

That this modest course of training in social skills should have a significant and lasting effect on the peer relationships of a group of problem children is an exciting lead, and should persuade many other researchers and clinicians to try this approach. Meanwhile, as Campbell and Paulaukas (1979) have pointed out, a great deal more work has to be done on defining the specific deficits in social skills of problem children. As an example of a specific deficit, Minkin, Braukmann, Minkin, Timbers, Timbers, Fixsen, Phillips, and Wolf (1976) found that delinquent girls had poor conversational skills. They were able to train them to a normal or better level.

Training in Assertiveness.   There is a growing literature on the measurement of assertiveness in adults; the relationships of deficits in this skill to anxiety, depression, and low self esteem, and the effects of training (Orenstein, Orenstein, & Carr, 1975; Pachman & Foy, 1978; Rathus, 1973). So far, the research has not spread to work with children. However, the authors and their colleagues have applied the techniques used with adults to a number of children and young adolescents. It is their impression that this treatment has been helpful for both those with social anxiety and those with undue aggressiveness. In fact, it is not uncommon to see children who have these difficulties in combination. They lack confidence in relating to other children and, when they find themselves in situations they cannot handle, they lose their tempers and lash out. Training them to express their feelings openly and deliberately in naturally occurring or engineered challenges leads to their being able to deal with frustration successfully.

Training in Impulse Control and Problem Solving.   This approach has a relatively long history and stems in large part from the ideas of Luria that were mentioned earlier (Luria, 1961). This distinguished Russian psychologist carried out experiments to determine how children of different ages used speech while they performed tasks. Luria observed that children went through the phases of commenting on tasks out loud, directing themselves through tasks, and finally thinking their plans out before starting tasks. From his findings, he argued that children develop control over their behavior by internalizing the directions they have learned from adults. His theory led naturally to experiments in teaching impulsive children to be more deliberate. Commonly, these experiments have involved children carrying out a mildly frustrating task, such as finding a path through a maze, while instructing themselves to "stop, look, and think" (Palkes, Stewart, & Kahana, 1968).

Two quite serious tests of this treatment have been reported. Douglas, Parry, Marton, and Garson (1976) used modeling, self instruction, and self reinforcement to teach hyperactive children effective ways of solving various problems. Twenty-nine boys who had been diagnosed as hyperactive, but who were not taking drugs, were recruited for the study. All these boys had also been rated as impulsive by their parents and teachers, and had low latency scores on the *Kagan Matching Familiar Figures Test* (i.e., below 10 seconds). Eighteen boys were given training and 11 served as controls. The training took place in 24 one-hour sessions spread over a period of 3 months and was based on the methods described by Meichenbaum and Goodman (1969, 1971). The instructor demonstrated problem-solving skills on various tasks and talked his or her way through the task. The subject then rehearsed the same procedures. In succeeding sessions, subjects were encouraged to internalize the directions they gave themselves. They were also taught to plan ahead, how to remember vital cues, and how to take account of other children's feelings when playing with them.

At the end of treatment, the experimental group had made modest but significant improvements in performance on the *MFF* and the *Bender Gestalt,* and gave healthier responses on a story-completion test that was designed to assess a child's response to frustration. The controls had not changed. Three months later, both groups were assessed again and the results were almost the same as immediately after treatment. The authors include enough detail on the assessment and treatment for the report to be useful for the practicing clinician.

Camp, Blom, Hebert, and van Doorninck (1977) described the results of a similar program, but one that focused more on verbal mediation and self control. The subjects were 23 boys in second grade who had been rated by their teachers as very aggressive. Twelve received treatment; 11 were controls. Three subtests of the *WISC–R,* a standard test of reading, part of the *Illinois Test of Psycholinguistic Abilities,* and the *MFF* were given before and after treatment. In addition, subjects' speech during the test was recorded. The authors' treatment, known as "Think Aloud," was derived from the work of Meichenbaum and Goodman (1971) and from that of Shure and Spivack (1974); the former source provided the approach for the cognitive aspects and the latter for the social aspects of the treatment. Half hour sessions were held every school day for six weeks. The results of treatment were quite impressive. Irrelevant, self distracting speech during the testing was reduced, and the experimental subjects were more reflective. There was little evidence however that their classroom behavior had improved.

The authors feel that these early studies present quite a heartening picture. As we come to know what a given method can accomplish and as more time and effort are put into such programs, we may find the treatment affects behavior in natural settings as well as on tests.

Wilderness Experiences

This approach has its roots in a program known as Outward Bound, which began in Great Britain in World War II as survival training for merchant seamen. The original concepts of the physical and psychological aspects of survival training are being applied in natural settings such as the wilderness area of northeast Minnesota. Activities such as canoeing, rappelling, rock and mountain climbing, orienteering, camping, and backpacking provide stresses that challenge an individual's personal and social resources. In meeting challenges that are both physical (climbing a rock face, portaging a canoe) and social (the team work and cooperation required to canoe or handle a belay in a rappel), the rewards of both positive and negative behavior are immediate and obvious.

Such programs have become widespread in the United States since the 1960's. Byers (1979) reviewed the literature on wilderness camping as therapy. She concluded that although some changes could be documented after the outdoor programs, changes in specific referral behaviors, either during the experience or on follow-up, had not yet been proven. Furthermore, although reports of the philosophy and objectives of outdoor-therapy programs have been published, little has been written on the specifics of programs and the skills needed in counselors.

Kelly and Baer (1971) reported the results of a 1 year follow-up on parolees using recidivism (the need for reinstitutionalization) as the criterion for change. They compared boys adjudicated delinquent who participated in an Outward-Bound program for 27 days with matched boys who received conventional intervention. At 1 year, they reported a 20% recidivism rate in the Outward-Bound group and a 42% rate in the control group. In a 5-year follow-up study, there was no difference between the groups if recidivism was used as the sole criterion. However, recidivism was delayed in the Outward-Bound group, suggesting that the treatment kept boys out of trouble for awhile (Kelly, 1974).

Smith, Gabriel, Schott, and Padia (1975) studied the effects of Outward Bound on self assertion, self awareness, self esteem, and acceptance of others. They concluded that Outward Bound had increased assertiveness and self esteem, but that acceptance of others and self awareness were not affected. They also describe a participant observation of the experience that would interest those who are not familiar with this type of program.

Nold and Wilpers (1975) discuss the idea of using wilderness programs as part of an integrated community-based program. They emphasize the wilderness experience as an "ignition phase" of the treatment process and as a catalyst for further intervention. The present authors' experience with wilderness survival programs for both boys and girls aged 10–16 supports the positive feelings of others. They are now systematically evaluating the impact of this program on children referred for a variety of behavior problems.

Treatment with Stimulant Drugs

The authors deal with this subject only briefly because many reviews have already been published in the past few years. They present issues that still have to be settled.

Many writers have stated that hyperactive children respond paradoxically to stimulant drugs by becoming calmer rather than more excited. This assertion has been one of the supports for the argument that hyperactivity is a medical disorder for which there is a specific drug treatment. Sroufe and Stewart (1973) presented reasons for being skeptical that the drugs' effects on children with hyperactivity or other problems differed from the known effects on normal adults. It was established experimentally as early as the 1950's that stimulants improved adults' attention to and performance on routine tasks. Their most striking effect was to counteract the decline in performance that came with boredom and fatigue. An elegant demonstration of how amphetamine affects academic performance in normal adults was reported by Smith, Weitzner, Levenson, and Beecher (1963). These workers compared the effect of amphetamine, secobarbital, and placebo on the performance of 78 graduate and undergraduate students doing a series of calculus problems and a digit–letter coding test. Amphetamine did not influence performance on the calculus problems, but it strongly affected how the student performed on the coding test. This investigation and many others suggest that stimulant drugs function to take up a motivational slack. When the subject is completely engaged in a task, there will be no effect. When he or she is not very interested or is fatigued, the stimulants will have an obvious effect.

The apparent calming of children with behavior problems may well reflect an increase in "on-task" behavior. Concentrating on one's school work is not compatible with getting up and down from one's seat, talking to one's neighbor, and disrupting the class. A side effect of the drug that may also account for some part of the apparent calming is that children tend to become mildly depressed and to lose some of their natural spontaneity and drive when they are taking therapeutic doses of stimulants (Rie, Rie, & Stewart, & Ambuel 1976; Whalen, Henker, Collins, McAuliffe, & Vaux, 1979). Finally, Rapoport, Buchsbaum, Zahn, Weingartner, Ludlow, and Mikkelsen (1978) have reported a detailed study of the effects of dextroamphetamine on normal and hyperactive children. The effects on the two groups of children were much the same. A clear implication of these findings is that response to stimulants should not be used as a criterion for diagnosing hyperactivity.

It is not clear yet which types of handicapped children respond to stimulants. What the clinician would most like is a drug that would effectively increase attention in those children who have severely disorganized behavior and who may be relatively resistant to behavioral treatment. Unfortunately, the tiny amount of evidence suggests that those who are definitely brain damaged or have some specific dysfunction, such as epilepsy, less often benefit from taking stimulants (Ounsted, 1955; Sleator & von Neumann, 1974). The authors' experience on an inpatient unit bears this idea out; children who have a span of attention measured in seconds and who are grossly distractible seldom change when given these drugs. Such patients are usually epileptic or brain damaged, and at least moderately retarded.

Recent research on drug treatment has been increasingly rigorous, relying on counts of specific behaviors by independent observers rather than ratings by parents and teachers. It has become clearer as a result that some behaviors are markedly affected by the drugs, at least in certain situations, and that others are probably not affected at all. Whalen, Henker, Collins, Finck, and Dotemoto (1979) carried out a painstaking study of how methylphenidate affected the behavior of hyperactive boys in a classroom. These boys were being treated by pediatricians and were already known to have responded well to the drug. The behavior of the subjects on active drug was compared with their behavior on placebo and with the behavior of a group of normal boys. Significant differences were observed between the placebo-treated hyperactive boys and the normal boys on several different kinds of behavior—for example, attention to task, moving around, talking, making noises, and interacting with other children, all during class. Drug-treated hyperactive children behaved more like the normal boys than did the untreated. There was no significant difference between these two groups.

In a different study with the same subjects, Whalen, Henker, Collins, McAuliffe, and Vaux (1979) found that the active drug did not alter the performance of a referential communication task by hyperactive boys. In fact, the performance of the hyperactive boys did not differ materially from that of the normal boys, whether the former were treated or not. However, there were differences in the way that the two groups of boys did the task, and the drug tended to influence qualities of behavior such as the amount of positive feedback given to the partner and the speed at which the boy worked. This study involved a task and a setting quite different from the one carried out in a classroom. However, the authors' general conclusion that stimulants alter style of behavior more than content seems justified and is consistent with results from a number of other studies.

Surprisingly little work has been done on the vital question of whether children with hyperactivity or other problems presumed to affect learning make better progress in school when taking stimulants. It is often asserted that they do, but there is actually no hard evidence that this is so. In a number of studies, an apparent improvement in children's achievement has been observed after a period of drug treatment, but the subjects had been tested off drug at the beginning rather than on drug. Rie and Rie (1977) have shown that there is an immediate effect of drugs on achievement-test performance. Some experiments have shown faster learning of a simple task, but even these do not show improved recall.

Rie, Rie, Stewart, & Ambuel (1976) studied a group of children who had learning handicaps but normal intelligence. Half took methylphenidate for 12 weeks, whereas the other half took placebo. Treatments were then reversed for 12 weeks. The investigators were blind to the children's assignments. Intelligence and school-achievement tests were administered individually before the treatment and after each treatment. The drug produced no increment in learning. Nevertheless, parents and teachers both rated the treated children as doing significantly better on school achievement.

There is still only one work that tells us anything of the results of giving hyperactive children stimulants over a period of years. Weiss, Kruger, Danielson, and Elman (1975) followed three groups of such children for 5 years and then assessed them. The measures of adjustment and progress in school were relatively crude, but no difference emerged between those who had taken methylphenidate for the 5 years, those who had taken a phenothiazine tranquilizer for part of that time, and those who had had no drug treatment at all.

In summary, the evidence collected so far suggests that stimulants do temporarily reduce the frequency of some silly and irritating behaviors, such as talking to the child at the next desk instead of working, or blurting out comments in class, but they do not cause children to do better at a task that engages their attention. Furthermore, there is no reason yet to think that stimulants help children to learn more readily and retain what they have learned, nor that they change general aspects of a child's social behavior over the years. In a sense, this is not as disappointing as it sounds, because the long-term outcome for the kind of children who were studied is benign anyway (Weiss & Hechtman, 1979). Many of the studies done on stimulant drugs have excluded children with serious behavior problems or with IQ's below 85. What is frustrating is that the drugs probably offer no more to those children who do seriously need help.

Treatments Involving Members of the Child's Family and Teachers

Occasionally, it is possible to treat aggressive and antisocial children successfully with no other methods than those described in the previous section. Almost always, however, it is necessary to change the environment as well. One needs to reduce as far as possible factors that tend to perpetuate the child's bad behavior—for example, mother's nagging or father's inability to set rules. In order to lower tension in the home and restore some harmony, it is also necessary to bring the family back to a natural balance between adults and children. Aggressive children tend to dominate their families. The helplessness this induces in the parents creates resentment and dislike toward the child. Parents need help to regain their authority if for no other reason than to restore a decent atmosphere in the home. Some of the other reasons for working on the family as well as on the child are touched on later.

A relatively simple way of teaching parents how to discipline their children has been developed by Patterson and his colleagues at the Oregon Social Learning Center. Considering the popularity of the method, there is rather little evidence to show how well it works and how long its effects last, but there are promising reports. Patterson (1974a and 1974b) has presented the results for 27 families in which the target child had problems such as aggressiveness, non-compliance, or stealing. There were significant reductions in the frequencies of most of these behaviors both at home and at school after parents and teachers were given short courses in child management. The children also showed a higher proportion of good behaviors in the classroom. Seventeen of the 27 children whose parents were trained were followed for a year after the end of treatment and their improvement was maintained. Ten of the 14 children who had problems in the classroom as well as at home were followed for 6 months after the teachers had been trained, and they also maintained their improvement.

Such studies of treatment are difficult to carry out, particularly in relatively small communities that do not have many potential subjects. Nevertheless, some reservation about Patterson's results is in order. The number of children treated was quite small; it is not clear how serious their problems were, and there were no untreated or placebo-treated controls. In the authors' experience, parents need a great deal of moral support to keep up the proper ways of dealing with their difficult child, and many competent and well-intentioned parents cannot sustain this effort. On the other hand, it is possible that the authors' patients tend to be more severely affected than those who were attending the clinic in Eugene.

Many factors in the home work against parents' successful practice of new ways to raise their child. The most obvious and challenging are the parents' own personalities, their moods, their health, the extent of their other responsibilities, and the support coming to them from relatives and friends. About half of the boys coming to a typical child-psychiatry clinic with aggressive conduct disorder have antisocial or alcoholic fathers (Stewart, deBlois, & Cummings, 1980). The father's disorder in turn is associated with wife and child abuse, extreme poverty, and rejection of the family by relatives and neighbors. Probably as a result of the father's behavior, the child's problem, and the associated isolation and hardship, a high proportion of mothers are clinically depressed (Tsai, Ashby & Stewart,

1980). Adequate management of an aggressive child may therefore include treatment for one or both parents, marriage counseling, and intensive casework. Little has been written about involving brothers and sisters in managing a child with behavior problems, but it is a vital part of a good program. The siblings deserve to have the problem explained to them and they should learn how to help the target child overcome the difficulty. Often, the siblings have important insights into the origins and the solutions. Family therapy is a vehicle for working with the other children in the family as well as for lowering tensions and changing attitudes in the parents. In coping with the logistics of a complicated and demanding treatment program, it is rather easy for the therapist to forget one simple and crucial aspect, that the problem child craves love. Without it he or she is likely to go on being hateful, no matter how scientific the treatment. In family therapy, one can see whether the necessary changes in people's attitudes are forthcoming and help them along.

This chapter would not be complete without mentioning the last resort, placing a child in a foster home or group home. It is an extraordinary fact that next to nothing is known about the effects of foster care on aggressive and antisocial children though thousands experience this every year and have done so for the past 70 years or more. In spite of our ignorance, we sometimes have little choice but to advise this step. There are families in which the parents seem incapable of loving the child or have such severe personality disorders themselves that almost any environment would be better.

CONCLUSION

In closing, the authors would like to make these observations: First, we know little of the natural history of aggressive conduct disorder. Robins' (1966) classic follow-up of antisocial children concerned patients who were mostly referred to a clinic by courts, who were on the average young adolescents rather than children, and who were delinquent rather than aggressive and noncompliant. Their bleak prognosis cannot be extrapolated to the common problem of the children discussed in this chapter. Perhaps their disorder has a better outcome, but without this knowledge, we have to be somewhat skeptical about the long-range effects of treatment. The children may improve without any treatment. The finding that few hyperactive children have any significant difficulties at work or at home by the time they are young adults (Weiss & Hechtman, 1979) is a good example of how vigorous treatments may be applied to problems that tend to disappear spontaneously.

The final comment is more philosophical. In going over the papers the authors have reviewed in this chapter, they were impressed with the range and quality of methods that seem promising, and with the ingenuity and persistence of the investigators. At the same time, their overall impression·is that what has been accomplished is only the first step or two in a long journey.

REFERENCES

Achenbach, T. M. The child behavior profile: I. Boys aged 6–11. *Journal of Consulting and Clinical Psychology,* 1978, *46,* 478–488.

Achenbach, T. M., & Edelbrock, C. S. The child behavior profile: II. Boys aged 12–16 and girls aged 6–11 and 12–16. *Journal of Consulting and Clinical Psychology,* 1979, *47,* 223–233.

Als, H., Tronick, E., Adamson, L., & Brazelton, T. B. The behavior of the full-term but underweight newborn infant. *Developmental Medicine and Child Neurology,* 1976, *18,* 590–602.

Bohman, M. A comparative study of adopted children, foster children and children in their biological environment born after undesired pregnancies. *Acta Paediatrica Scandinavica,* 1971, *Supplement 221,* 1–38.

Bronson, W. C. Central orientations: A study of behavior organization from childhood to adolescence. *Child Development,* 1966, *37,* 125–155. (a)

Bronson, W. C. Early antecedents of emotional expressiveness and reactivity control. *Child Development,* 1966, *37,* 793–810. (b)

Byers, E. S. Wilderness camping as a therapy for emotionally disturbed children: A critical review. *Exceptional Children,* 1979, *45,* 628–635.

Byles, J. A., & Maurice, A. The juvenile services project: An experiment in delinquency control. Canadian Journal of Criminology, 1979, *21,* 155–165.

Cadoret, R., & Gath, A. Biologic correlates of hyperactivity: Evidence for genetic factor. In S. Sells, R. Crandall, M. Roff, J. Strauss, & W. Pollin (Eds.), *Human functioning in longitudinal perspective.* Baltimore: Williams & Wilkins, 1980.

Camp, B. W. Verbal mediation in young aggressive boys. *Journal of Abnormal Psychology,* 1977, *86,* 145–153.

Camp, B. W., Blom, G. E., Hebert, F., & van Doorninck, W. J. "Think Aloud": A program for developing self-control in young aggressive boys. *Journal of Abnormal Child Psychology,* 1977, *5,* 157–169.

Campbell, S. B., & Paulauskas, S. Peer relations in hyperactive children. *Journal of Child Psychology & Psychiatry,* 1979, *20,* 233–246.

Cantwell, D. P. Psychiatric illness in the families of hyperactive children. *Archives of General Psychiatry,* 1972, *27,* 414–417.

Cantwell, D. P. *The hyperactive child.* New York: Spectrum, 1975.

Chandler, M. J. Egocentrism and antisocial behavior: The assessment and training of social perspective-taking skills. *Developmental Psychology,* 1973, *9,* 326–332.

Chandler, M. J., Greenspan, S., & Barenboim, C. Assessment and training of role-taking and referential communication skills in institutionalized emotionally disturbed children. *Developmental Psychology,* 1974, *10,* 546–553.

Christiansen, K. O. A preliminary study of criminality among twins. In S. A. Mednick & K. O. Christiansen (Eds.), *Biosocial bases of criminal behavior.* New York: Gardner, 1977.

Clark, R. A., & Delia, J. G. The development of functional persuasive skills in childhood and early adolescence. *Child Development,* 1976, *47,* 1003–1014.

Crowe, R. R. An adoption study of antisocial personality. *Archives of General Psychiatry,* 1974, *31,* 785–791.

Diener, E., & Wallbom, M. Effects of self-awareness on antinormative behavior. *Journal of Research in Personality,* 1976, *10,* 107–111.

Dollard, J., & Miller, N. E. *Personality and psychotherapy.* New York, McGraw-Hill, 1950.

Douglas, V. I., Parry, P., Marton, P., & Garson, C. Assessment of a cognitive training program for hyperactive children. *Journal of Abnormal Child Psychology,* 1976, *4,* 389–410.

Dykman, R. A., Murphree, O. D., & Reese, W. G. Familial anthropophobia in pointer dogs? *Archives of General Psychiatry,* 1979, *36,* 988–993.

Gersten, J. C., Langner, T. S., Eisenberg, J. G., Simcha-Fagan, O., & McCarthy, E. D. Stability and change in types of behavioral disturbance of children and adolescents. *Journal of Abnormal Child Psychology*, 1976, *4*, 111–127.

Goldstein, A. P., Sherman, M., Gershaw, N. J., Sprafkin, R. P., & Glick, B. Training aggressive adolescents in prosocial behavior. *Journal of Youth and Adolescence*, 1978, *7*, 73–92.

Graham, P., & Rutter, M. Psychiatric disorder in the young adolescent: A follow-up study. *Proceedings of the Royal Society of Medicine*, 1973, *66*, 1226–1229.

Hewitt, L., & Jenkins, R. L. *Fundamental patterns of maladjustment*. State of Illinois, 1946.

Hutchings, B., & Mednick, S. A. Criminality in adoptees and their adoptive and biological parents. In S. A. Mednick & K. O. Christiansen (Eds.), *Biosocial bases of criminal behavior*. New York: Gardner, 1977.

Ingram, T. T. S. A characteristic form of overactive behavior in brain damaged children. *Journal of Mental Science*, 1956, *102*, 550–558.

Kagan, J., & Moss, H. A. *Birth to maturity*. New York: Wiley, 1962.

Kelly, F. J. *Outward Bound and delinquency: A ten-year experience*. Paper presented at the Conference on Experiential Education, Estes Park, Colorado, October 1974.

Kelly, F. J., & Baer, D. J. Physical challenge as a treatment for delinquency. *Crime and Delinquency*, 1971, *14*, 437–445.

Loney, J., Langhorne, J. E., & Paternite, C. E. An empirical basis for sub-grouping the hyperkinetic/minimal brain dysfunction syndrome. *Journal of Abnormal Psychology*, 1978, *87*, 431–441.

Luria, A. R. *The role of speech in the regulation of normal and abnormal behavior*. New York: Liveright, 1961.

McCord, J. A thirty-year follow-up of treatment effects. *American Psychologist*, 1978, *33*, 284–289.

Meichenbaum, D., & Goodman, J. Reflection-impulsivity and verbal control of motor behavior. *Child Development*, 1969, *40*, 785–797.

Meichenbaum, D., & Goodman, J. Training impulsive children to talk to themselves: A means of developing self-control. *Journal of Abnormal Psychology*, 1971, *77*, 115–126.

Milich, R., & Loney, J. The role of hyperactive and aggressive symptomatology in predicting adolescent outcome among hyperactive children. *Journal of Pediatric Psychology*, 1979, *4*, 93–112.

Minkin, N., Braukmann, C. J., Minkin, B. L., Timbers, G. D., Timbers, B. J., Fixsen, D. L., Phillips, E. L., & Wolf, M. M. The social validation and training of conversational skills. *Journal of Applied Behavior Analysis*, 1976, *9*, 127–139.

Moore, D. R., Chamberlain, P., & Mukai, L. H. Children at risk for delinquency: A follow-up comparison of aggressive children and children who steal. *Journal of Abnormal Child Psychology*, 1979, *7*, 345–355.

Morris, H. H., Jr., Escoll, P. J., & Wexler, R. Aggressive behavior disorders of childhood: A follow-up study. *American Journal of Psychiatry*, 1956, *112*, 991–997.

Morrison, J. R., & Stewart, M. A. A family study of the hyperactive child syndrome. *Biological Psychiatry*, 1971, *3*, 189–195.

Morrison, J. R., & Stewart, M. A. The psychiatric status of the legal families of adopted hyperactive children. *Archives of General Psychiatry*, 1973, *28*, 888–891.

Moss, H. A. Sex, age, and state as determinants of mother–infant interaction. *Merrill-Palmer Quarterly*, 1967, *13*, 19–36.

Nold, J., & Wilpers, M. Wilderness training as an alternative to incarceration. In C. R. Dodge (Ed.), *A nation without prisons*. Lexington, Mass.: Lexington Books, 1975.

Oden, S., & Asher, S. R. Coaching children in social skills for friendship making. *Child Development*, 1977, *48*, 495–506.

Offord, D. R., Sullivan, K., Allen, N., & Abrams, N. Delinquency and hyperactivity. *Journal of Nervous & Mental Disease*, 1979, *167*, 734–741.

Orenstein, H., Orenstein, E., & Carr, J. E. Assertiveness and anxiety: A correlational study. *Journal of Behavioral Therapy and Experimental Psychiatry*, 1975, *6*, 203–207.

Osofsky, J. D., & Danzger, B. Relationships between neonatal characteristics and mother–infant interaction. *Developmental Psychology*, 1974, *10*, 124–130.

Ounsted, C. The hyperkinetic syndrome in epileptic children. *Lancet* 1955, *ii*, 303–311.

Pachman, J. S., & Foy, D. W. A correlational investigation of anxiety, self-esteem and depression: New findings with behavioral measures of assertiveness. *Journal of Behavioral Therapy and Experimental Psychiatry*, 1978, *9*, 97–101.

Palkes, H., Stewart, M., & Kahana, B. Porteus maze performance of hyperactive boys after training in self-directed verbal commands. *Child Development*, 1968, *39*, 817–826.

Patterson, G. R. Interventions for boys with conduct problems: Multiple settings, treatments, and criteria. *Journal of Consulting and Clinical Psychology*, 1974, *42*, 471–481. (a)

Patterson, G. R. Retraining of aggressive boys by their parents: Review of recent literature and follow-up evaluation. *Canadian Psychiatric Association Journal*, 1974, *19*, 142–161. (b)

Patterson, G. R., Littman, R. A., & Bricker, W. Assertive behavior in children: A step toward a theory of aggression. *Monographs of the Society for Research in Child Development*, 1967, *32*, 1–43.

Rapoport, J. L., Buchsbaum, M. S., Zahn, T. P., Weingartner, H., Ludlow, C., & Mikkelsen, E. J. Dextroamphetamine: Cognitive and behavioral effects in normal prepubertal boys. *Science*, 1978, *199*, 560–562.

Rathus, S. A. A 30-item schedule for assessing assertive behavior. *Behavior Therapy*, 1973, *4*, 398–406.

Rie, E. D., & Rie, H. E. Recall, retention, and ritalin. *Journal of Consulting and Clinical Psychology*, 1977, *45*, 967–972.

Rie, H. E., Rie, E. D., Stewart, S., & Ambuel, J. P. Effects of methylphenidate on underachieving children. *Journal of Consulting and Clinical Psychology*, 1976, *44*, 250–260.

Robins, L. *Deviant children grown up*. Baltimore: Williams & Wilkins, 1966.

Rutter, M. Parent–child separation: Psychological effects on the children. *Journal of Child Psychology and Psychiatry*, 1971, *12*, 233–260.

Rutter, M., Graham, P., & Yule, W. *A neuropsychiatric study in childhood*. Philadelphia: Lippincott, 1970.

Rutter, M., Tizard, J., & Whitmore, K. *Education, health and behavior*. London: Longman, 1970.

Sandberg, S. T., Rutter, M., & Taylor, E. Hyperkinetic disorder in psychiatric clinic attenders. *Developmental Medicine in Child Neurology*, 1978, *20*, 279–299.

Scheier, M. F., Fenigstein, A., & Buss, A. H. Self-awareness and physical aggression. *Journal of Experimental Social Psychology*, 1974, *10*, 264–273.

Schuckit, M. A., Petrich, J., & Chiles, J. Hyperactivity: Diagnostic confusion. *Journal of Nervous and Mental Disease*, 1978, *166*, 79–87.

Shaffer, D., McNamara, N., & Pincus, J. H. Controlled observations on patterns of activity, attention, and impulsivity in brain-damaged and psychiatrically disturbed boys. *Psychological Medicine*, 1974, *4*, 4–18.

Shaw, C. A comparison of the patterns of mother–baby interaction for a group of crying, irritable babies and a group of more amenable babies. *Child: Care, Health and Development*, 1977, *3*, 1–12.

Shure, M. B., & Spivack, G. *A mental health program for kindergarten children: A cognitive approach to solving interpersonal problems*. Philadelphia: Community Mental Health/Mental Retardation Center, Department of Mental Health Sciences, Hahnemann Medical College and Hospital, 1974.

Sleator, E. K., & von Neumann, A. W. Methylphenidate in the treatment of hyperkinetic children. *Clinical Pediatrics*, 1974, *13*, 19–24.

Smith, M. L., Gabriel, R., Schott, J., & Padia, W. L. Evaluation of the effects of Outward Bound. In *Evaluation Studies Review Annual*, University of Colorado, 1975, 400–421.

Smith, G. M., Weitzner, M., Levenson, S. R., & Beecher, H. K. Effects of amphetamine and secobarbital on coding and mathematical performance. *Journal of Pharmacology and Experimental Therapeutics*, 1963, *139*, 100–104.

Sroufe, L. A., & Stewart, M. A. Treating problem children with stimulant drugs. *New England Journal of Medicine*, 1973, *289*, 407–413.

Stewart, M. A., deBlois, C. S., & Cummings, C. Psychiatric disorder in the parents of hyperactive boys and those with conduct disorder. *Journal of Child Psychology and Psychiatry*, 1980, *21*, 283–292.

Stewart, M. A., de Blois, C. S., Meardon, J., & Cummings, C. Aggressive Conduct Disorder of Children. *Journal of Nervous and Mental Disease*, 1980, *168*, 604–610.

Stewart, M. A., deBlois, C. S., & Singer, S. Alcoholism and hyperactivity revisited: A preliminary report. In M. Galanter (Ed.), *Currents in Alcoholism* (Vol. 5). New York: Grune & Stratton, 1979.

Stewart, M. A., Cummings, C., Singer, S., & de Blois, C. S. The overlap between hyperactive and unsocialized aggressive children. *Journal of Child Psychology and Psychiatry*, 1981, *22*, 35–45.

Stewart, M. A., & Gath, A. *Psychological disorders of children*. Baltimore: Williams & Wilkins, 1978.

Stewart, M. A., & Leone, L. A family study of unsocialized aggressive boys. *Biological Psychiatry*, 1978, *13*, 107–117.

Thomas, A., & Chess, S. *Temperament and development*. New York: Brunner-Mazel, 1977.

Thomas, A., Chess, S., & Birch, H. G. *Temperament and behavior disorders in children*. New York: New York University Press, 1968.

Trower, P., Bryant, B., & Argyle, M. *Social skills and mental health*. Pittsburgh: University of Pittsburgh Press, 1978.

Tsai, L., Ashby, H., & Stewart, M. A. *A questionnaire with which to screen parents for depression*. Submitted for publication, 1980.

Waldrop, M. F., Bell, R. Q., & Goering, J. D. Minor physical anomalies and inhibited behavior in elementary school girls. *Journal of Child Psychology and Psychiatry*, 1976, *17*, 113–122.

Weiss, B., & Laties, V. G. Enhancement of human performance by caffeine and the amphetamines. *Pharmacology Review*, 1962, *14*, 1–36.

Weiss, G., & Hechtman, L. The hyperactive child syndrome. *Science*, 1979, *205*, 1348–1354.

Weiss, G., Kruger, E., Danielson, U., & Elman, M. Effect of long-term treatment of hyperactive children with methylphenidate. *Canadian Medical Association Journal*, 1975, *112*, 159–165.

Wicklund, R. A. The influence of self-awareness on human behavior. *American Scientist*, 1979, *67*, 187–193.

Whalen, C. K., Henker, B., Collins, B. E., Finck, D., & Dotemoto, S. A social ecology of hyperactive boys: Medication effects in structured classroom environments. *Journal of Applied Behavior Analysis*, 1979, *12*, 65–81.

Whalen, C. K., Henker, B., Collins, B. E., McAuliffe, S., & Vaux, A. Peer interaction in a structured communication task: comparisons of normal and hyperactive boys and of methylphenidate (Ritalin) and placebo effects. *Child Development*, 1979, *50*, 388–401.

Author Index

Italics denote pages with complete bibliographic information.

Subject Index

A

Adversarial evaluation, 181 (*see also* Program evaluation models and framework)
Antisocial children
  definition of, 308–309
Assertiveness training, 316

B

Behavioral assessment (*see also* Behavior therapy)
  Assumptions of, 240
  Characteristics of, 243–247
  Implications of, 240–242
  Uses of, 242–243
Behavioral model of process (*see* Process of mental health consultation)
Behavior therapy,
  Limits to, 312
  Role of assessment in, 237–247

C

Causal model validation, 266–268
Causal structure
  Temporal relations in, 265–266
  Theory of, 264–265
Child-school interaction model
  Assumptions of, 114
  Cost of, 126–128

Goals of, 121–123
Role of parents in, 123–244
Special education fundings, 124–126
Conduct disorder,
  Definition of, 208
  Nature of problem, 309–311
Consultant,
  Role in IEP process, 67–70
Client-centered case consultation, 138–139
Consultee-centered administrative consultation, 139
Consultee-centered case consultation, 139
Content validity, 233
Criterion-referenced assessment, 217–254
  Definition of, 217–219

D

Decision-oriented evaluation, 181 (*see also* Program evaluation models and framework)
Descriptive validity, 234
Direct services to teacher, 149–156
  Direct and indirect interventions in, 154–156
  Lack of confidence in, 151
  Lack of objectivity in, 151
  Lack of skill in, 150
  Lack of understanding in, 150
Domain achievement (*see* Ethnicity achievement)
Domain sampling validity (*see* Content validity)
Domain selection validity, 234